Samuel Johnson

Samuel Johnson

A LIFE

David Nokes

A JOHN MACRAE BOOK
HENRY HOLT AND COMPANY
NEW YORK

Henry Holt and Company, LLC
Publishers since 1866
175 Fifth Avenue
New York, New York 10010
www.henryholt.com

Henry Holt ® and 🛡® are registered trademarks of
Henry Holt and Company, LLC.

Distributed in Canada by H. B. Fenn and Company Ltd.

Originally published in Great Britain in 2009 by Faber & Faber

Library of Congress Cataloging-in-Publication Data

Nokes, David.
    Samuel Johnson : a life / David Nokes. — 1st ed.
        p. cm.
    ISBN 978-0-8050-8651-5
    1. Johnson, Samuel, 1709–1784.   2. Authors, English—18th
century—Biography.   3. Great Britain—Intellectual life—18th century.
4. Lexicographers—Great Britain—Biography.   5. Intellectuals—Great
Britain—Biography.   I. Title.
    PR3533.N55 2010
    828'.609—dc22
    [B]   2009032522

Henry Holt books are available for special promotions and premiums.
For details contact: Director, Special Markets.

First Edition 2010

Printed in the United States of America

1 3 5 7 9 10 8 6 4 2

To the Memory of

ANTHONY JOHN NOKES

1922–1999

. . . the business of the biographer is often to pass slightly over those performances and incidents which produce vulgar greatness, to lead the thoughts into domestick privacies, and display the minute details of daily life . . .

SAMUEL JOHNSON, *Rambler* 60

Contents

Preface

preface n.s. *(Fr.* Praefatio, *Lat.) Something spoken introductory to the main design; introduction; something proemial.*

> Heav'n's high behest no *preface* needs;
> Sufficient that thy pray'rs are heard, and death
> Defeated of his seizure.
>
> Milton's *Par. Lost*, b. xi.

When I came to King's College, on the Strand, thirty-five years ago, I was delighted to be upon the spot where many of the literary figures I spent time studying lived. On the corner of Surrey Street, where I now work, Congreve had once written. Fielding had presided as magistrate across the way at Bow Street and Swift had cowered from the Mohock gangs in his lodgings at Panton Street away past what is now Trafalgar Square. In the eighteenth century the alleyways congregating there, near the Royal Mews, included the New Exchange where John Gay worked as a draper's assistant, before opening out, later in the century, to Leicester Square, where Sir Joshua Reynolds had his fashionable dwelling place. In Covent Garden stood Button's coffee-house which Addison, Pope and Steele made the centre of the literary world, and in Russell Street, a generation later, James Boswell first met Samuel Johnson in Tom Davies's bookshop. Garrick, Fielding and innumerable others studied at the Inns of Court; Goldsmith put up at Wine Office Court and Boswell had his lodgings in Downing Street.

All these and many other literary persons existed within a mile of where I now have my office; but above all of them stood Johnson. His statue, erected a hundred years ago, stands behind St Clement Dane's

xiii

church, staring down the length of Fleet Street in whose courts and alleyways he lived, at Gough Square and Bolt Court. London dominated not just Johnson's work, but his essential being; the 'full tide of human existence', he once declared, 'is at Charing-cross'. Though he was born in Lichfield, which he loved, commemorated and many times returned to, it was London that gave life to all he wrote. In the *Dictionary* we find *Grubstreet* ('originally the name of a street in Moorfields in London, much inhabited by writers of small histories, dictionaries and temporary poems'), where, both metaphorically and physically, Johnson lived. The *fleet* ('A creek; an inlet of water') of Fleet Street, where he had his habitation, drew its name from the insalubrious Fleet Ditch ('A provincial word, from which the Fleet-prison and Fleet-street are named') which carried all kinds of refuse away to the Thames. If he turned right and walked up the *Strand* ('the verge of the sea, or of any water') he breathed more easily, and if he ventured as far as Pall Mall (*sc. Pallmall*, 'a play in which the ball is struck with a mallet through an iron ring') he could exercise himself but, if he ventured further and strolled upon the *Mall* ('A walk where they formerly played with malls and balls'), he might view the aristocracy at play. If, another day, he turned eastwards from Fleet Street and walked into the City, he might hear people exchanging *billingsgate* ('a cant word, borrowed from *Billingsgate* in London, a place where there is always a croud of low people, and frequent brawls and foul language'). He could then decide whether such people more nearly belonged to the *Marshalsea* ('the prison in Southwark belonging to the marshal of the king's household') or to *Bedlam*, 'corrupted from *Bethlehem*, the name of a religious house in London, converted afterwards into an hospital for the mad and lunatick'. All round him, as he walked, he would hear the cries of trade, with people proclaiming what they sold was cheap, without reckoning that 'cheap' itself came from *cheping*, 'an old word for *market*; whence *Eastcheap, Cheapside*'.

Johnson, more than any writer before Dickens, lived the life of London, from impecunious nocturnal rambles round St James's Square with Savage to accidental consultations with George III in Buckingham House on the state of British libraries. On the long central street which begins at Charing Cross as the Strand and waggles its way eastward to St Paul's Churchyard as Fleet Street, he memorialised his way at every inn and chop-house, from the Fountain Tavern where he read his play *Irene* (unsuccessfully) to David Garrick's elder brother, Peter, to the Mitre where he often dined and declared that 'when a man is tired of London, he is tired of life; for there is in London all that life can afford'.

In the course of writing this book I have roamed Fleet Street, the Strand and elsewhere in the country from Lichfield, where Johnson learnt his trade, to Armadale on the Isle of Skye, where he (rightly) judged the Highland weather 'not pleasing'. And I have accumulated many debts of helpful assistance from innumerable people which I should like to acknowledge here. In particular I should like to thank Joanne Peck and Diane Challenor of the Staffordshire and Stoke on Trent Archive, and the very valuable help, including delicious cups of tea, I received from Annette French at the Samuel Johnson Birthplace Museum in Lichfield. In Oxford I should like to thank Jane Richmond and Lynda Mugglestone of Pembroke College, together with the former Master of the College, Sir Roger Bannister, as well as Freya Johnston of St Anne's College. I received invaluable advice, in many areas, over several years from Adam Phillips, and would wish to pay my very great thanks to O M Brack, Jr. for the gift of several books and manuscripts, without which this book would have been far less comprehensive in its coverage. I should like to thank King's College, London, for granting me the time off from normal teaching duties to complete the book, and to acknowledge particular obligations to Petonelle Archer and Kate Chisholm for doing much research work to assist me in the British Library and to Christine Rees for offering very valuable advice. I also wish to thank David and Joan Boswell of the Boswell Society for making me President of the Boswell Society for 2006, and for offering me handsome accommodation at Auchinleck. I wish to thank Patricia Clarke, Jane Darcy, Valerie Glencross, Marilyn Imrie, Shearer West, Michael Bundock, Tom Deveson, Henry Hitchings, Max Saunders and Gordon Wise for help with this biography in several ways; but I wish to acknowledge that my chief debt, for research, for patience and for innumerable other things, is to my wife, Marie. I dismiss this book not with the tranquillity – frigid or otherwise – that Johnson wished upon the *Dictionary*, but trusting with him that whatever censure it receives is due to myself alone.

DAVID NOKES
London

'Till I Am Solitary'

biographer n.s. *(βιος and γραφω) A writer of lives;*
a relator not of the history of nations but of the actions of
particular persons.

Our Grubstreet biographers watch for the death of a great man,
like so many undertakers, on purpose to make a penny of him.

Addison, Freeholder, No. 35

On 16 April 1755 the London *Daily Advertiser* carried a brief
announcement: 'This day is published – a Dictionary of the English
Language . . . By Samuel Johnson, A.M.' Johnson, aged forty-five,
had arrived at last, with his highly prized degree not two months old.
His struggles since leaving Pembroke College, Oxford, in 1729 after
little more than a year's residence had been hard. Poverty had driven
him away without graduating and he had not set foot back in the city
until, needing books to complete the History and Grammar of the
language, he returned in 1754. It had not been a happy experience. He
had called at the Master's Lodge, occupied by John Radcliffe, formerly the bursar when as an undergraduate Johnson had not
reclaimed the £7 of caution money the college charged. Now he
found him hardly more forthcoming. Radcliffe received him coldly,
neither ordered a copy of the *Dictionary* to stand in the college library
nor chose to discuss it, and even failed to invite Johnson to stay to
dinner. In a fit of pique Johnson angrily declared, '*There* lives a man,
who lives by the revenues of literature, and will not move a finger to
support it.' It was a dream he secretly cherished that, as a reward for
furnishing the nation with a dictionary of its language, he might be
offered an Oxford fellowship; he used it to vent his anger at
Radcliffe, and at Pembroke. 'If I come to live at Oxford I shall take

up my abode at Trinity,' he pronounced. He spent his evenings in the city with college servants who recalled, or said they did, Johnson as a young man of nineteen; in particular he conversed happily with an ancient butler and expressed 'great satisfaction' he should still be recognised after staying so short a time, so very long ago. It was as if his youth, which had ended so abruptly in December 1729, could yet be rediscovered.[1]

The dream revived in conversations with Francis Wise, librarian at the Radcliffe Library, who thought it 'more apropos' and certainly 'more to Mr Johnson's good liking' if Oxford were to honour him before the *Dictionary* was published and to grant his degree, thereby allowing him 'to write himself A.M. in the title page'. Wise wrote this to Thomas Warton at Trinity College, little guessing how much the degree would mean to Johnson. He looked back with bitterness and frustration on all his youthful hopes and dreams which had ended, so abruptly, on leaving Oxford without a degree. He had attempted twice before to gain one to qualify himself as a schoolmaster, using Pope and Swift and even the Earl of Gower as intermediaries. But his efforts had all proved vain. At the end of December he wrote to Warton, 'extremely sensible' of the favour promised yet desperately anxious lest, once again, it prove fruitless. The *Dictionary* would 'be printed in less than six weeks' but he promised to 'keep back the titlepage for such an insertion'. On Christmas Eve he sent thanks in anticipation of the honour, but heard nothing. Again in February he offered a 'great sense of the favour' he believed had been done him, yet still he waited. Ten days later he wrote to Warton having 'heard nothing', not knowing 'in what state my little affair stands'; he begged to be informed 'if you can, tomorrow', for the printing of the *Dictionary* was all but done and he might be 'forced to delay the setting of the title page'.[2]

He took out his frustration on a man whose title, wit and knowledge of the fashionable world had allowed him to become an arbiter of correctness and an authority on the conduct of civilised conversation – the Earl of Chesterfield. Nine years before Robert Dodsley, head of the publishers employing Johnson to produce the *Dictionary*, well aware the authority of such a work would be 'imperilled without consensus', had been keen to involve Chesterfield in the enterprise. Johnson's *Plan* of a dictionary which circulated in manuscript to many notable persons in August 1747 was sent particularly to Chesterfield, to whom it was graciously dedicated. Chesterfield advised on spellings and pronunciation and it was from him that Johnson learnt 'the word *great* should be pronounced so as to rhyme to *state*': which was something of a nuisance as 'Sir William Yonge sent me word that it should be pronounced so as to rhyme to *seat*.' Only 'an Irishman', Sir William had declared, 'would pronounce it "*grait*" '. 'In lexicography', as in many other arts, Johnson sighed, 'naked science is too delicate for the purposes of life.'[3]

Writing the *Dictionary's* Preface he struck an elegiac note, remembering that both his wife Tetty and his former publisher and friend, Edward Cave, were now deceased. The work, he wrote, 'was written' (*not* compiled, but *written*) with little 'assistance of the learned' and with no 'patronage of the great', not in 'the soft obscurities of retirement' nor under 'the shelter of academick bowers' but amidst 'inconvenience and distraction, in sickness and in sorrow'. The tone he struck was truculent. It was with 'frigid tranquillity' that he affected to dismiss the *Dictionary* from him; but though this intensely personal statement goes beyond good taste, it makes one thing unmistakable. The *Dictionary* that he produced would be recognised as *his*. Johnson acknowledged, even revelled in the status he had awarded himself as a lexicographer of being a 'harmless drudge' and it came as a rather disagreeable shock to find the Earl of Chesterfield affecting to defer to him as a dictator. In a couple of brief essays, published in *The World*, Chesterfield claimed to find the *Dictionary* if not perfect (perfection was 'not to be expected from man'), 'as near to perfection as any one man could do'. Such fulsome praise might have been tolerable had his lordship left it at that, but Chesterfield's whimsy took him further. Writing anonymously, yet with a touch of aristocratic levity that was only too recognisable, he disclaimed the least hint of producing 'a hired and interested puff' for the *Dictionary* since Johnson had never offered him 'the usual compliment of a pair of gloves or a bottle of wine'. Good order and authority were now required, he declared, making 'a total surrender of all my rights and privileges in the English language' to the said Mr Johnson.[4]

Chesterfield's essays were supremely elegant performances. Boswell, clearly delighted by them, later declared that Johnson would have been so too, had there been no 'previous offence'; the offence being a story that Johnson, waiting in his lordship's antechamber and learning it was Colley Cibber who monopolised his lordship's attention, 'went away in a passion, and never would return'. Had Boswell, or Chesterfield, attended to Johnson's fierce sense of independence (evident in his last *Rambler* essay which refused to violate 'the dignity of virtue' by degrading it with 'the meanness of dedication') they would have been less surprised by what followed. Where Johnson had laboured for nine years, Chesterfield presumed to add his own literary *bonnes bouches* in a couple of weekends, and the essays' verbal cleverness may well have irritated Johnson as much as any previous slight. Sitting alone at Gough Square and wondering whether, at the last moment, his own university might disown him, he sought the precise tone of voice for his reply; stylish, civilized and dry, with just an adequate smattering of classical allusions to indicate what he and his lordship shared but, more importantly, what divided them. Citing the two essays in *The World* he appeared at first to offer thanks for them, then hesitated: 'being very little accustomed to favours from the Great, I know not well how to receive, or in what terms to acknowledge,' he wrote, making his failure to appreciate them both evident and significant. He had received 'some slight encouragement' but, slyly turning flattery to contempt, used a grandiose phrase *in French* (the language of 'disproportionate magnitude') to express it. 'I might boast myself Le Vainqueur du Vainqueur de la Terre,' he begins, affecting the courtly style of commendation, but ends with plain English common sense: 'no Man is well pleased to have his all neglected, be it ever so little.'

Is not a Patron, My Lord, one who looks with unconcern on a Man struggling for Life in the water and when he has reached ground encumbers him with help. The notice which you have been pleased to take of my Labours, had it been early, had been kind; but it has been delayed till I am indifferent and cannot enjoy it, till I am solitary and cannot impart it, till I am known and do not want it.[5]

'Till I am solitary'; the loss of his wife Tetty became a weapon Johnson could use. While she had been alive he was always wary of offending those with powers to damage him; now that she was dead, he became more outspoken, audacious even, turning what had previously been a mere grumble into a clear voice of independence. 'Those whom I wished to please, have sunk into the grave', he writes, leaving him wrapped in their memory, articulating sentiments more boldly than, had they still lived, he might have dared. He changed his definition of the word *patron* in the *Dictionary* to sound his own decisive and personal note: 'commonly a wretch who supports with insolence, and is paid with flattery'. There may have been patrons after 1755, but their era was gone, replaced in the nineteenth century by publisher's advances, in the twentieth and twenty-first centuries by advertising agencies and the university system.

Chesterfield was by no means affronted by the letter. Dodsley, distinctly irritated by it and believing that his lordship's patronage might have assisted sales of the *Dictionary* which, at £4 10s each, might need whatever aid was possible, apologised to Chesterfield. But his lordship waved aside the apology and insisted upon reading to him excerpts from Johnson's letter, which lay 'upon his table, where any body might see it' commending the 'severest passages', noting 'how well they were expressed.' In his *Letters* to his son, which Johnson described to Boswell as teaching 'the morals of a whore, and the manners of a dancing-master', Chesterfield explained: 'join in the laugh of the company against yourself' and 'play off the whole thing in seeming good-humour'. In this he was undoubtedly correct; many more have heard the tale of how he was *not* the *Dictionary*'s dedicatee, than would have remembered his name had he been so.[6]

A fortnight later, Johnson's degree diploma at last arrived from Oxford, brought to him in person by William King, Principal of St Mary's Hall. 'I have now the full effect of your care, and benevolence, and am far from thinking it a slight honour', he wrote with great relief to Thomas Warton, enclosing a letter of thanks to Vice Chancellor Huddesford, written in his best Latin.[7] The title page of the *Dictionary* could at last be printed with 'by Samuel Johnson A.M.' boldly emblazoned on it, in red. Here at last was something substantial (the two volumes of the *Dictionary* weighed almost a stone apiece) to set against his appearance – shaking, twitching, pock-marked, half-blind and distinctly careless about his dress – which might often be distinctly shocking to those who did not know him. Some years earlier the satirical artist William Hogarth had paid a visit to Samuel Richardson.

> While he was talking, he perceived a person standing at a window in the room, shaking his head, and rolling himself about in a strange ridiculous manner. He concluded that he was an ideot, whom his relations had put under the care of Mr Richardson, as a very good man. To his great surprise, however, this figure stalked forwards to where he and Mr Richardson were sitting, and . . . displayed such a power of eloquence, that Hogarth looked at him with astonishment, and actually imagined that this ideot had been at the moment inspired.[8]

It was a shock effect to which Johnson often resorted, making use of his grotesque appearance as the perfect preliminary to his remarkable powers of locution. 'I have indeed published my Book,' he wrote to Bennet Langton in May 1755, pointing out that it had neither patrons nor opponents 'except the Criticks of the coffeehouses, whose outcries are soon dispersed into the air'. He was at last 'at liberty', he declared, a solitary man who planned to make a summer's progress, wandering through the country whose language he had just regulated; from Oxford with the Wartons he would travel on to Birmingham with Edmund Hector and then to Lichfield which he had not visited for over twenty years.[9]

A map of London

Bunhill
Fields

Burying Place

Artillery
Ground

75

63

Fleet Street

The
Temple

V
E
R
R

T
H

Samuel Johnson

PART ONE

The Midlander

Lichfield

*Lichfield, the field of the dead, a city in Staffordshire, so
named from martyred Christians.* Salve magna parens.

September 7, 1709, I was born at Lichfield.

Johnson, *Annals*

Lichfield has changed little in appearance in the past fifty years,
though possibly it is more pleasant to explore on foot than formerly.
James Clifford, in his biography of Johnson, described 'thundering
trucks and streams of motor-cars' making the market-place a scene of
noise and danger, but now that the city centre has been pedestrianised
the walk from Bird Street, along Bore Street and down to Tamworth
Street is an agreeable saunter.[1] St Mary's Church, opposite the
Birthplace, where young Samuel should have been christened (he was
not expected to live and it was done hurriedly, in his mother's
bedroom), is no longer a complete church; three-quarters of it has
been transformed into the Lichfield Heritage Centre offering local
history, tea and coffee. On the corner of Sadler and Breadmarket
Streets is the Birthplace Museum, opposite the squat statue of the
Doctor presented to the city by its citizens in August 1838. 'Every
man has a lurking wish to appear considerable in his native place',
proclaims its plinth, though often lost in the market throng of green-
grocers, jewellery and pastry stalls.

Lichfield is a city of commemoration. Along Dam Street, leading
to Minster Pool and the cathedral, is Dame Oliver's School with,
above it, a neat metal plaque to commemorate the spot where Lord
Brooke, leader of the besieging parliamentary forces, was killed by a
bullet fired by a local royalist sharpshooter high up in the cathedral.
In Breadmarket Street, just past the Johnson Birthplace a plaque

commemorates Elias Ashmole, antiquarian and founder of the Ashmolean Museum, born there in 1617; outside the George Hotel in Bird Street another commemorates the residence of the playwright George Farquhar; further down the street yet another points out Garrick's house, and along Cathedral Close is where Joseph Addison lived when his father was the Dean. High up on the wall outside old St Mary's Church a small tablet commemorates three martyrs 'burnt at the stake in this market place' in the 1550s. Another signifies that George Fox, founder of the Quakers, stood 'without shoes' in the market in the winter of 1651, after his release from prison in Derby, 'and denounced the City of Lichfield'.[2]

Michael Johnson lived virtually his whole life in Lichfield, rising to become, in the year of Samuel's birth, its sheriff. It was a notable achievement for a man whose start had not been easy. In later years Samuel refused to be drawn on the subject of his forebears, informing Boswell he 'could scarcely tell' who his grandfather had been. Quite possibly he felt a sense of shame acknowledging William Johnson, born in Cubley, Derbyshire, about whose status there is a certain ambiguity; some documents describe him as a 'gentleman', others merely as a 'yeoman'. He first appears in Lichfield records in 1664, living in Tamworth Street with his wife Catherine and four children of whom Michael was the eldest.[3] The family found life in Lichfield unrewarding and were forced to scuttle round from place to place with little money until eventually William died in 1671, whereupon Catherine threw herself on local charity and was granted 'a waistcoat' to keep her warm. Apart from the physical benefit this gift conferred, it also indicated she was a perfectly respectable person for the Smith Charity to support. It was another charitable donation, this time from the Conduit Lands Trust, which provided Michael with an apprenticeship to a stationer in London, something he never forgot.[4] Once the eight-year term of his indenture was completed he returned to Lichfield and took up residence in Sadler Street in a substantial property with room both for his mother and a handsome bookshop. Soon he was not only selling books but publishing them; the title page of one boasts of 'shops at Litchfield and Uttoxiter, in Staffordshire; and Ashby-de-la-Zouch, in Leicestershire', while he also maintained stalls

4

at Abbots Bromley, Birmingham and Burton.[5] A file of letters between him and a trusted client, Sir William Boothby of Ashbourne, reveals the baronet complaining of his 'hurry at Uttoxiter', grumbling that 'the paper booke was not goode paper will not beare ink well'. In December 1684 Sir William, who was very free with objections, lamented that 'Xinophon is misplaced in the binding (a great fault you must be careful to prevent)'; but he was considerably less forthcoming when it came to settling his account. In October 1684 he sent Michael £10 by the bearer 'wh: is all I can spare at present'; in February he wrote: 'I cannot yet help you to money', and in December complained again of Michael's charges; although he lacked time to examine the books, he thought 'many of them to deare'.[6]

In 1691 Michael published *The Happy Sinner; or the Penitent Malefactor*, a collection of last prayers by the army surgeon Richard Cromwell, executed on 3 July in Lichfield for murder. Cromwell left behind him only his 'seven sovereign remedies for the ills of the flesh', the ingredients of which might be had from apothecaries 'except the Queen of Hungarie's Water', which, Michael noted, he retailed himself. The following year, when his mother died, Michael was a churchwarden of St Mary's, had purchased a 'sitting' in the church, was employing apprentices of his own and, by 1697, was even wealthy enough to advance £80 to the Corporation of Lichfield.[7]

Sir William Boothby's criticisms still rankled in Michael's mind. At one point the baronet had complained that 'most of yr books . . . are so ill Bund that I cannot open them to reade without much difficulty'. This was, he said, 'a great fault'. By the middle of the decade this was a fault Michael planned to correct by setting up as a manufacturer of parchment, vellum and leather and publishing his own books. So assiduous was he in his new enterprise that he obtained a summons against Jonathan Drayton, a tanner and potential rival. Michael travelled throughout the Midlands selling and repairing books, becoming a success and building up his trade, apparently reconciled to allowing the more personal side of life to take care of itself. But in June 1706, almost fifty and anxious for the future of his flourishing business, he negotiated a lengthy marriage contract between himself and Sarah Ford of King's Norton. Within the week they were married.[8] He drew up a further contract assigning his several mortgages into one deed and spent a great deal both of time and money planning a grand new house for them to live in, on the corner of Sadler and Breadmarket Streets, on four floors with at least fifteen rooms, overlooking the market. So grand was his new edifice that it encroached on all the neighbouring properties, for which he had to pay an annual indemnity of 2s 6d for forty years.[9] But it was worth it; Michael Johnson had finally arrived and it was in this house that, on 7 September 1709, his son Samuel was born.

Sarah, forty and bearing her first child, had 'a very difficult and dangerous labour', but it was a difficulty in which young Samuel, when he heard of it, took pride. 'I was born almost dead', he announced, 'and could not cry for some time.' Sarah Johnson was attended by the notable man-midwife George Hector, by whose efforts Johnson was safely delivered and celebrated in the words, 'Here is a brave boy.' The next day, Rogation Sunday, his father, who had risen that year to be sheriff of Lichfield, was due to ride the circuit of the city, a ceremony which was then performed with considerable solemnity. Asked by his wife 'whom he would invite', Michael replied 'All the town now.'[10] Michael Johnson's feasting of his Riding was almost the last to be maintained with 'uncommon magnificence' and splendour; nothing in his later life would match the eminence of that day.

Samuel was put *'by my father's persuasion'* to be suckled by 'one Marklew, commonly called Bellison' in George Lane; it was a further tiny mark of the sheriff's status that his wife should not feed the infant herself. Sarah Johnson came to visit every day though, conscious of her husband's dignity, 'used to go different ways, that her assiduity might not expose her to ridicule'. She would leave little things behind her, a fan or gloves, to have an excuse to return unexpectedly but 'never discovered any token of neglect'. It was Samuel who showed signs, not of neglect, but of tubercular infection from this status-seeking wet-nursing. The *Annals*, Johnson's partial memoir of his early years, speak of an 'inflammation' discovered after 'a few weeks' on his buttocks 'which was at first, I think, taken for a burn; but soon appeared to be a natural disorder'. From this point on diseases multiplied and Samuel narrates the evidence of 'scrofulous sores' afflicting every part of his body.[11] It was soon discovered that his eyes were affected and 'an issue was cut in my left arm, of which I took no great notice, as I think my mother has told me, having my little hand in a custard'. His mother immediately felt guilty and 'thought my diseases derived from her family' but Dr Swinfen, Johnson's godfather, told her the sores proceeded from 'the bad humours of the nurse'. The result was the same. 'In ten weeks I was taken home, a poor, diseased infant, almost blind. I remember my aunt Nath. Ford told me, when I was about [. . .] years old, that she would not have picked such a poor creature up in the street.'

There is a defiant swagger about the way Johnson, writing in about 1770, parades his early physical misfortunes proudly, not underplaying but rather exaggerating and exploiting them, taking his disadvantages and learning to use them to his advantage. In telling of his infant life he patronised his parents and, without consciously belittling them, took away the dignity they had so much striven to create. 'My father had much vanity', wrote Johnson, 'which his adversity hindered from being fully exerted.' In one anecdote Johnson says that his father 'never had much kindness' for Mrs Harriots, his mother's relative, and 'willingly disgusted her, by sending his horses from home on Sunday'. This behaviour, apparently criticised, is actually cherished as a symbol of masculine independence. But it was a kind of behaviour which vanished when, later, poverty enforced a cowed compliance. 'I remember, that, mentioning her legacy in the humility of distress, he called her *our good Cousin Harriots*.' Mrs Harriots, a childless widow, made a special point of Sunday observances; Johnson later noted the 'regularity' of her household, observing that 'he who may live as he will, seldom lives long in the observation of his own rules'.[12] On her death in February 1728 she bequeathed Mrs Johnson 'a pair of her best flaxen sheets and pillow cases, as well as a large pewter dish and a dozen pewter plates' along with £40 'for her own separate use'.[13]

A great deal of these scrappy, mutilated *Annals* concern troubles between his parents. 'My mother had no value for his relations,' Johnson recalled; 'those indeed whom we knew of were much lower than hers.' Not just *lower*, note, but *much lower*. The sentiment he singled out to characterise his childhood home is contempt. 'This contempt began, I know not on which side, very early: but, as my father was little at home, it had not much effect.' Johnson too spent as much time as he could away from home; at the age of sixteen he went to Stourbridge where he found the influence of his cousin Cornelius Ford more benign than his parents' contemptuous sniping. 'They seldom conversed; for my father could not bear to talk of his affairs; and my mother, being unacquainted with books, cared not to talk of any thing else.' There, neatly combined in a witty paradox, is Johnson's vision of life at Lichfield; but the wit comes from his years away from it, and the death of both parents.

> Had my mother been more literate, they had been better companions. She might have sometimes introduced her unwelcome topick with more success, if she could have diversified her conversation. Of business she had no distinct conception: and therefore her discourse was composed only of complaint, fear, and suspicion. Neither of them ever tried to calculate the profits of trade, or the expenses of living.

Though attempting to be even-handed in estimating why his father and mother 'had not much happiness from each other', his criticisms are most acute when reckoning up his mother's faults.

> My mother concluded that we were poor, because we lost by some of our trades; but the truth was, that my father, having in the early part of his life contracted debts, never had trade sufficient to enable him to pay them, and maintain his family; he got something, but not enough.[14]

His father was a romantic, so lost in the grand gestures of building his own Market Street mansion or celebrating his city 'Riding' with a feast of uncommon magnificence that he would not reckon up the cost. Coming from a background of poverty and apprenticed by charity, he was anxious to make his mark in the city. In 1706 he acquired the Earl of Derby's library, all 2,900 volumes of it, a tremendous coup but one which, considering this was the year in which he rebuilt his house *and* was married, showed a tendency to overreach himself.

Mrs Johnson brought with her a considerable dowry of some £430, but 'he had been unable to carry out his part of the bargain in adding £100 to a trust fund'. 'It was not till about 1768, that I thought to calculate the returns of my father's trade, and by that estimate his probable profits,' Johnson remarks. 'This, I believe, my parents never did.' Oddly, no record of his calculation has been found. He writes in his *Welsh Diary* of his intention 'To note down my Father's stock, expences, and profit'. But apparently he never did.[15]

Michael was over-ambitious and may have known it, but could do nothing about it. Buying up a small twelve-shilling parcel of books, including Troutback's sermons or a speech of Haversham's on the death of Dr Fowke, he was in his element. He enjoyed haggling with tight-fisted customers who reminded him that they bought an almanac 'every year'. But his purchase of the Earl of Derby's library, together with his manufacture of parchment and leather, were enterprises that went beyond his abilities. In 1718 he was tried 'for using ye Trade of a Tanner' without having been apprenticed to it and, in drawing up his defence, he gave evidence of his pride in his achievements. He was, he said, a merchant 'tradeing to Ireland, Scotland and the furter most parts on England', dealing in commodities, 'more perticuler in Hydes and Skins', who vehemently denied having done any actual tanning himself. He turned the hides over to John Barton who had 'a tanhouse of his own where he tans the Defend's amongst other goods'. Evidence of the court verdict has been lost but it seems Michael was cleared since he continued working for the locality, and was elected junior bailiff on 25 July 1718, fortuitously just as his trial was due to begin.[16]

When Samuel was two and a half he was taken by his mother to London, to be touched by Queen Anne for the 'King's evil' as scrofula was called. Anne was the last monarch to perform a rite which appeared, even then, rather anachronistic, but Johnson believed in it, and wore around his neck the amulet with Michael the archangel on one side, a sailing ship on the other, throughout his life.* This visit to

---

* Michael Johnson had probably been present when in 1687 James II had touched 'divers persons'.

London, towards the end of March 1712, was his first memory of the city and the 'speckled linen frock' his mother bought him was always remembered as his 'London frock'. She herself wore a stout petticoat with two guineas sewn into it 'lest she should be robbed'. They stayed with a colleague of his father, John Nicholson, 'the famous bookseller, in Little Britain'.

Johnson's memories of odd incidents in the visit seem real enough though, as he said, recalling a cat with a white collar and the dog, Chops, leaping over a stick, 'I know not whether I remember the thing, or the talk of it.' He recalled 'a little dark room behind the kitchen, where the jack-weight fell through a hole in the floor, into which I once slipped my leg', recollected 'that I played with a string and a bell, which my cousin Isaac Johnson gave me' and remembered, with pride, being asked 'on which side of the shop was the counter' and answering 'on the left from the entrance'. Many years later he verified what he said had been true. His memories of the 'touching' itself are those of an infant. Of the queen he recalled nothing; 'some confused Remembrance of a Lady in a black Hood', he told Mrs Thrale; but he remembered 'a boy crying at the palace' quite clearly.[7] Also the visit seemed to involve a kind of demotion, going to London 'in the stage-coach' but returning 'in the waggon'. His mother had told him it was his fault 'because my cough was violent'. On their way to London she had been embarrassed; 'I was sick; one woman fondled me, the other was disgusted.' But, recollecting these events, he drew a different conclusion: 'The hope of saving a few shillings was no slight motive; for she, not having been accustomed to money, was afraid of such expenses as now seem very small.' His mother had spent some of her money buying, besides the speckled frock, 'a small silver cup and spoon, marked SAM.I. lest if they had been marked S.I. which was her name, they should, upon her death, have been taken from me'. The silver cup 'was one of the last pieces of plate which dear Tetty sold in our distress' but 'I have now the spoon.'[18]

All these incidents are remembered as if from a golden age when, if they travelled in a wagon, it was from a desire not to spread his germs, rather than from simple economy. Sarah had been forty when he was born; Michael, over fifty, was more concerned with business than with his family. But the family equilibrium changed some three years later when, to everyone's surprise, his mother bore a second son, Nathaniel. Until that moment Samuel, a sickly infant, had been the cynosure of his elderly parents' affections, and it cannot be surprising that from that time a sense of rebellion entered his general demeanour. 'I never believed what my father said,' he told Boswell; 'I always thought that he spoke *ex officio*, as a priest does.' Sarah made what efforts she could to break down any jealousies, teaching Samuel, at Nathaniel's christening in October 1712, to 'spell and pronounce the words *little Natty*, syllable by syllable' and getting him 'to say it over in the evening to her husband and his guests'. This kind of ritual, requiring him to display his talents before onlookers, soon became a source of contention. As a youngster 'in petticoats' Samuel is supposed to have trodden on a duckling, killing it, and to have made up these lines on burying it:

> Under this stone lyes Mr Duck
> Whom Samuel Johnson trode on
> He might have liv'd if he had luck;
> But then he'd been an odd one.

As an adult Johnson denied the story, claiming the lines were made up by his father, 'a foolish old man, that is to say . . . foolish in talking of his children'. Both his parents were in his view equally guilty of basking in the reflected glory of their precocious infant; he would often 'run up a tree when company was expected, that he might escape the plague of being showed off to them'.[19]

The first school Samuel attended was in Dam Street, run by Dame Oliver, a widow who managed to survive by selling confectionery, tending her school and receiving charity from St Mary's. Her school was just around the corner from the bookshop but Samuel was so disabled by poor sight that he was seen home past the cesspool in the market-place. According to tradition, one day he insisted on going home alone, feeling his way on all fours, but Dame Oliver followed at a discreet distance, monitoring his progress. When he realised she was watching, he leapt up and attacked her; an early example of his fierce attachment to independence. From there he progressed to the school of Thomas Browne, also in Dam Street, who boasted of having once produced a spelling book which he dedicated to 'the Universe'. Browne died in July 1717 and from the inventory of his will the simplicity of his pedagogy can be gauged: in the kitchen there is 'a parcell of old bookes' valued at 5s, and 'in ye School . . . 1 Table & old cheer' at the same price. Yet from these sources Johnson learnt to read, to write, to spell correctly, and the rudiments of English syntax.[20]

His education in Christianity began at home and was largely the work of his mother who, while he still shared a bed with her, informed him of the twofold nature of the 'future state', one part of which consisted of 'a fine place filled with happiness, called Heaven; the other a *sad* place, called Hell'. In his sixties Johnson recalled his mother's wonderment 'that she should begin such talk so late' of these alternative future states. He told Mrs Thrale that 'I did not respect my own mother, though I loved her'. On Easter Sunday 1716 the roof of St Mary's Church collapsed 'with a rumbling noise, upon the lower leads of the south aisle'. Some members of the congregation cried out 'murder'; others 'Oh the Presbyterians.' The church was closed for repairs and Johnson seized the opportunity to declare his opposition to further church attendance, citing his poor eyesight as his excuse.

He entered Lichfield Grammar School the same year, the start of a lifelong learning process which he remembered always 'with pleasure'. 'Perhaps it is not possible that any other period can make the same impression on the memory,' he confessed.[21] For two years he was in the lower school, taught by the elderly Humphrey Hawkins who indulged him with the result that he 'really excelled the rest'. Whereas most people, then and now, regard the syllabus of their schooldays as eminently forgettable, Johnson spends page after page of his *Annals* attempting to recreate details of a way of life which struck him with delight as the blueprint for escape. On Thursday nights and Friday mornings they studied Aesop; on Friday afternoons *Quae Genus*, a section of the Latin grammar introducing nouns and pronouns, which 'was to me always pleasing'. By contrast *As in Praesenti*, on the conjugation of verbs, 'was, I know not why, always disgusting'. That precious phrase 'I know not why' is a poor pretence of misunderstanding the schoolboy joke which got 'arse' from *As*. For him, learning Latin was a feature of school life at which he excelled, which would lead away from crawling half-blind in Lichfield to a wider world, and he failed to comprehend the sniggers of boys who took amusement from the lamest of jokes. To Johnson the supposed difficulties of preparation were no such thing: '*Propria quae Maribus* I could repeat without any effort of recollection. I used to repeat it to my mother and Tom Johnson.' For the first time he had a skill to be proud of, which he loved to display, being truly *his* and not, as the buried Duck had been, something his father had made up so poor-sighted Samuel would be one of the company. It was particularly in front of his mother, and his non-Latin-speaking cousin Tom, who was living with them at the time, that he showed off his erudition. Tom's father, Andrew, had 'kept the ring at Smithfield (where they wrestled and boxed) for a whole year, and', Johnson later boasted, 'never was thrown or conquered'.[22]

The Latin so intoxicated Johnson that he dreamt of it: 'I once went as far as the middle of the paragraph, "*Mascula dicuntur monosyllaba*" in a dream', he recalled in his *Annals*, which are partly composed in Latin. Once, though, his memory failed and he was deeply discouraged till his mother comforted him. He told her of his 'good escape', but she was not in the least surprised: 'we often come off best when we are most afraid,' she said. She told him that when forming verbs he had once announced he 'did not form them in an ugly shape' and she had been very proud. There is an unfinished, irregular organisation to these memories in the *Annals*; thought follows thought seemingly at random with a 'dear mother!' interjected amid other thoughts, which 'sooth my mind'. He recalls a 'Moral' he learnt as a boy, of a man who had hated another and found that it 'had made him rich'. This he repeated 'emphatically' within his mother's hearing, but this was a test she failed. 'She remarked it, as I expected,' the elderly Johnson comments. Intentionally or not, his memory had reversed the terms of the aphorism. His mother said she could 'never conceive that riches could bring any evil', a naive enough reaction to her increasing poverty. Her son more emphatically repeated that it was hatred that had 'made him rich'.

When Samuel was ten, his class of eleven pupils ('the number was always fixed in my memory') progressed to the upper school, managed by the Reverend Edward Holbrooke; 'a peevish and ill-tempered man', noted Johnson, though others disagreed. Their removal from the lower school, rather earlier than was the custom, followed a 'reproof' of Hawkins by Richard Wakefield, town clerk and Johnson's godfather, who claimed he was 'intent upon his boarders' and let the town boys fester in the lower school. Hawkins complained that 'he had lost half his profit' by the move and Johnson noted that he 'cried' at the removal. From this point on he no longer noted the pleasure of study; instead, an apparent indolence which would be characteristic of his adult enterprises crept into his work. Assigned sixteen exercises to do, he did twenty-five but 'never shewed all mine; five lay long after in a drawer in the shop'. He could work quickly, but often dawdled; he once showed his mother an exercise he had tarried over and she said she knew that he *could* do them but *would* he 'as soon as you should'?

At Whitsun he and Natty were sent to stay in Birmingham ('Why such boys were sent to trouble other houses, I cannot tell'). His mother seemingly believed in widening their acquaintance on *her* (socially superior) side of the family. They stayed with their uncle Ford whose wife was easy, talkative but prone 'to find something to censure in the absent'; they met their uncle Harrison (whose wife had died) and their seventeen-year-old cousin Sally, about whom, Johnson remembered, he 'used to say she had no fault'.[23] About his uncle Harrison Johnson was terse: 'He was a very mean and vulgar man, drunk every night, but drunk with little drink, very peevish, very proud, very ostentatious, but luckily, not rich.' As Johnson writes these memories the thoughts come flooding back; there was the boiled leg of mutton he had gorged himself on at aunt Ford's, who 'used to talk of it', and his mother had told him, seriously, 'that it would hardly ever be forgotten'; there was himself sitting, lost in thought by the kitchen window, doing his school exercise while just behind him, quite unnoticed, his cousin Sally danced. He had a deep sense of pleasure as he recalled occasional glimpses of this early, apparently charmed, life: his having a rattle to his whip; the sense of time elapsing, while Sally danced, and he *had not perceived it*. 'This close attention I have seldom in my whole life obtained.'

About this time, too, he found his love of Shakespeare; he was sitting in the kitchen at home one day, reading through the early pages of *Hamlet*, and was so moved by the ghost scene that he rushed upstairs, to the outside door, to see living people about him. In a bookseller's house he found much to lose himself among, and quickly developed his lifelong habit of reading deeply but haphazardly, never following a book to the end; often he annotated, as he did to a copy of *Visscher's Atlas*, numbering its pages and writing out a contents table in the back. But with these memories, the sense of deep-seated grievances returns to the *Annals*. His father had come to fetch his sons home on Thursday of the first school week as Johnson *alone* had desired him, but had called out to the ostler that 'he had twelve miles home, and two boys under his care'. That cry had deeply offended Samuel, not only taking away his independence, but lumping him in with his brother as simply 'two boys'. Little wonder that in the paragraph before are more examples of the first person singular than anywhere else in Johnson.[24]

He recollected more of his school exercises, from Aesop to Phaedrus, the wolf and the lamb, translating and parsing. What reconciles schoolmasters to long lessons, opines Johnson (the failed schoolmaster), 'is the pleasure of tasking'. In one exercise he reverses the terms of Horace's lament that weapons used in civil strife might more properly be used to expand the empire and denounces European depredations of the world. 'Every age seems ambitious of surpassing its predecessor in wickedness', he translates: 'So insatiable is our avarice that . . . new regions unknown to our ancestors are sought out, and their inhabitants subjugated.' In another exercise he takes delight in exploiting the irony that 'if crimes had not been perpetrated, no one would have made laws against them'.[25] Sometimes the boys, uncertain of the meaning of a word, asked for guidance, only to find that Holbrooke himself 'did not know the meaning of *Uvae Crispae*' (a species of gooseberry). Upon being sent for punishment they complained they 'could not get' the passage only to be told they should have asked: they had, they said, but 'the assistant would not tell us'. This is rendered quite feelingly by Johnson, who complains that their headmaster, John Hunter, was 'wrong-headedly severe. He used . . . to beat us unmercifully; and he did not distinguish between ignorance and negligence; for he would beat a boy equally for not knowing a thing, as for neglecting to know it.' It is the *unfairness* of the sentence, not its severity, that Johnson criticises, for he was a great believer in corporal punishment:

> I would rather (said he) have the rod to be the general terrour to all, to make them learn, than tell a child, if you do thus, or thus, you will be more esteemed than your brothers or sisters. The rod produces an effect which terminates in itself. A child is afraid of being whipped, and gets his task, and there's an end on't; whereas by exciting emulation and comparisons of superiority, you lay the foundation of lasting mischief; you make brothers and sisters hate each other.[26]

One wonders if the gentle method of 'comparisons of superiority' had been tried at the bookshop in Market Street and became a reason for a growing dislike there between Samuel and Nathaniel. He himself well knew the virtues of a whipping. 'My master whipt me very well,' he told his friend Bennet Langton cheerfully. 'Without that, Sir, I should have done nothing.' These two, diametrically opposed, opinions of Hunter are quite characteristic. As Johnson grew older his impatience with the extreme tenderness and partiality of parents towards their offspring increased. Asked to listen to two boys reciting Gray's *Elegy* one after another, and judge which of them did it best, he protested: 'No, pray Sir, let the dears both speak it at once; more noise will by that means be made, and the noise will be sooner over.'

At home he ate oatmeal porridge in the mornings before his day at school but well remembered, years later, the tarts he and Edmund Hector used to buy from the pastry cook, Dame Reid. Too blind and clumsy to be good at games, he made sure his schoolfellows knew how far he exceeded them in intellect. 'They never thought to raise me by comparing me to anyone,' he told Boswell; 'they never said, Johnson is as good a scholar as such a one; but such a one is as good a scholar as Johnson.' The 'such a one' who might have borne comparison was Lowe, another town boy, but Johnson did not believe 'he was as good a scholar'. Hector recalled,

> As his uncommon abilities for learning far exceeded us, we endeavoured by every boyish piece of flattery to gain his assistance, and three of us, by turns, used to call on him in a morning, on one of whose backs, supported by the other two, he rode triumphantly to school.[27]

Boswell in his *Life* calls the boys whose backs Johnson used to ride upon his 'favourites' who showed him 'submission and deference' and who, in turn, 'used to receive very liberal assistance from him'. With only such partial evidence to draw upon it is hard to be precise, but there is an unpleasant hint of bullying about this anecdote. He recalled that in winter, when the city's Stowe Pool was frozen over, he used to take 'a pleasure in being drawn upon the ice *by a boy barefooted*, who pulled him along by a garter fixed round him'. His intelligence and bulk combined to make him compensate for early physical weaknesses by domineering both at home and school.

St Mary's Church, its repairs completed, reopened at the end of 1721, by which time Johnson was airing adolescent doubts: he 'came to be a sort of lax talker, rather against religion' and thought himself a 'clever fellow'. He 'used to talk to my mother' in just such a way, he told Boswell, showing off his cleverness. 'She ought to have whipped me for it.' Johnson's *Annals*, brief and interspersed as they are, cease in 1719 at the age of ten, but other records tell us of gradual family breakdown and bids for independence. Michael was always unable to meet the terms of the marriage settlement that required £100 from him, plus £200 of Sarah's dowry that should be placed in the hands of trustees. In March 1721 Dr Ford, one of the trustees, died, and responsibility passed to his son, Sarah's nephew Cornelius. Beset by problems with the excise, Michael signed a document with Cornelius Ford in September 1725, presumably at Lichfield, for it was then that Cornelius met Samuel and the two formed an immediate bond. Before long Cornelius had invited Samuel to stay with him at Pedmore.

Samuel was just sixteen; Cornelius was thirty-one with a charming, sophisticated manner. He had been a Cambridge don and a London wit, knew Lord Chesterfield and Alexander Pope, and had accumulated fashionable debts which he eventually settled, equally fashionably, by marrying a rich spinster and entering the Church. He had been married for eighteen months to Judith Crowley, who was thirteen years his senior and formerly a Quaker, by the time he met Johnson. Cornelius was just the person to dazzle a bright adolescent and his importance for the young Johnson is indicated by the fact that in the *Annales* compiled in late 1734, Johnson mentions his visit to Ford second only to his birth. Nothing else is noted as memorable until he enters Oxford, three years later.

The visit started as an autumn excursion but lasted until the following Whitsun; it was, in Johnson's view, his awakening to a world in which he felt at home. It was at Pedmore that he learnt to discuss books with Cornelius, whose 'mastery of the classics, and elegant *Latin* and *English* style was conspicuous'. He may also have attempted his first verses, 'On a Daffodill', in which, although the adjectives ('lambent zephyrs', 'balmy spirits') may be utterly conventional, the final stanza has a certain distinction:

> With grief this emblem of mankind I see,
> Like one awaken'd from a pleasing dream,
> Cleora's self, fair flower, shall fade like thee,
> Alike must fall the poet and his theme.[28]

The personal pronoun 'I' places Johnson at the centre of his poem. Awakening from a dream may be conventional enough, but for Johnson, dreams were unpleasantly real. Much later, watching Mrs Thrale's son go off to school, he said, abruptly: 'Make your boy tell you his dreams: the first corruption that entered into my heart was communicated in a dream.' When she urged him to say more he retorted, '*Do not* ask me.' Dreams of his brother Nathaniel, who died very young, were a constant source of terror in his later years.

During this brief, all-important phase of his development, Johnson wrote some of the more piquant versions of Horace that survive among his *Juvenilia*; these include Epode XI in which the poet, made voluble by drink ('when repeated bowls unlock'd the heart'), complains of the mercenary nature of even the tenderest affairs ('all the fair their favours sold'). The final stanza of the poem runs thus:

> Lyciscus whose soft arms excel
> A girl's, inflames me with desire;
> Nor counsels nor reproach expel
> The raging of the kindled fire
> But the next blooming virgin's beauteous face
> Or boy, whose snowy neck the flowing ringlets grace.[29]

It seems unlikely that Johnson allowed himself to follow through the homosexual idea adumbrated here; the thought alone excited him. But Ford was a tempter to the young Johnson, drinking hard and daring him to experience life in all its forms. In later years he was presented to the Rectory of South Luffenham in Rutland but found it considerably less agreeable than life in London. Allegedly it was Ford who served as model for the drunken clergyman, smoking his pipe and contemplating a vast punch-bowl, in Hogarth's *A Midnight Modern Conversation* from 1733. As Johnson left, Ford gave him, as a final thought, the advice to 'dispute no man's claim to conversation excellence' that they might 'more willingly allow your pretensions as a writer'. It was not advice that Johnson ever followed, though the image of Ford remained with him for many years.[30]

When he returned home it was inevitable he should suffer a reverse, quarrelling with his younger brother, tiring of both his father and his somewhat snobbish mother. He was cock among his fellows, riding on their backs to class, and felt no anxiety at taking six months away from school. But revenge was waiting. Hunter, resentful at his pupil's arrogance, refused to have him back; attempts were made to get him to Newport School in Shropshire, but without success. In the end it was Ford who intervened to get him admitted to school at Stourbridge, to live in the headmaster's house, giving rise to one of the smart epigrams for which Johnson was becoming noted. In Lichfield, he claimed, he learnt 'nothing from the master but a good deal in his school', whereas at Stourbridge the situation was reversed: he learnt 'a great deal from the master but nothing in his school'. The headmaster was John Wentworth and probably, in return for teaching the youngest boys, Johnson paid nothing for his own instruction. It was a time of arrogance and untrustworthiness; Johnson was, he confesses, 'idle, mischievous, and stole'; *what* he stole is unknown, but the statement is interesting for the truculence it reveals. Wentworth was good, but lazy; 'a very able man, but an idle man', said Johnson. He himself was a 'big boy', full of his own abilities and ready to mock anyone who pretended to teach him. 'I was too good a scholar,' he commented boastfully. 'He could get no honour by me.'[31]

From some translations of his surviving Latin verse exercises we can judge how good his vaunted scholarship was. His versions of Virgil are conventional enough, but those of Horace involve him more directly; much later he told Boswell that Horace's odes were the poems which gave him most delight. There is a noticeable antithesis between his translation of Horace's Ode II.xx and his English poem *'Festina Lente'* which appears to have been written immediately after-wards.[32] In the ode a strong first-person voice ponders on literary fame; like a bird the poet will soar:

> I spring,
> And cut with joy the wond'ring skies.

Though 'from no princes I descend', his talent shall take him to 'Quaff nectar with th'immortal Gods' and 'My works shall propagate my fame'. By using an unusual word ('unballast'), previously employed by Addison, Johnson appears to give the poem a personal edge. But in *'Festina Lente'* he presents the other side of the dilemma.

> Be careful to command
> Your passion . . .

it advises, strongly urging a pursuit of reason to 'guide the reins with steady hand'. Opposed to the rush of the ode, the steady pentameters of this poem have a clear target: 'Rashness! thou spring from whence misfortunes flow!' For Johnson the antithesis was clear.[33] The poem

'Upon the Feast of St Simon and St Jude' indicates he was still in Stourbridge on 28 October but left soon afterwards to return to Lichfield where bookselling seemed still his likeliest career option. He may have desired to quaff nectar with the gods, but he realised that his father, however capable as a bibliophile, was sinking further into debt: that year it was £10 he borrowed from Richard Rider, but loans from friends became a regular expedient.

The previous year Michael had been charged with matters arising from the excise. In a private note the commissioner wrote that 'the justices would not give judgement against Mr Michael Johnson, *the tanner*', and advocated that 'next time he offends', instead of making the information public, it would be better to convey the matter privately, with an affidavit, 'that he may be prosecuted in the Exchequer'. Johnson was of an age to defy his father at every turn ('there must always be a struggle between a father and son') but when in the *Dictionary*, long after Michael's death, he defined collectors of excise as 'wretches hired by those to whom excise is paid', this memory must have been in his mind.[34] Michael was elected senior bailiff to coincide, quite fortuitously, with these excise troubles, his name having been proposed, unsuccessfully, in 1722 and 1724. He appears not to have been particularly assiduous as a magistrate, attending only six of the fourteen 'Common Halls' in his first year. But he attracted no fine, and avoided all charges from the excise, running the Quarter Sessions alongside Jonathan Kilbey with whom he swore his oath of fidelity to the crown. The child of an old man, said Johnson, 'leads much the same sort of life as a child's dog; teased like that with fondness through folly, and exhibited like that to every company, through idle and empty vanity'.[35]

Many years later, when Johnson's reputation was established, he could return to the Lichfield bookshop, pull down a book and recollect its binding 'to be the work of his own hands'. But this routine was a display, designed to shock more genteel company and prove there were few things he could not achieve. At the time, he disliked the book trade intensely, both for itself, and for the fence it put before his ambitions. 'When I was running about this town a very poor fellow, I was a great arguer for the advantages of poverty,' he declared, 'but I was, at the same time, very sorry to be poor.' Throughout the next two years he read widely, looking in 'a great many books, which were not commonly known at the universities, where they seldom read any books but what are put into their hands by their tutors'. He read Latin and Greek, 'all literature, Sir, all ancient writers, all manly'; when upbraided for not paying enough attention to the shop, he replied that 'to supersede the pleasures of reading, by the attentions of traffic, was a task he never could master'.[36]

As a teenager he came to know Gilbert Walmesley, a middle-aged native of the city who had studied at Trinity College, Oxford and at the Inner Temple. Crippled by gout, Walmesley now maintained himself in some style in the bishop's palace in Lichfield. In his younger days he had been a figure in London society, spending time with the literary figures, discussing with them Swift's *Conduct of the Allies* and agreeing 'how low human nature is sometimes capable of sinking'.[37] His rabid anti-government Whiggery caused occasional difficulties and when the pro-Tory Peace of Utrecht was proclaimed in Lichfield by the pealing of bells, he left the city, 'as 'tis supposed', *The Post Boy* reported, 'disturbed by the music of the bells'. Perhaps on account of the violence of his opinions, he became known to Johnson through the bookshop, which sent a regular series of books and pamphlets to the bishop's palace. Johnson later acknowledged that Walmesley was 'one of the first friends that literature procured me' and in *The Lives of the Poets* he gives a frank estimate of their relationship.

> He was of an advanced age, and I was only not a boy; yet he never received my notions with contempt. He was a Whig, with all the virulence and malevolence of his party; yet difference of opinion did not keep us apart. I honoured him, and he endured me. He had mingled with the gay world without exemption from its vices or its follies, but had never neglected the cultivation of his mind; his belief of Revelation was unshaken; his learning preserved his principles; he grew first regular, and then pious . . . Such was his amplitude of learning and such his copiousness of communication that it may be doubted whether a day now passes in which I have not some advantage from his friendship.[38]

Just as at Pedmore where the older, more cultivated Ford led Johnson to sharpen his wits, so at Lichfield's bishop's palace he found someone who would let him speak his mind and argue against him with wit and fervour. Many years later Johnson told the novelist and diarist Fanny Burney: 'When I was beginning the world, and was nothing and nobody, the joy of my life was to fire at all the established wits! And then everybody loved to halloo me on.' Walmesley loved his spark of wit and Johnson found an environment in which his physical disabilities, his near-blindness and tendency to shake were as nothing compared to the lucidity of his speech. When, some years later, the bishop attempted to regain his rightful possession of the palace the tone of Walmesley's letters gives an indication of his style of argument. 'I thank God, I am not more afraid of him than I am of the lowest curate in the diocese,' he wrote to the bishop's son, warning that his father should beware of 'needless oppressive lawsuits'. Though Walmesley and Johnson argued fiercely, indeed *because* they did, a bond was forged between them. Years later Johnson declared, 'There was a violent Whig with whom I used to contend with great eagerness. After his death I felt my Toryism much abated.' Undoubtedly he was thinking of Gilbert Walmesley.[39]

2

Oxford

university: n.s. *(universitas, Lat.) A school, where all the arts and faculties are taught and studied.*

While I play the good husband at home, my son and servants spend all at the university.

Shakesp. Taming of the Shrew

In February 1728 Mrs Harriots of Trysull died, leaving in her will forty pounds for Sarah Johnson's 'own separate use'. The money was not released to her until Michael signed an affidavit saying it was hers alone, and not for him to use in hopeless efforts to keep the bookshop solvent. This was the second important intervention in Johnson's life by Mrs Harriots. It came as no surprise that his mother had no better notion of using the money than to send him to Oxford, where his schoolfellow Andrew Corbet undertook to 'support him . . . in the character of his companion'. This was exactly Johnson's wish; he entered it in his *Annals*, where only dates of particular significance are marked: '1728 NOVRIS 1mo S. J. Oxonium se contulit.'*

Reading through the surviving stories of the thirteen months Johnson spent at Pembroke College, it appears that he behaved with remarkable insouciance towards this chance to raise his prospects.[2] Brought to Oxford by his father, who lost no time in telling William Jorden, his son's tutor, that he was a truly excellent scholar, Johnson immediately did everything to undermine that impression. He waited on Jorden the next day, but stayed away for the rest of the week: asked by Jorden to give a reason he replied he had been 'sliding in Christ-Church meadow' where there was ice on the ground. His

---

* 'On 1 November 1728 Oxford accepted him.'[1]

remembered anecdotes of his year at Oxford all have this quality of insubordination. He cut Jorden's lectures and when fined, allegedly retorted: 'Sir, you have sconced me two-pence for non-attendance at a lecture not worth a penny.' He neglected to hand in his weekly essay on Saturday, when the Hall bell was rung, for which the fine was half a crown and he refused to perform his exercises for 5 November, a date kept 'with great solemnity' in Pembroke. Instead, there survives the image of him 'lounging at the College gate, with a circle of young students round him', entertaining them with wit, keeping them from their studies, and spiriting them up 'to rebellion against the College discipline'.[3]

These stories, and many like them, present the picture of a young man who, rather than accept the college or university authorities, went out of his way to defy them. His reason for this conscious insubordination was that they failed to measure up to his own exacting standards. When his school friend John Taylor enthused about joining him at Pembroke, Johnson told him with 'rigid honesty' that he 'could not, in conscience, suffer him to enter where he knew he could not have an able tutor'. Making enquiries he found that Edmund Bateman of Christ Church had the reputation of being the finest tutor, and Taylor was entered there. His disappointment with his tutor Jorden stemmed from that first evening when, in the course of general conversation, Johnson had quoted Macrobius and been amazed that it was seen as evidence of extensive reading. He later said that Jorden was 'no scholar', though as a man he was excellent and defended his pupils 'to the last'. Johnson would not have scrupled to send any sons of his own to Jorden for a tutor.[4] It was as a scholar, the kind of man Johnson had come to Oxford to meet, that Jorden failed. That first evening he found *his own father*, whom he could not wait to leave, knew more of books than his Oxford tutor. It was a bitter pill.

Allegedly he found the weekly college exercises dull and hence neglected them. He began with great hopes, writing his first exercise 'twice over', something he rarely or never did again throughout his life. William Windham says of that first performance that Johnson told him he had 'neglected to write it' till the morning, and so could only get 'part of it by heart'. Undergraduates were then expected to learn their exercises thoroughly, and to recite them quite unaided by notes. Hester Thrale records that Johnson confessed to her that, having given in his copy of the exercise to Jorden, he 'was obliged to begin by chance and continue on how he could'. In later life Johnson made light of the apparent risk he took: 'No man I suppose leaps at once into deep water who does not know how to swim.'[5] However, to judge not by these well-rehearsed stories but by existing records, his behaviour was not quite so offhand. It is not known when the two surviving manuscript themes were due to be submitted, but the first of them, '*Adjacere bonae paulo*', seems, both in style and content, an ardent expression of his Oxford hopes. '*Academia Castra Musarum est*,' he writes; the academy is the camp of the Muses. 'By daily [*quotidianus*, not weekly, one should note] exercises the powers of the mind are strengthened; and the whole scholarly art of arms is also learned.' He goes on: 'The academy forms and polishes the rough and rude mind . . . the earth furnishes marble, the material of a statue; but it is the hand of Phidias that makes the stone image breathe.'[6] There is an open, unguarded quality in this essay's expression which leaves the reader scanning it in vain for irony towards Jorden. Instead, we have a clear, open sense of hope and freshness. The second surviving essay includes two tiny errors and is light-hearted, affectionately devoted to the idea of drinking as a tribute to friendship. It concludes with a joke at the inferior quality of college beer: 'Do you want our poets to write better songs? Direct that a purer drink nourish our wit.' There is so much buoyant wit in this piece, such a premium put on *amorem* (love) and *sinceram puramque amicitiam* (sincere friendship), that the whole piece comes alive, while the grammatical errors and reference to the buttery's inferior beer help give it a genuinely collegiate quality.[7] He kept company in the college buttery with Philip Jones whose features – a long nose and pock-marked face – were recorded in the buttery books with such scribbled comments as 'Jones is an ass and a foolish long guts' or 'Philip Jones is an affected fellow, foppish dog, alias Coxcomb'.[8] Only these two of Johnson's signed essays survive, but they are sufficient to suggest the idea of him as a moody adolescent may be far from true.

They are eager, youthful, a little naive, but optimistic. It is a tone, from Johnson, we should not forget.

He had brought with him to Oxford a library of almost a hundred books, more than all but the most learned would have read by the time they left. But, for him, they were books to read for amusement, not tomes to study: 'what he read *solidly* at Oxford was Greek; not the Grecian historians, but Homer and Euripides, and now and then a little Epigram.' His own collection included Virgil, Horace and Ovid along with More's *Utopia* and Erasmus's *Colloquies*. Among English authors the poets figured largely: Spenser and Milton, Garth and Prior, five volumes of Dryden's translations and eleven of Pope's *Homer*: there was a bible and prayer book, surprisingly no Shakespeare, Chaucer or Swift, but four volumes of Addison. Other books came his way by serendipity; on the stairs to his room he found the *Essay on the Theory of Painting* by Jonathan Richardson, 'took it up with me to my chamber, and read it through, and truly I did not think it possible to say so much upon the art'.[9] With such volumes he would sit in his room, two flights up over the gateway looking out towards St Aldate's Church which served the college for daily prayers. Pembroke was then confined to a single quadrangle and total numbers in residence never rose to more than fifty-four, including Fellows.[10]

Among his undergraduate friends were Jack Meeke, John Carew ('alias Longguts Shanks') and Oliver Edwards. Of these Meeke became a Fellow, spending his life in Oxford, and when, in 1754, Johnson visited his old college haunts with Thomas Warton, the two received 'a most cordial greeting' from him. Afterwards Johnson boasted that Meeke had been 'left behind at Oxford to feed on a Fellowship' whereas he had gone to London to get his living: 'now, Sir, see the difference of our literary characters!' Edwards, who wore a wig of many curls, met Johnson quite by accident in Butcher Row in 1778, when Johnson did not remember him, but returning to his house and sharing memories he at last recollected them drinking together in 'an alehouse near Pembroke gate' and exchanging lines of Latin verse. It was then that Edwards made his celebrated remark, 'You are a philosopher, Dr Johnson. I have tried too in my time to be a philosopher; but, I don't know how, cheerfulness was always break-ing in.' Even in Oxford, Johnson could not escape from Lichfield memories; once, he recalled, 'as he was turning the key of his cham-ber, he heard his mother distinctly call *Sam*'. It was a chastening reminder of what it had cost his family to send him there.[11]

Johnson ate and drank well, as far as can be deciphered from col-lege battels (accounts), and lived in college for his whole thirteen months at Pembroke.[12] His mornings, after chapel, were given over to such college pursuits as Latin compositions, translations, tutorials or lectures, but the afternoons were free. Compensating for not writing on the Gunpowder Plot, he submitted verses entitled '*Somnium*', containing the thought 'that the Muse had come to him in his sleep, and whispered, that it did not become him to write on such subjects as politicks . . .'[13] These verses are not preserved, but Jorden, upon hearing them, asked Johnson to translate Pope's 'Messiah' into Latin verse 'as a Christmas exercise'; this he did so rapidly and 'in so masterly a manner' it earned him high esteem in 'all the University'. There is a story of the verses being sent to Lichfield where Michael proudly printed them, which caused Samuel to rage and (with unconscious Oedipal associations) to declare that 'if it had not been his father he would have cut his throat'. No copy of the offensive printing is known, but the piece was published by John Husbands, of Pembroke, in his *Miscellany of Poems* in 1731, by which time Johnson would have left, knowing nothing of this first appear-ance in print. Pope is said to have seen a copy and noted that 'the writer of this poem will leave it a question for posterity, whether his or mine be the original'.[14]

Once arrived, he stayed full-time in Oxford, not going back to Lichfield for vacations, indicating a wish, made obvious by his *Annals* entry, to register his time at Oxford as decisive. But he received dis-turbing news from home concerning his financial situation and began his second year by inscribing in his new diary: '*OCT. Desidiae vale dixi syrenis istius Cantibus surdam posthac aurem obversus*', translated by Boswell as 'I bid farewell to Sloth, being resolved henceforth not to listen to her siren strains.'[15] He listed the ancient Latin authors he most wanted, including Lucretius and Cicero, but though he had bidden sloth farewell he found it far less easy to make it go away. Another entry in the diary indicates an unfulfilled wish to recall what he had done ('*quod feci*') on 9, 12, 17, 19, 22, 28 and 26 September. There may be various speculations as to what a healthy undergraduate of twenty years old might guiltily record himself doing twice or three times a week from his birthday, but such speculations must remain unproven. A month later he was at his diary again, trying to create a grid to work out how many lines he could commit to memory a day, a week, a month or a year. He started at ten lines per day, which would be very easy, and went up by progressive stages (thirty, sixty lines per day) until he reached 14,400 a month. All these mental calculations were very impressive but actually prevented him from doing what they were designed to promote, that is, reading and memorising.[16] It was a device which he very often attempted when under stress; refusing to attempt the effort of what he could do, in favour of doing something else at which he frequently committed errors. This time he made no mistakes, but was unable to see whether he could actually memorise 17,280 lines in a year which, at sixty lines a day, he reckoned a decent average. In December 1729 he left Pembroke and did not return for twenty-three years.

His reasons for leaving Pembroke at the end of that Michaelmas term were financial.[17] Details of his father's debts have not survived, but only a rigorous reverse could have led him to abandon his studies at a place he later, perhaps consequently, treated with such reverence. An anecdote of how he came to leave, no doubt factually false, accurately encapsulates a truth about his situation at Pembroke. Having recommended Taylor to enrol at Christ Church to benefit from Bateman's teaching, Johnson would come across from Pembroke to get the lectures 'at second-hand' from him:

> till his poverty being so extreme, that his shoes were worn out, and his feet appeared through them, he saw that this humiliating circumstance was perceived by the Christ-Church-men, and he came no more. He was too proud to accept of money, and somebody having set a pair of new shoes at his door, he threw them away with indignation.

He later commented that he was 'mad and violent. It was bitterness which they mistook for frolick.'[8] His name disappears from the Pembroke buttery book on 12 December 1729 although from subsequent entries, down to 1 October 1731, it would appear that he had not made a final decision to quit Oxford. He left his books, a valuable resource, with Taylor at Christ Church, making no effort to remove them for six years. Dr Adam, subsequently Master of Pembroke, declared he was 'loved by all about him' and readily confessed that Johnson was 'above my mark'. The evidence is that Johnson regarded his departure, in December, as purely temporary. Dr Panting, another later Master of Pembroke, had allegedly heard him utter his hopes to sample foreign universities after Oxford: 'I'll go to France and Italy. I'll go to Padua . . . For an *Athenian* blockhead is the worst of all blockheads.'[9] It was in Oxford that he came to a more serious acknowledgement of religion, taking up William Law's *Serious Call to a Holy Life* 'expecting to find it a dull book, (as such books generally are)' but finding it 'quite an overmatch'.[20] But any thoughts that Law provoked were put aside as he journeyed back to Lichfield.

According to his old school friend Edmund Hector, Johnson was 'in his 20th year', and at Oxford, when he wrote his draft poem 'The Young Author', later printed in the *Gentleman's Magazine*. In it, dreams of 'future millions' raise the poet's soul:

> In blissful dreams he digs the golden mine,
> And raptur'd sees the new-found ruby shine.[21]

'Joys insincere!' warns the callow Johnson, trusting neither the acclamations of a living audience ('More false, more cruel, than the seas and wind') nor the 'imagin'd laurels' of posterity. Wise as these insincere declamations might be, they concealed the harsher cruelty of a life apparently deprived of all worldly hopes for lack of money. Between December 1729 when he left Oxford and early 1733 when he went to Birmingham, records of Johnson's life are few, and bleak. His *Annals* for 1731 mention the death of Cornelius Ford: '*Mensibus Aestivitis S. J. C. F. amisit*' ('In the summer months S. J. lost C. F.'), followed shortly afterwards by that of his father: 'DECEMB. *Patre orbatus est'* ('bereaved of his father').[22] Ford had been louche, but had taken Johnson seriously. Newspaper reports of Ford's death 'at the Hummums [hotel] in Covent Garden', where he had gone after incarceration in the Fleet prison, spiced up the details of his final days and concluded he was 'well known to the world for his great wit and abilities'.

> Ford is not dead, but sleepeth; spare his fame, I charge ye,
> One ounce of Mother-wit is worth a pound of Clergy.

Coming as it did at this low point in Johnson's own existence, the death of Cornelius was another example of a free, independent life snuffed out. The death of his father left him with more ambivalent feelings. There would be no more of the awkward encounters he had so detested; yet, deprived of them, he realised how much his father had meant to him. In his awkward, outspoken way, Michael had given much to Johnson. In their last two years in Lichfield the two of them, both in their own ways radically dissatisfied, had many arguments. Michael continued to attend his civic obligations, and was present in 1729 when the commissioners of the Turnpike Trust came to discuss improvements to the local highways. He was fairly conscientious about attending meetings of the Lichfield Corporation and 'the fact that he remained a magistrate up to the end proves that he could not have died bankrupt'.[23] Nevertheless his financial situation had for years been tottering, as Mrs Harriots's special benefaction to Sarah Johnson makes very clear. Michael was kept afloat by credit provided by William Innys, a bookseller in St Paul's churchyard in the capital, which he acknowledged and, on his deathbed, promised to repay. In 1731 the Conduit Lands Trust of Lichfield, which had granted him his apprenticeship many years before and of which he had once been a warden, gave him a generous payment of ten guineas as 'a decayed tradesman'.[24] It is worth remembering this charitable disbursement of a larger amount than was provided to almost anyone else, since it indicated the deep respect in which Michael was held in the city and in the bookselling business.

But for Samuel, newly returned from Oxford, these were signs of shame. He had as little as possible to do with bookselling, despite the fact that both his parents, and even Nathaniel, were keen for him to take it up. It seemed an obvious occupation for a young man who was so evidently fond of books; yet Johnson, more as a mark of independence than for any practical reason, refused to consider it. One day, towards the end of his life, Michael asked that he might accompany him to Uttoxeter market but Samuel adamantly refused. Years later this disobedience still haunted him. 'Pride was the source of that refusal, and the remembrance of it was painful.' He attempted to atone for the fault: 'I went to Uttoxeter in very bad weather, and stood for a considerable time bareheaded in the rain, on the spot where my father's stall used to stand. In contrition I stood, and I hope the penance was expiatory.' This act of expiation, while no doubt genuine, is a *public* act, an example of Johnson using Boswell, who recorded the act, to turn a personal sense of guilt into a public spectacle of contrition.[25] Such pride as he had was only redoubled by the sight of Michael working doggedly on, unable to rectify the causes of his progressive failure which were bound up with his attempt to manufacture his own parchment. When, in 1730, the lease of the factory lands by Stowe Pool came due, Michael was keen to have it renewed though the factory workshop was almost derelict 'for want of money to repair it'. He was 'not less diligent to lock the door every night' though even he could see 'that anybody might walk in at the back part'. Johnson told Mrs Thrale this anecdote as proof of what he most feared, insanity. '*This* . . . was madness, you see . . . but poverty prevented it from playing such tricks as riches and leisure encourage.'[26] The madness that he felt he saw in his father's behaviour played into Johnson's own obsessive fears of insanity, as acute when he came back from Oxford as at any later time. Boswell described them as a 'morbid melancholy' or 'horrible hypochondria' and concluded that Johnson 'never afterwards was perfectly relieved' from this melancholy, but performed his 'labours' and partook of his (occasional) enjoyments as 'temporary interruptions of its baleful influence'. He became so 'languid and inefficient that he could not distinguish the hour upon the town-clock', Boswell relates, mentioning as an astonishing fact something with which Johnson, afflicted with wretchedly poor eyesight, always had problems. More characteristically Johnsonian are the remedies – the 'forcible exertions' – he undertook, walking back and forth to Birmingham, a distance of over thirty miles, and 'many other expedients, but all in vain . . . "I inherited, (said he,) a vile melancholy from my father, which has made me mad all my life, at least not sober." '[27]

This fear of insanity, so much insisted upon by Boswell in his *Life* and Mrs Thrale in her *Anecdotes*, has become part of the accepted version of Johnson's life: 'To Johnson, whose supreme enjoyment was the exercise of his reason, the disturbance or obscuration of that faculty was the evil most to be dreaded. Insanity, therefore, was the object of his most dismal apprehension.'[28] Yet Johnson lived till the age of seventy-five, and his doings and his sayings were recorded, in detail, as for none other. Apart from one or two ominously revealing remarks, he lived a life of good sense in an age which had no Valium to calm the nerves. Similarly the 'madman' Michael also lived to be seventy-five, rising from nothing to become the mayor of Lichfield, a magistrate, and to own a well-stocked bookshop in the market-square. There are many myths of Johnson the deranged genius, even a rumour that Johnson 'strongly entertained thoughts of suicide' and talked to John Taylor of doing it.[29] By contrast what we know as fact about Michael's death was that it occurred in December 1731 and that Catherine Chambers, his wife's maid, arranged for the funeral ceremony.[30] These distinctions between Johnson *fact* and Johnson the biographer's *fancy* must be borne in mind when considering the life of the man who invented biography as a medium, and starred in one of the greatest biographies ever written.

During these empty years Johnson wrote poems to young ladies, which all have a noticeable tendency to speak of love. 'To a Young Lady on Her Birthday' is a 'tributary verse' sent by an 'ardent lover' which warns her that 'Alas! 'tis hard for beauty to be just'. 'An Epilogue to *The Distrest Mother*' was apparently never used in a performance of the play (an adaptation of Racine's *Andromaque*), though its lively tone, referring to young ladies' 'snowy breasts' and borrowing quite freely from *The Rape of the Lock*, suggests close, indeed intimate, female associations. Edmund Hector confirmed 'some young ladies at Lichfield' had indeed proposed to act the play, whereupon Johnson had gladly written the poem. The exact reason why it was not used is unknown, but Johnson's clumsy appearance and impecunious background cannot have helped his cause. His 'Ode on a Lady Leaving Her Place of Abode' and lines 'On a Daffodill' are addressed to 'Cleora', who may have been Ann Hector, Edmund's sister; almost fifty years later he told Boswell that Ann 'was the first woman with whom I was in love . . . She and I shall always have a kindness for each other.'[31] The last verses we have from 1731 are those 'On A Lady's Presenting a Sprig of Myrtle to a Gentleman' which were written for Morgan Graves, brother to Richard (author of *The Spiritual Quixote*) Graves, who received the sprig when the lady left the neighbourhood. Applying to Johnson for a poetic reply, Hector received the verses 'in about half an hour' and sent them off to Graves to use as a complimentary gift. This added sense of detachment allowed Johnson to indulge in playful anatomisations of both the role and meaning of the 'ambiguous emblem', at once crowning the 'happy lovers' heads' and spreading a tribute over their graves. He could never have guessed that his innocuous fourteen-line poem would become so popular or so controversial; reprinted at least twenty times in his lifetime it was tussled over after his death by Hester Thrale, who said the lines were 'nonsense' written for 'dear [Ed]Mund' in 'five minutes', and Boswell who believed them serious verses, addressed to Lucy Porter.[32] Boswell mentions friendships begun at this time with Hill Boothby, Molly Aston and Olivia Lloyd (a young Quaker whom Johnson met and loved while a master at Stourbridge school) but emphasises that Johnson's 'juvenile attachments' were 'very transient'.[33] It is clear that Johnson found the company of young women captivating, particularly when circumstances at home were dull; he must bitterly have regretted that his appearance and lack of social graces made entry into the fields of amorous display at best a puzzle, at worst a farce.

Johnson was mainly occupied at this time trying to get enough money to resume his studies in Oxford; failing which, to enable him to live somewhere other than at Lichfield. In Stourbridge that summer disputes at the grammar school resulted in a vacancy for an usher, and he immediately dashed off verses to Dorothy, the seventeen-year-old daughter of Gregory Hickman, who was half-brother to Cornelius Ford, praising the adroitness with which she played her spinet. In his poem Johnson presents himself enslaved to her melodious charms, blessing her tyranny and hugging his chain. Actually, he was 'very insensible to the power of musick', but, whether it was proximity to Dorothy Hickman or the possibility of the usher's post that inspired him, he described himself as quite helpless before her music's 'dreadfull pow'r'.[34] Sadly he was also helpless before the headmaster of Stourbridge grammar school and it was not Johnson but John Hughes, with a degree from Oxford, who was chosen for the usher's post. Hickman told him not to despair, and, much taken with the lines on his daughter, suggested a satire on disputes at the school. Johnson, unable to view the situation in quite such a merry mood, did not respond for weeks; when eventually he did reply, there is little disguising the bleakness of his tone. 'Versifying against ones inclination is the most disagreable thing in the World,' he writes, begging to be let off the task but asking Hickman in his last sentence that 'As I am yet unemploy'd' he would remember him 'if anything should offer'.[35]

More friends and acquaintances were approached over the winter and he at last gained a post at Market Bosworth grammar school which promised twenty pounds a year. It also offered him a house, according to the statutes, which went on to stipulate that the successful applicant should hold a BA degree and be free from all contagious infections. Sir Wolstan Dixie, a boorish, bullying lover of violent old-fashioned sports, was chief patron of the school and no stickler for the statutes. Johnson was accepted for the post and received accommodation in Sir Wolstan's residence, Bosworth Park, set in its own grounds, a few minutes' walk from the school. In March 1732 Johnson wrote optimistically in his *Annals*, 'S. J. Bosvorthiam petivit',* but his optimism did not last long. Sir Wolstan was legendary for his ignorance, matched only by his pugnacity. When he was presented to George II as 'Sir Wolstan Dixie of Bosworth Park', His majesty replied that he had heard of the battle of Bosworth, to which Dixie replied, 'Yes, Sire. But I thrashed him.'[36]

* 'S. J. went to Bosworth'.

Apart from teaching at the school, Johnson acted as a kind of lay chaplain to Sir Wolstan, saying grace at table, but, from the start, 'was treated with what he represented as intolerable harshness'. Severity was apparently quite common; another writer declares the inhabitants of Bosworth 'set their dogs at me merely because I was a stranger'. In the school there was no relief; Johnson did not know 'whether it was more disagreeable for him to teach, or the boys to learn, the grammar rules'. He had a job, but it was as 'unvaried as the note of the cuckow'; ' "*Vitam continet una dies*" (one day contains the whole of my life),' he declared.[37] In June, which in his excitement he miswrote as July, he received word from Lichfield that since Michael's will was to be proved, his presence was required. The results of the reading he recorded thus:

> I laid by eleven guineas; on which day I received all of my father's effects which I can hope for till the death of my mother, (which I pray may be late), that is to say, nineteen pounds; so that I have my fortune to make, and care must be taken, that in the mean time, the powers of my mind may not grow languid through poverty, nor want drive me into wickedness. Note: of twenty pounds I had taken out one before.[38]

It is tempting to read a lot into Johnson's scrappy notes, but this is a deliberate reminder to himself that he had 'my fortune to make'. For the first time, at the age of twenty-two, he had money of his own and was careful to add it up exactly; so careful that in doing so he made two errors, reckoning it first at twenty, later at eighteen pounds, and misspelling 'pounds' (*Libris* for *Libras*) completely. He had borrowed a pound from his father for some small necessity and was careful to deduct it from the total. He had a whole nineteen pounds, plus whatever he was owed from Market Bosworth, to make his fortune and he was determined to treat it seriously: so much so that, as he noted in his *Annals*, he returned to Bosworth the next day *on foot* ('*Bosvortiam pedes petii*'). His period at the school had been a mistake and he would not waste a single penny on retrieving his position. It lay some twenty-five miles from Lichfield and on his way Johnson did some serious thinking. The next day, during dinner with Sir Wolstan's brother, the Reverend Beaumont Dixie, he was reintroduced to John Corbet, brother to the Andrew Corbet who had promised Johnson financial help at Oxford but then had slipped away. He 'used to be most delightful to me,' Johnson comments, but there is a strong sense of the past about this meeting. He promptly gave his notice to Sir Wolstan, working it out so that he should have all the money due to him. By July he was back in Lichfield, correcting errors in a seventeenth-century book, *Manuductio ad Coelum*, by Giovanni Bona.[39] A fortnight later he wrote to John Taylor to enquire about a possible vacancy at Ashbourne grammar school that had been mentioned to him by John Corbet, possibly as a way of making amends. 'If there be any reason for my coming to Ashburne, I shall readily do it,' he declared, assuming Corbet would have acquainted Taylor with his reasons for leaving Bosworth: 'It was really *e Carcere exire*,' he writes; 'getting out of prison'. There is a new confidence in his tone and although when the school's governors met in August they elected Thomas Bourne, Johnson was not unduly concerned.[40] It was not schoolmastering but schoolmastering *at Bosworth* that he recalled with aversion, remembering it, long afterwards, with a kind of horror. Thomas Bourne had been without a degree, but still appointed, he noted.

3

Marriage

marriage n.s. *(*mariage, *French;* maritagium, *low Latin, from* maritus.*)* *The act of uniting a man and a woman for life.*

The *marriage* with his brother's wife
Has crept too near his conscience.
Shakesp. *Henry VIII*

That autumn Samuel received an invitation from his old school friend, Edmund Hector, to come to Birmingham, a grubby town mainly notable for the importance of its ironworks. Johnson went expecting nothing, anticipating a stay of a couple of weeks: he remained there for four years and, by the time he left, was married.

It cannot have been accidental that he stayed there. Or that he married. Ever since he had quitted Lichfield four years earlier he had been determined to find a place away from the city of his birth in which to make his name. The opportunities for him to publish and sell books in Lichfield were just too limited and, ever since being forced to abandon his hopes of Oxford, he had been making efforts to get away. His mother could not see why he had to go, which only made the need more pressing, forcing him to make his brother Nathaniel his excuse; which, though plausible enough, was a contingent, not necessary reason. Had he so wished, he could have controlled his spendthrift brother easily enough.

He escaped to Birmingham where he roomed with Hector in the house of Thomas Warren, the town's only bookseller, in the High Street. Warren was a man of boundless ambitions with plans to start a local weekly paper, the *Birmingham Journal*, to furnish all the news, foreign and domestic, to the Midlands. The foreign news he would 'borrow' from London papers while for domestic news he would rely on his own network of contacts; the paper would be set up in his own best type, with one page of its four devoted to advertisements. In everything it would be as good *and* cheap as anything they had in London. Johnson was intrigued; they fell to an agreement, and he began his first work as a journalist on Warren's *Birmingham Journal*.

Only a single issue of the *Journal* survives, for 21 May, from which a single item, the advertisement of a 'new melch'd ass, with a foul [*sic*] not a month old' to be sold by 'Mr Holmes at the George Inn in Lichfield', can, with any plausibility, be attributed to Johnson.[1] The rest of the items indicate the kind of news he dealt in. A Spanish fleet fired its guns 'with great Fury' off Leghorn; the French queen was delivered of a princess, while from Hamburg came whispers of court intrigues 'capable not only of kindling a dangerous Fire in the Kingdom of Poland, but also of engaging all Europe in a general war'. From the streets of Dublin came mortifying news: in Stephen's Street the five-year-old child of Jones the plasterer fell down a well 'of a very great Depth' while in Hammond Lane a shoemaker named Terryl poisoned himself, 'being jealous of his Wife'. In Kent, a grampus landed on the flats at Sandwich, proved 'very troublesome' and made 'a hideous Roaring', while in London a workman from Mr Tomkins's glass-house, 'being cheerful and seemingly in good Health', suddenly trembled and died. Tales of smugglers and highwaymen, footpads and perjurers filled the crammed columns to cater for the interests of the *Journal*'s Midlands readership.

Warren introduced Johnson to many people, including the Porters: Harry, who kept a drapery shop, and Elizabeth, his wife. By June Johnson felt sufficiently settled to take up lodgings on his own account. The *Annals* note him occupying a room '*apud F. Jervis Birminghamiae*' ('in the home of F. Jervis of Birmingham'); since Jervis was the maiden name of Elizabeth Porter it would seem the house belonged to her family and that she was already strengthening her hold on the young man from Lichfield.[2] Shortly afterwards the *Annals* mention an occupation to go with his new status as a tenant; '*Mensibus hibernis Iter ad Abisiniam Anglicè reddidi*,' he wrote ('Spent the winter months translating a *Voyage to Abyssinia*'). But the active force of his past-tense *'reddidi'* was, like so much else in Johnson's *Annals*, a matter of wish rather than attainment. One night he mentioned having read Father Lobo's *Voyage to Abyssinia* at Oxford and said an English translation would do well; both Warren and Hector immediately agreed, 'urging him to undertake it'. Warren promised five guineas for the completed work, which is when Johnson hit upon a problem.[3] It was fine to propose suggestions of what he *might* do; it was very different to have his bluff called.

At first the problem could be postponed since the only copy that he knew of the French translation of Lobo's *Voyage* was in the library of Pembroke College. Johnson happily bewailed the fact until, that winter, Hector went and asked to borrow it.[4] There was now nothing to prevent him from getting on with a translation except his own 'constitutional indolence'. Johnson took to his bed, declaring himself utterly incapable of achieving the task. But Hector, who had grown to know his man, told him the printer and his family were suffering while waiting for the translation to be done. Reluctantly Johnson was brought to 'exert the powers of his mind' upon the translation, though physically he still resisted. In bed he dictated his version to Hector which was given to Warren to be printed. Hector even corrected the proofs, which were almost totally unseen by Johnson. It was as if he did not wish to be associated in any way with the work, which represented his first book-length publication. *A Voyage to Abyssinia by Father Jerome Lobo* appeared in December 1734, with 'LONDON upon the title-page, though it was in reality printed in Birmingham, a device too common with provincial publishers'.[5]

Johnson was never proud of his first published work. He had dipped into Lobo's book and memorised notable passages but translating it gave him serious misgivings; the much-quoted Preface, however, is a masterpiece of his style which changed remarkably little throughout his life. It placed a strong emphasis upon stability. Here are 'no romantick absurdities or incredible fictions', he declares; Lobo has 'copied nature from the life', consulting 'his senses not his imagination'. The reader of his narrative meets with no basilisks that destroy with their eyes, his crocodiles devour their prey without tears, and his cataracts fall from the-rock without deafening the neighbouring inhabitants. The reader will here find no regions cursed with irremediable barren-ness, or bless'd with spontaneous fecundity, no perpetual gloom or unceasing sunshine . . . he will discover, *what will always be discover'd by a diligent and impartial enquirer*, that wherever human nature is to be found, there is a mixture of vice and virtue . . .[6]

In his translation, he acknowledged (even boasted, uncertain whether *translation* was the word he wanted) that 'great liberties have been taken' with the text, though usually he followed Lobo, even in such bizarre moments as the description of a serpent in whose head is found 'a stone about the bigness of an egg, resembling bezoar, and of great efficacy, as it is said, against all kinds of poison'. Occasionally Johnson's own sense of decorum led him to omit details of a sexual nature, including the custom of the Maracates who, valuing female chastity, sewed up the genitals of young girls, the stitching only to be undone by future husbands. Lobo conceded that '*cette coûtume soit un peu barbare*' but '*on ne peut s'empêcher d'estimer le soin qu'ils ont de con-server parmi eux une vertu si rare par tout ailleurs.*'* Johnson resisted, or even occasionally challenged, the strong Jesuit tone of the original, translating '*hérétiques*' or '*schismatiques*' as those 'opposed to the Church of Rome'.[7]

These details are from the first two sections of the *Voyage*, whose latter parts were written down and carried off by Hector without great thought or consideration. Johnson gradually withdrew his mind from the translation as indicated by the increased number of simple errors occurring in the text. Numbers are particularly subject to mistakes. '*Dix*' becomes 'six' more than once; '*trois hommes*' becomes 'four of their company' though elsewhere '*trois*' is given as 'two'. Nor is this an occasional matter; it occurs at least ten times, with some of the errors ('twenty four' used to express '*quatre vingt*') making for

---

* 'This custom may appear barbaric, but yet one cannot help applauding the care with which they seek to preserve a virtue which has, elsewhere, become so rare.'

significant blunders. The reason for these errors was not misunder-standing of the French but a psychological blockage in translating it. In the words of Adam Phillips, a psychoanalyst:

> His mistakes are an unconscious protest about accuracy and order; as though unconsciously there is a part of him that feels that getting it right is an act of submission or compliance, so in a comparatively minor way, in the text, he makes a bid for freedom. He permits himself the minimal numerical error that can easily be understood as a mistake and yet under cover of this rationalisation frees him to do something else (like Dostoyevsky's *Underground Man* insisting that 2 + 2 = 5).[8]

Reading Boswell's version of the translation process, one can see Johnson's 'bid for freedom' being enacted: 'He lay in bed with the book, which was a quarto, before him, and dictated while Hector wrote. Mr Hector carried the sheets to the press, and corrected almost all the proof sheets, very few of which were even seen by Johnson.'[9]

Reasons for this unconscious refusal to be associated with the processes of production must be conjectural; Johnson had not got over the feeling of rejection from Pembroke, which duplicated his earlier expulsion from Lichfield Grammar. The first rejection, he had boasted, had been 'his own fault' for treating Hunter, his schoolmaster at Lichfield, with condescension. But when he tried something of the same nature at Pembroke, happily reproving tutors for not being up to the task of teaching him, he flew, like Icarus, too near the sun. His family's financial collapse and his withdrawal from the college were terrible warnings to him. Since then he had been alternately lying on his bed in a state of psychological collapse or working feverishly to try to get back to the state that 'belonged' to him. Now at last he was gaining a foothold on a literary life, yet his surroundings made him bitterly self-conscious. His entrance into the literary world should have been with a volume of poems from an Oxford don or a play from a London man-about-town, not with the translation of a mediocre book from Birmingham.

Although he affected to be uninterested in the volume's publica-tion, its fate went deeply into his subconscious. When, twenty-five years later, he was forced back to this mental dark spot by the death of his mother, he returned to the same Abyssinian 'barren summit' in his fable *Rasselas, Prince of Abyssinia*. Here, 'princes of the blood-royal pass'd their melancholy life' guarded by officers who 'treated them often with great rigour and severity'.[10] In March 1735 the *Voyage* was mentioned in the *Literary Magazine*, which devoted several pages to excerpts, but, if Johnson knew of the publication, he made no comment on it.

In February he returned to Lichfield to receive £5 willed to him by his godfather, Richard Wakefield, and to issue new proposals for an edition of Politian, the Italian Renaissance poet.[11] Again, the original of the book he wanted was in Pembroke College library from where, when he heard of a clergyman visiting Oxford, he begged the chance to borrow it. The loan of the book was noted but not its return, and it was found among Johnson's posthumous possessions.[12] The fact that he kept it, and his own extensive library at Christ Church, indicate his reluctance to sever links with Oxford. His proposals for publishing, by subscription, the Latin poems of Politian have never been discovered, but it seems he promised a volume of some thirty sheets at the modest price of 2s 6d, 'at the delivery of a perfect book in quires', subscriptions being taken in 'by the Editor, or by N. Johnson, bookseller, of Lichfield'. In September he solicited an unknown correspondent, taking 'the liberty' of despatching him 'twelve of my Proposals' and hoping earnestly for his recommendation. Despite all these efforts his proposals were unsuccessful and, 'not meeting with sufficient encouragement, Johnson dropped the design'.[13]

Sometime that year he wrote his diary with poverty uppermost in his mind: 'To a man short of money . . .' he began, then crossed it out as being, even in an ancient language, too personal. He tried again: 'For a poor man going among strangers, I have found out the signs: silk thread (of which the stockings are knitted) and buckles of the same colour as the clothes.' He had been struck, walking about Lichfield, by the way this kind of clothing became a kind of uniform of the indigent and was more than a little ashamed to recognise he wore just such apparel himself. He attempted, noting it *in Latin*, to place a certain distance between himself and the observation, adding a touch of class to his aphorism by putting the word for stockings in Greek.[14] He also attempted, as he had in his last weeks at Pembroke, to regularise and stimulate his reading by writing down a number of Greek and Latin works, from the *Medea* of Euripides to Horace's *Ars Poetica* and Virgil's *Aeneid*, calculating the precise amount of lines that each one comprised and setting himself to read a certain number of lines each week. As he tried to fill his days in Lichfield with these useful occupations, he received word that would change his plans. In Birmingham Harry Porter had died, aged only forty-three. Johnson had heard something in the weeks beforehand of Harry Porter's sudden decline, but his death at such a youthful age was still a shock. More importantly, it offered him an opportunity.

Elizabeth Porter, née Jervis, was a plump widow of forty-five, a little older than her deceased husband, and mother to three children: Lucy, eighteen, Jervis Henry, sixteen, and Joseph, ten. She had kept herself remarkably handsome, for her hair, Johnson later claimed, 'was eminently beautiful, quite *blonde* like that of a baby'.[15] The comment, mentioned to her, pleased her, and she would play up to it with her fleshy figure, large eyes and pouting lips. Johnson had grown close to 'Tetty', as she allowed him to call her, by being attracted to her daughter, Lucy, as he was attracted to several pretty eighteen-year-olds, Mollies, Anns or Olivias. They had joked about it, both together. No doubt, while he was renting a room from her Jervis relation, they had often been in contact and, freed by her status as a married woman who was old enough to be his mother, the three of them, Samuel, Harry and 'Tetty', formed a relaxed trio. Lucy later recalled the horror of Johnson's appearance: his 'immense structure of bones . . . hideously striking', his 'scars of the scrophula . . . deeply visible'; himself 'lean and lank', his hair 'straight and stiff', with 'convulsive starts and odd gesticulations, which tended to excite at once surprize and ridicule'. But her mother had time to become engaged by his conversation and to overlook such superficial blemishes. She told her daughter that Johnson was 'the most sensible man that I ever saw in my life'.[16] That this 'most sensible man', twenty years her junior, should have fallen in love with her is, however, a somewhat improbable proposition and deserves to be fully explored.

The main commentators on the match, Boswell and Mrs Thrale, never met Tetty and each had their own reasons for minimising her position in Johnson's life. They relied on Garrick, who *had* known her, for the grotesque versions they depict. This is Mrs Thrale: 'she was a little painted puppet, of no value at all, and quite disguised with affectation, full of odd airs of rural elegance: and he made out some comical scenes, by mimicking her in a dialogue he pretended to have overheard . . .' This is Boswell, who narrates how Garrick described her:

> . . . as very fat, with a bosom of more than ordinary protuber-ance, with swelled cheeks, of a florid red, produced by thick painting, and increased by the liberal use of cordials; flaring and fantastick in her dress, and affected both in her speech and her general behaviour. I have seen Garrick exhibit her, by his exquisite talent for mimickry, so as to excite the heartiest bursts of laughter; but he, probably, as is the case in all such represen-tations, considerably aggravated the picture.[17]

Garrick first encountered Mrs Johnson as his schoolmaster's wife and many of his versions were based upon scenes allegedly glimpsed through the school bedroom keyhole. It is evident that neither Johnson nor Tetty was good-looking, though both had fairly large sexual appetites which, on Johnson's side at least, had only with difficulty been kept under control. It is obvious the girls he most admired were those whom any twenty-five-year-old would have found attractive; but not only did his physical disabilities place him at a marked disadvantage, he also had no money to set aside this initial effect. Tetty Porter was a woman whom he had come to know and, in a curious way, to trust. It has been maliciously suggested that poor eyesight may have misled him into not remarking Tetty's signs of maturity, but the real calculation of Johnson's proposal, with less potential for mockery, has been less widely discussed. Tetty was rich.[18]

Mrs Porter, born on 4 February 1689, the daughter of a comfortable Warwickshire squire, brought a dowry of £600 to her marriage with

Harry Porter which, their marriage document stipulated, remained her property if he should die before her. In 1734 £600 was a very large sum of money, a multiple of 100 generally being used to give a twenty-first-century equivalent. Johnson had endured the mortification of 'teaching' at Bosworth Hall for £20 a year and had thrown it up exultingly at receiving £19 in his father's will. Thirty years later he counselled Boswell that '£30 a year was enough to make a man live without being contemptible'. Now he had the prospect of a fortune of £600 before him. 'The first advances probably proceeded from her, as her attachment to Johnson was in opposition to the advice and desire of all her relations,' says Boswell.[19] Johnson was twenty-five, ugly and penniless; she was forty-five, portly, sentimental and rich. Walter Jackson Bate comments that 'no one with even the slightest acquaintance with Johnson ever did make or has made the suggestion' that Johnson married Tetty for money. But her family did. Her elder son, Jervis Henry, training to be a naval officer, was so affronted by his mother's conduct in marrying Johnson that he never saw her again; her younger son, Joseph, took years to overcome the same disgust. Her brother-in-law, a wealthy London merchant, 'offered to settle a very handsome annuity on her for life' *if* she gave up the engagement, but she refused. Only Lucy sided with her mother.[20] For Johnson, at the start of adult life, it was an almost incredible opportunity and, having had his hopes of Oxford rudely smashed, it was not one he was prepared to relinquish. Out of courtesy, he asked his mother for her consent which, according to Anna Seward's colourful version given to friends in Lichfield, she refused to give, on the grounds of Mrs Porter's age; 'she is turned fifty' was her reported comment.[21]

In view of all these discouragements, Johnson made a last serious effort to attain a position that would remove him entirely from all such problems. At the end of November he wrote to Edward Cave, proprietor of the *Gentleman's Magazine*. This journal, the most significant of the time, was widely read, and Johnson offered bold ideas 'to the improvement of it'. Cave should cut back his 'Wit of the Month' section and fill the space with literary dissertations, critical remarks or 'forgotten poems that deserve revival'. By this means the magazine would do much better than by 'low jests, awkward buffoonery, or the dull scurrilities of either party'. Johnson's tone is deliberately audacious; if Cave is interested 'be pleased to inform me in two posts', he writes. He has even decided on the amount of money he would need in London; 'Your late offer gives me no reason to distrust your generosity,' he tells Cave, having in mind the £50 prize for the best poem, in Latin or English, offered in the October issue. For £50 he would give up marriage and life in the Midlands and move to London; Cave must decide. 'Your letter, by being directed to S. Smith to be left at the Castle in Birmingham,' he concludes, offering a pseudonym for this fanciful request. He had decided what he would most like to do and was writing his request in his most confident voice, but really he did not expect a reply. 'S. Smith' would wait till the end of the year; if he did not receive a summons to London by then, he would propose to Tetty. The letter is endorsed 'Answered Dec. 2' but we do not know what Cave may have told him.[22]

By the end of the year he had made up his mind. He proposed and was accepted. To earn himself some additional funds and allow his bride some time for mourning her previous husband, he accepted a post as tutor to the son of Thomas Whitby of Great Haywood to prepare him for university. In consultation with Elizabeth, he had decided to invest the money she would bring him in a school. Although his experience of school-teaching had been far from ideal, he had a belief, strengthened by his present position, that the post of schoolmaster was one he might accomplish with distinction.[23] In May he wrote to his former schoolfellow Gilbert Repington who was now at Christ Church, Oxford, to have his library of eighty-six books collected and 'with what care you can' transmitted to him 'at the Castle in Birmingham'. He would 'very thankfully repay the expences of Boxes, Porters, and Letters to your Brother', feeling considerable relief, at long last, of being able to spend money with freedom. A month later he wrote to Richard Congreve of Christ Church to supply him with 'an account of the different ways of teaching' at Charterhouse and Westminster. He was about to 'keep a private boarding-school for Young Gentlemen' which, he cared to fancy, would be maintained by methods 'more rational than those commonly practised'. Still at Great Haywood he dreamt of doing notable things in education, after the little matter of the wedding which, though the letter is filled with friendly blandishments, he never thinks to mention.

Lacking goodwill on either side towards their marriage, the odd couple proceeded alone to Derby's St Werburgh's church to be married on 9 July 1735. 'I know not for what reason the marriage was not performed at Birmingham,' Boswell states, innocuously. The reason is quite clear: neither family approved the match. Tetty, conscious of their constant sniping, or from simple vanity, stretched the truth and gave her age as 'forty' on the marriage licence. A great reader, she had consumed several old romances and 'had got into her head the fantastical notion that a woman of spirit should use her lover like a dog'. She had the notion that young Johnson liked to be attentive to her, flattering her with pretty verses. For Johnson, it was most important that he stamp out that feeling immediately, and, apparently, he did so 'upon the nuptial morn':

> . . . at first she told me that I rode too fast, and she could not keep up with me; and, when I rode a little slower, she passed me, and complained that I lagged behind. I was not to be made the slave of caprice; and I resolved to begin as I meant to end. I therefore pushed on briskly, till I was fairly out of her sight. The road lay between two hedges, so I was sure she could not miss it; and I contrived that she should soon come up with me. When she did, I observed her to be in tears.[24]

'This, it must be allowed, was a singular beginning of connubial felicity,' comments Boswell, though it was a detail mentioned both to him and Mrs Thrale.[25] Clearly Johnson was determined to be master in his own house, even if it was his wife's money that paid for it. 'It was a love-marriage upon both sides,' Boswell alleges Johnson told Topham Beauclerk 'with much gravity', phrases which Beauclerk 'archly' recalled. It is not clear what inference Boswell draws from these marmoreal sentences, though it is clear the Johnsons' marriage did not conform to his notions. There would be no children, that was plain. The recollection of the journey of the affianced couple to church in July 1735 has a fabliau quality recalling Petruchio's interrogation of Katherina in *The Taming of the Shrew* and, many years later, when Johnson came to edit the play, he found that scene 'eminently spritely and diverting'.[26]

He delayed the opening of his school though, rightly wondering whether it were the occupation for him and, while he hesitated, a schoolmaster's post came up at Solihull. His old mentor Gilbert Walmesley wrote on his behalf and the answer, when it came, might have caused him further thought. The governors were satisfied he was an 'excellent scholar', but found his character 'very haughty, ill-natured' and were afraid his appearance ('distorting his face') might adversely affect his pupils.[27] Rather provoked by this reaction than dissuaded, Johnson soon found a building to rent for his proposed school at Edial (pronounced 'Edjal'), two miles west of Lichfield. Several alterations to the building were necessary, which accounted for the low rental, and while the work of refurbishment went ahead he busied himself formulating 'Schemes' of the education he would practise. As always, he went into precise detail: there would be examinations 'every Thursday and Saturday', starting with the colloquies of Cordery and Erasmus, going on through Eutropius and Cornelius Nepos, proceeding to Ovid's *Metamorphoses* and the *Commentaries* of Caesar, and concluding with Virgil, Horace and some Greek. On paper the scheme was well worked out and existed in several versions. Consulted for advice on books to study by his cousin Samuel Ford, who was going up to Oxford, Johnson advised him to apply himself 'wholly to the languages, till you go to the University', mentioning Homer for the Ionic dialect and Theocritus for the Doric. Among Latin authors he advises those 'of the purest ages' including Caesar, Virgil and Horace and recommends that Ford attain 'a habit of expression' without which all knowledge is of little use.[28] Written in his best pedagogic manner the letter gives a clear indication of Johnson's teaching style and his emphasis on a simple but strict syllabus.

The school opened in 1735 but only attracted somewhere between three and eight pupils, with most later commentators opting for the lower figure; those who give the higher figure make clear that 'not all' those who attended were boarders.[29] Johnson was twenty-six, without a university degree and with a most forbidding appearance: even without the existence nearby of the excellent Lichfield Grammar School, such disadvantages would have been enough to discourage most potential pupils. His own education had been acquired 'by fits and starts' and it places too much reliance on his undoubted zeal to think inspired enthusiasm might take the place of dogged persistence. His eccentricities of manner were quickly ridiculed by pupils amongst whom young David Garrick showed a particular gift for pantomime. In later years he would entertain close friends with those scenes which he claimed were spied through the bedroom keyhole; the clumsy Johnson, in dishevelled bed-linen, calling out, 'I'm coming, my Tetsie', which struck them as 'ludicrous, when applied to a woman of her age and appearance'; or absent-mindedly tucking the bedclothes instead of his shirt down his breeches, leaving poor Tetty to freeze.[30] Things became so bad in June and July of the following year that the *Gentleman's Magazine* carried this advertisement: 'At Edial, near Litchfield, in Staffordshire, young gentlemen are boarded and taught the Latin and Greek languages by Samuel Johnson.' There were no takers. One night, at the end of August 1736 Johnson took up his *Annals*, but had nothing to record. 'This day I have trifled away', he wrote, 'except that I have attended the school in the morning.' He could see the school was going broke but, like his father, did not care to investigate too closely. Instead, he read sermons and made a resolution to eat no more till Sunday, when he would take communion.[31] The following week he took stock of himself, promising to 'review the rules I have at any time had lain down in order to practice them', a moral reflection deepened by news he had just received from Lichfield.

In late September 1736 his mother had received a letter from her younger son, Nathaniel, who was in London planning, so the letter informed her, to 'go to Georgia', the newly founded American colony, 'in about a fortnight'. Although he was now twenty-three years old Mrs Johnson still thought of him as her 'young Natty' and the letter was an example of what she was used to, his trying terribly hard to be strong, but failing completely. 'I know not nor do I much care in what Way of Life I shall heafter [*sic*] live,' he had written, 'but this I know, yt it shall be an honest one and yt can't be more unpleasant yn some part of my life past.'[32] In the absence of any co-operation from Samuel, Nathaniel had tried his hand at the book trade, starting off in Stourbridge where Sarah Johnson's family could keep an eye on him. But, sadly, Nathaniel did not have the true way of bookselling, being too easily led, too merry and too fond of a drink. Mrs Johnson would have given him enough to make a 'Positive Bargain' for a shop there which might have allowed him to live happily enough and not to have slipped into the 'crime' which a recent visit from Samuel had revealed. Nathaniel's crimes went beyond such minor peccadilloes as running up large debts and cheating his customers. He admitted and apologised for faults which, as he put it, 'have given both you & me so much trouble' and even complained that he had now 'neither Money nor Credit to buy one Quire of paper'. He knew his mother would not begrudge the 'Working Tools' he had borrowed from the Lichfield shop. But his brother took a very different view. Fearing lest rumours of Nathaniel's criminality might put an end to whatever slim hopes he still clung to of maintaining his school, he ruled that nowhere in England would do for Nathaniel's rehabilitation. America was the only place. 'As to My Brothers assisting me I had but little Reason to expect it', Nathaniel wrote, 'when he would scarce ever use me with common civility & to whose Advice was owing that unwillingness you shewd to my going to Stourbridge.' He signed off with a last apology for all the trouble and expense he had caused the family. 'Have courage my dear Mother,' he wrote. 'God will lead you through all your troubles. If my brother did design doing anything for me I am obliged to him & thank him . . .'

Michaelmas brought no new boys to the school and when, in November, Lawrence Offley was admitted to Clare College, Cambridge, Johnson's school at Edial was left almost without pupils. In February Gilbert Walmesley wrote to his friend Mr Colson in Rochester requesting him to prepare David Garrick for the bar; his brother George was sent to Appleby Grammar and, without them, the school finally closed.[33] How much of Tetty's money Johnson lost in the venture is not known, but it was considerable. Now he was left not only without a means of support, but with his wife's expectations to maintain. He spent the last few weeks at Edial hastily concocting a tragedy, *Mahomet and Irene*, sketched from Knolles's *General History of the Turks* which he had borrowed from David Garrick's elder brother, Peter. David, meanwhile, was planning to set out imminently for London and Johnson decided to accompany him. On 2 March Walmesley informed Colson that Garrick and 'another neighbour of mine, one Mr Samuel Johnson', were setting out that morning for London, with Johnson hoping 'to try his fate with a tragedy'.

The urge to move and try his hand elsewhere received a further incentive when Samuel heard that Nathaniel, having finally lost the nerve to risk himself on an ocean voyage to Georgia, had hidden himself away in the West Country. No one knew him in Somerset and it seemed even possible that he might gain a living as a bookbinder. But something essential to Nathaniel's life had been extinguished and, in early March, he died. Samuel said nothing; his charity was all exhausted, and he had the failure of his own attempt as a schoolmaster, and with it the loss of almost all of Tetty's money, to consider. He was, wrote Walmesley, 'a very good scholar and poet, and I have great hopes will turn out a fine tragedy-writer'. Whether Johnson shared these hopes is rather doubtful, but clearly something of the kind had been said in order to pacify Tetty's troubled mind. On the very day that Nathaniel died, Samuel and 'Davy' Garrick took one horse between them for the journey to the capital, which they 'rode and tied'; that is, each taking turns to ride ahead, tie up the horse to a wayside post and walk on. In later years, they liked to joke about that journey, and about the poverty which drove them to it; Johnson declared, 'I came with twopence halfpenny in *my* pockets, and thou, Davy, with three halfpence in thine.'[34]

Three days after they set out Johnson's brother, Nathaniel, was buried in St Michael's Church at Lichfield. That Samuel knew of his reappearance and of his death is certain, but by then the decision to leave had been made and he would not change it, even for his brother's funeral. How Nathaniel's body was brought back to Lichfield; how his debts (if any) were paid, and how Nathaniel himself was buried he did not allow himself to deal with, leaving all such matters to his mother's care. He evaded responsibilities which had rightfully become his on his father's death and left Sarah Johnson to mourn for her son alone. His only obituary message was the words 'my brother' scribbled alongside the words 'the sufferings which our Blessed Saviour underwent in his body were more afflictive to him than the same would have been to another man' in John Norris's *Collection of Miscellanies* (1699). Just as his wedding was conducted in private, in a city where neither he nor Tetty had relatives, so his brother's funeral was concluded without his participation. He left behind him in Lichfield a dead brother buried, whose sudden death had been made mysterious by suspicions of crime, and in Edial a spectacular financial failure. 'It is necessary to hope', he later wrote, 'tho' hope should be always deluded; for hope itself is happiness, and its frustrations, however frequent, are less dreadful than its extinction.'[35] He came to London, at the age of twenty-six, trusting to the very thinnest of hopes.

PART TWO

The Londoner

4

London

magazine. 2. Of late this word has signified a miscella-neous pamphlet, from a periodical miscellany named the Gentleman's Magazine, *by Edward Cave.*

If Johnson had serious hopes of becoming a playwright, he had chosen his time badly. That spring Drury Lane was in uproar over galleries reserved for footmen who, waiting for their employers, engaged in horseplay, hurling orange peel, apple cores and ribald repartee. By February, audiences had had enough; they broke out in a riot and would not allow a production of Addison's *Cato* to proceed until the manager, Theophilus Cibber, cleared the gallery. Instead of quietening down as bidden, the footmen assaulted the theatre with hatchets, 'huzzaing, tossing of Hats and the most obstreperous Vociferation' until the chief magistrate for Westminster was called out to read the Riot Act. *Cato* had never been so dramatic.[1] A few streets away at the Little Haymarket, Henry Fielding's afterpieces were the fashion, interrupted only by such occasional mishaps as the appropriation of the theatre by a gang of tradesmen. A fortnight later Fielding presented his topical *Historical Register for 1736*, full of broad political satire and outright attacks on the government. Robert Walpole immediately rushed a licensing bill through parliament to gag the stage. The Earl of Chesterfield protested the bill was an attack on property: 'Wit, my lords, is a sort of property: the property of those who have it, and too often the only property they have to depend on'; but his words were unavailing.[2] On 21 June the Theatrical Licensing Act became law, remaining in force until 1968.

With no money of their own Johnson and Garrick sought out the simplest lodgings, and found them 'at the house of Mr Norris, a stay-maker, in Exeter-street, adjoining Catharine-street, in the Strand'.

Johnson prided himself on his methods for living well at very modest expense. 'I dined (said he) very well for eight-pence, with very good company, at the Pine Apple in New-street, just by.' It cost his companions 'a shilling, for they drank wine' but Johnson abstained, had 'a cut of meat for six-pence, and bread for a penny, and gave the waiter a penny'.[3] Financially, Garrick's position was far better than Johnson's, his uncle having died as the pair left Lichfield, leaving him a legacy of £1,000. In March Garrick was entered at Lincoln's Inn, a gesture towards studying the law which, as Fielding was already finding, could prove immensely valuable when the London theatre was inhospitable. He played his part of a struggling young artist, which Johnson was condemned to live, with full conviction; both men counted every farthing while enjoying the time they spent in Exeter Street. On an odd scrap of paper Johnson noted the heads of items that struck him during this period: 'fair Esther – w. the cat – children – inspection of the hand – stays returned – lodging – guinea at the stairs – Esther died – ordered to want nothing – house broken up – advertisement – eldest son quarrel.'[4] Condensed and random, these notes indicate the sense of informality which Johnson easily struck up in new surroundings. Far from the anxieties of his failed school, his brother's death and Tetty's lost money, he caught something of the old familiarity of childhood memories of Birmingham and Lichfield. But 'fair Esther's' death in 1743 and the subsequent break-up of the household reminded him that nothing lasts.

Short of money the pair applied to Wilcox, a bookseller in the Strand known to Garrick, representing themselves as two young men, travellers from Lichfield, just arrived in London with a view to settling. Wilcox was so moved by their artless tale he advanced them the entirety of the modest amount (£5) they sought, which was soon afterwards repaid. Asked by Wilcox how he meant to earn his living in London, Johnson replied, 'By my literary labours', at which Wilcox burst out laughing. Taking a survey of his massive physique he replied, 'Young man, you had better buy a porter's knot.'[5] Wilcox was to remain a firm friend, as was Henry Hervey whom Johnson had come to know as an officer in the 11th Dragoons, stationed in Lichfield. Known as the 'wildest of the wild' Hervey exuded charm and lived, considerably beyond his means, at a house where the pair were always welcome and where they met much hard-drinking society which, to Johnson, was a kind of liberation. Years later, recalling Hervey to Boswell, he admitted he was a vicious man, but 'very kind to me. If you call a dog HERVEY, I shall love him'.[6]

In Lichfield Johnson had left behind a situation which it was his duty to rectify, quickly. The failure of the school at Edial was not exactly a surprise to Tetty, but its consequences were distinctly mortifying. Not only had a considerable amount of her £600 dowry been sunk in its decline; her place of refuge became the Lichfield bookshop where she briefly took up residence, but it was hardly a success, either in her eyes or in those of Sarah Johnson. Her daughter Lucy, now twenty-one, was able to do whatever might be necessary in the way of tending the shop, but Sarah, who at almost seventy had neither the skill nor the inclination to pursue her business, rested content in exercising her tongue. Once before she had informed Samuel that his widowed bride was not only 'turned fifty' (when she was only forty-five) but had 'expensive habits'; now it was quickly borne in upon him that the two dowagers could not long survive together beneath a single roof. He was made aware that he should quickly allow Tetty to join him in a fashionable part of London, to carry on her life among the social gatherings she had become vicariously acquainted with in the *Spectator*.

In his first weeks in London, looking for work, Johnson explored the capital, rambling from the village of Hampstead to the stairs of Southwark, from Chelsea in the west to Bow in the east. On 5 March, the day he arrived, another Johnson, a rich farmer from Surrey, was robbed of £20 in Clapham by 'two Highwaymen, dressed like Gentlemen'. Twelve condemned men were hanged at Tyburn and, a few days later, thousands of onlookers crowded to Shepherd's Bush 'to see Maw the Soldier, and Morat the Black, hang in chains'. The roads out to the west were lined with people, many of whom had their pockets picked as they stared towards the gibbet where the black man, face quite exposed and mouth open, hung, his tongue dangling, looking frightful. All along the roadway, at every hundred yards or so, were stalls selling 'Gallons of Gin' with, here and there, a little gingerbread to soak up the alcohol. North of the Thames the notorious highwayman Dick Turpin, a bounty of £100 on his head, shot and killed a gamekeeper 'dead on the spot' in May, forcing his companion to run away 'even though he had a gun'. In July Captain Thomas Coram petitioned the king to build a hospital for foundlings, supported by aristocratic ladies, ashamed at 'the frequent Murders committed on poor Miserable Infant Children at the Birth'. All those bringing children to the hospital were requested 'to affix on each child some particular writing or other distinguishing mark' by which the child could be identified. But despite the most philanthropic aims, results were sadly disappointing. Four hundred babies were received in the hospital's first four weeks, and numbers of admissions grew until between 1756 and 1760 they stood at over fifteen thousand; impossible to maintain, had not at least ten thousand of them perished.

Across the river the impresario Jonathan Tyers was making Vauxhall Gardens a resort of masquerades and gaiety for the polite, free from the threats of prostitutes or thieves.[7] Horse-racing and betting had become crazes; in March on Wimbledon Common Mr Paterson's bay mare Miss Molly beat Mr Jones's grey mare Lightfoot for twenty guineas; in April Mr Bradley's chestnut gelding took on Mr Peters's bay in a race twice round Chelsea Common for the same amount. Newspapers relied on deaths, the more macabre the better, to fill their columns: in early June a waterman who plied the Thames near Whitehall was found to have 'hung himself with his garters' in a hedge near Chelsea; the jury brought in the verdict: lunacy. More frequently the cause was rather simpler; when at the end of March Mr Swale, a carman, was found to have drowned in the Thames, it was supposed 'he was in liquor'. In his series of paintings *Four Times of the Day* Hogarth depicted 'Noon' with satisfied appetites and 'Night' with a woman tumbling from a coach and urine tossed from an upper window.

That first summer he spent in London, Johnson, inspired by bibulous conversations with Garrick, was full of ambitions to be a playwright and retired to lodgings 'next door to the golden Heart, Church Street' in Greenwich to finish his play *Irene*. Having completed it he persuaded Peter Garrick, David's brother, to offer it to Drury Lane where the managers promptly turned it down.[8] Still penniless he turned from plays to poetry, wrote a draft of his poem 'London' and contacted the only person he knew in literary London, Edward Cave at the *Gentleman's Magazine*. To Cave he promised to write almost anything, offering, as a first suggestion, a new translation of Father Sarpi's *History of the Council of Trent*. Using his own name (suggesting greater confidence or greater desperation than the last time he had written), he said he was 'a stranger in London' and requested a 'speedy' reply. Apparently it worked. Johnson met Cave and some undertakings were given sufficient for him to invite Tetty, with whatever money she still possessed, to join him in the capital.[9] Her daughter Lucy stayed on in Lichfield with his mother who, since Nathaniel's death, had been very low in spirit. Dimly recalling her own brief visit to London, Mrs Johnson remembered disagreements between those who kept and those who gave the wall, but Johnson rather intemperately (and inaccurately) told her that '*Now*' it was 'fixed'; every man 'keeps to the right . . . it is never a dispute'.[10]

Mr and Mrs Johnson arrived in London in late autumn and took up lodgings near Hanover Square while Johnson hunted out an appropriately prestigious, but economical home. He found one at Mrs Crow's house at No. 6 Castle Street, in the fashionable west end of town. Tetty immediately pronounced its quarters cramped, but he assured her they would only stay there until his play *Irene* met with the triumph it undoubtedly deserved. Whether he had any reason to anticipate success with *Irene* is uncertain, but such expectations were necessary to the wife of a celebrated poet and playwright and helped assuage Tetty's distinctly uneasy sense of status. The house they took had the requisite stylish address, and had even been supplied with the latest offices; some years later the *Daily Advertiser* boasted of a small family house near Cavendish Square where 'water comes into the area and back kitchen twice a week'.

In January 1731 Cave had started the *Gentleman's Magazine*, a monthly digest of urban newspapers for readers in the country. Johnson made his first appearance in its pages in March 1738 with the Latin poem '*Ad Urbanem*', rebutting criticisms that Cave ('Sylvanus

Urban') attracted from his rivals on the *London Magazine*.[11] The poem may be somewhat overblown but, disguised and elevated by its Latin phrasing, the sentiments appear quite modest. Johnson wrote again in the April issue, publishing a Greek epigram to Elizabeth Carter, probably 'the most highly regarded learned woman in England', whom he later praised, without the least irony, by saying she 'could make a pudding, as well as translate Epictetus from the Greek, and work a handkerchief as well as compose a poem'. Eight years younger than Johnson, Carter had the love of learning which he most admired, having already taught herself nine languages, but, being wealthy and independent, she preferred the company of Catherine Talbot and Elizabeth Montagu (neither of whom were pudding-makers) to that of David Garrick and Henry Hervey. Carter passed only the winter months in town, spending the rest of the year at Deal, in Kent.[12]

Early in 1738 Johnson wrote again to Cave, this time rather more desperately, enclosing his finished poem 'London'. Since Tetty had arrived in London with her careless attitude to money, he found himself rapidly made penniless, but attempted to disguise the situation and wrote of himself in the third person. Very 'disadvantageous circumstances of fortune' had occurred to Mr Johnson, he said, begging to be informed 'what you can afford to allow him'. He stressed Cave's remarkable 'generosity', particularly his 'generous encouragement of poetry', apologising for the 'coarseness' of appearance of Mr Johnson's poem; he was sure Mr Johnson would rapidly agree to alter any 'stroke of satire which you may dislike'. Cave did indeed prove generous, sending Johnson a 'present' directly, but without indicating whether or not he would print the poem. Johnson volunteered to 'read the lines' aloud to the publisher Robert Dodsley in order to have 'his name on the Title-page', maintaining a sense of self-promotion despite the ever-present threat of poverty. Calculating the costs of printing five hundred copies, he reckoned any profits, after costs, should be 'set aside for the Authour's use' excepting for Cave's generous 'present' which, if the poem should make a profit, he would instantly repay. Awkward references to 'the Author' suggest that even while writing of his poem he hardly dared aspire to have composed it, presenting himself merely as 'the Authours Friend'. In the event either he or Cave was successful and Dodsley paid ten guineas to acquire the copyright of the poem; Johnson would have taken less but 'Paul Whitehead had a little before got ten guineas for a poem'. Though prepared to act the suppliant if forced to, he had a proud sense of his relative value.[13]

At this time, while seeking any means to make a living Johnson made the acquaintance of a man for whom impecuniosity had become a way of life. Richard Savage was a debonair man of forty with a spark of danger and excitement which proceeded partly from his repeated claims to be the bastard son of Earl Rivers and Lady Macclesfield (something she vehemently denied), partly from the elan he acquired by stabbing a man to death, being found guilty of murder and released only after a pardon from the king. In 1738 both Johnson and Savage were penurious, writing for the *Gentleman's Magazine* and well enough acquainted for these lines by Johnson 'To Richard Savage, Bearer of Arms, Lover of Mankind' to be printed in the magazine that April:

> Devotion to your Fellow Man burns brightly in your Breast,
> O! that Fellow Man may cherish and protect Thee in return.

This was how Johnson, writing in 1744, recalled Savage on their first meeting:

> He was of a middle stature, of a thin habit of body, a long visage, coarse features, and melancholy aspect; of a grave and manly deportment, a solemn dignity of mien, but which, upon a nearer acquaintance softened into an engaging easiness of manners. His walk was slow, and his voice tremulous and mournful. He was easily excited to smiles, but very seldom provoked to laughter.[14]

Savage had recently lost the £200 a year paid to him by Lord Tyrconnel, with whom Savage loudly boasted kinship when reputation cast him as a minor illegitimate celebrity; he attempted, unsuccessfully, to restore his diminished notoriety by addressing Tyrconnel in letters, as 'Right Honourable Brute, and Booby'. He had also lost the annual £50 paid to her 'Volunteer Laureate' by Queen Caroline who had the ill grace to die in November 1737. He was thus currently destitute, a state he may have exaggerated to secure Johnson's sympathy. The two of them became instant friends but, as Johnson quickly found, receiving Savage at home in Castle Street proved not entirely successful: '. . . they soon discovered him to be a very incommodious inmate; for being always accustomed to an irregular manner of life, he could not confine himself to any stated hours, or pay any regard to the rules of a family . . .' Tetty, in particular, found Johnson's new acquaintance rather wearing. He was, allegedly, heir to a title, but had neither the money to make that claim credible nor the manners she expected of aristocratic society. Rather, he sat at their dining table into the hours of the morning, drinking wine that she had paid for, berating the players for acting plays he had, apparently, written, but from which he received no money. Soon, rather than discompose his wife's slumbers, Johnson began embarking with Savage on nighttime rambles through the squares and alleyways of London, discoursing volubly all the while. Although the queen was dead Savage adjusted to the situation, writing a poem to her memory which was addressed to King George. He was mortally offended to discover in September that, as a reward, he was 'struck out (& am y'e only Person struck out) of y'e Late Queen's List of Pensions'. The two men walked round the town, not weighed down by rejection but making endless schemes to bring them both to riches. One night they took St James's Square in their rambles and 'were not at all depressed by their situation; but in high spirits and brimful of patriotism, traversed the square for several hours, inveighed against the minister'. They resolved 'they would *stand by their country*', talked politics boldly and boasted of their patriotism which, in an England ruled by a German monarch, could be a highly subversive subject. They walked not about Clerkenwell where the *Gentleman's Magazine* had brought them together, but around the newly fashionable square and further west to Tyburn, surveying the gallows where men were hanged for crimes much inferior to stabbing a man to death. And, unless the final flourishes are exaggerations put in by Joshua Reynolds to spice up the anecdote, they were well furnished with drink. Here, for comparison, is the description given by Johnson's first biographer, John Hawkins:

. . . they had both felt the pangs of poverty and the want of patronage . . . they seemed both to agree in the vulgar opinion, that the world is divided into two classes, of men of merit without riches, and men of wealth without merit . . . Johnson has told me, that whole nights have been spent by him and Savage in conversations of this kind, not under the hospitable roof of a tavern, where warmth might have invigorated their spirits, and wine dispelled their care; but in a perambulation round the squares of Westminster, St James's in particular, when all the money they could both raise was less than sufficient to purchase for them the shelter and sordid comforts of a night cellar.[15]

Thoroughly disapproving of Savage, Hawkins viewed these adolescently rebellious night walks with barely concealed displeasure, noting in particular the heavy drinking and 'temporary separation' that had driven young Johnson away from his wife. Two later descriptions of these nocturnal perambulations, by Arthur Murphy and Boswell, make it clear that Johnson dwelt upon his memories of them long after Savage had died. They were of vital importance to him, recapturing something of the limitless horizons of London, of the night, and the drunken excess he had first experienced, as a nostalgic dream, with his cousin Cornelius.

It is impossible to say exactly when Johnson first met Savage but, if it was in Greenwich, then the character of Thales in his poem *London*, who seeks the 'Cambrian shade', was based on Savage's proposed removal from penury in London to the calm of a cottage in Wales:

> Resolved at length, from vice and London far,
> To breathe in distant fields a purer air . . .

Boswell thought the identification of Thales with Savage 'entirely groundless', but that tells us more of his own desire to be central to Johnson's life than it does of the poem. Johnson stressed to Cave that parallels with living people were 'part of the beauty of the performance (if any beauty be allow'd it)', saying he had worked at 'adapting Juvenals Sentiments to modern facts and Persons'.

London was published on 13 May, the same day that Pope launched his satire 'One Thousand Seven Hundred and Thirty-Eight', a coincidence which served Johnson well. Pope's enemies talked up and, more importantly, bought up his poem which quickly sold out three editions; Pope, sending to learn the author's name, allegedly remarked that he would soon be brought to prominence.[16]

London begins at Greenwich where 'All crimes are safe, but hated poverty'. In a letter to Cave the previous summer Johnson asked to be given an exact time to meet, 'for it' – the distance between Castle Street and Cave's office in St John's Gate, Clerkenwell – 'is a long way to walk'. He had spent much of his first year in London walking its streets, writing poetry and attempting to launch a production of his tragedy *Irene*; in *London*, he laments his woeful lack of success.

> This mournful truth is ev'ry where confess'd,
> SLOW RISES WORTH, BY POVERTY DEPRESS'D:
> But here more slow, where all are slaves to gold,
> Where looks are merchandise, and smiles are sold:

Addison's career showed that a willingness to become involved in politics was a sure way to get noticed and in *London* Johnson follows the Addisonian model, but any similarity between political sentiments articulated here and those he later supported is purely coincidental. Robert Walpole, effective ruler of Britain for fifteen years, was in decline and Johnson attempted to benefit from his fall. Imitating Juvenal's Third Satire he created in the poem's spokesman, Thales, a man who, waiting to board his vessel of departure, views the vices of London with growing despair. *London* strikes at many of Johnson's most pressing concerns, among which the lack of money ('And ev'ry moment leaves my little less') is the clearest. The poem's answer, a retreat to some place of rural seclusion where 'honesty and sense are no disgrace', had more than once occurred to him, but being only recently arrived in the capital, it seemed too great a confession of failure to leave. Where Juvenal mentioned the Greeks, Johnson attacks Spain and France, attempting to sound both bellicose and Shakespearean, naming Edward III at Crécy and Henry V at Agincourt. In Thales' name he even abandons his Oxford dreams of

European culture, turning his former pledge ('I'll go to France and Italy') into 'I cannot bear a French metropolis.'[7]

The mood throughout is chauvinistic, though literary borrowings remind us Johnson was not as crude as his poetic persona; at times his couplets have a Popeian subtlety as here, where he catches the tone and movement of flattering courtiers.

> To shake with laughter ere the joke they hear,
> To pour at will the counterfeited tear,
> And as their patron hints the cold or heat,
> To shake in dog-days, in December sweat.

By contrast, his 'mischievously gay' lines following some 'frolick drunkard' reeling homeward from a feast and casually stabbing some poor man in his way 'for a jest' come rather close to a reflection on Savage. It was in just such a misadventure, some ten years earlier, that Savage had killed James Sinclair and wounded Mary Rock in a coffee-house down the alleyways near Charing Cross. In this poem Savage merges with the figure of Thales, but, just for a moment, Johnson allows the disguise to slip to reveal the sordid underside to his life. At the end, the poem's tone is raised as Thales gathers himself for a political coda:

> Propose your schemes, ye Senatorian band,
> Whose *Ways and Means* support the sinking Land;
> Lest ropes be wanting in the tempting spring,
> To rig another convoy for the k—g.

Representatives of the British nation found it rather annoying, not to say expensive, that their monarch, George II, should travel to Hanover each year, and in a note Johnson glosses '*Ways and Means*' as a 'cant term in the House of Commons for methods of raising money'. Many years later his *Dictionary* refined this insult by defining 'cant' as 'a whining pretension to goodness, in formal and affected terms'. By contrast, Thales recalls 'Alfred's golden reign' when 'a single jail' could 'half the nation's criminals contain' and 'Fair justice' was adored 'without constraint'. Thales sailed off to a more pleasant land where 'ev'ry bush with nature's musick rings' while Johnson remained behind in treacherous, murderous London, signalling that, if politics are the way to power, he could be as tasteless as any.[18]

The success of *London* brought a fresh burst of marital harmony and Johnson resumed the habit of reading plays together with his wife, which they had abandoned long before. He later recalled that Tetty read comedies 'better than ever he heard anybody' though in tragedy he could not help regretting 'she always mouthed too much'. He wrote excitedly to Cave that he would 'not fail to attend you to-morrow with *Irene*' on receiving Dodsley's promise to promote the play.[19] But while Cave was happy enough at Johnson's success, *Irene* presumed too far on his good nature. Instead, Johnson prepared his translation of Sarpi's *History of the Council of Trent*, for which he received £49 7s, 'in sums of one, two, three and sometimes four guineas at a time, most frequently two'. It amused Boswell to note down the 'scrupulous accuracy with which Johnson pasted upon it a slip of paper entitled "Small Account" ', which contains one article, 'Sept. 9th Mr Cave laid down 2s 6d.'; but for Johnson the money was not risible.[20]

He may, briefly, have been tempted to think himself a literary success, but Cave expected to receive ready copy for his money; in a terse missive to Johnson a month later, he demanded to know where it was. Irritated, Johnson penned a terser reply, distinctly annoyed that Cave should insinuate he 'had promised more than I am ready to perform'. If he had forgotten anything he was very sorry for it, he said, begging to be reminded of it, while at the same time making an inordinate list of all the things he *had* remembered. If there were fewer alterations than usual to the parliamentary debates he published, it was because fewer were necessary, he said, and waited to be corrected. The verses on Lady Firebrace might be had whenever Cave wished; 'such a subject neither deserves much thought', he declared, 'nor requires it.' Johnson's lines on Firebrace's 'lovely face' appeared in the September issue, their limpness rather underlining his point.[21] But in the matter of selecting a prize for the *Gentleman's Magazine*'s verse competition, Johnson threw up his hands; it would '*hardly* end to my own Satisfaction and *certainly* not to the satisfaction of the parties concerned', he wrote. Cave had been publishing verse entries on 'the Divine Attributes' since the previous spring but, faced with the task of selecting a winner, he too finally evaded the issue. Readers of the *Magazine* were informed, after three years' prevarication, that 'it was left to them to vote among themselves, excepting their own Poems'.[22]

Still Johnson had not finished; he conceded he had 'not been just to my proposal' but explained that he had met with 'impediments'. These 'impediments' might have included a considerable amount of time spent with delightful Elizabeth Carter and the eager historian Thomas Birch, whose diary indicates at least two convivial supper parties. Johnson opted not to specify, preferring to dwell in the Latinate imprecision of his epigram. Evidently his reunion with Tetty, briefly achieved after the success of *London*, had been discontinued with the non-appearance of *Irene*. 'If any, or all these have contributed to your discontent, I will endeavour to remove it,' he signs off to Cave who remained his sole reliable employer in the capital.[23]

In April 1738 the Commons declared any publication of its debates to be a breach of privilege, aiming its blow at the *Gentleman's Magazine* and the lengthier accounts in the *London Magazine* from which Cave filched his copy. Resourceful editors thought up historical disguises to evade the ban; in May the *London Magazine* began the 'Proceedings of the Political Club' including the speeches of brave Romans, featuring Walpole as a rather unconvincing Cicero. The following month Cave produced 'Debates in the Senate of Lilliput', using undemanding anagrams ('Walelop' for Walpole, 'Ptit' for Pitt). It was not until 1747 that Cave was summoned to the House of Lords to be charged; asked how he acquired the materials to publish, Cave bravely lied, claiming that he personally had taken the speeches down by hand, in pencilled notes which were later written up and published. The truth was they were copied out by William Guthrie from notes taken by the *London Magazine*, altered and disguised by Johnson.[24] Cave's defence, benign in intention, recognised that any reasonably educated man could do the job. Johnson's view that there was 'less need of alteration' in preparing them for publication was a compliment to Guthrie, and a desire to taunt the parliamentary authorities, but chiefly it manifested his own lack of interest in such a tedious subject.

* * *

On his twenty-ninth birthday Johnson began what came to be a solemn duty, writing a prayer. 'O Lord, enable me by thy Grace to use all diligence in redeeming the time which I have spent in Sloth, Vanity, and wickedness.' When, in 1768, Johnson transcribed his prayers, he noted this one from thirty years earlier as the first: 'Whether I composed any before this, I question.' It is difficult to speculate on how and why he came to begin this solemn ritual, other than observing that for him the past year had been full of new experiences, from coming to the capital and publishing his poem 'London', to meeting the remarkable Richard Savage, who knew the vanities he confessed to, having been present at the commission of many. Savage related how once he had been reduced to act a part in his own play, *Sir Thomas Overbury*, shortly to be relaunched in an entirely more favourable guise. The theatre was very fickle, he confided, and run by entirely unscrupulous men; why, once his 'friends', so called, had sent for a tailor to measure him for clothes, so ashamed were they at his appearance. Now, reduced to utter distress, Savage awaited from Pope's group of philanthropic friends a pension of £50 per annum to send him away to Wales, but still conversed with anyone prepared to buy him a drink with the utmost lack of pretension.

For Tetty the year they had been living in London was a time of much readjustment. She had come to the capital fondly believing her husband was to be a leading playwright, with Garrick his principal actor; the reality, that he wrote for the *Gentleman's Magazine* on anything from Chinese tales to ladies' faces, was something she tried to get used to but never quite achieved. We know little of how she filled her days while Johnson worked; she corresponded with her daughter Lucy in Lichfield and argued daily with the servant she considered absolutely essential. In the warmer months she sauntered the streets of the metropolis, gazing in shop windows, feeding her imagination with all the things she saw in newspapers that would soon be theirs, once Samuel's play was the great success he promised. She read of the *Royal Guardian* which docked in the pool of London, giving forth its rich East Indies cargo of dimities, ginghams and masses of Bohea tea. The 'Royal Beautifying Fluid' which was 'exceedingly valued by the Ladies of Quality' was just the thing for her hands, her face and neck, now nearing their fiftieth year, and possibly she made a private note of a 'short and infallible Cure for the Hemorrhoids' which was daily advertised. She was intrigued to observe a piece of valuable advice on the mineral waters which Samuel was always trying to get her to drink; apparently they contained 'false Waters', as she had always thought. On the whole she preferred to stick to proper alcohol, and noted that 'upwards of Three Thousand Gallons' of Jamaican rum was waiting to be tasted 'in the cellars under the Punch House' on the corner of Bartholomew Lane. Reading through the *Daily Gazetteer* she was shocked to read that a child 'about 4 years of age' had been run over by a coach just outside a house in Castle Street, where she was at present, and had been 'killed on the spot'. It was a mortifying thing to read, and had her reaching for the claret, if not the rum bottle.[25]

Meanwhile Johnson worked on proposals for translating Sarpi's *Council of Trent*. Throughout October advertisements appeared for a handsome two-volume edition and would-be subscribers were advised to resign their cares 'into the hands of God'. This work would at last establish Johnson's reputation and he felt no qualms about placing his name prominently in the advertisement. In his summary for the *Gentleman's Magazine* he revealed Sarpi was 'born for Study, having a natural Aversion to Pleasure and Gaiety, and a Memory so tenacious, that he could repeat thirty Verses upon once hearing them'.[26] Here was a man to whom he could unreservedly devote himself. He set to and had done most of his translation when, in October, he received a devastating blow; the *Daily Advertiser* published a letter from a certain *John* Johnson claiming that *he* had made 'considerable progress in a new translation' of Sarpi. Cave published an instant reply insisting not only that their translation had been the first, but that 'Mr Johnson's sirname is no new acquisition'. But the damage was already done. Subscriptions for (Samuel) Johnson's translation continued to trickle in, but his enthusiasm for the project had gone. By the end of the year *both* Johnsons' translations had come to a halt.

Similar controversial circumstances surrounded Johnson's involvement with translations of the Swiss theologian Crousaz's attacks on

Pope's *Essay on Man*.[27] An English translation of Crousaz's *Examen* begun by Elizabeth Carter that summer was announced as 'speedily' to be published, but speed and Cave rarely went together. Elizabeth's father, annoyed at the delay in publication, wrote that 'Dilatoriness is an inseparable Part of his Constitution'. When in November the *Daily Advertiser* announced 'this day is publish'd' a translation of Crousaz's *Commentaire* by Charles Forman, it came as a complete surprise.[28] Cave wrote to Johnson seeking advice but Johnson, still gloomy over Sarpi, was distinctly unenthusiastic. 'I am pretty much of your Opinion,' he wrote; 'the Commentary cannot be prosecuted with any appearance of success.' He urged Cave to promote Elizabeth Carter's *Examination* 'with utmost expedition', making clear it was a wholly different work from the *Commentaire*, and Cave rapidly inserted a notice in that day's *Daily Advertiser*, adding that 'A COMMENTARY on MR POPE'S *Principles of Morality*' might '*speedily*' be had '*having been some Weeks in the Press*'. This was the same deception Johnson had used a month before in the Sarpi controversy, declaring that 'to snatch the hint and supplant the first undertaker, is mean and disingenuous'.

Throughout November Cave and his rival Edmund Curll promoted their respective versions of the *Commentaire* keenly, despite the fact that Forman's translation of the first epistle sold badly and Cave's version, advertised as '*some Weeks in the Press*', was actually only starting to be translated. Years later Johnson told of having written 'six sheets in one day: forty-eight quarto pages of a translation of Crousaz on Pope, published by itself in 1740 or 1741'; actually it was 1742 when it was published, appearing without announcement or advertisement.[29] Charles Forman died before completing his translation and Johnson's *Commentary* was held back to help sales of the *Examination*. Elizabeth Carter possessed a copy, so she and Johnson worked together through the summer with him providing brief notes on her work, giving readers such invaluable snippets of erudition as 'The Illinois are a people of North America'. He also composed Greek and Latin epigrams for her, believing she should 'be celebrated in as many different languages as Lewis le Grand'. From Deal, Carter's father wrote to his daughter to beware of Johnson, a name, he said, 'with which I am unacquainted . . . I a little suspect his judgement, if he is very fond of Martial.'[30]

Throughout the *Commentary* Johnson cribbed shamelessly from Forman: where Forman found an argument smelling 'of the slave' Johnson transferred the detecting organ from nose to ear; it was, he said, 'the murmur of a slave'. Although later describing the *Essay on Man* as 'not the happiest of Pope's performances', it was far superior to the French writer Du Resnel's 'miserable version' on which Crousaz had based his works, something Johnson proved by rendering Du Resnel's translation of Pope's poem *literally*, down to the order of the words: where Du Resnel offered,

> Sur des mondes sans nombre, eloignes de tes yeux,
> Garde-toi de porter des regards curieux.

Johnson followed him, word for word:

> On worlds without number, remote from thy eyes,
> Beware of carrying views curious. (I.ll.31-2)

By contrast, whenever Crousaz selected a passage for analysis, Johnson was sure to substitute Pope's original.[31]

As in his translation of *A Voyage to Abyssinia*, certain errors occur so frequently they indicate Johnson's subconscious refusal to take the arguments seriously. Numbers are particularly revealing: '*cent*' is translated as 'thousand', '*milliers*' becomes 'millions', '*quatre Chants*' is rendered as 'five cantos', '*un million de personnes*' is amplified in space but *not* in number by 'thousands and ten thousands'; where the French has '*plus*' the English offers 'less'. Such errors, like confusing '*ôter*' with '*oser*', prove that while the French may appear to be daring, the English easily outdoes it. Johnson's lack of interest is clear in the declining number of footnotes he supplies: twenty-seven in Epistle I, only one in Epistle IV. 'To comment on a translation is a very adventurous task,' he notes towards the end of Epistle III, restricting himself to only two thereafter. Antagonism to his sources built up as the chances of publication lessened. There is an early snort against the French language ('as good a translation of the *English* as perhaps his language will admit') and an eloquent defence of Pope against Crousaz ('he has . . . done a voluntary wrong to the *English* poet') but at last he can take no more, and explodes in a chauvinistic aside:

> Tho' I shall not mention all the defects in the translation of this passage, I cannot, however, forbear observing, in the second couplet, the evident marks of a *Frenchman's* genius, who snatches every opportunity of talking of love, and misses not the least hint that can serve to guide him to his darling subject . . . But it is the general genius of that airy people.[32]

That word 'darling', used here so scornfully, suggests guilt towards Tetty, from whom his separation lengthened as he continued to be fascinated by Elizabeth Carter.

To earn back the money lost on Crousaz, Cave set Johnson to write short pieces on different topics, using a selection of noms de plume. As 'Pamphilus' he reprimanded John Gay for his monument in Westminster Abbey which challenged the Almighty with an irreverent witticism:

> Life is a Jest, and all Things show it;
> I thought so once, but now I know it.

Such a sentiment should be 'in its proper place', Pamphilus thundered; 'the window of a brothel'. As a youth in Lichfield he may have found church attendance tiresome, but now felt reverence was required. 'A childish levity has of late infected our conversation,' he soberly intoned; 'let it not make its way into our churches.'[33]

He forced himself to dabble in political invective, inspired by the partial success of *London*. His lines in the poem on the 'tempting spring' had been designed to remind readers of the king's annual visits to his Hanoverian mistress Amelie von Wallmoden. Such reminders became more appropriate when, following Queen Caroline's death, the king declared, '*J'aurais des maîtresses*', and imported von Wallmoden to England. Pamphilus lavishes ironic praise on the king for having discovered an 'effectual remedy' against regal melancholy which allowed him to demonstrate his 'tender affection to his people'. Hard pressed to make readable copy out of the work which piled up on his desk he offered vague comments on Chinese manners, aware that his own ignorance would only compound that of his readers, and engaged in journalistic banter against rival papers when Cave wished it. He attacked *Common Sense*, the *London Magazine* and 'almost twenty' imitations of the *Gentleman's Magazine* 'which are either all dead, or very little regarded by the world'. *Common Sense*, he declared, was so malicious it deserved 'no other fate than to be hissed, torn and forgotten', feeling only slight misgivings that there might, on one of these other journals, be some individual who, like him, waited for his chance to prove himself.[34]

Gradually London was beginning to develop a shape recognisable to the twenty-first century reader. London and Westminster were still quite distinct, though their Restoration identifications with puritan merchants (London) and royalist rakes (Westminster) were beginning to soften and merge. Royal stables occupied what would become Trafalgar Square though Arlington House, rather than Buckingham Palace, commanded the view over St James's Park. The northernmost extremities of London's buildings extended no further than Old Street and Bunhill Fields in the east, or the Oxford Road, past recent developments at Golden Square and Bond Street, in the west. Around Leicester Fields a new wall and rails were erected with 'a Bason in the Middle, after the Manner of Lincoln's-Inn-Fields . . . to be done by a voluntary Subscription of the Inhabitants'. Tetty, as she took her walk along Portugal Street, across to Piccadilly, past Burlington House, and down Hay-Market wearing her best shoes of Spanish or Morocco hide, carrying her umbrella, more for show than use, would breathe in the perfumes from the shops along her way and feel that this was London. She had arrived, and soon, when her husband was a famous playwright, she would enjoy tea and conversation in the houses that, at present, were only buildings to her.[35]

Johnson continued to toil away, to provide his wife with the trivialities she believed so essential to life in a capital city. He began work on his life of the Dutch physician Dr Herman Boerhaave in January 1739 with the comment that some students 'not well acquainted with the Constitution of the human Body, sometimes fly for Relief to Wine instead of Exercise'; words which had a baleful resonance for him.[36] Politically he remained an opposition hack, rather for the work it put in his way than from any conviction. He quickly penned *Marmor Norfolciense*, a pamphlet based on Swift's *Windsor Prophecy*, in the same spirit of opportunism that animated many Grub Street writers before, and after, him. Swift had a Windsor gravedigger unearthing a parchment that, decoded, was a satire on the Duchess of Somerset; Johnson has a farmer discovering an inscribed stone in a field 'near Lynn in Norfolk', the constituency represented by Robert Walpole. Reading Swift for the *Debates in Lilliput* clearly influenced Johnson's style as may be seen when he describes how easily officials may be housed in Greenwich Hospital by the simple expedient of expelling seamen 'as have no pretensions to the settlement there, but fractur'd limbs, loss of eyes, or decay'd constitutions'. Pope found *Marmor Norfolciense* 'very humorous', a judgement which has not been widely shared; most commentators find its wit laboured and its subtlety impenetrable. Mentioning the lion 'melting in a lewd embrace' (a gibe at the king's sexual improprieties), the lines occasionally catch fire but are immediately doused by lengthy commentary. Among touches which confirm Johnson's authorship are closing remarks that £2,000 a year is 'more than the regular stipend of a commissioner of excise' or that the salary of officials may easily be raised 'by a general poll-tax, or excise upon bread'. His father's difficulties with excise-men were never quite forgotten, or forgiven.[37] Printed by John Brett, publisher of *Common Sense*, *Marmor Norfolciense* caused a stir as soon as it went on sale. Hawkins speaks of an arrest warrant being issued and of Johnson taking 'an obscure lodging in a house in Lambeth marsh', but no evidence of such a hiding place has ever been unearthed. Two months later, though, John Brett was arrested for a passage in *Common Sense*. These were the real dangers Johnson faced as a journalist.[38]

He rushed out his *Compleat Vindication of the Licensers of the Stage* barely three weeks after Henry Brooke's play *Gustavus Vasa*, which had been banned from public performances, sought redress in immediate publication; and, though it has attracted far less attention than *Marmor*, this pamphlet is easily the more incisive. It suggests, ironically, the political virtues of suppressing works by inconvenient writers; what is power, Johnson asks, 'but the liberty of acting without being accountable?'[39] 'Our intention was to invest him [the Lord Chamberlain] with new privilege and to empower him to do that *without* reason, which *with* reason he could do before.' A poet seeking to know the licenser's reasons for rejecting his play is simply told 'there are reasons which he cannot understand', since authority is far more important than understanding. 'It may be made felony to teach to read, without a license from the Lord Chamberlain', the pamphlet warns. Short, politically unimportant and not attributed to Johnson until 1785, this pamphlet is an unrecognised journalistic gem.[40]

Such occasional flashes of brilliance brought no diminution of his daily toil. That summer, while Tetty wondered over advertisements to cure her toothache without arranging for a painful and expensive extraction, Johnson laboured to produce a defence for Joseph Trapp's sermons on the dangers of Methodism. Cave marvelled at the thirty numbered clauses Johnson produced so quickly, indicating his instinctive gift for such forensic tasks; but Tetty, studying crude illustrations of a smiling man in the paper, wanted to know if he believed this powder could really make 'the foulest teeth as white as Ivory'. Johnson's arguments needed some slight diminution of tone, Cave believed, a modest suggestion which unexpectedly brought Johnson close to despair. Tetty attempted to comfort him; reading *Read's Weekly Journal* she had discovered an ideal way for enterprising persons to make money. One 'Gentleman of Distinction' had made a wager for fifty guineas that he could walk 'eight times, up and down the Mall, in Boots that weigh'd 5lbs' in an hour. He won his bet, having performed the task 'in fifty-seven Minutes'.[41]

In July Savage, having extracted as much money from Pope and others, less his well-wishers than those who wanted rid of him, decided the time had come to leave the capital and finally headed for rural Wales. Till the end Johnson exhorted him to remain in London and when they parted he had 'tears in his eyes'. When he came to write his *Life of Savage* a mere four years later, having not seen him since that day, he reckoned up the brave, yet foolish nature of his friend, who had never in his life before ventured upon country living:

> . . . he could not bear to debar himself from the happiness which was to be found in the calm of a cottage, or lose the opportunity of listening, without intermission, to the melody of the nightingale, which he believ'd was to be heard from every bramble, and which he did not fail to mention as a very important part of the happiness of a country life.[42]

Despite all his faults and weaknesses, Savage was a man, like Cornelius or Hervey, who had a sense of the endless possibilities of life which made those difficulties worth bearing. With him gone, Johnson found the constant pressure of working in London intolerable. He heard of, and suddenly applied for, a teaching post at Appleby in Leicestershire, not far from Market Bosworth. It was a reckless but apparently serious move. Pope, who knew Johnson only by his written works, wrote a letter of recommendation to the local peer, Lord Gower. Johnson's lack of a degree was a difficulty but, on the evidence of his journalistic style, it was believed Swift might be able to procure him one from Trinity College, Dublin. Gower, highly sceptical, wrote to a friend of Swift, endorsing the claims of 'Mr Samuel Johnson (author of *London* . . .)':

> They say he is not afraid of the strictest examination, though he is of so long a journey; and will venture it, if the Dean thinks it necessary; choosing rather to die upon the road, *than be starved to death in translating for booksellers*; which has been his only subsistence for some time past.[43]

This letter sounds the true melodramatic note of Johnson's desperation; the pledge, of dying rather than again translating, sounds like the authentic declaration of a man approaching his thirtieth birthday. With Tetty, now in her fiftieth year, forever complaining about her husband's lack of fame and failure to become a famous playwright, there was no chance to discuss things in a rational way. At present she was marvelling over the several fine ladies she had read about who 'used to wear French silks, French Hoops of Four Yards wide' and

'Tête de Mounton [*sic*]' hairstyles but who had suddenly 'turned Methodist', joined the followers of Mr Whitefield and were now to be seen in 'plain Stuff gowns' with 'no hoops' at all. There was no way for Johnson to contrive an interest in their plight. He took his leave, set off for the Midlands and would not see his wife again for the greater part of a year.

5

Love

to love v.a. *(* lufian, *Saxon.)* *1. To regard with passionate affection, as that of one sex to the other.*

Johnson didn't get the Appleby job, which went to Thomas Mould, MA, who remained in post for forty years. No one was very surprised, except Johnson. He had been rejected as a schoolmaster at Ashbourne, Solihull, Brewood and Appleby and had failed abysmally at Market Bosworth and at his own school at Edial. It was not particularly the lack of an MA that ruined his chances; it was the appearance that his affliction, a version of Tourette's syndrome, gave him which school governors thought, quite reasonably, might prove risible or alarming to the boys. 'He has an Infirmity of the convulsive kind, that attacks him sometimes', noted Pope, 'so as to make Him a sad Spectacle.'[1]

Instead of going home, to London, he went to what he still thought of as his real home, the Midlands. But at Lichfield there were awkward questions to be answered or evaded (his mother being one of the few who *would* ask) about his wife and prospects. Mrs Johnson and Lucy Porter worked quite steadily together in the bookshop, but without any of his father's flair; Gilbert Walmesley's account book lists only one bill paid to Mrs Johnson, though there are frequent payments to 'Mr Bayley', 'Robt. Shaw', even 'Thomas Warren' of Birmingham, all more adventurous rivals in the bookselling trade.[2] He spent his time instead at Ashbourne with his easygoing school friend John Taylor who was thinking of entering the Church, less for spiritual than remunerative reasons. When he did go to Lichfield, it was to visit Walmesley at the bishop's palace, which is where he met, and fell in love with, Molly Aston, Walmesley's sister-in-law.

Years later, when it was all over and both Tetty and Molly were dead, he confessed to Hester Thrale, by then the woman he loved, that the only occasion on which he had experienced 'measureless delight' was 'the first Evening I spent Teste a Teste with Molly Aston'. It had not been happiness, he said, but 'rapture'; thoughts of it had 'sweetened the whole year'. Molly 'was a beauty and a scholar, and a wit and a whig', but, as with Walmesley, her whiggism only acted as a spur; 'she talked all in praise of liberty: and so I made this epigram upon her – She was the loveliest creature I ever saw!!!'[3] The epigram, translated by Hester Thrale, reads:

> Persuasions to Freedom fall oddly from you,
> If Freedom we seek, fair Maria Adieu!

Thrale's memories, or possibly Johnson's, are not entirely accurate. He had first placed the Latin epigram in the columns of the *Gentleman's Magazine* two years earlier, alongside similar effusions in praise of Elizabeth Carter. It was, if not false exactly, a highly flattering piece of deference. By late summer the following year, bereft of his close friend Savage, escaping from a dreary life of translating commentaries, the situation had altered. Molly was older than him by just three years, not twenty, like his wife. She was tall, well-read, brilliant in conversation and not afraid to put others in their place – quite unlike Tetty. Many men quailed before her, but not Johnson; he blossomed. A group of poems which have 'Stella' as their common link ('Stella in Mourning', 'An Evening Ode', 'To Stella') date from this period and speak of his passionate feelings. In 'An Evening Ode' he bids Stella walk with him, beneath the darkening sky:

> Silence, best, and conscious shades
> Please the hearts that Love invades;
> Other pleasures give them pain,
> Lovers all but Love disdain.

'Invades' gestures to a feeling, close to love, which may not be articulated in prose, much less acted upon in fact; it may only be lightly breathed in verse.

> Let us now, in whisper'd joy,
> Ev'ning's silent hours employ . . .[4]

Hester Thrale asked what his wife thought of this emotional attachment. It was thirty years since Tetty had died and, in Hester's company, he felt able to be merry on the subject.

> She was jealous to be sure (said he), and teized me sometimes when I would let her; and one day, as a fortune-telling gipsey passed us when we were walking out in company with two or three friends in the country, she made the wench look at my hand, but soon repented her curiosity; for (says the gipsey) Your heart is divided, Sir, between a Betty and a Molly: Betty loves you best, but you take most delight in Molly's company: when I turned about to laugh, I saw my wife was crying.[5]

Boswell records him remembering Tetty 'to be in tears' on their nuptial morn and here too Tetty is crying; or so Hester Thrale recalls. The anecdotes are far distant and those remembering them of radically different sensibilities; yet one senses a certain relish, on Johnson's part, in boasting to them both of his mastery of the relationship. The situation was considerably less amusing in 1739 when, enjoying Molly's company, he allowed his stay at Lichfield to run on over his birthday, over Christmas and into the new year. At last, in January, Tetty wrote to him. Her letter no longer exists: we have none of Tetty's letters from which to determine the quality of the Johnsons' marriage, which is worth a moment's pause. Why do we have none of her letters? Did she not write to him when he was first in London? Did he destroy her letters, and if so, why? Did he feel her lack of literary skills might place a question mark against his own? What kind of perspective might her solitary voice, unmediated by his explicatory tone, have cast over his endeavours? The tone of her letter may be judged only from his reply, the sole surviving letter from this important, opaque relationship, and it is very revealing. He begins with explicit concern for the tendon of her leg, which she had, apparently, damaged:

> After hearing that You are in so much danger, as I apprehend from a hurt on a tendon, I shall be very uneasy till I know that

You are recovered, and beg that You will omit nothing that can contribute to it, nor deny Yourself any thing that may make confinement less melancholy.

Here, and throughout the letter, he is not only solicitous for her health; he is most careful she should recognise his solicitude. He mentions eminent surgeons she must consult, John Ranby and John Shipton, who had members of the royal family as their patients. She must not scruple about expense: 'you need not fear to part with [a guinea] on so pressing an occasion', he writes, 'for I can send You twenty pouns more on Monday, which I have received this night.' Together with his mother he had mortgaged the family house which his father had been so proud of, in Lichfield's Market Square, to Theophilus Levett for £80; and here he is, making a conspicuous display of all that wealth, offering her his entire share of the money, to spend on surgeons' bills. Remembering how much money meant to him; how he had been forced to leave Oxford for want of it, how he and Garrick had come to London with just *fourpence* between them, this sudden generosity with 'twenty pouns' seems really rather extraordinary. 'You have already suffered more than I can bear to reflect upon,' he goes on; 'and I hope more than either of us shall suffer again . . . for the future our troubles will surely never separate us more.' There, for a moment his tone wavers. Irony was never Johnson's strong point and, despite the fact he had recently studied Swift to improve his political journalism, rarely enters his letter-writing style. But there are no other letters to Tetty to compare and one wonders whether 'you are in *so* much danger' or 'you need not fear to part with on *so pressing* an occasion' betray a hint of implicit criticism as Johnson *happily* abandons a portion of his birthright to soothe Tetty's bruises on her leg.

He moves on to mention his play *Irene*, attempting once again to bring Tetty to recognise that she may, very soon, be the wife of a famous playwright. The play has at last become 'a kind of Favourite among the Players', he writes; 'Mr Fletewood promises to give a promise in writing that it shall be the first next season.' Mr Chetwood (the prompter at Drury Lane) 'is desirous of bargaining for the copy, and offers fifty Guineas for the right of printing after it shall be played'. The thing, he implies, is as good as settled. Having thereby given the impression of tireless work for their joint benefit, with seventy pounds *at least* to show for it, he risks a sentence which, he knows, is the heart of the letter:

> Be assured, my dear Girl, that I have seen nobody in these rambles upon which I have been forced, that has not contributed to confirm my esteem and affection for thee, though that esteem and affection only contributed to encrease my unhappiness when I reflected that the most amiable woman in the world was exposed by my means to miseries which I could not relieve.

He is here working himself up into an apparently intimate tone; that much is evident from the awkward tone adopted towards his 'dear Girl' of fifty years old. The sense of being 'forced' upon rambles which had taken up at least six months was clearly exaggerated; that cannot be said about Tetty's 'miseries'. Johnson knew his wife's ailments were emotional as much as physical, but he shields himself from the knowledge and concentrates on her bruised tendon, offering to pay for treatment and pretending to be unaware of any other ills. But being with her meant *not* being with anyone else, and, as he wrote this sentence, Johnson admits what has, in reality, been affecting his heart and paralysing his movements. Whether he acknowledged anything of his feelings to Molly Aston is very doubtful; what he did, instead, was to write another poem, 'The Winter Walk'.

> Enliv'ning hope, and fond desire,
> Resign the heart to spleen and care,
> Scarce frighted love maintains his fire,
> And rapture saddens to despair.
>
> In groundless hope, and causeless fear,
> Unhappy man! Behold thy doom,
> Still changing with the changeful year,
> The slave of sunshine and of gloom.

> Tir'd with vain joys, and false alarms,
> With mental and corporeal strife,
> Snatch me, my Stella, to thy arms,
> And screen me from the ills of life.

We have here something which, as Richard Holmes remarks, is not 'usually recognised about Johnson's sensibility . . . his gloomy longings for physical tenderness in a world of "ills" '.[6] Stella 'snatches' the poet, shielding him from 'the ills of life'. But Molly did not, was not asked to, 'screen' Johnson. Remarks of hers are mentioned in the Lives of Pope and Gray, proving that Johnson had not forgotten her, but as far as his winter interlude in Staffordshire was concerned, it was over. Many years later Boswell records Johnson speaking of 'the dreadful winter of Forty' when it was colder in London than in Hudson's Bay and many people froze to death. On 15 January, 'a Sheep was roasted whole on the Ice upon the Thames off Pepper-Alley Stairs' and, a fortnight later, press-gangs operated among the young men there and 'picked up several idle young Fellows, who had nothing in their pockets but their Hands, to preserve them from the cold'.[7] But Johnson did not hurry back to London to relieve Tetty's ills; he sent money instead.

How long he stayed away from London is uncertain. Seven letters from Johnson to Edward Cave exist for 1738, dealing with subjects as diverse as a Greek epigram for Elizabeth Carter and Chinese stories. Two letters to Lewis Paul exist for 1741; but for the years 1739 and 1740 there is only this one long and tortuous letter to Tetty. Biographers disagree about this period.[8] For Clifford it is a time when Johnson enjoyed an agreeable social round, moved in 'the best society of Derbyshire', got up 'when he pleased' and enjoyed 'a profusion of food'. DeMaria buries it in a welter of Johnson's miscellaneous prose and notes that when he returned to London in 1740 he 'was confirmed in his choice of life'. Bate, usually keen to proclaim his biography's Freudian credentials, senses no disturbance here: 'everything was at his disposal: good food, pleasant surroundings, servants, leisure, and hours of conversation.' Only Holmes feels something odd about Johnson's absence from Elizabeth, guessing the reason for it is love. ' "Abandon" does not seem too strong a word' for the way Johnson treated his wife, he says, reminding us that Boswell 'slides over this whole separation'. Johnson did come back to London. The first instance we have of his return is the Prologue to Garrick's production of *Lethe* on 15 April, showing his awareness of theatrical fashions and reluctant readiness to defer to them. But it was in a mood of determination, to make not just the best of what he had in London, but something of which he might be justly proud.

The next half a dozen years began the slow and gradual decline of Tetty. It is not certain how early she took to opium, which was available at a price and without criminal associations, for ills of every kind. For her damaged tendon some draughts of laudanum (opium mixed with alcohol) might well have been prescribed. Increasingly she took it, or alcohol alone, allowing the mixture to fuddle her brain and drive her to hypochondria. Robert Levet, who practised physic to the poor, told Hester Thrale she 'was always drunk & reading Romances in her Bed, where she killed herself by taking Opium'.[9] Johnson tried to make good his promise of 'many happy years from your tenderness and affection' by stopping drinking himself, as an example to her; but she took it as an insult, and drank even more. Throughout his life Johnson loved his food, giving it as his opinion that there was something 'grossly wrong' if a family's dinner was 'ill'; but about his own dinner he 'huffed' his wife so much that 'at last she called to me, and said, Nay, hold Mr Johnson, and do not make a farce of thanking God for a dinner which in a few minutes you will protest not eatable'.[10] Even at their poorest Tetty kept a maid, using the greater part of the £100 annual salary which Johnson persuaded Cave to pay him on domestic's wages, doctor's bills and alcohol. As to the physical side of their relationship, she was too ill, she claimed, even to attempt it.[11]

The lively prologue to *Lethe* marked a period when Garrick, still losing money with his brother in the wine trade, sought employment before the cash was gone. The repertoire at Drury Lane was dull, switching only from *Timon of Athens* and *Henry VIII* to revivals of Fielding's farce *Tom Thumb the Great*, so that summer Garrick went on tour with Giffard's company, keeping his identity a secret, blacking up for *Oroonoko* and assuming a false name for Farquhar's *The Inconstant*. A year later he would shine forth at Goodman's Fields as 'a theatrical Newton' in *Richard III* but for the moment he and Johnson amused themselves in drinking tea, to which Johnson was becoming habituated, and outdoing each other's verse. Johnson composed an epitaph for the Welsh violinist Claudy Phillips who was 'distress'd by poverty no more', a glimpse of posthumous bliss after which both must, if only occasionally, have dreamt.[12] Tea, considered by Johnson's father as 'very expensive', was discouraged at home in Lichfield: the *London Daily Post* advertised all sorts of teas costing from 15s a pound for 'superfine' tea to fine green tea at 10s 6d. Johnson did not merely disobey this parental ruling, but developed his tea-drinking into a fetish for which, in later years, he was well known. At a dinner party at Richard Cumberland's, Sir Joshua Reynolds risked commenting on the number of cups of tea Johnson was taking, to which he retorted: 'Sir, I did not count your glasses of wine; why should you number my cups of tea?' On his trip to Devon he countered Mrs Mudge's rudeness ('What? Another, Dr Johnson?') by relating how he had taken revenge on 'a certain lady' by swallowing '*five and twenty* cups of tea, and did not treat her with as many words'.[13]

Britain had recently engaged in a naval war with Spain and the *Gentleman's Magazine* hurried to join the ranks of those applauding the country's sudden bellicose endeavour. Widespread festivities greeted Admiral Vernon's daring capture of Portobello and a spirit flourished which only the composition of such rousing anthems as 'God Save the King' and 'Rule, Britannia' could meet. 'We hear that all his Majesty's Land Forces in Great Britain are order'd to be augmented,' reported the *Daily Post*; 'they are busy at Woolwich in preparing warlike Stores, &c for the Garrison of Gibraltar.' The mood suddenly was eager for British heroes and Johnson was there to supply it. He published the suitably jingoistic *Life of Admiral Blake* and followed it with the *Life of Admiral Drake* which ran, in monthly instalments, from August 1740 till January 1741. The Tories were great supporters of the war, and Johnson could write tales of heroism and adventure, full of sinking ships and burning men-of-war,

without worrying overmuch about religion, merely acknowledging that Blake was religious 'according to the pretended Purity of
these Times'.

The pieces that he wrote revel in action and stereotypical characters:
the Dutch enemy is 'arrogant' and fights 'without any regard to the
Customs of War'. Van Trump's insolence in 'carrying a Broom at his
Top-mast' to sweep the English from the Channel is mentioned, only
to be triumphantly overturned when eventually he cries out: '*The
English are our Masters, and by consequence Masters of the Sea*.'[14] The *Life
of Drake* displays similar characteristics: the hero is wise, brave and
thoroughly English, a 'rigid Observer of the Laws of War' who 'never
permitted his Arrows to be poison'd'; he was a man 'whose good or ill
Success never prevailed over his Piety'. At times Johnson's eulogies
become formulaic, as when Drake's 'Penetration immediately discovered all the Circumstances and Inconveniencies of every Scheme', but
he is attempting to create an heroic image and the word 'Nation' is
endlessly repeated. But just occasionally Johnson reminds his readers
that this is no ordinary Grub Street tract they are reading. In the last
instalment he pauses to discuss the conditions of the Indians among
whom Drake travels; are they, or we, the happier? There follows a
lengthy antithetical debate, such as would later characterise his
Rambler essays, in which he examines the argument that 'we enlarge
our Vices with our Knowledge, and multiply our Wants with our
Attainments'. His conclusion, that the 'Happiness of Life' is best
secured by 'Ignorance of Vice' rather than 'Knowledge of Virtue', may
not be satisfying, but is a small indication that the author of this heroic
tale is not content with gold and jewels and coney-skins.[15]

Johnson was drawn into trying to help Lewis Paul establish a
cotton mill in Birmingham, though he felt the venture was ill-
conceived, and negotiations for the establishment of the mill were
interminably protracted.*[16] It was a time when he knew real poverty
and discovered, all around him, dreamers and enthusiasts surviving

---

* The scheme was not a success and the mill failed a few years later. The friends
included Dr Robert James, a former schoolmate, and Thomas Warren, the publisher of
the *Birmingham Journal*. Johnson moved to 'the black Boy over against Durham Yard'
where Garrick had previously stored his stock while attempting to be a wine merchant.

on the fringes of Grub Street, sharing his condition. Some wrote poems or plays or acted the party hack, writing pamphlets for or against the government; some, like Johnson, worked on magazines, but all eked out their lives in the back streets of the metropolis, keeping to their cherished dreams of fame and success. George Psalmanazar made a profession of his life on Formosa, not only inventing a detailed language for his chosen island but publishing a history and even visiting Oxford to teach the tongue to a group of would-be missionaries. Then, at the height of his fame he suddenly converted and confessed his Formosa gambit was all a lie. He had never been to Formosa at all! Rather than being condemned as a cheat his confession was so effective that he was taken for a true penitent. Johnson told an amazed Boswell that he was happiest when sitting and talking with Psalmanazar at an alehouse in the city.[17] When Hester Thrale asked who was the best man he had ever known his reply was immediate and unequivocal: 'Psalmanazar,' he said; his 'piety, penitence, and virtue exceeded almost what we read as wonderful even in the lives of saints'.[18] Another eccentric he knew was Samuel Boyse, minor poet and major wit, who had recently modernised Chaucer's *Canterbury Tales*. Johnson recalled money being collected to buy Boyse a meal who, having 'got a bit of roast beef', promptly declared he could not eat it without ketchup. Like Savage, he would not relinquish his exotic tastes even to allay desperate hunger, and laid out his last half-guinea in truffles and mushrooms. He wrote to Cave from a coffee-house, 'entreating your answer', 'having not tasted anything since Tuesday evening I came in here, and my coat will be taken off my back, for the charge of the bed. So that I must go into prison naked, which is too shocking for me to think of.' Cave sent him the money he required and endorsed the note, 'Mr S. Boyse poetical writer. A singular character.'

Johnson met many such singular characters as he wandered the streets of London, or sat in taverns reading of their exploits. On 13 August Alexander Flack, described by the *Daily Post* as 'notorious', was committed to prison for several burglaries. Troubled by neither the verdict nor sentence, Flack behaved 'very insolently' before the justices, telling them that 'all the *Squeakers*' (glossed by the *Daily Post* as 'Witnesses') would be unable 'to *Jamm* him this Time'. The same paper carried a report of a woman who entered a distillery at Dorset Stairs for some 'spirituous liquors', after which she became 'heated' and had 'some Words' with a man in the shop who 'in his Rage' hurled 'a Cann of Boiling Liquor' at her. The consequence was that, despite the efforts of St Bartholomew's hospital, she died. The paper does not say what happened to the man but, for those with a taste for justice, it did report the execution of James Hall, to be held 'in the Strand, over against Somerset House' being 'as near the Place where the Fact was committed as could conveniently be found'. It noted that the gibbet was specially made 'of an extraordinary Height', the better to expose 'so notorious a Fellow to the View of Spectators'.[19]

Johnson kept moving his lodgings, initially from Durham Yard to Bow Street, then later round the corner to Fetter Lane, in this way keeping his working hours with Blake or Drake quite separate from domestic life at Castle Street. This arrangement meant ceding more than half his earnings to maintain Tetty's fading sense of style, leaving him teetering on the brink of poverty. But it also meant that while he was away from Castle Street, he was free of her anxieties. If he *chose* to leave his books and papers in what *appeared* to be a mess, he was free to do so. 'She was extremely neat in her disposition', he told Hester Thrale, '& always fretful that I made the House so dirty – a clean Floor is *so* comfortable she would say by way of twitting; till at last I told her, I thought we had had Talk enough about the Floor, we would now have a Touch at the *Ceiling*.' By this time anyway, Tetty was mainly drunk and, increasingly, Johnson found the serendipitous friendships he struck up in the alehouse or chophouse, in the bookshop or the printing press, more fulfilling.[20]

As he entered his fourth decade his prospects seemed distinctly gloomy. The men he had cherished for their enlivening wit were either dead like Ford or gone like Savage, and what memorials would ever record them? In the *Magazine* he turned to epitaphs, which became a favourite subject for him since 'every man may expect to be recorded in an epitaph'. The pyramids in Egypt were epitaphs, erected by the pharaohs in attempts to preserve their own memory; but 'the best subject for epitaphs is private virtue . . . exerted in the same circumstances in which the bulk of mankind are placed'. In that conviction he thought not only of the epitaphs of famous men, like Newton, but of Claudy Phillips and even Epictetus, a beggar, cripple and a slave, remembered as 'the favourite of Heaven'.

That Johnson was not blessed as being the favourite here (he did not care to presume about hereafter) was clear as he settled down to produce a series of essays on topical (or what Cave thought were topical) themes.[21] Considering debates between Oliver Cromwell and the Commons he wrote on the 'necessity' of Cromwell becoming king because Cave was seized by the idea that readers would spot parallels between the tyranny of Cromwell a century ago and the rule of their present 'Screenmaster-General' Sir Robert Walpole. Johnson was unconvinced of this but wrote the essay anyway, dwelling only lightly on parallels, using the objective style he had acquired for writing the parliamentary *Debates* which, increasingly, became his principal duty. Occasionally he contributed translations of the *Jests of Hierocles* which made him smile while his other chores drove him almost to tears, or he translated portions of Guyon's *Histoire des Amazones* in which shy virgins were forbidden to engage in sexual congress until they had 'killed three men' to show 'how much they detested them'.

Cave offered to assist him in attempts to sell the manuscript of *Irene* but, with no prospect of a production, there was little interest. Among the *Jests* was one which featured a philosopher who, hearing crows lived 'two hundred years', procured a young one, just 'to try'. Johnson rather liked that one. Perhaps even *Irene* might be produced in two hundred years? How long would he continue grinding out the *Debates* which, though allegedly a favourite with readers, were anything but a favourite for him? At the end of 1741 he wrote a Preface to the *Gentleman's Magazine* claiming it was read 'as far as the English language extends' and offered a jest in which Man A greeted Man B who had 'just buried a twin brother'; Man A enquired of Man B 'whether it was he or his brother that was lately buried?' The dark humour of that disturbed his sleep, dreaming of Nathaniel laid to rest at St Michael's Church.[22]

He confessed nothing of the fact that, day after day, he worked at producing the *Gentleman's Magazine*'s version of the parliamentary *Debates* and it was not till much later that he acknowledged, disingenuously, in another magazine, that he knew anything of their composition. 'The speeches inserted in other papers', he wrote, 'have been long known to be fictitious, and produced sometimes by men who have never heard the debate, nor had any authentic information.' He acknowledged authorship of a speech 'by' Pitt because of the applause which greeted it among guests at a dinner party: 'That speech I wrote in a garret in Exeter Street,' he declared, unable to resist basking in the sudden praise for making the *Debates* not merely readable but enjoyable. He relished the occasional sense of being privy to state affairs. In a confidential letter to John Taylor he mentioned a report which appointed Lord Chesterfield to be Lord Lieutenant of Ireland: 'if I hear more, I will inform You', and mentioned the king of Prussia in the same self-important fashion, telling Taylor he proposed 'to get Charles of Sweden ready for this winter'. Sadly, few of these whispered snippets actually turned out to be true. Johnson never produced a play on Charles XII of Sweden and the Duke of Devonshire remained in his Irish post for a further three years. The letter merely indicates Johnson's tendency to preen towards his old school friend, now a parson in Leicestershire. Even this had its limitations. His next letter to Taylor begs his understanding for neglect in answering a letter; 'Mrs Johnson was seized with such an illness' twelve weeks ago that she has not even 'walked about [her] chamber'. Taylor would know what to make of that. 'She was the plague of Johnson's life,' he said later, 'abominably drunken and despicable.'[23] Robert Walpole's administration, lasting for twenty years from 1720, was not a period of parliamentary principle or constitutional progress; rather the opposite. The few Tories who still existed were split by nostalgic hankerings for a Stuart monarch who, though he lived abroad, at least spoke English; sadly, he was also a Roman Catholic. Walpole's rise to power exploited just such splits, utilising the utmost guile, deploying royal patronage, the privy purses and an extensive secret service. He displayed consummate skill manipulating parliament and negotiating such potentially awkward transitions as that between the courts of

George I and George II. His powers only began to wane with the death of Queen Caroline in 1737, who had been his trusted friend and confidante. Still, carefully arranging parliamentary debates on such vexed issues as the matter of buttons and buttonholes or the registration of British seamen, he managed to maintain his control over matters of state.

Johnson's style in the *Debates*, using an august vocabulary to discuss the most humdrum subjects, always maintains a full sense of decorum. 'Branard' (Sir John Barnard) mentions the complexities of marine insurance 'more perplex'd with an endless Diversity of Circumstances than those which relate to commercial Affairs . . .' 'Blatimore' (Baltimore) takes up the issue, pointing out Britain's thriving economy. 'If our Insurers gain by securing the Ships of our Enemies, the Nation is benefited, for all national Gain must circulate through the Hands of Individuals.' For three years Johnson wrote the debates in this fashion, compressing the numbers of speakers and having each orate in a style which, as Philip Francis, who translated Horace, declared, put Demosthenes to shame. The Lilliputian Senate appeared so dignified in deploying arguments that many readers declared the speeches were 'the best [they] had ever read'.[24] On major issues, such as the fall of 'Walelop' (Walpole), Johnson might use a certain piquant irony, but such touches were limited. Walelop complains all he has gained for his service is 'a little house at a small Distance from this City, worth about seven Hundred *Sprugs*', and the sound of *sprugs* (pounds) makes a fine satiric comment on his extensive estate of Houghton. No speaker is ridiculed and though Johnson told Boswell he 'took care that the WHIG DOGS should not have the best of it', the tone is always neutral. 'Were I in power', Boswell recalls him saying, 'I would turn out every man who dared to oppose me', but this is definitely not the way of the *Debates*; even Walelop is allowed some telling barbs, as when he hints that a fellow 'Clinab' (member of the House of Commons) 'may perhaps not intend long to retain his Senatorial Character' for delivering his opinions 'only as a Merchant'.[25]

In particular, the role of liberty struck Johnson as important. In a debate on the compulsory registration of all 'Seafaring Men capable of Service at Sea', Branard rejects the idea that Britons should 'think it necessary to punish them for asserting their Birthright, by depriving them of the Appearance of Freedom'. If such a register should ever come about, he argues, 'a Sailor and a Slave will be terms of the same Signification . . . let the Brave, the Hardy, the Honest Seaman retain his liberty'. What makes the difference between a freeman and a slave, demands 'Snadsy' (Lord Sandys), 'except that the Happiness of one is in his own Power; and that of the other in the Hand of his Master?' Preserving liberty emerges as a guarantee of a government's health. The 'Hurgoes' (Lords) express displeasure that the king should secretly ask the Clinabs for two hundred thousand sprugs to finance a clandestine expedition. Commending the spirit of the young Hurgoes for expressing their objections, 'Quadrert' (Carteret) argues it shows their mettle. 'My Lords, it is with Pleasure that I perceive a Spirit of Virtue and Liberty beginning to prevail among the young peers.' 'Haxilaf' (Lord Halifax) agrees: 'What a melancholy Prospect should we present to our Countrymen, whose expiring Liberties call loudly for our Aid, if we, the Guardians of their Rights, could no longer protect our own?'[26]

The *Debates* are now little read and Johnson made no attempt to retrieve them or distinguish which of the many lengthy speeches were written by him. Speaking at the end of his life, they were the only part of his voluminous writings which caused him anxiety; 'but that at the time he wrote them, he had no conception he was imposing upon the world, though they were frequently written from very slender materials.' From those materials he composed debates which, as he wrote in the 1743 Preface to the *Gentleman's Magazine*, 'are considered as the most faithful and accurate representations of senatorial proceedings'.[27] However, the need to write them resulted in a sense of drudgery which could easily turn to cynicism: asked to review the Duchess of Marlborough's *Account* of political affairs he produced the telling comment that 'distrust is a necessary qualification of a student in history'.

Producing Lives for the *Gentleman's Magazine* often brought him to the same conclusion, but he calmed his doubts by glossing over panegyric details of the synopses with which he was presented. Did

Dr Morin really confine himself 'to Bread and Water' and allow himself 'no Indulgence beyond Fruits'? Being a great lover of his food, Johnson was distinctly sceptical: 'Some people (said he,) have a foolish way of not minding, or pretending not to mind, what they eat. For my part, I mind my belly very studiously.' He attempted to reduce Peter Burmann's narrative 'to Credibility' by suggesting he was only 'moderately skilled' in Latin and taught only 'the first Rudiments' of Greek. He developed a pragmatic sense when sifting through these supposed biographic facts, seeking for authenticity. Barretier was supposedly 'Master of Five Languages at the Age of Nine' yet Johnson cut much corroborating detail, 'being unwilling to demand the Belief of others to that which appears incredible to myself'. When it came to China, though, he admitted total ignorance, and restricted himself to mundane remarks on Du Halde's *Description of China* and his life of Confucius. Already he was making rules for fashioning biographies, of which the first rule was, did he believe it himself?[28]

Towards the end of 1742 Johnson became involved in an enterprise large enough to raise him to another level altogether when he was hired to catalogue the books and manuscripts that had been amassed by Robert and Edward Harley, with the view to putting them on sale. Robert Harley, first Earl of Oxford and friend of Swift, had been a great book collector, but ever since the death of his son in 1741 there had been rumours of a sale; when it was revealed that the books had passed to Thomas Osborne it was quite as expected. The price, £13,000, was steep, but no more 'than the binding of the books had cost', said a rival bookseller, and therefore wholly appropriate for Osborne who prided himself on such deals. Two years earlier he had splashed out on the whole front page of the *London Daily Post* to advertise a book sale at his Gray's Inn premises; Pope included him in the revised *Dunciad* for having sold off copies of the *Iliad* at half price.[29] In October Osborne negotiated with Johnson to write proposals for the library sale, notable for one distinctive detail: the catalogues themselves would cost ten shillings. As Johnson argued that November, the collection would excel 'any library that was ever yet offered to public sale'. Contemplating his task of making up the catalogue, he allowed his imagination to soar.

> Nor is the use of catalogues of less importance to those whom curiosity has engaged in the study of literary history, and who think the intellectual revolutions of the world more worthy of their attention, than the ravages of tyrants, the desolation of kingdoms, the rout of armies, and the fall of empires.[30]

If, briefly, he allowed his mind to travel back to his father, buying up the Earl of Derby's library of nearly three thousand books, he gave no signs of it. Arming himself for this mighty duty, more valuable to him than the rout of armies, Johnson was ably assisted by William Oldys, Lord Oxford's secretary, a man of indefatigable diligence who 'resembled a lion in harness'. By March 1743 the first two volumes of the *Catalogus Bibliothecae Harleianae* were ready and the books exhibited at Marylebone.[31] By the following Christmas Johnson issued '*flying sheets*' of the collection in separate weekly instalments, boasting that 'among the natives of *England* is to be found a greater variety of humour than in any other country'. However, there were objections to the *Miscellany*, not to the work he had put in, but to the price he charged. The public, unaccustomed to *buy* such items, resented the cost, no matter how handsomely they were annotated. Osborne, rejecting these objections, reluctantly agreed to allow those taking catalogues to use them 'in exchange for books', his sole priority being how fast the books were sold. Having lost money on the catalogues he became a trial to Johnson whose interest, naturally, was in the books themselves. Osborne begrudged the time spent preparing volumes to be sold and the amount of annotations done on them till Johnson described him as 'a man entirely destitute of shame, without a sense of any disgrace but that of poverty'.[32] Arranged in almost a hundred separate heads from 'Admiralty' to 'Witchcraft' and amounting to 'near forty thousand volumes', the library was of unprecedented size and Johnson and Oldys made valiant efforts at cataloguing it, entering their annotations, sometimes a single sentence, sometimes a page, erratically throughout the volumes. But the serendipitous nature of their researches through the stacks made for delays.[33] So it was that Osborne, expecting a rapid completion of the task, arrived to find Johnson *reading* a book, instead of cataloguing it. What happened next exists in several variants; here is Boswell's version:

> It has been confidently related, with many embellishments, that Johnson one day knocked Osborne down in his shop, with a folio, and put his foot upon his neck. The simple truth I had from Johnson himself. 'Sir, he was impertinent to me, and I beat him. But it was not in his shop: it was in my own chamber.'[34]

Mrs Thrale adds a touch which sounds authentically Johnsonian, reporting his boast that he 'beat many a fellow, but the rest had the wit to hold their tongues'. Johnson was clearly willing for the incident to be as violent as possible since Osborne had pointed out, quite succinctly, a tension which haunted him all his life: the love of books but the necessity of money.

On 1 December 1743 Johnson wrote to Theophilus Levett in Lichfield from 'Mr Osborne's, Bookseller in Grey's Inn', begging 'two months' forbearance on the twelve pounds' mortgage of his Lichfield family home, acknowledging that he owed the sum, but begging Levett 'not to mention it to my dear Mother'. The two-month term to which Levett happily agreed was brief, but news had just reached Johnson that encouraged him to hope it might soon be discharged. He had just heard of the death of Richard Savage, which came as a blow, but offered him a timely opportunity. He wrote immediately to Cave promising a life of Savage which would 'speedily be published'. Here, at last, was his opportunity and he meant to make the most of it.

He rapidly completed his work of supplying a dedication to his school friend Robert James's *Medicinal Dictionary* for which he had previously written proposals. This was a favour which was done on account of James's reputation for skill in medicine, and not at all in return for the five guineas he received for it, or to feelings of responsibility for the collapse of Lewis Paul's cotton mill in which James had had a share. Johnson wrote brief biographies of Actuarius, who specialised in urine, and Asclepiades, who gave his patients wine, though the fact that most of the medical men whose lives he wrote had names beginning with 'A' suggests a lack of continuing interest. 'Credulity, obstinacy and folly are hourly making havoc in the world,' he wrote, sentiments which his work on the Harleian collection only confirmed.[35]

In later years Johnson boasted of having written 'forty-eight of the printed octavo pages of the *Life of Savage* at a sitting; but then I sat up all night'. Writing the life of a man he had known on his first entrance to literary London, with whom he had experienced the heights and depths of fortune, to whom he had confessed his inner-most thoughts and from whom he had heard incredible tales of duplicity was providential. He insisted on doing justice to Savage as raconteur, poet and philosopher, not forgetting that his friend had been the most charming sponger. 'What more have you got?' he demanded of Cave, listing 'his trial etc.' and any magazines 'that have any thing of his or relating to him'. Cave was presently besieged by demands for money and he joked that he 'would *not* press you too hard', desiring only 'two Guineas for a Sheet of Copy'. The money could 'lye by in your hands' until 'it may be more convenient' but, he warned him, it would be 'very expensive'. Johnson worked hard on the *Life*, but always there were other projects to be completed; Cave had proposed to him a history of parliament and then, as always, there were the *Debates*: 'With the debates shall I not have business enough?' he hinted to Cave, prompting him with the suggestion: 'if I had but good Pens . . .'

There is a distinct tremor of excitement in Johnson's tone as he turned to the *Life of Savage*, which took longer than expected to finish because he was anxious to get the tone just right. Cave paid him fifteen guineas for the completed work in the middle of December 1743 and two months later the full volume of 180 pages went on sale. In the three years since his own tearful farewell to Savage (which he carefully records) Johnson had had time to come to a balanced view of this 'child' who 'mistook the love for the practice of virtue'. In the *Life* he presents his considered findings. He begins very much on Savage's side, never doubting that Savage was the illegitimate offspring of the Countess of Macclesfield whom he condemns for her 'implacable and restless cruelty' in exposing her son 'to slavery and want'. Referring to her constantly as 'the Mother', Johnson generates such fierce denunciation of her wickedness that feelings against his own mother, whom he would never see again, are surely hinted at. But gradually, as he unfolds the tale, although his heart's sympathy for Savage never wavers, Johnson's head moves in a different direction. He tells tales of Savage's life which are very funny; on one occasion Savage is dining with Sir Richard Steele amid an 'expensive Train of Domestics' who turn out to be bailiffs; on another, Savage writes to a friend when incarcerated in Bristol, 'I *absolutely command* you not to offer me any pecuniary Assistance', thus asking for the very thing he so vehemently forbids. But the reader slowly moves to a sense that Savage is not only a danger to himself but to those who trust him, of whom Johnson had been one. He is forced to realise that 'when once [Savage] had entered a Tavern, or engaged in a scheme of Pleasure, he never retired till want of money obliged him to some new expedient'. However often Savage promised a change of direction, his life was set upon a downward trajectory; yet, despite the bleakness of his circumstances, he always contrived to sound positive: 'His Distresses, however afflictive, never dejected him; in his lowest State he wanted not Spirit to assert the natural Dignity of Wit.' The essential charm of Savage was that of a man who always seemed on the point of rising above present distresses:

> On a Bulk, in a Cellar, or in a Glass-house among Thieves and Beggars, was to be found the Author of the *Wanderer*, the Man of exalted Sentiments, extensive Views, and curious Observations, the Man whose Remarks on Life might have assisted the Statesman, whose Ideas of Virtue might have enlightened the Moralist, whose Eloquence might have influenced Senates, and whose Delicacy might have polished Courts.

Reaching the end of the life, Johnson had drawn hard lessons from the career of a man to whom friendship was a thing 'of little value'. By elevating Savage's life to the status of a moral exemplum, he universalised but depersonalised the lessons, enabling him to preserve something, however illusory, of a friendship once so important to him.[36]

Boswell records Joshua Reynolds reading the *Life of Savage* before ever he knew anything of Johnson, 'with his arm leaning against a chimney-piece. It seized his attention so strongly, that, not being able to lay down the book till he had finished it, when he attempted to move, he found his arm totally benumbed.'[37]

At the age of thirty-five Johnson had composed his first major biography, describing the dreams of literary fame, the reality of life in literary London and the hard choices between them; in composing this spellbinding *Life*, Johnson had chosen his path.

As he enjoyed his successful emergence as a writer, Johnson learnt that the attorneys of the deceased Thomas Perks of Birmingham, to whom Harry Porter had loaned £100, were offering a composition. They agreed to disburse a little over a third of the sum, giving £36 to Tetty and himself. He immediately sent directions to Lucy to open his cabinet and bring the money directly to Levett. It was a moment to rejoice; his first successful biography and the repayment of a debt. Sadly it seems Levett never received a penny; but the thought that the money was promised to him, and coming, would have soothed Johnson's conscience. It allowed him, briefly, to bask in his literary prospects and not worry about the £12 debt still owed.[38]

Other liabilities, less easily forgotten, could at least be concealed. Cave dined with Walter Harte, tutor to Lord Chesterfield's son, at St John's Gate, where Harte made many appreciative comments on the *Life of Savage*. Meeting him a little later, Cave said he had made a man 'very happy t'other day'. 'How could that be,' said Harte; 'nobody was there but ourselves.' Cave reminded him of a plate of food, sent behind the screen to Johnson, his clothes so shabby he dared not appear; he had been 'highly delighted with the encomiums on his book'. On New Year's Day at the start of 1745 Johnson thanked God that he had 'hitherto forborn to snatch me away in the midst of Sin and Folly'.[39]

Johnson always loved major challenges which, in addition to fully exercising his mind, brought in the most money. In eighteenth-century English publishing there was no greater challenge than

Shakespeare and so, in the early winter of 1745, puffed up by the success of *Savage*, he offered to tackle Shakespeare. He produced a bold provisional pamphlet on *Macbeth* to demonstrate he was the man to offer an innovative edition of the Complete Works.[40] From his first remarks he sought to prove he had the skills to make evident Shakespeare's 'abilities and merits as a writer'. In a masterly demonstration he asserted that belief in witchcraft has 'in all ages and countries been credited by the common people', amongst whom he includes King James I whose *Daemonologie* was read 'by all who desired either to gain preferment or not to lose it'. He recalled the empress Placidia who was kind enough to kill the magician who had promised her marvellous victories, 'cutting him off at a time so convenient for his reputation'. From Hall's *Soliloquies* to Cervantes's *Don Quixote* he spread around his sources, declaring aphoristically that 'the greatest part of mankind have no other reason for their opinions than that they are in fashion' or that witchcraft or enchantment 'though not strictly the same, are confounded in this play' as evidence of both Shakespeare's wit and worldly intelligence. Maintaining a pose of knowing wit he refrained from criticising former editors of Shakespeare, preferring instead to reveal their faults by unconvincing excuses. He even refused to censure Theobald who, though often wrong, 'ought to be treated with indulgence'. This was even more the case with Shakespeare himself, whose numerous errors were put down to a variety of increasingly implausible excuses: 'something else was undoubtedly intended by the author,' says Johnson, implying that alterations to the text are necessary 'almost in every page'; Shakespeare 'never has six lines together without a fault', he later declared; this was the chance to correct them.

Changes that he offered to *Macbeth* indicate a magisterial self-confidence, no more so than when the shift he recommends is the alteration of a single letter. Macbeth's 'Safe tow'rds your love and honour' becomes '*Save* tow'rds . . .' and Lady Macbeth's 'nor keep peace between . . .' becomes 'nor keep *pace* . . .' He changes Macbeth's 'I pull in resolution' to 'I *pall* . . .', happily accepted by later editors; but his alteration of 'my Way of life/ Is fall'n into the sear . . .' to 'my *May* of life . . .' (arguing 'W' 'is only an "M" inverted') shows the tempting dangers of such a verbal game. Not only nouns and verbs but every grammatical form is subject to his playful scrutiny. He amends the punctuation of Macbeth's 'It will have blood, they say blood will have blood', inserting a dash and a capital T ('They . . .') and declaring it 'the general observation of mankind' – something he is always keen to identify – 'that murderers cannot escape'. Nor is rhythm safe; whenever Shakespeare attempts to write regular rhyme Johnson assists, clarifying scansion and removing 'two superfluous syllables' from 'That trace *him in* his line . . .' He applies his pruning shears to many famous lines, reducing Macbeth's lament for the dead Duncan, 'Unmannerly breech'd with gore', to 'Unmanly drench'd . . .', asserting that 'every word' in the line is 'equally faulty', and he dismisses '*Sir T. H.'s*' (Thomas Hanmer's) recent sumptuous edition of the plays with studied insouciance: 'Such harmless industry may, surely, be forgiven, if it cannot be praised.'[41]

Clearly anxious that his *Miscellaneous Observations* should be noticed, he appended, among the advertisements at the end of the pamphlet, his own *Proposals for Printing a New Edition of the Plays of William Shakespeare*, with subscriptions to be taken in by Cave. This was too much. Within the week Cave received a letter from Jacob Tonson, asserting his sole control over publishing Shakespeare and threatening a suit in Chancery against anyone who attempted to dispute it. Tonson, they knew, would be a very determined opponent and, reluctantly, Cave and Johnson backed down.[42]

Instead, Johnson settled for a small audience, a congregation in fact, who came to hear a sermon written by him preached by his old friend Henry Hervey who, having thrown over his commission of dragoons and changed his name to Hervey *Aston*, assumed holy orders and took up the rectorship of Shottley in Suffolk. The change which converted the 'wildest of the wild', whom Johnson called 'a vicious man', into a man of the cloth is not easily, or perhaps it is *too* easily, explained. The occasion of Johnson's sermon was the annual feast of a body known as the Sons of the Clergy, a prestigious affair in May, with a service beforehand at St Paul's Cathedral graced by the Archbishop of Canterbury. For a modest two-guinea fee which, Hawkins records, Johnson made 'no scruple of', he wrote and gave up his sermons as 'absolutely the property of the purchaser'. This sermon, Johnson's first, preached before a charitable commission, was on the theme of charity: 'To do good and to distribute forget not: for with such sacrifices, God is well pleased.' Generalised, as appropriate for a commissioned sermon, it provides hints of the occasion by telling the congregation not 'to neglect the universal happiness of mankind' but to 'practice every duty consistently with nature'. The feast at Merchant Taylors' Hall, appropriately combining happiness with duty, contributed a collection of £180, the 'largest hitherto made on the occasion'.[43]

Two months later, on 14 July 1745 (NS), Charles Edward Stuart embarked from St Nazaire and landed in Scotland at the start of August; there he raised his standard, at Glenfinnan, and began his Jacobite quest to wrest the crown of Britain from the Hanoverian monarch. Initially he enjoyed considerable success, winning the battle of Prestonpans, near Edinburgh, though in England his advance did not provoke particular concerns. The *Westminster Journal* estimated the Pretender's followers at fifteen hundred on 8 September, increasing the number to 'not together above 2,500 Men' a fortnight later, while it entertained its readers with a new ballad, entitled 'The Highland Invasion'. On its front page it carried a large advertisement for John Williams's pesticide, under the title 'BUGGS Destroyed', noting that 'Palaces' were a particular speciality. But as the invasion continued its southern march, gathering supporters as it moved, the tone became less frivolous. In October the *Journal* estimated the rebels at '8,000 effective men, exclusive of what they call his guards', and as it described the Pretender himself, dressed in a Highland garb of 'fine silk tartan, red velvet breeches and a blue velvet bonnet, with Gold Lace round it', his popularity became more tangible. So much so that in its issue for 16 November the *Journal*'s whole front page was occupied by an engraving of the Pretender as a Highland warrior, labelled 'The POPE'S SCOURGE, or an exact Portraiture of a Pope's Pretender' with ' 'Tis time for Vengeance' coming from his mouth. Worse was to come; later in November, Carlisle fell and by December the *Westminster Journal* was reporting that the Pretender and his forces had reached Derby, by which time their correspondent was 'confidently told that they were complete 16,000 effective men'. The militia of Essex and Suffolk were being raised, to prevent 'foreign Troops from Landing on the coast'.[44]

During all this time we have no knowledge of Johnson's movements and there has been considerable speculation as to his sympathies: 'it is a realistic possibility', argues a recent historian, 'rather than a romantic speculation that for a time in 1745–6 he held himself in readiness for dramatic events in circumstances which may have arisen.'[45] To support this proposition we have his known Toryism which, in *London* and *Marmor Norfolciense*, had assumed a public face; from his association with Savage he had acquired a desperate hardiness, a desire to see things change and for people like Robert Walpole or the erstwhile Countess of Macclesfield to be brought low. But Walpole *had* fallen by 1745 and the Countess (now Mrs Brett) lived alone in Bond Street. In his *Life of Savage* Johnson had brought the cold, dry light of reason to shine on drunken nocturnal fantasies and he may well, during the winter of 1745–6, simply have kept his own counsel. Boswell notes that 'none of his letters' for the period exist, and wonders aloud; 'it is somewhat curious, that his literary career appears to have been almost totally suspended in the years 1745 and 1746, those years which were marked by a civil war in Great-Britain.' Johnson was neither blind to the political significance of what was going on nor unprincipled in his consideration of political affairs. Ten years later, at the time Admiral Byng was sentenced to death, he insisted there were times when 'every Englishman expects to be informed of the national affairs'. But, in the winter of 1745–6, having just written the *Life of Savage* and contemplated an edition of Shakespeare, the time was not right for him to engage in political debates, or even to let his particular prejudices be known. The battle of Culloden, ending the Jacobite adventure, occurred on 16 April 1746 and two months later Johnson signed the contract to produce a dictionary which would extend the rule of the English language throughout the civilised world, whether the England from which the language came were Protestant-Hanoverian or Catholic-Jacobite. It was to be the most significant moment of his life though, inevitably with Johnson, the money was what counted most; the matter of £1,500 could not be neglected.[46]

Almost thirty years later, when making his tour of the Western Isles of Scotland, Johnson passed within a couple of miles, between Fort George and Inverness, of the point where the rebellion ended, at Culloden; yet he makes no mention of it. This is despite the fact that his narrative is full of memories of former glories. St Andrews is a city that has 'gradually decayed', now presenting 'the silence and solitude of inactive indigence and gloomy depopulation'; at Aberbrothick (Arbroath) he surveys the ruins of the famous monastery and notes that they 'afford ample testimony of its ancient magnificence'. Of Culloden he says nothing, but is entertained, at Fort George, by the governor, Sir Eyre Coote, with great elegance and, in consequence, arrived 'somewhat late' at Inverness.[47] Boswell diverts the company with dinner-table talk of Arabs and Shakespeare, and confides that, to him, the whole evening was 'like enchantment'. He records Johnson saying that 'here was a large sum of money expended in building a fort' but the reason for that large expenditure is never mentioned. Later on their tour Johnson lies on the same bed, in Flora Macdonald's house on Skye, that Charles Edward Stuart had lain on, but assures Boswell he has 'no ambitious thoughts'. Clearly, by then in receipt of a government pension, he may have felt constrained in what he said and wrote since, though thirty years in the past, the fear of Jacobitism remained, and the kilt, a word not mentioned in either the *Journey* or the *Dictionary*, was still proscribed. But Johnson was not a man to accept artificial curbs on his conversation; pressed endlessly by Boswell to utter his thoughts on Jacobitism, the most he would utter was his declaration that 'if holding up his right hand would have secured victory at Culloden to Prince Charles's army, he was not sure he would have held it up'.[48] Whatever thoughts he may have felt in 1738, there is no evidence that in 1745 he was anything but a loyal Hanoverian Englishman.

6

A Harmless Drudge

lexicographer n.s. *A writer of dictionaries; a harmless drudge, that busies himself in tracing the original, and detailing the signification of words.*

ADAMS: But, Sir, how can you do this in three years?
JOHNSON: Sir, I have no doubt that I can do it in three years.
ADAMS: But the French Academy, which consists of forty members, took forty years to compile their Dictionary.
JOHNSON: Sir, thus it is. This is the proportion. Let me see; forty times forty is sixteen hundred. As three to sixteen hundred, so is the proportion of an Englishman to a Frenchman.[1]

Johnson claimed he had long thought of the idea of a dictionary, but when Robert Dodsley first suggested the project to him, he turned it down. Though vastly flattered to be asked (the last man to be made such an offer was Addison) he said 'in his abrupt decisive manner, "I believe I shall not undertake it." '[2] Something happened to change his mind, which was partly the realisation by Tetty that with £1,500 they could finally quit Castle Street and move to a more elegant address, partly his own recognition that by completing such a task he would earn himself an undeniable reputation, and a biography.

Dictionaries had been done before. Nathan Bailey had produced his *Universal Etymological Dictionary* in 1736 to give normal words their etymologies and meanings; Ephraim Chambers's *Cyclopaedia* furnished accounts of the most recent technical innovations, and a host of other dictionaries, hard-word books and lexicons existed for all kinds of linguistic usage from the argot of Canting Crew to lawyers' Latin slang. But none of them provided what Pope required when he lamented that 'such as Chaucer is, shall Dryden be' or of which Swift signalled the need when he published *Proposal for Correcting . . . the English Tongue* and signed it with his own name. Such people required more than a guide to current vocabulary; they demanded a prescriptive definition of usage which would put an end to linguistic devaluation. Pope had started the work by compiling impeccable authorities; Addison, who, like Swift, envisaged an academy to maintain standards, marked quotations in Tillotson's sermons to be used in his 'voluminous dictionary' advertised in June 1717; the bookseller Jacob Tonson promised him £3,000 for the work. When Addison died his materials passed to Ambrose Philips who published proposals. But there the project stalled.[3]

The main problem about attracting a well-known name like Addison was the amount of laborious toil the enterprise would entail. But Robert Dodsley, who had been observing Johnson since he published *London*, reckoned he had the knowledge and tenacity for such a major undertaking; more importantly, he had the thirst for recognition such a dictionary would bring. Dodsley formed a group of leading publishers to sponsor the project and, through a mixture of bribery and flattery, tempted Johnson to sign up. *The Plan of a Dictionary* was published in 1747 after the circulation of the scheme in manuscript; notable among those expressing opinions on it was Lord Chesterfield to whom it was dedicated. Even Johnson nodded in deference to his lordship, an act which only hindsight suggests lacked conviction. Had Shakespeare had the benefit of such a dictionary, which would correctly signify the proper names of plants, he would not so erroneously have intermingled the woodbine with the honeysuckle, the *Plan* made clear; and an exact taxonomy of reptiles would certainly have prevented Milton from disposing 'so improperly' of the ellops and the scorpion. In settling these and many similar errors Johnson arrogated no authority to himself, but threw all such questions back upon the arbitration of Lord Chesterfield, on whose behalf he exercised only 'a kind of vicarious jurisdiction'.[4]

The one 'great end' of the work would be to fix the English language for ever. 'All change is of itself an evil,' Johnson declared, vowing he would secure the tongue from being 'over-run with cant'. But, though his claims were large, he carefully played down all thought of personal fame; 'unhappy lexicographers' held the lowest place as candidates for literary fame; they did no more than beat 'the track of the alphabet with sluggish resolution'. Such declarations of humble status may have been designed to flatter Chesterfield's linguistic vanity, but possibly Johnson sought to distance himself from the enormous task upon which he was embarking. He was genuinely 'frighted' by the extent of work that lay before him, 'like the soldiers of Caesar' viewing the shores of Britain 'as a new world, which it is almost madness to invade'. Recalling the bold terms in which he set out to edit Shakespeare, the differences are obvious. That was a role in which he hoped to dazzle readers by deploying the latest techniques; this was a well-paid but tedious task, promising little chance to show off personal skill but many thousand opportunities to register inattention, lack of comprehension or plain ignorance. Little wonder he attempted to slough off responsibilities of the office of dictionary-maker on to his lordship, the publishers and the language of which he assumed custodianship. 'An ingenious document', Birch confided to Yorke when Johnson sent him a copy, 'but the style too flatulent.' On the continent of Europe, though, the *Plan* was well received; the *Bibliothèque raisonnée des ouvrages des savants de l'Europe* believed it was written '*avec une pureté et une elegance peu communes*'. The sum agreed was £1,575, far more than Johnson could have obtained for any comparable task; when he signed the contract on 16 June he promised to have his *Dictionary* ready for publication in three years' time.

Undoubtedly the money was a great incentive to both himself and Tetty; 'No man but a block-head ever wrote, except for money,' he declared. He immediately used the wealth to acquire a fine dwelling place in Gough Square to put an end to their years of living separately.[5] The house, which still exists, was quite substantial, having three main floors, a cellar and an extensive garret. Ascending from a basement kitchen, the ground floor comprised a dining room and sitting room; above these was a large bedroom with a withdrawing room and, above these, two more bedrooms. In the garret Johnson 'fitted up a room with desks and other accommodations for amanuenses, who, to the number of five or six, he kept constantly under his eye'.[6] It was furnished with 'an old crazy deal table' and an even older elbow-chair 'with only three legs and one arm' at which he constantly presided, 'having, with considerable dexterity and evident practice, first drawn it up against the wall, which served to support it on that side on which the leg was deficient'. This chair on which he balanced to compose not just the *Dictionary* but also his main periodical essays had a large part in his mental organisation. Since he wished always to create a sense of order in whatever area he worked, it provided a valuable incentive to him that the balance he sought would have to be imposed, even in this, his most instinctive working environment.[7]

Johnson hired six amanuenses to assist him copying passages for the *Dictionary*: Francis Stewart, Alexander and William Macbean, V. J. Peyton, Robert Shiels and a man called Maitland, all of them, with the exception of Peyton, Scotsmen. He did not employ them all at once. Stewart he hired on the day he signed the contract, requiring a receipt for the £3 3s 'by way of advance', to be repaid at the rate of twelve shillings a week. Stewart was 'a porter-drinking man', a source of 'low cant phrases', but he died early on, as did Shiels. William Macbean and Peyton were recruited to replace them; Peyton was, according to Johnson's friend Giuseppe Baretti, 'a fool and a drunkard. I never saw so nauseous a fellow.'[8] Johnson, who was always better with metaphors than men, wrote in exasperation to William Strahan, the printer, confessing he knew not 'how to manage, I pay three and twenty shillings a week to my assistants, in truth without having much assistance from them'. In his new year prayer for the start of 1748 he begged to 'become every day more diligent in the duties which in thy Providence shall be assigned to me', but the signs were not good.[9]

During the following year he had much to harass him in organising his working practices on the *Dictionary*. When, occasionally, he was called upon to supply materials for other publications such as Dodsley's self-education work, *The Preceptor*, he did them quickly, often betraying his own concerns as he did so. Thomas Tyers writes that after a day in Holborn, Johnson composed 'in one night' his allegory of human existence, 'The Vision of Theodore, the Hermit of Teneriffe', concentrating on the intoxicating power of *habit*, which was 'so absolute' that 'neither Hope nor Fear' could withstand. Habit's subtle force left her victim 'always wishing for her presence' and, like a delicious drug, was so pleasantly numbing there was real effort involved in throwing her off. Many years later Johnson still thought this 'Vision' one of his best pieces. Defining *habit* in the *Dictionary* he concentrated on its pleasingly harmful influence, citing a phrase from Robert South's sermons to particularise its meaning: 'by frequent repetition of the sinful act . . . it settles into a fixed con-firmed *habit* of sin'.[10] Tetty's tendency to spend vast periods of the day in bed, drinking and finding innumerable things to complain about, from the squalid nature of Fleet Street air to the slippery nature of Chancery Lane footings, soon became the accepted habit of the house in Gough Square.

Meanwhile Garrick's theatrical career had blossomed. During the last five years he had amazed audiences with remarkable leading per-formances in *Hamlet, Lear* and *Macbeth* with his salary rising as his reputation grew. He now commanded some £500 for a season and seemed at the height of his fame. But in September 1747 he took one more ambitious step and, at the age of only thirty, embarked upon the management of Drury Lane. Johnson, aged thirty-eight, was uncer-tain whether to be proud of him or simply envious. He wrote a *Prologue* for the opening of the season which, in retrospect, he saw only as the source of further irritations. He had the entire sixty-two lines of verse composed in his head 'before I threw a single couplet on paper' but was forced to alter words 'at the remonstrance of Garrick'. He supposed 'it was necessary he should be satisfied with what he was to utter', he grudgingly confessed, thoughts of *Irene* swimming into mind. The verses are best remembered now for what they reprove, particularly their comments on playwrights of the Restoration era:

> Themselves they studied, as they felt, they writ,
> Intrigue was Plot, Obscenity was Wit.

Ostensibly he was supporting his now famous former pupil, who repeated his words on the Drury Lane stage, but there was jealousy implicit in them. 'Then Johnson came,' he wrote, recalling the 'Cold

Approbation' which had greeted his last great namesake on the English stage, Ben Jonson:

> A Mortal born he met the general Doom,
> But left, like *Egypt*'s Kings, a lasting Tomb.[11]

Would it be left to posthumous generations to appreciate his worth, while Garrick pranced in the limelight? Just ten days after the declamation of these lines he had some kind of answer; Birch wrote to his friend Yorke that *Irene* was threatened 'for our entertainment this winter'. The warning though was premature and a year later Birch wrote again with a revised prospectus; Johnson had indeed agreed with Garrick 'for bringing his *Irene* upon the stage next winter'.[12]

Problems with Tetty continued and were not lessened by his continuing failures to have his tragedy staged while the town all whispered that *of course* it would be put on, because Johnson so pestered his former pupil. Continuing to drink, she took opiates for the many illnesses to which she believed herself a prey and grumbled at the noise and noxious air she found at Gough Square. The place which had at first pleased her now became the source of her dissatisfaction and her discontents were maintained in the bedroom, where she became more inventive than ever manufacturing excuses to keep herself from Johnson's embraces. She insisted something must be done to remove her from the grime of Fleet Street and, to gain the advantages of country air, lodged herself in Hampstead, in a 'small house beyond the church', without worrying about expenses. Years later Johnson was threatened with legal action for a bill in which Tetty was charged 'for the sum of two pounds ever since August 12th, 1749'. Boswell endorsed the note: 'Proof of Dr Johnson's wretched circumstances in 1751.' Johnson often joined her in Hampstead and wrote 'the greatest part, if not the whole' of *The Vanity of Human Wishes* there; but still she kept him from her bed, pleading the excuse of her ill-health. Johnson, still under forty, had a vigorous sexual appetite, but Tetty had thought of that, as he confessed to Boswell.

> 'My wife told me I might lye with as many women as I pleased, provided I *loved* her alone.'

BOSWELL: She was not in earnest.

JOHNSON: But she was; consider, Sir, how gross it is in a wife to complain of her husband's going to other women, merely as women; it is that she has not enough of what she would be ashamed to avow.

BOSWELL: And was Mrs Johnson then so liberal, Sir? . . .

JOHNSON: Sir, if she refuses, she has no right to complain.

BOSWELL: Then, Sir, according to your doctrine, upon every such occasion a man may make a note in his pocket-book, and do as he pleases.[13]

Johnson was a continent and devout man whose marriage vows were sacred to him; yet he was also a man with strong sexual appetites. Elizabeth Desmoulins, daughter of Johnson's godfather Dr Swinfen, came to stay with Tetty at Hampstead and from her there are some noteworthy points, made to Boswell but subsequently suppressed by him. For one thing, she slept in the same room with Tetty, except when female visitors came to stay; then she slept in the same bed, but only after giving her word never to breathe a word of it to Johnson who was given to believe his wife could never tolerate a bedfellow. More significant are the nocturnal activities of Johnson, who might come in late, after an evening spent with Dr Bathurst, to find Tetty gone to bed and only Desmoulins waiting up for him, with a pan of coals from the fire to warm his bed. Often, when he had undressed, he would call her through to sit with him upon his bed and talk to him; sometimes she would even lie beside him with her head upon his pillow. Boswell and Mauritius Lowe, the painter, pressed her closely on this subject in 1783. Lowe began by saying, 'Now, Ma'am, let us be free. We are all married people. Pray tell us, do you really think Dr Johnson ever offended in point of chastity?' To which Desmoulins replied that 'there never was a man who had stronger amorous inclinations than Dr Johnson. But he conquered them.' They continued their close questioning, with Lowe affecting to believe that Johnson never had an 'inclination for women', to which Desmoulins replied that decidedly he had. Lowe said he believed the Johnsons' marriage was never consummated, which she emphatically denied, though admitting that 'they did not sleep together for many years'. When she mentioned laying her head upon his pillow Boswell became excited and asked, 'And he showed strong signs of that passion?' To which she agreed, but said she 'always respected him as a Father' (though he was only seven years older than her). Asked whether he had made any direct sexual advances, Mrs Desmoulins replied that 'he never did anything that was beyond the limits of decency'. She admitted that if he had urged her with more force she might have given way to him, but it was Johnson himself who finally resisted, pushing her from him and begging her to leave. Meanwhile Tetty slept, in a drunken stupor, only a room away.

In his prayer for New Year's Day that year Johnson begged for Heaven's bounteous mercy that had not yet 'suffered me to fall into the Grave'.[14] He was in such a mood when he wrote *The Vanity of Human Wishes*, composing the first seventy lines 'in the course of one morning', writing 'a hundred lines' a day and planning the whole poem in his head before committing a single couplet to paper. Written in the late summer of 1748, he presented the completed poem to Dodsley in November for fifteen guineas, but reserved to himself 'the right of printing one edition'. He chose badly; whereas there were five English editions (and one Irish) of *London*, this more philosophical poem was never reprinted in his lifetime. Garrick expressed the general view when he joked it was 'hard as Greek'; he hoped Johnson would not go on to imitate another satire which would inevitably be 'as hard as Hebrew'.[15]

The poem, which appeared that January with his name printed on the title page, expressed Johnson's view of life as he neared his fortieth birthday. Taking Juvenal's Tenth Satire as its model the tone is gloomy, only saved from despair by a final effort of will which calls upon celestial wisdom to calm the mind. By registering his identity upon the poem and owning its sentiments Johnson attempted to signal his arrival on the literary scene, hoping that as author of the *Dictionary* his words would soon have weight. But the total absence of critical comment, apart from a brief puff in the *Gentleman's Magazine* and Garrick's facetious jests, told him he had chosen his calling card badly. Serious poetry did not sell well and he did not write another major poem.

Johnson claimed to have carried *The Vanity of Human Wishes*, like many other of his poems, sketched out in his head before writing it; this was a remarkable feat of memory which, like his habit of writing entire *Rambler* papers at a sitting and not re-reading them, turned acts of composition into theatrical performances. He made his life a living theatre, fashioned his conversation into bouts of showmanship and wrote as an extension of his argumentative voice. Something of his mnemonic powers may be seen in his poetic language which repeats key rhyme words, particularly those of a single syllable ('Pow'r' with 'Tow'r', 'Dart' with both 'Art' and 'Heart'), stressing elements closer to the technique of Lego than of plasticine. Only occasionally does the poem rise above this quality, and one such moment is his memory of Oxford.

> When first the College Rolls receive his Name,
> The young Enthusiast quits his Ease for Fame;
> Through all his Veins the Fever of Renown
> Burns from the strong Contagion of the Gown;
> O'er *Bodley*'s Dome his future Labours spread,
> And *Bacon*'s Mansion trembles o'er his Head:
> Are these thy Views? Proceed, illustrious Youth,
> And Virtue guard thee to the Throne of Truth,
> Yet should thy Soul indulge the generous Heat,
> Till captive Science yields her last Retreat;
> Should Reason guide thee with her brightest Ray,
> And pour on misty Doubt resistless Day;
> Should no false Kindness lure to loose Delight,
> Nor Praise relax, nor Difficulty fright;
> Should tempting Novelty thy Cell refrain,
> And Sloth effuse her opiate Fumes in vain;
> Should Beauty blunt on Fops her fatal Dart,
> Nor claim the Triumph of a letter'd Heart;
> Should no Disease thy torpid Veins invade,
> Nor Melancholy's Phantoms haunt thy Shade;

Yet hope not Life from Grief or Danger free,
Nor think the Doom of Man revers'd for thee:
Deign on the passing World to turn thine Eyes,
And pause awhile from Letters to be wise;
There mark what Ills the Scholar's Life assail,
Toil, Envy, Want, the Garret, and the Jail.[16]

This passage is clearly autobiographical and, later, Hester Thrale would often say that Johnson burst into tears on reading it. Yet it is noticeable that, while mentioning the temptations which distract the scholar (Novelty, Sloth, Beauty), he mentions 'Want' only as an abstraction, rather than poverty as a fact. Twenty years had passed since he had been forced to leave Oxford yet still he found it impossible to acknowledge the shaming condition that had driven him from Bodley's dome and Bacon's mansion.

Yet he did not confess any particular application of these generalised remarks, and the lines were finally given a personal bite in March 1755 when, having sent his famous letter to Chesterfield the previous month, Johnson substituted the insidious word 'Patron' for the poor, but honest 'Garret'. In the *Dictionary* he defines *patron* as 'commonly a wretch who supports with insolence, and is paid with flattery'.[17]

It was a bitter winter. One despairing woman attempted to drown herself in the water reservoir at Marylebone but, according to the *London Evening Post*, 'could not break the ice'. Her miseries were less easily frustrated, though, and she contrived to hang herself. Many people believed that Johnson's poem, published in January 1749, was intended as a preparation for *Irene* (or *Mahomet and Irene* as Garrick insisted on re-titling it), currently in rehearsal at Drury Lane. Well aware of the importance of publicity, particularly for a play about which he had severe reservations, Garrick had an article placed two weeks before the opening night which spoke of 'everyone' being 'big with expectation' to see a tragedy which was reckoned 'the highest pitch of dramatic performance'.[18] All through rehearsals rows kept breaking out between Johnson, keen to preserve every line, and Garrick who knew that without judicious trimming the play would not be playable at all. Johnson complained to Dr Taylor of Ashbourne who was called in to mediate between them; 'the fellow' (as he called Garrick) wanted 'to make Mahomet run mad, that he may have an opportunity of tossing his hands and kicking his heels'. With tactful patience a kind of truce was made between them both but, never satisfied, Johnson sat through all the performances 'expressing his disapprobation aloud'.[19]

Part of his disappointment had nothing to do with Garrick's production (though he pretended otherwise) but came from Tetty's reaction. Thirteen years earlier, his Edial dreams in ruins, he presented *Irene* as a peace-offering between them; since then whatever tensions there might be could be calmed by reading the play and talking of its prospects. He added to the cast the character of Aspasia in an idealised portrait of Tetty, attempting to convince her that soon he would not be a dull journalist or drudging lexicographer but a tragedian, enjoying something of the fame in which Garrick basked. But it had taken nine years for the play to be produced, in which time Tetty's interest had waned. Now, although he dressed himself up, ridiculously he thought, in scarlet waistcoat and gold-laced hat to frequent the Green Room of the theatre and mix in 'the sprightly chit-chat of the motley circle then to be found there', he did so all alone. Not that he didn't find amusement in the company of players; probably too much so with regard to the 'rigid virtue' he espoused. Garrick reported him saying that he would 'come no more behind your scenes, David; for the silk stockings and white bosoms of your actresses do make my genitals to quiver'.[20]

The run of *Irene* went strangely well; the audience only objected to one incident on the opening night, which came near the end. Hannah Pritchard, in the role of Irene, preparing to be strangled on stage, came forward to speak her lines with a bowstring tied around her neck. Such realism greatly offended the audience who, accustomed to the more decorous conventions of neoclassical tragedy, 'cried out *"Murder! Murder!"* She several times attempted to speak; but all in vain. At last she was obliged to go off the stage alive.' The incident, an innovation by Garrick, was dropped, Mrs Pritchard died off stage and Johnson made much of the importance of observing the tragedian's wishes. The rest of the run went off successfully, making Johnson a final profit of £195, plus £100 from Dodsley for the copyright. Garrick bulked up the audience for the last three nights with comic afterpieces and the result was, if not outstanding, at least quite respectable attendances.

For Johnson, the heart of the play was the scene in which Aspasia counsels Irene to pursue virtuous ends by virtuous means and value a life of 'chearful poverty' in a 'quiet cottage'. Her words are all in vain; Irene disparages a life of 'dull obscurity' and the tragedy proceeds to its conclusion.[21] The *Gentleman's Magazine* was, unsurprisingly, full of praise and even the *General Advertiser* called *Mahomet and Irene* 'the best tragedy which this age has produced'; yet there were less amiable comments. Aaron Hill thought it contained 'strong sense' but was 'ungraced by sweetness'; John Blair noted the play was not kept in repertory.[22] Considering it thirty years later Boswell thought it contained 'noble sentiments' but was 'deficient in pathos'. Johnson, though, was frank; he regarded it as quite dead, 'like a Monument'. The silence that greeted the publication of *The Vanity of Human Wishes* meant he would not attempt another major poem; now the lack of success of *Irene* decided him not to write another play.

From Johnson's own perspective as he approached his fortieth birthday, the prospects did not look good. He had been in London for ten years, had tried his hand at writing poetry and tragedy, but with indifferent results; meanwhile his pupil, Garrick, was a tremendous success. He dearly hoped his latest enterprise, the *Dictionary*, would triumph, though the prospects for it were not benign.[23] He had been working on it now for two years and the task, though tedious, was progressing. In August Birch told Yorke the amanuenses' work would 'soon be over' and Johnson would 'begin to connect their papers, and draw them up into form'. There seemed every reason to hope that his rash prediction ('Sir, I have no doubt that I can do it in three years') would be fulfilled. Newspapers constantly reminded the public the work was in a state of 'great forwardness'. When Joseph Ames told Peter Thompson in September 1749 that the *Dictionary* was 'ready for the press' it was no more than was expected.[24]

Johnson worked hard to establish schemes for the selection, definition and illustration of words, but the more he read, the more he felt it necessary to refine his techniques. Sorting through the definitions of a simple word like *bear*, with thirty-eight potential meanings, was a complicated task, 'of such latitude', he said, 'that it is not easily explained'. Gradually he became aware that what he had first envisaged as a straightforward, almost mechanical task was no such matter. Bishop Percy, highly annoyed at Boswell's blithe summary of Johnson's methods for composing entries ('B. utterly ignorant of the Manner in wch Johnson collected Material for & composed his Dict.'), set down how Johnson began with the 'diligent perusal' of the most correct English authors and, under a sentence which he meant to quote, 'drew a line, and noted in the margin the first letter of the word under which it was to occur'.[25] Johnson made a special search of books from 1550 to 1650, the 'well of English undefiled', he said, quoting Spenser's praise of Chaucer, 'from which we date the golden age of our language', and marked up quotations in black pencil, leaving out only such authors as Thomas Hobbes whom he refused to cite 'because I did not like his principles'. Hester Thrale, noting the absence of the Earl of Shaftesbury and several other 'wicked writers' from the *Dictionary*, confirmed the exclusion was deliberate; 'lest it should send People to look in a Book that might injure them forever'.[26]

Having grown up surrounded by books Johnson had no particular reverence for them, often returning works that he had borrowed 'so defaced as to be scarce worth owning'. Boswell commented on his 'ravenous' way with books, tearing into them like 'a dog who holds a bone in his paws in reserve, while he eats something else which has been thrown to him'. Garrick, who made difficulties over lending Johnson early quartos of Shakespeare for his later work on an edition, complained of his breaking his own rule about not including living writers as authorities in the *Dictionary*; specifically Richardson, he said. Johnson retorted he had done far worse than that: 'I have cited *thee*, David.' Whether being cited as the authority for *giggle* ('to laugh idly, to titter, to grin with merry levity') constituted approbation, or the opposite, for Garrick's talents is arguable.[27]

At some point in early 1750, as he worked on the letter C, Johnson came to have doubts about his methods. Quite simply, he recognised that by transcribing entries on to *both* sides of a manuscript page he had not left space enough for additional material, which in turn led him to have to serious misgivings about the whole nature of the task. The *Plan* had declared his intention to 'fix the English language', but in working on his method to bring that possibility about, his reservations about it grew. One day he happened to read Benjamin Martin's *Lingua Britannica Reformata* and his doubts became a certainty. In his 'Physico-Grammatical Essay' Martin declared 'the pretence of fixing a standard to the purity and perfection of any language . . . is utterly vain and impertinent, because no language as depending on arbitrary use and custom, can ever be permanently the same'. This was exactly the conclusion Johnson was reaching after two solid years of work. So while Thomas Birch was assuring Mrs Yorke that the *Dictionary* was 'almost ready for the Press' it was, in fact completely at a stand.[28]

That July Johnson wrote a secret, lover-like letter to the 'little Gipsy' Lucy Porter away in Lichfield in which he pretended to tick her off for frightening him with her black-edged paper; he feared it must contain 'ill news of my mother, whose death is one of the few calamities on which I think with horrour'. But the tone of his letter is quite light-hearted; he says he wishes to know how his mother does, but the emphasis is in the added half-line 'how you all do'. He had recently been ill, a condition exacerbated by frustrations with the *Dictionary* and the melancholy duty of coping with Tetty, 'your poor Mamma' who was 'very weak'. She will 'grow better,' he writes, or else 'shall go into the country'; but the last line reveals a hidden intimacy: 'She is now up stairs and knows not of my writing.' There is a sense of a younger generation, writing to each other in secret, while above their heads their elderly mothers sleep.

He turned to other work as a relief, producing a Preface for Robert Dodsley's teaching aid *The Preceptor* in which he remarked that 'every man who has been engaged in teaching knows with how much difficulty youthful minds are confined'; nevertheless, he set himself to capture their 'restless desire of novelty' with enthusiasm.[29] He also wrote a Preface for William Lauder, a man first met in 1747 for whom he felt immediate sympathy on account of his wooden leg, the result of a limb lost playing golf. Lauder claimed to have gathered materials together proving parts of Milton's *Paradise Lost* were plagiarised, which greatly intrigued Johnson, who had little sympathy for the puritan poet. Writing as 'W.L.', Lauder penned several pieces for the *Gentleman's Magazine* in which he suggested the strong influence of several writers on the poem, not accusing Milton directly of plagiarism but making the implication clear. Then in 1749, using proposals which Johnson had written for an unsuccessful edition of Grotius as his Preface, he went on to publish an *Essay on Milton's Use . . . of the Moderns*, concluding with a postscript, also by Johnson, in which he sought support for Milton's granddaughter, a 'good, plain sensible woman' fallen on hard times.[30]

Johnson, who later described Milton's political notions as those of 'an acrimonious and surly republican', paid no special attention to the claims Lauder made in the *Essay*, but others, notably the Reverend Dr John Douglas, later Bishop of Salisbury, did. Douglas published a pamphlet, *Milton Vindicated . . . and Lauder Himself Convicted of Several Forgeries*, which soon became a major talking point. Catherine Talbot wrote to Elizabeth Carter rejoicing over 'the public infamy of that villainous forger Lauder'; Lady Anson set about devising 'some grievous punishment' for him and thought Caligula's decree on bad authors, making each one 'lick out all his lies', would be no bad idea.[31] A notice appeared in the *London Gazetteer* offering to make good any losses suffered by readers of Lauder's book by advertising it for sale at half price 'as a masterpiece of fraud'.

Something had to be done. In the new year *A Letter to the Reverend Mr Douglas* appeared, ostensibly by Lauder, actually by Johnson, listing twenty-five falsifications made by Lauder, not the seven which had been detected by Douglas. In the closing paragraph 'he' made a full confession of guilt.

> But for the violation of truth, I offer no excuse, because I well know, that nothing can excuse it. Nor will I aggravate my crime, by disingenuous palliations. I confess it, I repent it, and resolve

my first offence shall be my last. More I cannot perform, and more therefore cannot be required.

That should have put an end to the affair, had not Lauder added a short Postscript in which he claimed the falsifications were part of a well-wrought stratagem to find out just how clever Milton's admirers were. When Johnson read the published *Letter*, and postscript, his heart sank. In April he had written to advertise a benefit performance of *Comus* for Milton's impecunious granddaughter, followed by 'a dramatick satire, called *Lethe*' performed by Garrick. It was into Lethe he now longed to sink but, in place of it, took his solace with several companions in the formation of a new club.

Johnson always relished the society of intelligent, loquacious men, willing to spend an evening debating anything from books (he confessed to liking the old black-letter volumes) to boxing (people should 'not be alarmed at seeing their own blood') and from envy (which he acknowledged) to dread (of which, he said, he was free). If he were in company with talkative friends, their previous faults, such as having killed a man (Savage) or invented an exotic childhood in some far-flung part of the globe (Psalmanazar), were forgiven.[32] He began meeting new friends each Tuesday evening at the King's Head in Ivy Lane, between Paternoster Row and Newgate, and soon these acquaintanceships formed themselves into a club. Membership of the Ivy Lane Club may have been less celebrated than of his later literary clubs, but its importance for him was no less important, for it was at the Ivy Lane that he developed his celebrated capacity to argue in friendly company. Hawkins records that members of the club included Richard Bathurst whom Johnson declared he loved better 'than ever I loved any human creature' because Bathurst 'hated a fool, and he hated a rogue, and he hated a *whig*; he was a very good *hater*'. The club acted as a forcing-house, facilitating relationships on which subsequent literary careers were built; John Hawkesworth not only followed Johnson at the *Gentleman's Magazine* but later edited the *Adventurer*, which in turn was published by John Payne who also published the *Rambler* and was a member of the club. All members were at the outset of careers, apart from Samuel Salter, aged seventy, and full of sprightly wit. Hawkins, whom Johnson described as 'a most *unclubable* man', wrote up their convivial meetings, but in a carping style that tinged each recollection with criticism, recalling Johnson looking on 'in a state of mental bondage'. The difference may be seen by glimpsing a meeting of the club in December 1750 to celebrate the publication of Charlotte Lennox's novel *The Life of Harriet Stuart*. It was the first and, by surviving evidence, the only time female guests were admitted.

Johnson was in the mood for something new. In that week's *Rambler* he had written of the human soul 'always impatient for novelty'; wherever he turned his eye he found things to stimulate his curiosity. It was only natural for a man to demand 'new gratifications' and Charlotte Lennox, a young, ambitious lady, barely twenty-one, from America, stirred him to new feats of literary showmanship. In her novel Lennox had done her best to create a fuss, deliberately creating a female patron identifiable as Lady Isabella Finch, whose companion she had briefly been, rousing the 'surprise and indignation' of Lady Mary Wortley Montagu. Lennox unashamedly used her sexual allure to further her ambitions, arguing, in 'The Art of Coquetry', that by such means a 'nymph' could 'unsubdu'd control the world'.

At eight o' clock that December evening Lennox arrived at the Devil Tavern, accompanied by her husband and a female friend. John Payne had published *Harriet Stuart* and staged the dinner for its launch, but the celebration party, which numbered almost twenty, was quite unprecedented. Johnson called the book her first 'literary child' and demanded readings from it while Edmund Barker, recently set up as a physician, wielded his long yellow-hilted sword. The company sat down to an elegant supper, while Johnson, continuing as architect of the evening, directed that 'a magnificent hot apple-pie should make a part' of the feast, 'stuck with bay leaves' because 'Mrs Lennox was an authoress'. Having 'prepared for her a crown of laurel' he invoked the Muses and ceremonially encircled her brows with it, while the whole company applauded. Mrs Lennox, whose principal desire was to be noticed, made no objection, having envisaged in an early poem, 'To Aurelia', just such a coronation.

> . . . from the slighted Tree he tears
> Its Leaves, to deck Aurelia's Hairs.
> A Poet now by all she's own'd,
> And with immortal Honour crown'd.[33]

Johnson may have liked the poem for casting him in the unlikely role of Apollo. The night went on with port and brandy, tea and coffee circulating, but Johnson, drinking only lemonade, indulged in his favourite sport, conversation with a sprightly woman. At five in the morning, while others yawned he maintained his rational discussions, continuing while sleepy waiters made out the bill; finally, at eight, 'the creaking of the street door gave the signal for our departure'. Hawkins, having spent the night afflicted by toothache, sensed shame at the morning light, feeling the night's activities had resembled a 'debauch'; Johnson by contrast felt exhilaration, boasting in his next *Rambler* of possessing 'a snail that has crawled upon the wall of China'.

Johnson needed the company of people of wit to challenge his mental abilities and loved contending in conversational bouts in which he always strove 'for victory' rather than 'for truth'. He remained in touch with Cave at the *Gentleman's Magazine* and kept up connections with such friends as Thomas Birch and Elizabeth Carter but, whenever they met, awkward questions were sure to be asked about the *Dictionary*. The three years he had boasted of were up, and Johnson found himself languishing between *cabbage* ('a plant'), of which in an extensive entry he identifies twenty-two varieties, and *carious* ('rotten').

The truth was that Johnson had ceased working on the *Dictionary*, having read through the first seventy sheets and recognised that some important changes must be made. The decisions he took then, making definitions more concise and marking them up on loose sheets rather than in notebooks, seem straightforward, but it took enormous self-discipline to go back over entries he had already prepared and rewrite them. He did not begin again entirely and his entries for the letter 'A' are more expansive than those for later letters, but he determined on a new working method which would see him through to the end. Time had been lost, though; the next fifty sheets, from the twenty-second meaning of *carry* to the second of *dame*, took him sixteen months, and the next batch, from *dame* to *grate*, took even longer, being delivered in October 1753. The publishers' faith began to waver. They asked Strahan to arrange a meeting to review progress which, if not agreed to, might result in financial backing being withdrawn. Johnson's reply was splendid, sending back a defiant message: 'My citadel shall not be taken by storm while I can defend it,' he asserted; 'if a blockade is intended, the country is under the command of my batteries.' But his sense of his own failings is clearly visible through the vainglory of the military metaphors he employed. In a somewhat calmer frame of mind he wrote to Strahan: 'I will try to take some more care but can promise nothing,' he said; 'one cannot always be on the watch.'

At some point a new system of payment was agreed to; the publishers now gave him a guinea for every sheet of copy produced, which suited Johnson perfectly but was less acceptable to his amanuenses, who, he complained, gave him little assistance; 'but they tell me they shall be able to fall better in method, as I intend they shall.' Piecework pay encouraged temptations to bulk up the manuscripts by slipping in sheets of old copy, as 'W.N.', a printer in Strahan's shop, later admitted, but offenders were sacked and others hired who stuck to their tasks. Gradually they became good friends, who might be mocked for their weaknesses.[34] Sitting with Robert Shiels one day, Johnson picked up a volume of Thomson's verses, read some of it and then asked: 'Is not this fine?' To which, when Shiels agreed, Johnson said he had 'omitted every other line'.[35]

At the start of 1750 'after 3 in the morning' Johnson offered up his new year prayer to promote God's glory in his latest venture, a twice-weekly periodical called *The Rambler* which, though it went on to include some of Johnson's best occasional writing, was begun purely for financial reasons. The large sum he had been granted on starting the *Dictionary* was all used up and the piecework money he now received was to pay his staff. Something was necessary to keep himself and Tetty from starving until work on the *Dictionary* was completed: hence the *Rambler* was born. He received four guineas a week for the essays, which should have been enough, and would have been for him alone; but not infrequently he was put to borrowing small additional sums, a guinea or perhaps two, from his friend John Newberry, the bookseller in St Paul's Churchyard, for Tetty's impulsive needs. 'I hope not much to tire those whom I shall not happen to please,' he wrote in the first number of the *Rambler*, keeping his essays to a regular fifteen hundred words through all 208 issues. 'A man may write at any time, if he will set himself doggedly to it,' he declared, writing his essays twice a week, whatever his 'constitutional indolence, his depression of spirits, and his labours . . . on his Dictionary'. Finding a title for the periodical proved troublesome; he confessed he could not think of one till, sitting on his bed one night, he resolved, 'I would not go to sleep till I had fixed its title.' The *Rambler* was the best one that occurred to him and so 'I took it'. It was quite memorable too, though its suggestion of easy, strolling reflections on life was not quite true; in the *Dictionary* Johnson defined 'ramble' as 'to rove loosely in lust' – definitely *not* what his *Rambler* proposed.

Each essay was headed by a Latin motto followed by its English translation by his friend James Elphinston who, he noted in the collected edition, 'now keeps an academy for young gentlemen, at Brompton'. On hearing of the death of Elphinston's mother he wrote a letter, advising James to give up 'useless grief'; he too had a mother, 'now eighty-two years of age', whom he must soon lose unless 'she rather should mourn for me'. The thought struck him that he might die with the *Dictionary* still halted at the word *carry*, which was bleak indeed.[36] 'The natural flights of the human mind are not from pleasure to pleasure, but from hope to hope . . . The general remedy of those, who are uneasy without knowing the cause, is change of place; they are willing to imagine that their pain is the consequence of some local inconvenience, and endeavour to fly from it, as children from their shadows.' He wrote that latter sentence in *Rambler* 6, having the image of a dissatisfied Tetty, constantly flitting between rural Hampstead and urban Gough Square, before him. In April he wrote: 'We desire, we pursue, we obtain, we are satiated; we desire something else, and begin a new persuit', and found that, by accident, he had discovered his natural style as a moralist. He was disappointed that numbers of the *Rambler* sold so poorly with his print run seldom exceeding five hundred copies; his model, Addison's *Spectator*, had frequently run to three thousand, which, allowing 'twenty readers to every paper', had given him 'threescore thousand disciples in *London* and *Westminster*'. Johnson's liking for 'hard words' was a principal difficulty, conceded as such by Boswell who said 'the structure of his sentences . . . often has somewhat of the inversion of Latin'. Marchioness Grey agreed; there were 'so many hard words' in the *Rambler* that it 'really breaks my teeth to speak them'. But Johnson, disappointed at his sales, was unrepentant about his style; Samuel Rogers's *Table-Talk* records him saying his other works were wine and water, 'but my *Rambler* is pure wine'.[37]

'No man is so much abstracted from common life, as not to feel a particular pleasure from the regard of the female world,' he wrote, coaxing Tetty's blessing. Walking back from fractious weekends in Hampstead he formulated phrases to tackle the subject of unhappiness in marriage. 'This general unhappiness has given occasion to many sage maxims among the serious, and smart remarks among the gay; the moralist and the writer of epigrams have equally shown their abilities upon it . . .' He rested and looked down the hill towards where the dome of St Paul's was clearly visible; on all sides married people could be seen, working in the fields, enjoying the sun, squabbling or taking drinks in the various beer-shops of Kentish Town.

> . . . some have lamented, and some have ridiculed it; but as the faculty of writing has been chiefly a masculine endowment, the reproach of making the world miserable has been always thrown upon the women, and the grave and the merry have equally thought themselves at liberty to conclude either with declamatory complaints, or satirical censures, of female folly or fickleness, ambition or cruelty, extravagance or lust.

He arrived back at Gough Square with this, his longest sentence (ninety-nine words), worked out in his head and thus distanced from a problem best tackled in abstraction. In the intricate arrangement of paired clauses and antitheses, culminating in a final triumphal triplet, he found a neatness to soothe away his cares. 'A man writes much better than he lives,' he conceded, leaving his readers 'not to wonder that most fail, amidst tumult, and snares, and danger'.[38]

He developed the habit of leaving himself as little time as possible to compose the essays. Cave remarked that each one was 'seldom sent to the press till late in the night before the day of publication' and it made no difference whether Johnson was alone or in company when he composed them. Mrs Gastrell was astonished that 'the printer's boy would often come after him to their house and wait while he wrote off a paper for the press in a room full of company'. He did not have time, he said, to *re*read what he wrote, sending them off as soon as they were written, turning a personal failing into a general boast. Having the wit to make himself the topic of their general conversation, he attempted to develop a corresponding style of writing, but found it very difficult.

Biography ranked high among his preoccupations. Johnson declared there was 'no species of writing . . . more worthy of cultivation', which was 'more delightful or more useful' or could 'enchain the heart' more irresistibly. Yet forcing himself to write entertainingly on different topics twice a week took a degree of invention to which he could only occasionally rise; his main difficulty lay in attempting to create and maintain an acceptable persona for himself as the 'Rambler'. His *Life of Savage* was written with clear personal feelings, which could not be said for his thoughts on novelty, politeness or even plagiarism. Arguing at the Ivy Lane Club he cultivated a gruff persona from whom his forceful verbal polemics flowed quite easily; but inventing himself to an unseen audience was rather different.[39]

The essays, all but four by Johnson himself, are remarkably consistent in both subject and style. Some sixty essays, written as letters 'to the editor', offered the opportunity of varying his narrating voice or introducing different characters, but it was a chance he did not take. His attempts at counterfeiting a woman's hand are particularly poor, as he is the first to acknowledge: 'it is much easier not to write like a man, than to write like a woman.' His best essays often take the business of writing as their theme. 'Nothing is more unjust, however common, than to charge with hypocrisy him that expresses zeal for those virtues which he neglects to practise,' he writes in *Rambler* 14, taking the tribulations of writers as his subject and carrying readers from the spires and turrets of the imagination to see the 'narrow passages . . . embarrassed with obstructions, and clouded with smoke' of home.[40] In June, three months into his task, he addressed complaints of readers who, brought up on the *Tatler* and *Spectator*, accused him of wanting 'mirth and humour' and, in particular, of neglecting to 'take the ladies under his protection'. Such readers certainly existed. The *Gentleman's Magazine* may have esteemed the *Rambler* to exceed 'anything of the kind ever published in this kingdom', but others did not agree. Jemima Grey told Catherine Talbot she saw 'nothing new or clever in his essays', William Duncombe thought they needed 'more sprinklings of humour' to make them popular and Thomas Birch confided to Charles Lyttleton that Johnson had insufficient 'knowledge of the world' to make them entertaining. Mrs Talbot, deeply moved by *Rambler* 78 on death ('what a noble paper'), suggested to Elizabeth Carter, who 'could talk more persuasively to the author than anybody', that she should steer Johnson towards 'the living manner of the times', but spoke 'with fear and trembling' for 'humour and manners of the world are not his fort'. In the face of such criticism, Johnson felt he was like 'a ship in a poetical tempest' but resolved to gain 'the favour of the publick by following the direction of my own reason'.[41]

Although applause was not counted 'among the necessaries of life' he gained it from a surprising quarter. Tetty, after reading the first few issues, declared that though she thought well of him before, she 'did not imagine you could have written any thing equal to this'. The printer Samuel Richardson, who had risen to sudden literary eminence with the runaway success first of *Pamela* (1740) and subsequently of *Clarissa* (1748), said he read the *Ramblers* 'with honour' and was proud to have 'procured them admirers; that is to say, *readers*'. He wrote to Cave, expressing vexation 'that I have not taken larger draughts of them before'. Cave wrote back, confirming Richardson's guess at the Rambler's identity: 'Mr Johnson is the *Great Rambler*, being, as you observe, the only man who can furnish two such papers in a week, besides his other great business.' Johnson quickly wrote to

Richardson, returning the compliment and praising the latest edition of *Clarissa*, in which, he said (without a trace of irony), Richardson had risen above his 'fears of prolixity' to restore some passages 'hitherto suppressed'. It was a *Rambler* by Richardson (no. 97) that had the widest sale, something that caused them both embarrassment: 'The encouragement, as to sale, is not in proportion to the high character given to the work by the judicious,' Richardson wrote, and Johnson claimed he understood.[42]

Still, Johnson felt disappointed not to reach a wider public, and to be so frequently criticised. 'I have never been much a favourite of the publick,' he wrote, demonstrating in a gloomy final essay his pride in proclaiming what he had *not* done ('descended to the arts by which favour is obtained') and making a virtue of what he had: 'I have at least . . . laboured to refine our language to grammatical purity.'[43] Some essays claim a place in journalistic history. The life of Misella, a prostitute, follows her to the 'dismal receptacle' where whores spend their nights, 'crowded together, mad with intemperance, ghastly with famine, nauseous with filth, and noisome with disease'. The accuracy of what Johnson depicts might be seen at St Luke's parish poorhouse which admitted over fifty babies from illicit relationships in the early 1750s, all of whom perished from cold, hunger or disease. Sometimes Johnson appeals for independence ('There is no state more contrary to the dignity of wisdom than perpetual and unlimited dependence'), but there is always a self-deprecating quality behind his elevated generalisations ('No place affords a more striking conviction of the vanity of human hopes, than a publick library'). If Johnson was indeed kept waiting in Lord Chesterfield's antechamber by Colley Cibber, the incident would seem to have occurred in the summer of 1751, judging from a *Rambler* written then which excoriated patrons as 'corrupt, licentious, and oppressive' and labelled writers who praised them the 'hirelings of vanity' prepared to flatter 'cheats, and robbers, and publick nuisances'.[44]

Johnson nervously anticipated the reception of the *Dictionary* when it was, at last, completed. ('When a writer has with long toil produced a work . . . he is seldom contented to wait long without the enjoyment of his new praises.') He feared the worst: 'no man is much regarded by the rest of the world.' In literary criticism he was at home, whether checking his risibility at the avengers of guilt 'peeping through a blanket' in *Macbeth*, commending the 'graces of versifica-tion' in Virgil's works or outlining the task of criticism which, he argued, was 'to establish principles'. He displayed his own literary skill with occasional powerful aphorisms, such as 'Curiosity is the thirst of the soul' and 'Sorrow is a kind of rust of the soul, which every new idea contributes in its passage to scour away.'[45]

Throughout the *Rambler* the weakness to which he devotes most attention is vanity. The 'greatest human virtue bears no proportion to human vanity,' he writes; 'we always think ourselves better than we are.' Against vanity he champions hope, which 'is necessary in every condition'. As he comes to the end of the *Rambler*, this thought remains unchanged: 'Hope is the chief blessing of man, and that hope only is rational, of which we are certain that it cannot deceive us.'[46] His comments upon marriage as 'the strictest tye of perpetual friend-ship' are respectful, but not passionate, and the word 'love' is hardly mentioned. Instead, the Rambler places his emphasis on duty, arguing, in an essay on 'Friendship', that it is important 'superiority on one side is reduced by some equivalent advantage on the other. Benefits which cannot be repaid . . . are not commonly found to increase affection.' Judging by the strict criteria mentioned here ('No man was ever in doubt about the moral qualities of a letter') the let-ter he sent to Tetty back in 1740 appears bleak indeed. Authors, like lovers, always 'suffer some infatuation' from which 'only absence can set them free'. For some years Tetty had lived in Hampstead, Johnson in Gough Square, which were not so far apart, but sufficient for absence to have the necessary distancing effect.[47]

Reasons for ending the *Rambler* in March 1752 were not such as he cared to explain, saying merely they were 'of little importance', particularly as 'no objection is made'. Tedium at the sameness of the project, coupled with a feeling that he had gained enough from the *Rambler* to pursue the *Dictionary* (which had progressed to the word *dame*) to its conclusion, were important, together with the fact that the *Rambler*, though respected, had never built up a notable reader-ship. But the most significant reasons were personal. When, in July, he had been forced to settle the tradesman William Mitchell's bill of £2 for one of Tetty's sprees, outstanding for two whole years, Mitchell had threatened court proceedings if it were not paid that week. Many more such minor but repeated debts would seriously diminish the funds he had accumulated to pay their joint expenses until the publication of the *Dictionary*. So, immediately upon writing his last *Rambler*, he sold the republication rights for £100, which he promised to John Levett for arrears on the mortgage of the family home in Lichfield, payable 'the first of May'. Money was still tight and, having opened his letter with bold promises, he closed it with a hasty postscript; if Levett needed money exceeding the £100, 'I must beg you to accept my Note for Six Months.'[48]

Over the past two years his situation had gradually changed, partly through his regular attendance at the agreeable dinners of the Ivy Lane Club, partly through friendship with Richardson who had become a major literary figure. Charlotte Lennox was immensely keen to meet the famous Samuel Richardson and badgered Johnson to take her; at last he agreed but, just as they were approaching the novelist's house, Charlotte suddenly begged Johnson to leave her, being under 'great restraint' in his company. Or at least that is how Fanny Burney recollects the occasion, writing twenty years later, adequately catching both his excitement and Charlotte Lennox's abrupt and thoughtless tone. She might have been more tactful, for on this first occasion Richardson was not, or *said* he was not, there: 'I have been much indisposed,' he claimed, thanking Johnson for the manuscript of *The Female Quixote* which he had not *quite* read. 'May I hope for a visit from you and that lady?' he tactfully enquired. Better than that, Lennox sent him more of the novel. The combined pressures of both Richardson and Johnson had their effect and Andrew Millar the publisher agreed to take it, though Richardson warned Mrs Lennox that as 'a young lady' – she was barely twenty-two – she had 'much time before you'. Johnson was delighted and wrote blithely of 'our Charlotte's Book' as of the production of a favourite child. In February she wrote to him again, saying it would be a 'particular favour' if he could 'hurry the printing' and begging him to help her find 'some employment in the translating way'. She wrote so guilelessly of his mind, 'so generous and compassionate', that Johnson, unused to such phrases, especially from the pens of young ladies, was smitten and readily agreed. She had been 'unkindly treated by Mr Richardson', he said (for not hastening the printing of *The Female Quixote*). 'I wish I could help it . . . I am much concerned.'[49]

Johnson wished Charlotte's novel the success it thoroughly deserved. When it was published in March, with a dedication to the Earl of Middlesex and some further sections written, Charlotte hastened to send him a presentation copy in which he found himself celebrated as 'the greatest genius in the present age' (Lennox was prodigious with her compliments). It was little surprise he felt the book's deserts were high, but he was otherwise preoccupied at present. 'Poor Tetty Johnson's Ilness will not suffer me to think of going any whither, out of her call. She is very ill, and I am much dejected.' That name has a strange formality: 'Tetty *Johnson*': neither the affectionate note of 'Tetty' (while he called Charlotte by her first name) nor the dignified formality of 'my wife'. Tetty *Johnson* is a subject for analysis between the two of them and already there is a faint sense that Tetty Johnson's function is what it will become, a deadening hold on Samuel Johnson, who might not be permitted to go 'out of her call'.[50]

At that time Johnson became interested in the aspirations, vain, but noble, of Zachariah Williams, aged over eighty, who had spent half his life and all his money attempting to win the £20,000 Admiralty prize for determining the longitude at sea. Since 1729 Williams had lodged at the Charterhouse as a poor pensioner, pursuing his grail of the longitude, supported by the efforts of his blind daughter Anna as a seamstress. When he became ill in the late 1740s she lodged in his room to tend him, but such behaviour, though fully understandable, went quite against the rules of the Charterhouse. Not only was he immediately expelled; his room was ransacked and his scientific instruments destroyed. In desperation Williams wrote to Johnson who had first mentioned his work in *Rambler* 19. *Rambler* 67 returns to the theme, speaking of him as a man 'on the point of discovering the longitude'. It did not matter that such a dream might be thought utopian; he listed it together with a plan to end slavery or to obtain a court place after 'twenty years soliciting' as examples of hope, and 'it is necessary to hope, though hope should always be deluded; for hope itself is happiness, and its frustrations, however frequent, are less dreadful than its extinction.'[51]

Johnson wrote many times, ineffectually, to the Admiralty for Williams over the autumn and winter of 1751/2 and published *An Account of an Attempt to Ascertain the Longitude at Sea* some four years later. But all to no avail.[52] He invited Anna and Zachariah to Gough Square where Anna and Tetty struck up a friendship, the last his wife ever made. By the start of March the various pressures of new contacts and old duties, the *Rambler* and the *Dictionary* were mounting. In *Rambler* 203 he wrote of 'the loss of friends and companions' impressing hourly upon us 'the necessity of our own departure'; in the penultimate number of the journal he confessed the vision enabling the endurance of any lengthy duty was 'the prospect of its end'. Three days later he presented Tetty with the first collection of *Rambler* essays. Her health had sunk badly, she was now barely alive, but it appears she appreciated the gift of these essays and signed the opening volume. It may be suspected she received Johnson's help to do so; the volume, with Tetty's signature, dated 13 March 1752, is the sole example of her handwriting that survives, but only the most rigorous or curmudgeonly of biographers would deny her that ghostly presence. By then opium had sadly fuddled her brain and four days later, on the night of 17 March, she sank and died. Above her, Johnson wrestled as always with finances, writing to Levett in Lichfield to offer him the profits from the reprinted *Ramblers*, and did not know what had happened, so that the blow, so long anticipated, fell upon him as a complete surprise. He was alone at last, and he was terrified.[53]

Or guilty. Immediately he 'dispatched a letter to his friend, the Reverend Dr. Taylor' which, Taylor told Boswell later, expressed 'grief in the strongest manner he had ever read'. The letter does not survive, and its disappearance is the first indication of a mystery surrounding Johnson's behaviour over his wife's death. At three in the morning Taylor rose and went to Johnson whom he found 'in tears and in extreme agitation'; together they 'prayed extempore' till his mind was 'soothed and composed', but not so much as to prevent him writing to Taylor the next day to 'let me have your company and instruction. Do not live away from me. My distress is great.' Johnson had a terror of being alone; everything he said and did at this time speaks of the intensity of that feeling. He no sooner asked for Taylor's company again than he worried over fussy details of mourning clothes for his mother and Lucy Porter. He begged Mrs Taylor for advice: 'Remember me in your prayers', he concluded, 'for vain is the help of man.'[54]

'He intended . . . to have deposited her remains in the chapel in Tothill Fields, Westminster,' claims Hawkins. But instead, a week later, Tetty was buried in Bromley parish church, where she had no known connection. John Hawkesworth, Johnson's friend from the Ivy Lane Club, lived in Bromley, and Johnson sent for him as peremptorily as he had summoned Taylor.[55] On 26 March 'Elizabeth Johnson of the Parish of St. Brides London' was buried by the curate of Bromley, Thomas Bagshawe, who conducted a service from which Johnson himself was absent. Also absent were Lucy, Tetty's sons Jervis Henry and Joseph, and anyone who had ever known her. Johnson tried to arrange a funeral service for her in London, but received little assistance since Robert Levet's view that she 'killed herself by taking Opium' was generally shared. Taylor refused to compose a funeral sermon for her because he 'would not commend a character he little esteemed'. Johnson wrote one for him in which he conceded 'that she had no failings, cannot be supposed', but thought it ill became those 'weak and sinful as herself' to recall faults 'which, we trust, Eternal Purity has pardoned'. But still Taylor refused, provoking Johnson 'to tear the manuscript', remembering words he had written, that 'they likewise are hastening to their end, and must soon . . . be buried and forgotten'. The sermon was written for a service which he and those around him would attend, in Tothill Fields. She 'surely may be remembered', he wrote, 'whom we have followed hither to the tomb'. But it was not to be. He removed her wedding ring, preserving it, for the rest of his life, in a little wooden box in which he noted the dates of her marriage and death, but made another tiny, telling error, giving the wedding as 1736 instead of 1735.

Apart from these calming measures he was in such an agitation of mind that, at the last minute, he absented himself from her funeral. Tetty Johnson was buried, with no special sermon to mark her passing, in a churchyard she had never visited, with no one who knew anything of her to mark her interment. Johnson may have visited her grave the following year but it was another thirty years before her burial place was commemorated with a gravestone.[56]

He grieved for over a month, taking to alcohol and, according to many, going close to death himself. 'I have been told that his grief for the loss of his wife went near to cost him his life, that is, despair drove him to drink which brought on a fever,' wrote a relative of Sir Joshua Reynolds. At last, in early May, he composed a sequence of prayers 'on the Death of My Wife' which he 'deposited among her Memorials' with a heavy Latin sigh: '*Deus exaudi. – Heu!*' ('Hear, o Lord – Alas!') In the first of these he begs not to 'languish in fruitless and unavailing sorrow', a plea reiterated in the next day's prayer in which he reminds the Lord, and himself, of purposes that he had 'recorded in thy sight, when she lay dead before me'. Finally, on the third day and 'after 12 at night', he pleads his 'departed wife' may 'have a care' of him that he might 'enjoy the good effects' of her attention and ministration. He was too late for Easter; Tetty was buried just one day before Good Friday, but he made up for it in quasi-ritualistic fashion, with three days of impassioned grieving. Then on 6 May he acts as though this devout period of mourning was over. He prayed he 'may now return to the duties of my present state' and, in a final note acknowledged that he had 'used this service, written April 24, 25, May 6, as preparatory to my return to life to-morrow'. The next day, 7 May, was Ascension Day that year. Before then, in April and just a fortnight after Tetty's death, Johnson accepted her replacement into his home in Gough Square.[57]

7

Frank Barber

negro n.s. *(Spanish;* negre, *Fr.) A blackmoore*

Negroes transplanted into cold and flegmatic habitations,
continue their hue in themselves and their generations.

Browne

servant n.s. *(*servant, *Fr.;* servus, *Latin.) 3. A word of
civility used to superiours or equals.*

This subjection, used from all men to all men, is something more
than the compliment of course, when our betters tell us they are
our humble *servants*, but understand us to be their slaves.

Swift

'Quashey! Where you go now, boy? Quashey!' Away in Jamaica, in
the plantations between Spanish Town and the sea, the boy remembered an old woman, Grace, calling out to him. She said she was his
mother and it may have been the truth. She had been there, calling
to them both, him and Luckey, where they lay and hid one night,
sheltering in their musty hollow amid the canes of sugar. Scipio made
them both a thick black syrup of molasses and kill-devil. The Colonel
was selling up, Scipio was saying, laughing a laugh as thick and dark
as the moon behind a cluster of clouds. 'You'll be all right though,
Quashey,' he said, flicking flying beetles away and grinning, his
mouth wide and teeth the colour of molasses. 'Him taking you with
him. Him paid £5 to take the lot of you.' Quashey didn't know what
had happened to Grace or to Luckey since they left the ship. They
docked one night when it was bleak and cold and he stared out at a
mass of harbour walls and ropes and grey faces. We are here,

Quashey, the Colonel said and lifted him with pock-marked hands grizzled by years in the sun; he took him from the wooden bulkhead and placed him on the deck surrounded by pasty-faced men. Quashey had grown used to the bulkhead, lying with his head on a coil of ropes beside Luckey and the woman with grey hair and the scar down her cheek who called herself his mother. But the Colonel carried him away in a rattling coach that shook like his mother shaking away the hornets that buzzed around the molasses.[1]

The Colonel gave him a new name – 'Barber' – for his new home in this frozen country. There were thick patterns of ice on his window in the morning, in circles and stars like the leaves of trees above Spanish Town. But by lunchtime they were gone, and the window was quite smooth. Quashey liked to watch as the barber-man scraped the Colonel's face each morning, scything away the tufts that sprouted up like little canes of sugar. That was his name now, Francis Barber. But just as Barber was learning to hear himself called by this new name, shouted out by footmen in the depths of cellars or chambermaids in the rafters of the attic, he was sent away, perched on the peak of a chilly coach, through Middlesex, Cambridgeshire and Lincolnshire to a tiny school in Yorkshire. There he was taught to write the name the Colonel had chosen for him, FRANCIS BARBER, and to forget all about Quashey who had belonged to quite a different world. He was taught his age, which was eight, and many other very important things such as the names of Bristol and York and the name of the king who was George the Second who ruled a vast empire, including the seaboard of America and the island of Jamaica. But when Francis Barber fell asleep he became Quashey again, recalling in dreams the warm syrupy taste of molasses and the sun through the coconut palms above Spanish Town.

Two years later, when he was used to thick snows that could lie for weeks, and to ice on the ponds that had to be shattered so horses could drink, Frank Barber was brought back to London, given livery to wear and told to be a servant boy to Richard Bathurst who was Colonel Bathurst's son. There was a large man in the front parlour in very shabby clothes who was lamenting the death of his wife though, they whispered below stairs, no one had liked her much; not even the man who lamented, which was why, they said, he lamented so much. Frank Barber went with his master Richard to sit with the man called Johnson who sat in rags that stank of the London streets, staring at the walls and drinking cups of tea. Sometimes there was another man too, Shiels, who tried to get the ragged man interested in a book they both were writing, but without success. The ragged man sat and occasionally sighed that *grate* would be as fine a place to end as any, stuck midway between the rank and slippery *grassy* fens and *grater*, which grinds all things to powder. Richard whispered that on Sunday, over a dinner of roast meat which Mr Johnson took with Miss Anna Williams, who was blind, and Mr Diamond the apothecary, Johnson had planned out for himself a voyage to the island of Iceland. He insisted on detailing every mile of it, in the most lugubrious detail, so bleakly did he now regard his state of life in London.[2] Something needed to be done, Richard said, and there was general agreement at that; but the solution, when it came, took them all by surprise. Richard Bathurst took the step of donating Barber to Johnson; he would raise his spirits, he said, in giving him someone to worry over.

As a solution it worked very well, especially when Frank Barber learnt they were not to go to Iceland, which had worried him, for ice was something he did not greatly care for. The man Johnson said he would always be eternally grateful to his '*dear, dear* Bathurst', and busied himself immediately. First he put Barber, whom he told that he would always call 'Francis', to board with Mrs Coxeter; secondly he sent him to school, to the school at Blackfriars with forty boys and thirty girls, to improve his reading and writing and to learn to keep books. On the way there Francis, still unaccustomed to the life of a city, noted the roads between Ludgate Street and Blackfriars Steps had deep channels in them, heaped with dirt and ashes, broken glass and offal; he saw cattle, pigs and sheep being driven through from London Bridge to Smithfield leaving a pattern of dung along their path; and he saw hundreds of men and women on foot, and riding on horses or in hackney carriages, all bustling about the noisy, smelly city. Francis was intoxicated by it all and spent the whole day taking it in. In the morning he was sick. The large man, Johnson, who said Francis was to call him Samuel, declared he had contracted the smallpox, a contagion of the London streets. He was not born to such pestilential sights, he said; so many people, five hundred thousand at least, crammed into the hectic five-mile area from Hyde Park in the west to Limehouse in the east, with Charing Cross as its centre.

Once Francis had recovered from the illness, which, luckily, was not severe, Samuel put him to general duties at his large but dirty town house at Gough Square; Francis would carry messages to Mr John Hawkins or Mr John Hawkesworth and answer the door to Miss Charlotte Lennox or Mr Samuel Richardson. Two years later came a day that Francis would always remember. The Colonel, who had been good to him, yet still owned him and in many little ways would show it, died. In his will he granted Francis Barber his liberty, and not only that; he also granted him the fortune of twelve whole pounds to spend. The date was 24 April 1754. At last Francis was freed from his status as a slave; he was a free man, aged eleven, with £12 in his pocket and his living to make for himself. Among those around him were many who still felt Samuel had need of him, though Mr Hawkins, who always disliked him strongly, ventured to disagree: 'Diogenes himself never wanted a servant less,' he said. So Francis Barber allowed himself to be sent away to Mr Desmoulins's writing school.[3]

8

The Dictionary

Dictionary, n.s. *(dictionarium, Latin) A book containing the words of any language in alphabetical order with
explanations of their meaning; a lexicon; a vocabulary; a
word-book.*

Johnson did several things to shake off his grief for Tetty. In addition
to taking charge of and becoming a virtual parent to Frank Barber he
set down, in November, a prayer to use 'Before Any New Study',
stimulated by thoughts of the new periodical *The Adventurer*,
just launched by fellow members of the Ivy Lane Club. Naturally, he
was invited to contribute, having now much more opportunity to
do so. No one wished to malign the dear departed, but he must
secretly be relieved. But although he expressed every good wish to
Hawkesworth, Johnson bowed out of making regular contributions,
in order to complete the *Dictionary*, he said. He prayed he might not
'lavish away the life which Thou hast given me on useless trifles' but,
a fortnight later, had to beg forgiveness for time 'negligently and
unprofitably spent'.[1] The new year began with prayers to consider
Tetty's death and resolutions to rise early, to keep a journal and 'to
lose no time'. He set 28 March aside 'with prayer & tears', praying for
Tetty 'conditionally' as long as 'it were lawful', but was uncertain of
the propriety of praying specifically for a dead individual. He was
most anxious his memorials should be exactly proper for a wife.[2] At
Eastertime he begged forgiveness for duties he had neglected in his
marriage and besought God to grant Tetty 'whatever is best in her
present state'. Clearly his thoughts, though *about* Tetty, were not
really *for* her, but rather for himself. His next entry, made the same
day, makes that very clear. 'As I purpose to try on Monday to seek a
new wife without any derogation from dear Tetty's memory I purpose

at sacrament in the morning to take my leave of Tetty in a solemn commendation of her soul to God.'

A new wife? This bald statement about seeking one (much as he might have sought out a new wig) makes it very evident his thoughts were not on Tetty at all, but on her replacement. He had no sooner written this than he posted down to Bromley 'where dear Tetty lies buried', took the sacrament and prayed fervently 'against unchastity, idleness & neglect of publick worship' during a sermon he could hardly hear. He prayed in French ('*larme à l'oeil'*), in Latin (*'fluunt lacrymae'*) and in English, all day and everywhere, 'at the altar . . . in the pew, in the garden before dinner, in the garden before departure, at home at night'. During all his prayers he pleaded earnestly, 'I was never once distracted by any thoughts of any other woman'. But that very thought implies its opposite. He recollected 'my design of a new wife which freedom of mind I remembered with gladness in the Garden'. The mention of 'gladness' strikes a surprisingly blithe note. It is the first time he has dared pronounce such a potentially heretical thought since his wife's death. 'I hope I did not sin,' he adds piously, hoping he may, at last, have made expiation. The following Sunday he worried that he might have over-indulged 'the vain longings of affection' but hoped such feelings might 'intenerate my heart'. That archaic word 'intenerate', meaning 'make tender', indicates the awkwardness he half-acknowledges, but was willing to risk.

Garrick was almost alone of his later companions in having known him throughout the period of his marriage, and his anecdotes, although often waspish, maintain a savour of Johnson the man. According to Garrick, Johnson, on being asked what he believed the greatest pleasure, answered 'fucking and the second was drinking. And therefore he wondered why there were not more drunkards, for all could drink though not all could fuck.' The fact that, for long periods of his life, Johnson abstained from *both* these pleasures indicates the strength of the moral control he exacted on himself.[3]

Amongst the marriageable women Johnson knew most would be affronted by his awkward physique, gloomy manner and continuing poverty; but there was one, Hill Boothby of Tissington, Derbyshire, who might be willing to rise to the challenge. He had first met and been attracted to Miss Boothby while visiting John Taylor in Ashbourne. She was one year older than himself, attractive and distinctly pious, but able to maintain a lively correspondence. His letters to her began to exude all his charm; he addressed her as 'My Sweet Angel' and argued the Cartesian maxim 'I think therefore I am' was no truer than his own: 'I am alive therefore I love Miss Boothby.'[4] Alas! by the time he wrote these tender greetings, he knew Hill Boothby would not become the second Mrs Johnson.

A year after Tetty's death, and just a month before Johnson confessed to his diary his desire of seeking a new wife, Miss Boothby's close friend Mrs Fitzherbert died, leaving Hill Boothby to fulfil her promise of assuming control of the widower's household of six children. That was Johnson's 'official' reason for giving up the chase. More candidly he explained to Mrs Thrale that, as he knew her better, he found Miss Boothby's holiness off-putting: 'she pushed her piety to bigotry, her devotion to enthusiasm' and 'somewhat disqualified herself for the duties of *this* life, by her perpetual aspirations after the *next*'.[5] There is a waspish Thralian tone to that comment, but the feelings it betrays were ones Johnson acknowledged. Hill Boothby wrote to him in July 1755 that she was desirous 'you should think as I do; and I am persuaded you some time will', but his only replies were flatteries, coupled with recommendations of favourite remedies 'for indigestion and lubricity of the bowels'.[6] When she died in January 1756 he transcribed a prayer returning thanks to the Lord 'for the good example of Hill Boothby', committing himself once more 'to the duties which thou hast set before me'. He does not, though, speak of seeking a new wife. That indiscretion was behind him.[7]

Also in his April prayers he mentioned the *Dictionary*. 'I began the 2d vol of my Dictionary', he writes; 'room being left in the first for Preface, Grammar & History none of them yet begun.' This, the first reference to the *Dictionary* he has made for well over a year, indicates that, for whatever combination of reasons, the loss of Tetty had enabled him to speed up efforts on his major literary undertaking. Not that it had ever been far from his mind: 'He might write his *Ramblers* to make a Dictionary necessary, and afterwards compile his dictionary to explain his *Ramblers*,' was a saying of the time. He quickly reached the second volume and began working far ahead of the printer, an increase of speed made possible by having a clear method, firmly understood by all his amanuenses. He curbed his mental exploration which had often sought, in the minutiae of lexicographical enquiries, a relief from the pressures of marital life, and abbreviated entries for his *Dictionary* from the standards established for the letters A and B.[8] In November his printer, Strahan, had only seven presses in his shop but by the following February this number was increased to nine. In July Johnson wrote to Thomas Warton in Oxford saying the *Dictionary* could not be finished without him 'visiting the Libraries of Oxford'. He had indeed made rapid progress since Tetty's death.[9]

These labours were accomplished at a great price. He wrote to Joseph Warton in March, soliciting him to write for *The Adventurer* 'at two Guineas a paper', and confessed he had 'no part' in the journal 'beyond now and then a Motto'.[10] Samuel Richardson thought he was being very helpful when he alerted him to the work of Thomas Edwards, arguing for a more logical spelling, but to Johnson such unsolicited aid came as just another burden. Thanking Richardson for his assistance, he made it clear the time for such philosophical aid was over: 'Help indeed now comes too late for me when a large part of my Book has passed the press.' He wrote often to Thomas Birch to borrow books to help him in the *Dictionary*, penned an ingratiating letter to Lord Orrery, full of flattering Greek, and introduced him to Charlotte Lennox with whom he maintained an affectionate correspondence, a little sharp but always sweet. He also wrote to John Levett, away in Lichfield, to whom he had promised £100 to pay off the mortgage, but been 'disappointed . . . I have not yet received a third part of the money.'[11] At least the transaction, though not complete, had given him credit to borrow money 'which I will immediately send you as soon as it comes to my hands'. This letter, simple and direct, conveys the real sense of irritation that the mortgage, which he had tried so hard to pay off, still remained. It was a judgement against him.[12]

During the summer of 1753, as he progressed rapidly through the *Dictionary*'s second volume, all his activities were bound up with finishing the project. He connived at, without exactly permitting, a series of wagers between Hamilton of Strahan's printing house and his amanuensis Macbean for expediting progress. 'You may easily see my end in it,' he wrote to the publisher Andrew Millar, 'that it will make both M— and H— push on the business, which is all that we both wish.' Soon, however, he became aware of the downside of this wager-system when he was warned by Strahan that submitted sheets were not tightly enough written, leading to overpayment. Annoyed, he said he would take more care of it, but was careful to promise nothing. He maintained a wide circle of friends and acquaintances to preclude the dangers of despair, to which he was always prone. He thanked Richardson for copies of *Sir Charles Grandison* presented to himself and Anna Williams, and sought to interest the novelist in Williams's attempts to launch a scientific dictionary, deflecting the burden from himself. He congratulated Joseph Warton on his 'papers of Criticism' for the *Adventurer* and sought urgent information on the condition of 'poor Collins' the poet, recently confined to MacDonald's madhouse in Chelsea. 'I knew him a few years ago full of hopes and full of projects,' he wrote. 'What do you hear of him? Are there hopes of his recovery?' As a young man 'high in fancy' Collins's *Odes* and *Persian Eclogues* had made him celebrated while still only thirty years old. To Johnson at forty-five, depressed and labouring to finish a lexicographical task which was 'generally considered as drudgery for the blind', it was an ominous sign.[13]

Robert Levet, whom Johnson had befriended as long ago as 1746, came to live at Gough Square about this time, busying himself at waiting on Johnson during their long, silent breakfasts. Born in Yorkshire, Levet's origins were humble; he had worked in London and Paris as a menial, waiting tables where amid the slops of claret and coffee he had picked up enough scraps of medical knowledge to practise as a physician to the poor. So, while Johnson sat 'in dishabille, as just risen from bed' (though it might often be midday), Levet poured out 'tea for himself and his patron alternately' and 'no conversation' passed between them. Levet's scraps of medical knowledge, rudimentary as they might be, were greatly prized 'from Houndsditch to Marybone' by those whose needs for treatment greatly exceeded their ability to pay. Levet's only failing was a tendency to drunkenness, though even that was brought on, Johnson observed, 'through motives of prudence'.

If he refused the gin or brandy offered him by some of his patients, he could have been no gainer by their cure, as they might have had nothing else to bestow on him. This habit of taking a fee, in whatever shape it was exhibited, could not be put off by advice . . . He would swallow what he did not like, nay what he knew would injure him, rather than go home with an idea that his skill had been exerted without recompense.

Johnson also became acquainted with Bennet Langton who, having known him only from his admiration of the *Rambler*, was shocked to meet a 'huge, uncouth figure' newly risen about noon 'with a little dark wig which scarcely covered his head, and his clothes hanging loose about him'.[14] Dinners at Ivy Lane were a constant reminder of the doings of the *Adventurer*, but Johnson stuck to his resolution of *not* writing for it, just occasionally giving ideas. When, on occasions, he did break this self-imposed restraint, he attempted to disguise his hand and write in a less serious, less *Rambler*-esque manner under the pseudonym 'Misargyrus'. Readers seemed to enjoy the lighter tone: Catherine Talbot wrote to Elizabeth Carter in January that she liked the *Adventurers* which did not 'abound in harsh words' but were 'varied with a thousand amusing stories' and 'touch with humour on the daily follies and peculiarities of the times'. The two ladies were soon ransacking their 'considering drawer' for 'old sketches' they might submit, particularly after Dodsley launched *The World* as a rival periodical.[15]

As the year neared its end and Johnson could feel confident that the *Dictionary* would be completed, he relaxed and wrote more of the later numbers of the *Adventurer*, producing a total of twenty-nine papers or, from autumn 1754, just under a third of its output. Stimulated by work on the *Dictionary*, he wrote of the intoxicating desire to 'imagine ourselves equal to great undertakings' for 'there are few things above human hope'. But Hawkins was naturally cynical about his motivation; 'gain was the only genuine stimulative to literary exertion,' he wrote.[16] Throughout the summer, as the presses rolled, Johnson's spirits rose. Briefly, it seemed almost reasonable 'to have perfection in our eye' and hope that 'we may always advance towards it'. 'Those who have attempted much, have seldom failed to perform more than those who never deviate from the common roads of action', for, even in failure, they 'benefit the world . . . by their miscarriages.' Johnson had not expressed, or felt, such optimism for years; one senses the shadow of a terrible guilt he had long felt over the death of Tetty being momentarily removed.

Inevitably these feelings could not last; by November his thoughts had resumed a more characteristic tone. He mourns the death of an unknown friend, sensing that 'perhaps' like him everyone had known a friend 'die with happiness in his grasp'. He realises publication of the *Dictionary* would make not the slightest difference to general ignorance; 'innumerable books and pamphlets . . . have overflowed the nation', scarcely one of which had 'made any addition to real knowledge', and he ends the year on a melancholy note; 'there is in the world more poverty than is generally imagined,' he reminds his readers; 'affliction is inseparable from our present state.'

Troubled always by the tension between the irresistible human imagination and the paucity of what it might achieve, he strove for something, anything to 'fill up the vacuities of life', considering 'the laborious cultivation of petty pleasures' to be more virtuous than simple, and potentially dangerous, idleness. 'We are not born to please ourselves,' he declared, with a tone of resignation; 'much of my time has sunk into nothing, and left no trace by which it can be distinguished.' Briefly, the previous summer, he had a rare glimpse of liberation as the *Dictionary*, which bore down on him like Sisyphus' boulder, entered its final phases, but this was gone by March 1754. 'The present life is to all a state of infelicity,' he wrote in the final issue of the *Adventurer*, trying to raise his tone from the 'common miseries of life' but managing only to achieve 'lenitives' and 'abatements'.[17]

Later that year he made arrangements to visit Oxford for materials to write the history and grammar of the language. He contacted Thomas Warton, hoping to see him 'in about a fortnight'; he was uncertain, he hinted, 'where I shall lodge'. Warton picked up the hint and arranged for Johnson to stay at Kettel-Hall, just by Trinity, for the five weeks of his stay. Yet before he left London he recorded a death which meant more to him than any other, even the death of Tetty, had done. This was the demise of his friend and supporter, Edward Cave, which he wrote up, as was most fitting, in the *Gentleman's Magazine*. Cave had helped him take his first steps in literary journalism and, in his obituary, Johnson gratefully acknowledged that Cave's 'money and his diligence were employed liberally for others'. Not that he had had an easy life. As a boy he had once been 'stigmatized' for stealing a chicken, not because he was more criminal than those who judged him, but because he was 'more easily reached by vindictive justice'. Cave had founded the *Gentleman's Magazine*, a 'periodical pamphlet of which the scheme is known wherever the English language is spoken', and when he died, as Johnson records, one of his last conscious acts was 'fondly to press the hand that is now writing this little narrative'. Johnson does not record that Cave's estate at death was a massive £8,708; he merely notes that it was large, but might have been 'yet larger' had he not 'rashly and wantonly impaired it' by engaging in countless projects, of which 'I know not that ever one succeeded'.[18]

Johnson's visit to Oxford that summer was his first return for twenty-five years to the alma mater he had celebrated so ambivalently in *The Vanity of Human Wishes*. It had taken that long for him to revisit on his own terms, as one for whom the 'Doom of Man' had been, if not reversed, at least delayed. The two people who had sheltered him in the worst of times, and shared with him his sense of the long and slow ascent to lexicographic fame, were now both dead. And it must have been with a strong desire for recognition from the place that had given him his first and deepest blow that he returned. If so, he was sadly disillusioned. The Master of Pembroke, John Radcliffe, not only 'received him very coldly' but did not even ask him to dine. Johnson retaliated by vowing that, should he return to Oxford, 'I shall take up my abode at Trinity', thus indicating his notion of what might be a decent show of gratitude for a lexicographer, worth sixteen hundred Frenchmen.[19]

The librarian Francis Wise furnished him the texts he sought and Johnson worked through them, taking many 'outright borrowings' for his History and Grammar. The word 'inconnection', not listed in the *Dictionary* proper, appears, as does the letter *C*, though Johnson offers his opinion that it might be omitted 'without loss', its sounds supplied by *S* and *K*. Under *O* he notes that *oe* 'being not an English diphthong' is best excluded, the words written 'as they are sounded, with only *e, economy*'; yet in the Preface to the *Dictionary* he spells the word 'oeconomy'. It seems odd, since she was so much on his mind, that he did not list 'Tetty' as a contraction of Elizabeth in his Grammar, but he did not, being content with *Betty* and *Bess*. 'My journey will come to very little', he wrote back to Strahan, 'beyond the satisfaction of knowing that there is nothing to be done, and that I leave few advantages here to those that shall come after me.'[20] One evening, returning to Oxford from Elsfield where Wise resided, Warton 'out-walked Johnson', who called out, '*Sufflamina*,' which, Warton notes, 'was as much as to say, *Put on your drag chain*'. It was a fitting mood in which to leave the university.

He did not travel on to see his mother and Lucy Porter in Lichfield but sent Lucy a letter, eighteen months later, to deny a report 'running in the town' that he was dead. 'I am afraid the story should get into the papers', he wrote, concealing a justifiable vanity as concern, 'and distress my dear Mother.' He wrote similarly to 'dearest' Hill Boothby lest she also should be alarmed. His concern for all three ladies is quite understandable, as is the secret pleasure he felt that as author of the *Dictionary* he was becoming, slowly, a person whose doings were reported, or *mis*reported, as matters of public interest. This, the first mention of his being noted by the papers, definitely excited him, yet the fact that he only allows it to register as a minor irritation is typical.[21]

In November an amanuensis drew up a chart marking out the remaining letters, 'R|S|S|T|T|U|V', and Johnson was told not only that the Master of Arts degree might now be granted to him, but that it might be 'more apropos' if it were granted soon, allowing him 'to write himself A.M. in the title page'. At the end of December Johnson wrote again, 'extremely sensible' of the favour, pointing out the *Dictionary* would be printed 'in less than six weeks' but promising to 'keep back the titlepage for such an insertion', a solicitation he continued for two long months until at last the degree diploma arrived, in February.[22]

It came as a great relief, for tensions had been building up since his return from Oxford, part of them resulting from his recent friendship with the impulsive young Italian Giuseppe Baretti, whom Charlotte Lennox had introduced to him the previous year. In June Baretti had gone to Headley Park in Surrey to assist the owner, William Huggins, translate Ariosto's *Orlando Furioso*. Baretti had passed a most agreeable summer, receiving the use of a house, venison for his table and a handsome gold watch for his help in the translation. Returning to London, Baretti pawned the watch and wrote to a friend in Milan of his good fortune; which is when his fortune began to change. He was accused of stealing the watch. Johnson heard details of the affair in Oxford from a clergyman, Charles Holloway, who noted in his diary that Baretti had used 'artifice' to gain the watch; he also noted that the translation of Ariosto was to be 'revised by Johnson'.[23]

Possibly Johnson may have thought of doing something of the kind for Huggins, who was clearly very generous. But then the accusations and counter-accusations, often extremely violent, began. He wrote to Huggins, recognising his intervention was 'likely to suffer the common fate of intermeddlers, and receive no thanks on either side', proposing an even-handed remedy which was 'certainly the most speedy, and I believe the cheapest'. But his words had been twisted by Baretti. He protested he had 'opposed Mr Baretti in the whole process of this difference' down to the matter of 'not even mend[ing] his English'. Had he known of verses which Baretti sent to Charlotte Lennox depicting Johnson as a harsh, prosaic villain, he might have said so even more clearly. His words, though, had a good effect, bringing an immediate apology from Huggins to which he as quickly replied, expressing his relief and indicating by brief phrases ('I never in my life saw either the Venetian Resident, or the Landlord') that 'fiction' – or Baretti's fanciful imagination – 'has no limits'.[24]

The poet William Collins, in his madhouse, was much on his mind and he wrote often to the Wartons, hoping that by abstinence 'he might yet recover'. Johnson had himself 'often been near his state', he confided to Joseph that winter, 'and therefore have it in great commiseration'. To Thomas he wrote a dismal paragraph, hearing Dodsley's wife had died, hoping he did not suffer quite as much as he did himself for Tetty. 'I have ever since seemed to myself broken off from mankind a kind of solitary wanderer in the wild of life, without any certain direction, or fixed point of view. A gloomy gazer on a World to which I have little relation.'

'I now begin to see land', he wrote a month later, 'in this vast Sea of words. What reception I shall meet with upon the Shore I know not.'[25] In the justly famous Preface to the *Dictionary* he sounds the same weary, combative note. Acknowledging that he has toiled on one of 'the lower employments of life', he yet makes clear the work has been of radical significance both for the language and himself. He writes in a simple style, abandoning the 'hard words' of the *Rambler* for a direct, some-times peremptory voice, stressing the many problems he has had to decide in the *Dictionary* and itemising the many difficulties of grammar, orthography and etymology he has overcome. 'Some words there are', he confesses, 'which I cannot explain, because I do not understand them'; these might have been omitted, but 'I would not so far indulge my vanity as to decline this confession'. This 'confession' of a fault – his ignorance – is actually a sly permission to pay himself the compliment of a comparison to 'Tully' (Cicero), who admitted not knowing 'whether *lessus* . . . means a *funeral song* or *mourning garment*', and to Aristotle, uncertain whether a word in Homer 'signifies a *mule*, or *muleteer*'. Linking his problems to theirs is a subtle indication of the heroic nature of his task. He will not 'magnify his labours' by clouding his meanings in 'involution and obscurity' but does, for a moment, allow his memory to revert to his first hopes to 'revel away in feasts of literature'. He feels a sense of triumph at displaying 'my acquisitions to mankind'. These, he says, 'were the dreams of a poet doomed at last to wake a lexicographer'.

One point he makes in elegiac form, recalling recent deaths; 'it remains that we retard what we cannot repel,' he writes; 'that we palliate what we cannot cure. Life may be lengthened by care, though death cannot be ultimately defeated.' Having established his concern in terms of bodily care, he broadens it to wider administrations: 'Tongues, like governments, have a natural tendency to degeneration; we have long preserved our constitution, let us make some struggles for our language.'[26] He repeats his point about the inconvenience of change, 'even from worse to better', which he had stated in the *Plan* and closes with a peroration in which he cedes the elegiac note to a highly personalised sense of struggle. The *Dictionary* which the reader has opened was indeed 'written with little assistance of the learned, and without any patronage of the great';

not in the soft obscurities of retirement, or under the shelter of academick bowers, but amidst inconvenience and distraction, in sickness and in sorrow. It may repress the triumph of malignant criticism to observe, that if our language is not here fully displayed, I have only failed in an attempt which no human powers have hitherto completed . . . I have protracted my work till most of those whom I wished to please, have sunk into the grave, and success and miscarriage are empty sounds: I therefore dismiss it with frigid tranquillity, having little to fear or hope from censure or from praise.

He may step beyond good taste in making this intensely personal statement, but, having completed the work, he was acutely anxious it should be recognised as *his*. The unmistakable tone of irritation in this lonely finale comes from his anger that his years of toil at this 'lower employment' should be abducted by the Earl of Chesterfield's casual piece of aristocratic whimsy in *The World* which threatened the fierce sense of independence that Johnson had been cultivating. In the final issue of the *Rambler* he had written: 'Having hitherto attempted only the propagation of truth, I will not at last violate it by the confession of terrors which I do not feel: Having laboured to maintain the dignity of virtue, I will not now degrade it by the meanness of dedication.' Chesterfield had evidently neglected to read this warning when he wrote that 'the publick in general' and the 'republick of letters in particular' were 'greatly obliged to Mr. Johnson' for having produced 'so great and desirable a work' as the *Dictionary*. 'Perfection is not to be expected from man; but if we are to judge by the various works of Johnson already published, we have good reason to believe, that he will bring this as near to perfection as any one man could do.' The apparent praise is offset, to Johnson's mind at least, by supposed humour as Chesterfield affects to give his vote for his assumption of the 'great and arduous post' of dictator, surrendering 'as a free-born British subject' all rights and responsibilities for his language 'to the said Mr. Johnson, during the term of his dictatorship'.[27] In the way of puffs this was indeed a witty piece, which may have been why it irritated Johnson so much. Writing back he affects to offer gratitude for his lordship's words of approbation, offering his devastating demolition of the Olympian stance from which they had been delivered. 'Is not a Patron, My Lord,' he asks, politeness only just covering his naked anger, 'one who looks with unconcern on a Man struggling for Life in the water and when he has reached ground encumbers him with help.' He did not receive a reply.[28]

The *Dictionary* neared completion in the early months of 1755, guided through its final stages in the press by Andrew Millar and William Strahan. Johnson asked the messenger who took the final sheet of it to Millar what he had said. 'Sir (answered the messenger) he said, thank GOD I have done with him.' 'I am glad (replied Johnson, with a smile,) that he thanks GOD for any thing.' Publication was presaged on 1 March by the reprinting of fifteen hundred copies of the *Plan*. 'I intend in the winter to open a Bibliotheque,' Johnson wrote to Warton at the end of March, quite blithe to be at last free of the thing: 'My Book is now coming *in luminis oras* what will be its fate I know not nor much think because thinking is to no purpose. It must stand the censures of *the great vulgar and the small*, of those that understand it and that understand it not.' On 15 April several London newspapers announced that 'This day is published – a Dictionary of the English Language . . . By Samuel Johnson, A.M.' The idea that Johnson expected a financial reward, and had arranged a meeting in a tavern to receive it, is untrue; though no 'very accurate accountant' he knew his monetary situation well. Boswell is nearer the truth in commiserating that Johnson did not receive more for the *Dictionary*: 'He said I am sorry too. However it was very well. He said the book-sellers were generous, liberal-minded men.' The *Dictionary* in two volumes, weighing almost 10 lb each, cost almost a year's wages for many literate labouring men, and only two thousand copies of the first edition were published.[29]

The *Gentleman's Magazine* was naturally full of praise for the work. Johnson's friend John Hawkesworth anonymously applauded it in words Johnson may have chosen. In seven years, he said, Johnson had brought about 'what the joint labour of forty academicians could not produce to a neighbouring nation in less than half a century'. A long, measured appreciation from the *Monthly Review* concluded with 'wonder and admiration to see how greatly he has succeeded' and in the June issue of the *Edinburgh Review* Adam Smith declared the author's merit was 'extraordinary' before quibbling on some points of detail. These were the favourable public reactions; in private Warton told his brother Joseph that there were many 'strokes of laxity and indolence' about these 'two most unwieldy volumes' and Thomas Edwards, a Whig, and friend to Richardson, disapproved of 'a vehicle for Jacobite and high-flying tracts'.[30] Johnson told Charles Burney, the music scholar, that he had 'no Dictionaries to dispose of for myself', but directed him and his friends 'to Mr Dodsley'; he enclosed the *Dictionary* in a 'strong box' for his old friend, Edmund Hector in Birmingham, asking that the money be remitted to his mother; he announced triumphantly to Bennet Langton that his book had 'you see, no patrons', declaring himself 'at liberty' for Lichfield, or for Langton.[31]

He wrote to Warton, promising to come to Oxford 'being resolved not to lose sight of the University' and informing him cheerfully that 'the Dictionary sells well'. A fortnight later he wrote again, apologising for his non-appearance, explaining that 'two of our partners', Thomas Longman and Paul Knapton, who had brought out the *Dictionary*, 'are dead' and 'death . . . hears not supplications'. The booksellers had agreed to produce a second edition in weekly instalments, at 6d each, beginning in June, making Johnson's *Dictionary* compete directly with Nathan Bailey's, also available weekly. Both the *Dictionary* proper and these weekly instalments sold quite well, but it was only when Strahan brought out the ten-shilling abridgement at the end of the year that sales really multiplied. In the twenty-eight years of copyright the full *Dictionary* sold five thousand copies, but the abridgement sold thirty-five thousand. For the preface to the abridgement Johnson made a direct appeal to 'common readers' engaged in 'the common business of life', hoping to have accommodated 'the nation with a vocabulary of daily use'. This drastically condensed version, its definitions abbreviated and its quotations omitted, became the standard authority on the language, going through 309 miniature versions, one of which was tossed from her departing coach by Becky Sharp as she quitted Miss Pinkerton's academy in Thackeray's *Vanity Fair*.[32]

Definitions in the *Dictionary* most often mentioned are those few eccentricities which Boswell conceded must be reckoned 'to the account of capricious and humorous indulgence'. These include *oats*, 'a grain, which in England is generally given to horses, but in Scotland supports the people'; *whig*, 'the name of a faction'; *Tory*, 'one who adheres to the ancient constitution of the state, and the apostolical hierarchy of the church of England; opposed to a *whig*'; and *pension*, 'an allowance made to any one without an equivalent. In England it is generally understood to mean pay given to a state hireling for treason to his country.' The definition of *network* ('Any thing reticulated or decussated, at equal distances, with interstices between the intersections') is commonly cited as an example of Johnson's technical vocabulary, and *pastern* ('knee of a horse') of his ignorance.[33] But other features are worth noting. He adhered to his stated aim of including 'no testimony of living authors', save where some 'uncommon excellence excited my veneration', such as Samuel Richardson for *romance* ('This is strange romancing') and Charlotte Lennox for *suppose*, though whether this should be regarded as a compliment ('One falsehood always supposes another, and renders all you can say suspected') is at least arguable. Less obvious reasons guide the inclusion of William Law for *gewgaw* ('Splendidly trifling; showy without value'), but the use of David Garrick for *giggle* which was 'retained in Scotland' managed to glance at two favourite adversaries. Finally he cites himself from the *Rambler* for *medicate* ('She secured the whiteness of my hand by *medicated* gloves'). Although he excludes the more notorious four-letter words, the *Dictionary* includes *arse* ('a vulgar phrase'), *bum, fart, turd* and *piss*. Praised by some ladies for having excluded the most 'naughty' four-letter words, he is alleged to have replied, 'What, my dears! Then you have been looking for them?' *Retromingency* is included, defined as 'the quality of staling backwards', which the supporting quotation explains as 'pissing backwards', 'something that hares do, apparently'.[34]

Love of his native city, Lichfield, led Johnson to scatter references to it throughout as the place of martyred Christians. *Cant*, a term he glosses as used 'by beggars and vagabonds', is employed by him to lump together several forms of slang, as *nervous* ('medical cant'), *plum* (meaning £100,000), 'cant of the city', *stout*, 'a cant name for strong beer', *bishop*, 'a cant word for a mixture of wine, oranges, and sugar', and *cabbage*, 'a cant word among tailors'. *Cabbage*, a word he had glossed in the early days of the *Dictionary* before retrenchment, is given, after its bald definition ('A plant'), a lengthy description taken from Philip Miller's *Gardener's Dictionary*, of which this is an extract:

> the turnep *cabbage* was formerly more cultivated in England than at present; and some esteem this kind for soups, but it is generally too strong, and seldom good, except in hard winters . . . The musk *cabbage* has, through negligence, been almost lost in England, though, for eating, it is one of the best kinds we have; for it is always looser, and the leaves more crisp and tender, and has a most agreeable musky scent when cut. It will be fit for use in October, November, and December . . .

He adds that the verb *to cabbage* ('a cant word among taylors') means 'to steal in cutting clothes'. Some definitions exhibit a moral distaste, such as *stockjobber*, 'a low wretch who gets money by buying and selling shares', and *gambler*, 'a knave whose practice it is to invite the unwary to game'. He offers many definitions of words which have significantly changed their meanings in the two and a half centuries since he included them. Thus for him *barbecue* is 'a hog dressed whole, in the West Indian manner', and *soho* 'a form of calling from a distant place'; he defines *urinator* as 'a diver; one who searches under water'.[35]

Johnson had most problems defining those words 'too frequent in the English language' whose meanings are 'so loose and general' that he strives 'to catch them on the brink of utter inanity'. 'Put' is one of these, with sixty-six primary meanings (expanded to sixty-eight in 1773) and fourteen secondary denotations, concluding, in the fourth edition, with a fifteenth in which he asks, in near despair, 'without synonymes and paraphrase, how can [words like these] be explained!' In attempting to give his definitions he does not merely list meanings; through his illustrative quotations he displays a wealth of connotations from sublime to absurd, beginning with Genesis, 'God planted a garden and there he *put* a man', and concluding with a fool, telling us that as a noun the word *put* means 'a rustic or clown'. The Bible, with thirty-seven references, supplies most quotations, but there are twenty-six from Shakespeare, fifteen from Dryden, ten from Milton and eight from Swift, one of which is advice to cooks, 'When you cannot get the dinner ready, *put the clock back.*' Shakespeare illustrates almost every sense of the word: his Julius Caesar *puts by* the crown; his King John *puts on* the dauntless spirit of resolution; his Lady Macbeth *puts it* (the murder) upon the spongy officers; and his Prince Hal *puts down* poor Falstaff. Mortimer's *Treatise on Husbandry* keeps us down to earth ('As for the time of *putting* the rams to the ewes, you must consider at what time your grass will maintain them'), yet shortly afterwards we are raised back to the heavens with Milton: 'Ye shall die perhaps, by *putting off* human, to *put on* Gods'. Johnson turns the quotations for this little auxiliary verb into a self-contained narrative of human hopes and fears.

There are undoubtedly many errors and omissions in the *Dictionary*. Nathan Bailey's *Dictionarium Britannicum* included fifty per cent more words and Johnson's attempts to seize this opportunity to make grand pronouncements are often particularly unwise. In the 'Grammar' his statement that 'X begins no English word' may have been, at the time he wrote it, true, but the same cannot be said of his equally authoritative view of the letter H. This letter, he takes it upon himself to state, 'seldom, perhaps never, begins any but the first syllable'. John Wilkes, writing in the *Public Advertiser*, had great fun with that pronouncement. 'The author of this remark must be a man of a quick *appre-hension*, and *compre-hensive* genius; but I can never forgive his *un-handsome be-haviour* to the poor *knight-hood, priest-hood*, and *widow-hood*, nor his *in-humanity* to all *man-hood* and *woman-hood*.' Wilkes had struck a hit, which Johnson immediately recognised; but he also knew and heartily disliked the man who made it, and was most unwilling to concede. Thus, in his fourth edition, he added some few words of explanation, beginning caustically, 'It sometimes begins middle or final syllables in words compounded, as *block-head*.'

Towards the end of his life Johnson made a judgement on the *Dictionary* which it is hard to better. Writing to Francesco Sastres he said, 'Dictionaries are like watches, the worst is better than none, and the best cannot be expected to go quite true.'[36]

PART THREE

The Pensioner

9

Nothing Is Concluded

conclude v.n. *To end.*

> And all around wore nuptial bonds, the ties
> Of love's assurance, and a train of lies,
> That, made in lust, *conclude* in perjuries.
>
> Dryden's *Fables*.

Having finally completed his 'Book', Johnson intended to spend the summer rambling through the country visiting old friends; his mother, now over eighty, counted the days till publication. He would pay her a 'duty' visit, he told Bennet Langton, and revisit old acquaintances like Edmund Hector in Birmingham and the Wartons in Oxford. Then he would come on and spend some time with him in Lincolnshire. But there was always something to hinder his journey. He wrote again apologising for delay, fully anticipating taking tea with Mr Wyse; a fortnight later he wrote again, sending more apologies, occasioned by the sudden deaths of Knapton and Longman. 'I have not laid aside my purpose,' he promised; 'every day makes me more impatient of staying from you.'[1] In mid-July he visited Frances Cotterell who had lived opposite him in Castle Street twenty years before, but she was not at home. They exchanged letters instead. So many minor things seemed determined to impede his longed-for relaxation.

Gradually his first enthusiasm at the publication of the *Dictionary* drained away and left him with the painful awareness that he must write to stay alive. He fell to his prayers, confessing he had lived 'in perpetual neglect of publick worship', designing an eight-point scheme 'of settled practice' which he hoped to follow, modelled on several he had made before (and would again). The scheme began, boldly: '1 To rise early.' Johnson found a psychological release in making such plans.

The fondness he felt for Hill Boothby was not unconnected with the rigidity of her spiritual practice. But between making out the plan, and following it, came life, and there Johnson strayed, constantly. He was now in a different world; the *Dictionary* which had kept him going for the last nine years was done, and the people, Tetty and Cave, who had been closest to him were dead. He had, once again, to find something to sustain his attention, but seemed unconcerned as to its nature. He planned writing a monthly review of all books, noting the 'infelicity' of current journals, and was asked, not impertinently, by his friend William Adams what precisely he knew of mathematics? Or natural history? He would do 'as well as I can', he replied, intemperately. When Adams suggested that Dr Maty, author of the *Bibliothèque Britannique*, might act as his assistant, Johnson was furious: 'I'd throw him into the Thames.'[2]

This conversation probably took place in Oxford where Johnson went in August. The idea of launching a review came to nothing, but the need to find work persisted. He thought of an edition of Thomas More, and begged Warton to 'pass an hour' procuring the first few lines of a dozen manuscripts 'that I may know whether they are yet unpublished'. What of an examination of languages? Or a study of philosophy 'as an Instrument of living'? He jotted down these and many other thoughts such that, if the Lord should please to 'intrust me with plenty' (the likelihood seemed remote), 'I may be ready to relieve the wants of others'. On leaving Oxford he sent a note to Robert Chambers, an ambitious young Fellow of Lincoln College, asking him to pay his barber whom he had forgotten. 'Call at Mrs Simpson's for a box of pills which I left behind me, and am loath to lose.' Having gained a lift to London, he did not wish to give it up, but neither did he wish to be thought of as a defaulter.[3]

Back in London, he was plunged again into the abyss of journalistic work; he wrote dedications, prefaces and reviews for the *Universal Visiter* [*sic*], the *Universal Chronicle*, the *Daily Advertiser* and the *Literary Magazine*, simply for the money. 'Poor dear Cave' was dead, he told Elizabeth Carter, and he must find work where he could. At Christmas he wrote a brief *Account* of Zachariah Williams's attempts to find the longitude, but it sold badly. Within the year Williams died and, in his brief obituary, Johnson wrote that he was 'worthy to have ended life with better fortune'.[4] Was that what they would say of him? He attempted to promote a benefit performance of *Merope* for Williams's daughter Anna at Drury Lane, wrote to a great many friends and eventually raised £260. He added several paragraphs to Baretti's *An Introduction to the Italian Language* and wrote Dedications for Charlotte Lennox's *Memoirs of . . . [the]Duke of Sully* and for William Payne's *Introduction to the Game of Draughts*. He proposed a *Dictionary of Trade and Commerce* to a collection of booksellers and had one of them retort, 'What the D—l do you know of trade and commerce?' Nothing, he acknowledged, 'in the *practical* line', but he was willing to 'glean' all that was required from 'authors of authority'.[5] Nothing came of that idea either, although he did compose a Preface for Rolt's *A New Dictionary of Trade and Commerce*. Tackled about it by Boswell, he said he had never met Rolt, nor had he even read the book, but 'I knew very well what such a Dictionary should be, and I wrote a Preface accordingly'. Dictionaries 'of every kind' were suddenly the fashion, he noted.[6]

Such comments appear to demonstrate a firm grip, but in reality he was suffering very badly. He had anticipated that as writer of the *Dictionary* he should be above such daily struggles, but it was not so. That winter he had a bout of hoarseness together with a cough, so violent 'that I once fainted under its convulsions'; he was bled for the ailment and lost fifty-four ounces of blood. His eye swelled up so badly that it closed, till he thought he might share Anna Williams's blindness, and remained like that until mid-February, when his eyesight was restored. He immediately composed a prayer of thanks for allowing him 'to persue again the studies which thou hast set before me' and told his stepdaughter Lucy he was coming soon, repeating sentiments expressed to Richard Congreve a few months earlier about passing 'some of the winter months with my mother'. But worse news came; he received disturbing rumours from Tissington. 'The Doctor is anxious about you,' he wrote to Hill Boothby on 30 December, adding 'You think . . . better of me than I deserve'. He wrote to her frequently, mixing detailed prescriptions for dried orange peel, cinnamon and nutmeg with tender sentiments ('Dear Angel . . . my heart is full of tenderness'). The end was not far off. 'Allmercifull God have mercy on You' were the last words he sent her; she died on 16 January 1756. Baretti reported Johnson to have been 'almost distracted' so that 'the friends about him had much ado to calm the violence of his emotion'. In the prayer he composed upon her death, Johnson thanked God for her 'good example' and prayed that he might improve 'the opportunity of instruction' she had provided.[7]

He attempted to assist Lewis Paul, whose factory in Northamptonshire was going broke, by suggesting people who might be approached for a loan. Dr James, who had refused to pay up for three boxes of tickets for *Merope*, he reckoned not a good prospect, but Paul might have better luck with young Richard Cave who 'cannot, I think want forty pounds'. He even volunteered to go in with him and make it '*our* request', affecting to be in funds, which might tempt Cave to risk it. But only four days later his elaborate disguise was punctured. A hurried note sent to Richardson on 16 March explained he was 'under an arrest for five pounds eighteen shillings . . . if you will be so good as to send me this sum. . .' This is a graphic reminder of the poverty, and possible consequences of it, that not only Johnson but thousands of Londoners suffered every year. The note is endorsed in Richardson's hand 'Sent Six Guineas', but Johnson's financial troubles were only just beginning. He had felt Tetty's extravagance had dragged them down, but was soon to learn financial disaster waited for anyone without a settled income. Two years later 'an accident' sent him in search of 'about forty pounds', this time to Jacob Tonson. That Johnson had no fear of Richardson's assistance is suggested by an anecdote in which he claims, 'I knew I could afford to joke with the rascal who had me in custody, and did so over a pint of adulterated wine.' He thanked Richardson two days later, enclosing a copy of Sir Thomas Browne's *Christian Morals* which he had edited and had just been published. 'The inflammation is come again into my eye, so that I can write very little,' he said in a brief acknowledgement, whose dismal tone seems more accurate than the tale of his joking over adulterated wine. He gave a copy of his *Life* of Browne to Birch 'by way [of] interest' on the loan of a book which he had kept far too long. Money was, as always, very scarce with him but books were a negotiable commodity. 'The reciprocal civility of authors is one of the most risible scenes in the farce of life,' he writes in his candid view of Browne, a comment looking beyond the man to the world he inhabited.[8]

The volume on Browne did not sell well. It was published by John Payne of the Ivy Lane Club, which was faltering as more of its original members grew old, died or, in Hawkins's case, married. 'Our symposium at the King's Head broke up,' he reports, leaving Johnson 'with fewer around him than were able to support it'. Desperate for work to bring in money, he helped out on the new periodical *The Universal Visiter*, set up the previous winter, since when Christopher Smart, who signed the contract, had shown signs of his emergent madness, though Johnson claimed he would 'as lief pray with Kit Smart as any one else'. He added that Smart 'did not love clean linen' but confessed he himself had 'no passion for it'. Johnson produced his *Further Thoughts on Agriculture* in March, arguing that agriculture alone could support us; commerce was a 'daughter of fortune', but when the ground was 'covered with corn and cattle, we can want nothing'.[9] That he should write this just before the outbreak of the Seven Years War is notable in that, even when not writing for political effect, it makes his patriotism clear. Shortly afterwards *Reflections on the Present State of Literature* demonstrates his true feelings at the time: 'If I were to form an adage of misery, or fix the lowest point to which humanity could fall', he writes, 'I should be tempted to name the life of an author.'

The first volume of Joseph Warton's *Essay on the Writings and Genius of Pope* appeared anonymously on 8 April and Johnson was surprised to have received neither a copy of it nor word of its publication. He wrote back to tell Warton 'that way of publishing' was 'a wicked trick'. The poet Collins he had written to, but received no answer; just the constant ill-paid demands of the periodical publishers, which left him feeling lonelier than ever. His eye remained inflamed, but he begged, 'let me not be long without a letter'. It is the cry of a man who had written a great work, the *Dictionary*, and, for a month at least, had been celebrated, yet now felt more isolated than ever.[10]

Years later he said his work on the *Universal Visiter* was to assist 'poor Smart', whose reputation as a journalist came from the *Midwife*, a paper engraved on its first number with a midwife sitting by a close-stool labelled 'The Jakes of Genius'. But it was a period of endurance, not enjoyment. Johnson quickly stopped writing for the *Visiter* as soon the *Literary Magazine*, brainchild of William Faden (formerly printer of the *Rambler*) and the publisher Joseph Richardson, took form. This was to be an altogether more purposeful publication, with plans and maps and illustrations, for which Johnson was offered, and accepted, the role of editor; his only problem was that the magazine's 'literary' identity extended no further than its title. The principal emphasis was political and since its first number appeared in May 1756, just as Britain declared war on France, the omens for success seemed excellent. But for Johnson, whose political instincts were never strong, such matters were of little consequence. He began with a long historical essay analysing British imperial interests since the time of Queen Elizabeth, questioning the rationale of maintaining colonies and seeing colonialism not from the perspective of the warring states of Europe but from that of the colonised natives. The French found Canada 'a cold uncomfortable uninviting region' which yielded only 'furrs and fish'; yet the greatest security they enjoyed was 'the friendship of the natives' to which they had a right as 'consequence of their virtue': 'surely they who intrude, uncalled, upon the country of a distant people, ought to consider the natives as worthy of common kindness, and content themselves to rob without insulting them.' This principle, so clear and humane, took priority even over Johnson's instinctive dislike of the French, and he returned to it in his *Letter* of a French refugee in America, writing to a '*Gentleman in England*': 'we should have endeavoured to have given [the Indians] just notions of life, natural, civil and religious.'[11]

Control of the editorial position of the *Literary Magazine* is difficult to determine but seems to have been linked with the Pittite faction in parliament. There was general delight at Johnson's hostile *Observations* on the British decision to pay £54,000 for the services of eight thousand Hessian troops, pouring 'the gains of our commerce' into foreign coffers, to buy men 'like sheep or oxen'. But when, the following month, he returned to the American war, likening the French and British troops to 'two robbers' quarrelling 'for the spoils of a passenger', his sentiments were not appreciated. Suddenly the *Observations* came to an end with a brief note, 'to be continued'; but, as is frequently the case with such notes, it came to nothing. Johnson's editorship was terminated and the next issue of the *Magazine* included a paean to Pitt's glorious war, not at all to his taste.[12] He apologised to Charlotte Lennox, who was anxious for a review of her *Memoirs of the Countess of Berci* to appear in the *Literary Magazine*; he would 'press for a place in the Gentleman's Magazine' for it, he said.[13]

It was three years since Charlotte Lennox had brought out *Shakespear Illustrated* and more than ten since Johnson had published his *Miscellaneous Observations* on Macbeth which had been so firmly slapped down by Jacob Tonson. In the intervening decade he had built up unrivalled familiarity with the plays, which were often used as explanatory sources for the *Dictionary*. He was thoroughly familiar with the strengths and weaknesses of Hanmer, Pope, Warburton and Theobald as editors and had shaken off his fascination with emendatory criticism. In short, his credentials were at last sufficient to convince Tonson that the idea of linking Johnson's name to Shakespeare's made sound commercial sense. Eleven years after Johnson had first proposed the notion, the two men signed a deal, in June, for an eight-volume subscription edition of Shakespeare's complete works to be published 'on or before Christmas 1757'.[14]

The fact that Johnson gave himself a mere eighteen months to complete the task indicates that he had, or *thought* he had, already done much of the work for this new edition. In his *Proposals* he had set out many of the problems to be tackled which were 'peculiar to Shakespeare': the plays were produced 'not to be printed, but to be played', copied out 'transcript after transcript, vitiated by the blunders of the penman, or changed by the affectation of the players'. 'No other author', he declared, 'ever gave up his works to fortune and time with so little care.' Johnson promised an edition which would surpass those of Rowe and Pope ('very ignorant'), of Warburton ('detained by more important studies') and of Theobald, who considered 'learning only as an instrument of gain'. Tackled by Charles Burney on the relative merits of Warburton and Theobald as editors he had not the slightest doubt that Warburton was the superior: 'Sir, he'd make two-and-fifty Theobalds, cut into slices!'

Giving every sign of keeping to his deadline, Johnson set about publicising his edition, selling subscriptions to it, for which he offered receipts. Within weeks he had recommended six to Birch, told Hector there were more to be had 'from my Mother' and sent a dozen receipts, already signed, to Mr Vaillant, a bookseller in the Strand.[15] Samuel Richardson enclosed a copy of the *Proposals* to Thomas Edwards, and Thomas Warton secured twelve subscriptions from Oxford. From Birch Johnson asked to borrow 'any of the contemporaries or Ancestors of Shakespeare', stressing he would only need them 'a short time', and within the year was telling Warton, 'I am printing my new Edition of Shakespeare.' Even when this wildly optimistic timetable began to slip, he was convinced, and tried to convince others, that the date of completion was very close. 'I shall publish about March,' he told Charles Burney on Christmas Eve; in March he wrote again, thanking him for several subscriptions, acknowledging the edition would 'not be out so soon as I promised' but certain it would be published 'before summer'.[16]

Still anxious for money, he continued writing for the *Literary Magazine*, but anonymously; 'you must not tell that I have any thing in it,' he wrote to Robert Chambers; 'I would not have it made certain.' He considered visiting the Midlands and wrote to Edmund Hector complaining he was never free of a kind of 'melancholy indisposition which I had when we lived together at Birmingham'. Now he was once again alone and poor, he thought more often of his schooldays 'than I did when I had just broken loose from a Master. Happy is he that can look back upon the past with pleasure,' he added, without saying whether he should be counted amongst that happy number.[17] The phrase about 'breaking loose' from a master was particularly on his mind since Frank, his manservant, had done exactly that. 'My Boy is run away', he wrote to Lewis Paul, 'and I know not whom to send.' Some months later he told Charlotte Lennox he had 'no servant, and write therefore by the post'.[18] Truly alone, he felt more melancholy than ever; 'I feel a pang for every moment that any human being has by my peevishness or obstinacy spent in unhappiness,' he told John Taylor, but then apologised: 'I know not how I have fallen upon this, I had no thought of it, when I began the letter.' It was not John Taylor whom he had made unhappy by his peevishness and obstinacy, but Frank Barber who, luckily, soon returned. 'Perhaps he found working for an apothecary more tiring than working for a dilatory hack writer.'[19]

He began to write rapid reviews for all kinds of different journals which were important only in the act and moment of composition but, once written, were just copy. He trumpeted his anti-imperialist sentiments in a review of Lewis Evans's *Map* of the British colonies in America for the *Literary Magazine*, concluding it would 'very little advance the power of the English to plant colonies on the Ohio by dispeopling their native country'. He fulminated in several articles on Admiral Byng's court martial for cowardice. Byng, 'stigmatized with infamy', had been shot to 'divert the public attention from the crimes and blunders of other men' or, as Voltaire appositely put it: '*il est bon de tuer de temps en temps un amiral pour encourager les autres.*' By the time of Byng's execution, Johnson had moved on, writing reviews both of Charlotte Lennox's *Memoirs of the Countess of Berci* and of *Memoirs of the King of Prussia* 'whose actions and designs', he noted, 'now keep Europe in attention'.[20] Starting in October, the *Memoirs* continued through the winter and ended with Frederick 'at the height of human greatness', but the outcome of the present war 'is yet too early to predict', wrote Johnson, having learnt the journalistic instinct for a sequel which might turn everything to ashes.[21]

He wrote reviews of many works, from William Payne's *An Introduction to the Game of Draughts* ('triflers may find anything a trifle') to Blackwell's *Memoirs of the Court of Augustus*, which proved that Rome grew great 'only by the misery of the rest of mankind'. When he liked a book he could be fulsome, as was the case with Stephen White's 'little tract' on *Collateral Bee-Boxes* which he found rich in 'benevolence and piety'. Though pushed by poverty to produce vast numbers of such pieces, it is noteworthy that his personal attention to each one never diminished.[22] In May he began a review, continued for three issues, of Soame Jenyns's *A Free Enquiry into the Nature and Origin of Evil*, which forced him to re-examine his own religious and political convictions. Jenyns's book, based on assumptions found in Pope's *Essay on Man*, was hardly original; it promulgated a belief in subordination to justify the conditions of the poor, to

which Johnson took fierce exception. 'That hope and fear are insepa-
rably or very frequently connected with poverty and riches my surveys
of life have not informed me,' he writes; 'This author and Pope perhaps never saw the miseries which they imagine thus easy to be
borne.' He proceeds to articulate principles which Jenyns's book
ignores and, in so doing, indicates the book has touched a nerve in the
body of one who knew too well what poverty was. 'Evil must be felt
before it is evil,' he declared, noting that Jenyns 'has at last thought on
a way by which human sufferings may produce good effects':

> He imagines that as we have not only animals for food, but
> choose some for our diversion, the same privilege may be
> allowed to some beings above us, *who may deceive, torment, or
> destroy us for the ends only of their own pleasure or utility . . .* Some
> of them, perhaps, are virtuosi, and delight in the operations of
> an asthma, as a human philosopher in the effects of an air pump.
> To swell a man with a tympany is as good a sport as to blow a
> frog. Many a merry bout have these frolic beings at the vicissi-
> tudes of an ague, and good sport it is to see a man tumble with
> an epilepsy, and revive and tumble again, and all this he knows
> not why.

Writing in a measured way Johnson explodes Jenyns's naivety, proving
the truth of an axiom, here buried in a paragraph, but soon to be picked
out in *Rasselas*: 'The only end of writing is to enable the readers better
to enjoy life, or better to endure it.'[23]

Reviewing Jonas Hanway's attack on his favourite drink (*An Essay
on Tea*) which denounced it as being as injurious as gin, Johnson
boldly confessed to being 'a hardened and shameless tea-drinker'. For
more than twenty years, he boasted, he had 'diluted his meals with
only the infusion of this fascinating plant' and could think of few
more agreeable people to know than the man (or woman) who 'with
tea amuses the evening, with tea solaces the midnight, and, with tea,
welcomes the morning'. He mentioned a recent visit to the Foundling
Hospital (of which Hanway was a governor), saying that he found the
children wholly uninstructed in Christian principles, a failure 'equally
pernicious with gin' or 'even tea'. Hanway replied; Johnson replied to

his reply (the only known occasion on which he took this trouble) and the matter quickly spiralled. The governors of the Hospital issued threats of writs for libel, but Joseph Richardson, publisher of the *Literary Magazine*, declared (quite falsely) he had no idea as to the identity of the author. The result of the spat was a disappointing compromise; Johnson was not prosecuted, but neither did he write any more reviews for the *Literary Magazine*. Tea, as events in Boston were to show, could be a very contentious commodity.[24]

To ease his parting, Richardson included a four-page announcement of Johnson's forthcoming edition of Shakespeare, hoping that by attracting subscribers to the work which (he confidently pronounced) would be published 'on or before next Christmas', he could minimise the force of Johnson's dismissal. Such a gesture was generous in a magazine that did not carry advertisements, characteristic of Richardson's style, but had an inevitable consequence; within the year the *Literary Magazine* ceased publication. Johnson found other means to voice his anti-imperialist views and, in November, sounded off about a recent naval fiasco off the west coast of France, when the army had done nothing more than fill 'their bellies with grapes'.[25]

It annoyed him not only that sales of the *Dictionary* should be so disappointing, but that praise for it was non-existent. Even among Johnson's acquaintance there were 'only two who upon the publication of my book did not endeavour to depress me with threats of censure from the publick', he told Charles Burney. The fame, or notoriety, it brought swelled his post with letters from would-be writers, to one of whom he wrote back recommending shorter paragraphs, less love of Thomson and less attention to the voice of the public. He did not think an author 'just to himself', he wrote, who 'rests in any opinion' but his own.[26] He thanked Edmund Hector in April for remitting money to his mother from Shakespeare receipts, which went on 'tolerably', he said, and should make 'some addition to my fortune'. Such additions were abruptly reversed in June, when Levett threatened Lucy Porter with foreclosure of the mortgage on the Lichfield property. Johnson immediately wrote to him to take no advantage of 'so small a lapse' and spare his mother 'all the trouble' of their financial dealings. She was 'too weak at present to bear the shock of such a thing'; Lucy reported back to him that 'the very naming of it would almost destroy her'. He set out, as carefully as he could ('I suppose you do not think I would cheat you of ten or twelve pounds'), the mortgage account for £146, indicating how and by whom it had been settled. That very day he had sent a bank bill 'of 100£' to his mother: 'You may easily settle the affair,' he wrote, exaggerating in an offhand way that indicates how deeply he was affected. To his mother, now eighty-eight, he wished only good things to be related, of his *Dictionary* or his edition of Shakespeare; nothing that would revive unpleasant memories of rows over who kept the wall in London, or of poor Natty. The money he sent was raised from Tonson, on the strength of receipts for Shakespeare. Levett, fortunately, was satisfied, though in the document he entered the sum as £98, saying that he 'allowed' to Johnson 'the sum of £44 (which was *alleged* to have been paid in part)'. Levett was keen to ensure that, whatever might be allowed, his arithmetic should not be faulty.[27]

Johnson continued to dream up money-making schemes. If he went to live in Oxford he might try a life of Richard I, or Edward the Confessor, or maybe even a history of the Reformation 'not of England only, but of Europe'. He sent these ideas 'in confidence' to a colleague, reminding him that 'the schemes of a writer are his property, and his revenue'. He treated the edition of Shakespeare as though it were a property completed, confidently borrowing the £100 for the mortgage on his family home, and it was not until he found himself *again* arrested for debt, and *again* troubling Tonson for £40, that some other journalistic work became not advisable but essential. He assured him that 'no other such vexation can happen to me' and within two months, on 15 April 1758, the first *Idler* essay appeared. Further essays continued to appear weekly for the following two years, providing him, at last, with a regular salary.[28]

What happened to Shakespeare, so confidently promised for the previous summer, but not appearing until 1765 – seven years later – is a mystery. Bertrand Bronson dismisses, rightly, accusations of indolence, but something prevented Johnson from completing the work he had seized on, two years earlier, to keep the bailiffs from his door.[29] From April there were his *Idler* essays, issued in a paper called the *Universal Chronicle*, but they could barely have occupied half a day a week. He was overtaken by a form of lethargy which prevented him from noting anything in his diary from the end of March and marked a very different persona from the erudite sage on his three-legged chair portrayed by Reynolds earlier that year. Bennet Langton's father offered him a living 'of considerable value' in Lincolnshire, were he to take holy orders, but Johnson declined, partly because he believed his 'temper and habits' were unfit for a clergyman. Instead, over the following two years he produced ninety-two of the 104 numbers of the *Idler*, for which he was paid a total of £292 19s; when the work was subsequently republished, he received a further £84. It was, for Johnson, a satisfying way of earning money which allowed Shakespeare to drift from the forefront of his mind. 'No man but a blockhead ever wrote, except for money,' he declared, and the *Idler* provided him with what he required. Hawkins said of his work on Shakespeare: 'Well! Doctor, now you have finished your *Dictionary*, I suppose you will labour your present work *con amore* for your reputation'; to which Johnson retorted, 'No, Sir . . . nothing excites a man to write but necessity.'[30]

As periodical essays, the *Idler* contributions have hardly recommended themselves to later critical opinion. The *Idler* has 'less body and more spirit' than the *Rambler*, comments Boswell, doing what he can to recommend them. More characteristic is the remark of the Yale editors that the 'confirmed Johnsonian' finds them thin. Johnson underlined the feeling by his neglect of the *Idler* compared with the *Rambler*, and 'less extensive revision of the *Idler* for the collected edition'.[31] Essays were brief, sentences briefer and often devoted to trivial subjects, at which Addison or Steele might excel but at which Johnson labours. There are few polysyllabic sentences of multiple clauses, previously so characteristic of his style; in their place we have essays on such inconsequential topics as advertisements, or the weather. 'Genius is shewn only by invention,' he comments as he examines wash-balls, 'duvets for bed-coverings' and a beautiful fluid to repel pimples and plump up the flesh. Early on he addresses papers to female readers, attempting to introduce light-hearted bulletins from the war, but fails to catch the right conversational tone. 'There is no crime more infamous', he comments, 'than the violation of truth.' When he writes that 'among the calamities of war' may be numbered 'the diminution of the love of truth' it seems he speaks of himself.[32] Amongst these early *Idlers*, though their tone is light, Johnson never disappears from view, as when he says of debtors that we have now 'imprisoned one generation of debtors after another, but we do not find that their numbers lessen'. In another paper on the same subject he writes of the 'corruption of confined air, the want of exercise, and sometimes of food' in debtors' prisons which 'put an end every year to the life of one in four' of those incarcerated within: 'If there are any made so obdurate by avarice or cruelty, as to revolve these consequences without dread or pity, I must leave them to be awakened by some other power, for I write only to human beings.'[33]

He sounds, in this essay, like Dickens and his increased solemnity of tone may have been occasioned by letters from Lichfield acquainting him with his mother's decline. 'The account which Miss gives me of your health, pierces my heart,' he wrote to her, borrowing money from his printer to send her twelve guineas.[34] He maintained his interest in Oxford, writing to Robert Chambers at Lincoln College encouraging his hopes of the new Vinerian Professorship of Law, and to Thomas Warton and Bennet Langton at Trinity. Langton came to Oxford bearing 'some of my plays with him', which he and Warton were at liberty to peruse, provided 'you both hide them from everybody else'. Shakespeare was still a current interest and he confidently played down Warton's fears over the loss of subscription receipts: 'The loss is nothing,' he assured him. To Langton he maintained a fatherly posture, advising him to write down his first thoughts of Oxford 'before custom has reconciled you to the scenes before you'; one feels the sense of Johnson reliving his own first experiences of Oxford through Langton's eyes. He wrote to Anna Maria Smart, wife of the poet recently incarcerated in St Luke's Hospital for the Insane, who had gone to Dublin, but found it very bleak; Johnson reminded her that 'though a place much worse than London' it was yet 'not so bad as Iceland'.[35]

Financially his state was still precarious, despite the money from the *Idler*. James Grainger told Thomas Percy that he had several times been to see Johnson 'to pay him part of your subscriptions: I say part, because he never thinks of working if he has a couple of guineas in his pocket.'[36] That jibe at Johnson's dependability is generally unworthy, but about this time came to have a certain truth. Finally unable to keep up the annual rent of £26 on Gough Square he moved out, leaving the place in such a state the next tenant had the rent reduced.[37] The last mention of Gough Square is a recollection Charles Burney gave to Boswell, of going there with him and finding 'five or six Greek folios, a deal writing desk, and a chair and a half'. Johnson, having given up his seat to his guest, 'tottered himself on one with only three legs and one arm'.

In this, the quintessential image of Dictionary Johnson, balanced precariously on his three-legged chair, the two happily debated the qualities of different editions of Shakespeare. The chair figures in a description of Johnson meeting Reynolds and the sculptor Louis-François Roubiliac in his garret where, 'besides his books, all covered with dust', there was 'an old crazy deal table, and a still worse and older elbow chair, having only three legs'. Finally there is a description by Reynolds's sister Frances, who, besides remarking Johnson's shabby appearance ('like a Beggar'), speaks of his living as one:

> wanting even a chair to sit on, particularly in his study, where a gentleman who frequently visited him whilst writing his *Idlers* always found him at his Desk, sitting on one with three legs; and on rising from it, he remark'd that Mr. Johnson never forgot its defect, but would either hold it in his hand, or place it with great composure against some support, taking no notice of its imperfection to his visitor.[38]

If Johnson had lived in the twenty-first century, in a world marked out by brand images, it is clear this would be his: a man alone, a half-blind widower balanced neatly by his own disproportionate bulk, making clarity in the *Dictionary* out of chaos.

Johnson's move, at least from the major tenancy of Gough Square (it has been credibly suggested that he lived in a room there until his occupancy of Staple Inn), had consequences for those who shared his lodgings. Miss Williams moved a little way down Fleet Street, to Bolt Court, where Johnson would call in and drink tea with her each night. Robert Levet had to move, and Frank Barber took this opportunity to join the navy, entering the service in July and not being discharged until two years later. It was in these penurious conditions that Johnson contrived to write his light-hearted *Idlers*, while pursuing his endeavours with Shakespeare, a project which '*movet sed non promovet*';* James Grainger wrote to Percy that he would 'feed him occasionally with guineas', making the distasteful but understandable comparison of Johnson with a chained-up bear.[39]

In the new year he wrote in his avuncular mode to Langton, advising him to learn from his example: 'When I was as you are now, towering in the confidence of twenty one little did I suspect that I should be at forty nine what I now am.' He gratified the young man's curiosity with green-room gossip about *Cleone*, a play of Robert Dodsley's which, since Garrick's refusal to produce it, went on at Covent Garden with Johnson's applause: 'I went the first night and supported it as publickly as I might.' Strangely, he made the statement 'I, who have no Sisters nor brothers', which might pass unnoticed but for the fact that he had said much the same ('I have no brother') in a letter to John Taylor two years earlier. It would have been more correct to say he had no brother *now*, but the implication of his remarks is not bereavement but solitary splendour. With Tetty gone, he recreated a sense of himself in splendid, if somewhat dirty, isolation, imagining the life he might have lived, at Oxford; in such a life, Nathaniel's shabby dealings at the Lichfield bookshop would simply not appear.[40]

As he wrote these words to Langton, his mother was slipping away, as letters from Lucy informed him. He wrote to her immediately, promising money, recommending a 'strong infusion' of tree bark which 'would do you good', and bidding earnestly for prayers and blessings: 'whatever you would have done . . . I shall endeavour to obey you.' There is, despite the sincere urgency of his reactions, a certain coldness about the letter: he addresses her as 'Honoured Madam', promising his best efforts to 'obey', as becomes her 'dutiful Son'. Three days later he wrote again to Lucy, promising to send more money 'in a few days', and to his mother, a short, submissive letter: 'Your weakness afflicts me beyond what I am willing to communicate to you.' Again, the letter is brief – a mere six lines, in which he has 'nothing to add to my last letter', but yet he does add something:

* 'He sets it going, but does not advance its progress.'

'Dear, dear Mother', he writes in signing off, attempting a closeness he had not used in over twenty years. 'You are too ill for long letters,' he wrote two days later, concluding his brief prayer for God's blessing with 'dear Mother', begging her to 'let Miss' (meaning Lucy Porter) write to him 'every post, however short'. In London he made every effort to raise the money to cover whatever expenses his mother might need. He wrote to William Strahan, spelling out the volume he had mentioned the night before, 'The title will be The choice of Life or The History of —— Prince of Abissinia.' He floated various ideas for the money to be raised by this publication; £75 (or seventy-five guineas) a volume for the two-volume first edition, with £25 for the second; or £60 for the first edition 'and the property then to revert to me, or for forty pounds, and share the profit that is retain half the copy'. Whichever way, Johnson had 'occasion for thirty pounds'; he promised to 'deliver the book' by 'Monday night', but entreated Strahan to get him the money by that time, ending his note with a further reminder: 'Get me the money if you can.' By the same post he wrote again to Lucy, promising, 'I will, if it be possible, come down to you', yet begging, 'Do not tell, lest I disappoint her. If I miss to write next post, I am on the road.' To his mother he wrote, 'You have been the best mother, and I believe the best woman in the world', a piece of forgivable flattery which never reached her. Mrs Johnson died on the night of Saturday 20 January, soon after he had finished writing.[41]

It was only at the end that he could make that effort to be close to her, feeling only then that he would not be spurned or laughed at. With women Johnson never had a controlling role. He had attempted to gain it once, with Tetty, as they rode to Derby to be married, and had come off very badly, losing half her money at Edial. His mother had expressed herself on the marriage, for which reason Johnson had stayed away from Lichfield for more than twenty years. Had the *Dictionary* been a great success or *Shakespeare* made his fortune, he would have returned; but, as it was, there was nothing to prove her wrong in thinking he should have stayed a bookseller in Lichfield. It took him a lot of effort to come back; ostensibly he was on the point of doing so – but she died.

On the day his mother was buried, Johnson, having decided not to go, as he had not gone to Tetty's funeral, wrote himself a special prayer. In the years since Tetty's death, her memory held a special place in his holy devotions: 'let the remembrance of her whom thy hand has separated from me, teach me to consider the shortness and uncertainty of life,' he prayed the previous Easter: 'Let my life be useful, and my death be happy.' Now, he had someone else to feel guilty about. 'Forgive me whatever I have done unkindly to my Mother,' he prayed; 'Make me to remember her good precepts and good example.' But it was not just for his mother's forgiveness he prayed; there were others whom he had tried, unsuccessfully, to forget. These are the last lines of his prayer:

> I returned thanks for my Mother's good example, and implored
>   pardon for neglecting it.
> I returned thanks for the alleviation of my sorrow.
> The dream of my Brother I shall remember.

The two first are reverential observations, to be entered into and ticked off, but the third strikes us, as it struck him, as a complete surprise. He does not say what form the dream took, but it was clearly memorable, and acted as a reproach for the artifice he had claimed when telling John Taylor, 'I have no brother.' That Easter, having finally moved from Gough Square to Staple Inn, he inscribed a prayer recalling them all to divine attention: 'I commend to thy fatherly goodness, my Father, my Brother, my Wife, my Mother.' He may have felt alone before, but now he really was solitary, with only their appearances in dreams to remind him of what was lost.[42]

In the *Idler* a different approach is clearly evident. Four days after the burial of his mother, he writes an essay on an affliction 'perhaps not necessary to be imparted to the publick', arguing that, while we may attempt to 'look with indifference on external things' and 'conceal our sorrow', nothing can assuage it. The following *Idlers* are even more sombre in tone, reminding readers that 'the night cometh when no man can work', that 'overburthened by the weight of life' we all 'shrink from recollection' and 'wish for an art of forgetfulness'.[43] His mother's death and funeral involved him in debts which he needed urgently to discharge. He had promised Lucy Porter 'twelve guineas' for curative measures, but added a further twenty when he received the news that these had failed and his mother had died. 'I [would] have done what you suppose my dear Mother would have directed,' he wrote on 27 January. A week later he wrote again, having 'nothing particular to say', only the desire to 'correspond with my dear Lucy, the only person now left in the world with whom I think myself connected'. He wanted everything to stay the same at Lichfield, with 'Kitty' (Catherine Chambers, his mother's former maid) continuing to carry on the book trade and living in the house; 'I shall not want to put her out of a house where she has lived so long and with so much virtue.' Above all, he insisted that Lucy herself should stay on 'in what part of the house you please' and flattered himself 'that you and I shall sometime pass our days together'. That thought gave him a certain comfort; he begged Lucy to continue in the old way, looking after affairs in the house and the shop, not bothering with accounts and receipts as she had so 'prudently' proposed. He wrote a week later, agreeing to all Lucy's ideas. 'I do not doubt but I shall like all that you do.' Again, a fortnight later, having received her inventory of 'little things' at the Breadmarket Street house: 'I could have taken your word for a matter of much greater value,' he insists, brushing aside her care to itemise the Johnson family goods. He begged her to go on, acting for him as she had done for his mother 'without the least scruple'. He relied absolutely 'upon your prudence' and felt sure they never would have reason 'to love each other less'. The tenderness he felt for her soothed his desolate mood and he urged her to write 'at least every week'; without her letters, he confided, he might be 'universally forgotten'. 'I am, Dear Sweet, your affectionate servant,' he signed off, varying this endearment with 'dear love', 'dear Miss' and 'dearest girl' in letters of the time, reviving an old-fashioned amour which, he assured her, might be prudently rekindled without the least scruple.[44]

The first person to be paid was Kitty; from his £20 he begged her to settle Sarah Johnson's 'London debts', after which she could 'close her mistress's account and begin her own'. To pay all these expenses Johnson had immediate need for substantial cash, and to get it he produced *The History of Rasselas, Prince of Abyssinia*. Boswell records Strahan saying Johnson wrote the book 'that with the profits he might defray the expence of his mother's funeral, and pay some little debts which she had left'. Joshua Reynolds said he composed it all 'in the evenings of one week, sent it to the press in portions as it was written, and had never since read it over'.[45] On 20 January Johnson recorded that he had spoken of it to Strahan 'last night'; three months later it went on sale, two small octavo volumes priced at five shillings, for which he received £100. He had £25 more for the second edition, which appeared two months later.[46] This was a time he needed all the skills of instant composition of which he liked often to boast. Visiting Oxford in July 1759, he asked Langton how long it was until the post went. On being told half an hour, 'he exclaimed "then we shall do very well"', sat down and wrote an *Idler*. When Langton expressed the wish to read it, he told him 'you shall not do more than I have done myself', folded it up and sent it.[47]

Rasselas has long been admired by critics who, nevertheless, differ as to its meaning. Its method is essentially that of comedy, declares one: 'Johnson recalls the distinctive manner of the oriental tale, but he does so in a delicate parody.' A second declares it to have 'the method of satire', which a third refines, invoking the name of Menippus. It has been linked to remote Greek allegories 'well known in the eighteenth century' and to nearer forms of literary pilgrimage, such as *Don Quixote* and *Robinson Crusoe*. All that is certain is that it is 'the most problematic' of his works.[48]

Johnson could write *Rasselas* quickly because the notion of an oriental moral tale, full, not of action but axioms, had long been in his mind. The plot contains few events and the one notable incident which does occur, the abduction of Pekuah by a troop of marauding Arabs, is treated with no hint of the sensations that flourish in the novels of Aphra Behn or John Cleland. Instead of details of threatened rape or lengthy torture Johnson has Imlac, operating throughout as a reflective, reasonable man, observing that 'our minds, like our bodies, are in continual flux; something is hourly lost, and something acquired'. Pekuah is restored to the company of her friends four chapters later for the price of two hundred ounces of gold, and this exchange, which might have been treated by Fielding or even Fanny Burney with narrative excitement, is handled by Johnson with no more drama than may be accommodated by a pair of well-wrought adages.

Not that the work is devoid of narrative incidents. It has moments of great comedy, as when a supremely confident artist, having fashioned wings for himself, leaps from a high rock in the expectation of flying, and 'in an instant dropped into the lake'; or when Imlac, feeling the 'enthusiastic fit' upon him, expounds 'the business of a poet' at such inordinate length that young Rasselas suddenly stands up and cries 'Enough! Thou hast convinced me, that no human being can ever be a poet.' On their journey the travellers are frequently surprised by incidents that, starting in comedy, end in something bleaker; yet such episodes may of instructional value. 'Discontent . . . will not always be without reason under the most just or vigilant administration of publick affairs.'[49]

Rasselas is a philosophic tale in which events occurring to Rasselas, Imlac, Nekayah and Pekuah are less important than the sentiments derived from them. For Rasselas, entombed within the Happy Valley, suffers the feeling that he has 'enjoyed too much'; the very happiness of his existence becomes a form of malignity: 'Give me something to desire,' he cries; 'I shall long to see the miseries of the world.' As the four innocent travellers set forth from the happy valley which is so perfect as to have become tedious, they seek a form of useful occupation with which to satisfy their lives. From reading pastoral myths they visualise the lives of ancient shepherds as embodiments of their ideal and rush to try the pastoral life, but they suffer rapid disillusionment. Observing shepherds tending their flocks they quickly find the hearts of those they watch are 'cankered with discontent', for they are 'condemned to labour for the luxury of the rich': what functions well enough as a literary trope is not the same when experienced as reality. Similarly, when they try out the wisdom of hermits they discover not solitude and contemplation but bitterness and vanity; 'the life of a solitary man will be certainly miserable, but not certainly devout.' About the lives of academics Imlac is rightly sceptical; 'they discourse like angels', he says of the professors, 'but they live like men.' At times Imlac's paradoxes are playful; inconsistencies, he notes, 'cannot both be right, but, imputed to man, they may both be true'. More often he utters sentiments which carry all the weight of Johnson's melancholia: 'Human life is everywhere a state in which much is to be endured, and little to be enjoyed.'[50]

At times it seems all Imlac's assertions have the imprint of Johnsonian obsessions. Encouraging Rasselas's efforts to escape the Happy Valley, he declares: 'He that shall walk with vigour three hours a day will pass in seven years a space equal to the circumference of the globe', an insight of which Johnson was fond, having tried out a variant in the *Adventurer* six years before. Testing out his calculations, Birkbeck Hill estimated Johnson 'must have reckoned vigorous walking at the rate of a little over three miles an hour'. Walking and performing repeated acts of mental calculation were among Johnson's most frequent methods of asserting control over his mind. 'When Mr Johnson felt his fancy, or fancied he felt it, disordered', says Mrs Thrale, 'his constant recurrence was to the study of arithmetic.'[51]

In Egypt the travellers are confronted by the pyramids in all their magnificent uselessness. Imlac, voicing another of Johnson's favourite tropes, declares that they seem

> . . . to have been erected only in compliance with that hunger of imagination which preys incessantly upon life . . . He that has built for use till use is supplied, must begin to build for vanity . . . I consider this mighty structure as a monument of the insufficiency of human enjoyments.

That sentiment, apparently so perfectly in place, had been anticipated by the *Idler* only weeks before: 'Where necessity ends curiosity begins, and no sooner are we supplied with everything that nature can demand, than we sit down to contrive artificial appetites.'[52]

A central debate in *Rasselas* concerns marriage, in which princess Nekayah articulates Johnson's thoughts, with only minimal disguise. 'Marriage has many pains, but celibacy has no pleasures,' she declares, tilting the balance, ever so slightly, in the former institution's favour. Personally, it was Johnson's view that 'even ill assorted marriages were preferable to cheerless celibacy'. Those who marry late 'are best pleased with their children', she says, and Johnson recalls his childhood; 'those who marry early, with their partners', she concludes and he tries, but fails, to recall his first happy days with Tetty.[53]

Imlac shifts the subject of debate away from marriage, reminding his fellow travellers that 'while you are making the choice of life you neglect to live'. He reflects: 'no mind is much employed upon the present: recollection and anticipation fill up almost all our moments.' This is one of several moments when *Rasselas* recalls sentiments from the *Rambler*; we 'relieve the vacuities of our being by recollection of former passages, or anticipation of events to come'. And if Imlac should ever seem to lack intelligence (the likelihood seems small), his powers of analysis are aided by an astronomer from Cairo, whose 'comprehension is vast, his memory capacious and retentive, his discourse is methodical, and his expression clear'. This astronomer, feeling the approach of old age and seeing the precision with which Imlac performs his duties, volunteers to pass on secrets entrusted to him alone. These include such celestial mysteries as the regulation of the weather, the division of the seasons and the command of the motions of the sun, which passes 'from tropic to tropic by my direction'. At last he has found 'a man of wisdom and virtue, to whom I can cheerfully bequeath the inheritance of the sun'. Nekayah, who hears him, smiles; Pekuah too finds herself 'convulsed . . . with laughter'; but Imlac, feeling neither mirth nor sorrow, observes that 'of the uncertainties of our present state, the most dreadful and alarming is the uncertain continuance of reason'.

> Disorders of intellect . . . happen much more often than superficial observers will easily believe. Perhaps, if we speak with rigorous exactness, no human mind is in its right state. There is no man whose imagination does not sometimes predominate over his reason, who can regulate his attention wholly by his will, and whose ideas will come and go at his command.[54]

Madness was the disorder Johnson most deeply feared. It was, says Boswell, 'the evil most to be dreaded'. Mrs Thrale noted Johnson's overanxiety to 'retain without blemish the perfect sanity of his mind' and said he watched out for 'diseases of the imagination' with a 'solicitude destructive of his own peace, and intolerable to those he trusted'.[55]

Towards the end of the tale, the travellers come to judge which *choice of life* has come through their journeys least disadvantaged; Imlac forbears 'to force upon them unwelcome knowledge, which time itself would soon impress'. 'None are happy', is the lesson

Nekayah has learnt, 'but by the anticipation of change: the change itself is nothing; when we have made it, the next wish is to change again.' Pekuah is drawn to a convent of pious maidens whereas Nekayah wishes to preside over a college of learned women. Rasselas desires a 'little kingdom' which he may rule 'in his own person', while Imlac and the astronomer are content 'to be driven along the stream of life without directing their course to any particular port'. Naturally, none of these wishes is fulfilled: 'of these wishes . . . they well knew that none could be obtained', and the four decide to return to Abyssinia for want of a better resolution. It is, as the chapter heading indicates, a conclusion 'in which nothing is concluded'.[56]

Many of the tenets articulated in *Rasselas* are given a stoic setting by Johnson as he considers his solitary life now that his mother, his last blood relative, has gone. In the *Idler* some weeks earlier he had considered the advantages of a life led in company against one lived in isolation but had come to no definite opinion. One thing he knew; he longed for an end to the dreams of father, brother, wife and mother which now continually tormented him. 'In solitude', he wrote, conscious he wrote of himself, 'we have our dreams to ourselves'; 'O Lord, let not my sorrow be without fruit.' His only comfort came on nights without dreams, when he enjoyed the bliss of utter forgetfulness; but now he was a man alone and more voices called to him in sleep than ever visited in the light of day.[57]

IO

The Pensioner

pension n.s. *(pension, Fr.) An allowance made to any one without an equivalent. In England it is generally understood to mean pay given to a state hireling for treason to his country.*

pensioner n.s. *(from pension) 1. One who is supported by an allowance paid at the will of another; a dependant. 2. A slave of state hired by a stipend to obey his master.*

'There is not, perhaps, among the multitudes of all conditions that swarm upon the earth, a single man who does not believe that he has something to relate of himself.' Writing this in the *Idler* gave Johnson pause, particularly when he followed it by his observation, which long experience seemed to prove, that 'let any man tell his own story' and 'nothing of all this' would be told. From the moment the last member of his family, his mother, died, his wish to have his own life memorialised came to be a minor obsession. 'Biography is, of the various kinds of narrative writing, that which is most eagerly read, and most easily applied to the purposes of life.' Quietly, and without conscious motive other than these occasional essays on the art, he began searching for someone who might measure up to his own existence, which, he felt certain, would consort well with 'the purposes of life'.[1]

'I have this day moved my things,' he told Lucy near the end of March 1759, giving her his new address at Staple Inn. He wrote again to thank her for her letters and to send copies of *Rasselas* to her, Kitty, Mr Howard (for help with the funeral) and Lucy Hunter, Tetty's sister-in-law, who had been with his mother when she died. He had been hindered, 'I hardly know how', from replying to her letters, but begged her not to cease from writing. *Lloyd's Evening Post* flattered him as the author of *Rasselas* ('Johnson his oriental pearl displays/ And shines a glory of unsully'd rays'), which may partially have offset reproaches from the *Critical Review*, whose readers might be decoyed 'into a kind of knowledge they had no inclination to be acquainted with'. But nothing could deflect the painful impact of Owen Ruffhead's comments in the *Monthly Review*: 'He wants that graceful ease, which is the ornament of romance; and he stalks in the solemn buskin, when he ought to tread in the light sock.'[2] 'Criticism is a study by which men grow important and formidable at very small expence,' Johnson remarked: 'No genius was ever blasted by the breath of crit-icks.' These experiences persuaded him to pen his most memorable *Idler*, on the dubious subject of pleasure. 'Nothing is more hopeless than a *scheme* of merriment,' he said; all that is possible for mortals is hope, as he had always known: 'It is necessary to hope, tho' hope should always be deluded, for hope itself is happiness, and its frustrations, however frequent, are less dreadful than its extinction.'[3]

In his prayer for Easter Day that year he confessed he was 'a sinner', beseeching Heaven's grace 'to break the chain of evil custom', begging his mother should not suffer 'by my fault'. He wrote a sheet of 'Scruples' which besought God's aid to enable him to break 'the chain of my sins' and 'reject sensuality'. 'Every revived idea reminds us of a time when something was enjoyed that is now lost,' he wrote in the *Idler*; 'overburthened by the weight of life, all shrink from recollection, and all wish for an art of forgetfulness.'[4]

Private opinions on *Rasselas* were divided: 'tell me', wrote Hester Mulso to her friend Elizabeth Carter, 'whether, with all your venera-tion for the author, you were not grievously disappointed in it?' Johnson, unheeding or unaware of such reactions, spent time in com-pany with literary friends. Thomas Percy, the ascetic and hot-tempered chaplain to the Earl of Sussex, dined with him in February, took tea with him and Mrs Williams on 1 March and called again the following day, separating these visits by viewing a live crocodile.[5] In June Johnson decamped to Oxford, which was rapidly becoming his second home, and stayed there seven weeks, wearing his 'new and handsome' MA gown 'almost *ostentatiously*'. He swam three times in the river and invited the thirty-year-old Robert Vansittart, Fellow of All Souls

College, to climb the college walls, 'but he has refused me'. Johnson, at fifty, was living out the exuberant excesses of the Oxford education that had been denied him all those years before, and doing it with gusto. 'I have clapped my hands till they are sore,' he reported of his attendance at the Chancellor's installation, revelling in his ability to attend such a ceremony. Yet, at the same time, he confided to Lucy that he had 'no great pleasure in any place', urging her 'to write to me often' for he had 'no greater pleasure than to hear from you'.[6]

Johnson's sense of fun was eager and boisterous, often striving for a kind of rivalry with men far younger than himself. Years before he had enjoyed a night of frolics with Topham Beauclerk and Bennet Langton: the pair had been supping at a London tavern 'till about three in the morning' before they noisily came to seek him out and 'rapped violently at the door of his chambers' until he appeared 'in his shirt, with his little black wig on the top of his head instead of a nightcap, and a poker in his hand'. When told their business, he announced, 'What, is it you, you dogs! I'll have a frisk with you.' The three of them then wandered into Covent Garden, drank a bowl of 'bishop' (made of wine, oranges and sugar) at a tavern, took to the Thames and rowed to Billingsgate, singing all the way,

> Short, O short then be thy reign,
> And give us to the world again.

Garrick, hearing of the frolic, announced 'You'll be in the *Chronicle*', to which Johnson riposted that he 'durst not do such a thing. His *wife* would not *let* him'. At the time Johnson must have been in his mid-forties, yet behaved as though he were twenty years younger, the decade of struggle, from leaving Oxford until meeting Richard Savage, simply wiped from his memory.[7]

Coming back to London he was hurt by the reception granted to *Rasselas*. Words 'are only hard to those who do not understand them', he argued, inviting any critic who was so troubled to ask himself 'whether he is incommoded by the fault of the writer, or by his own'. In September, in a paper devoted to the memory, he wrote a sentence capable of interesting psychoanalysis: 'No man will read with much advantage, who is not able, at pleasure, to evacuate his mind, or who brings not to his author an intellect defecated and pure, neither turbid with care nor agitated by pleasure.'[8] In the *Dictionary* neither 'defecate' ('to purge liquors from lees or foulness; to cleanse) nor 'evacuate' ('to make empty; to clear') is given a specifically faecal meaning, though Johnson's bowels were causing serious disturbance at the time and Reynolds was suddenly called upon to replace him as writer of the *Idler*. 'Johnson required them [the *Idler*s] from him on a sudden emergency, and on that account he sat up the whole night'. Reynolds recalled writing numbers 76, 79 and 82; but[9] Johnson was back in charge by November, slipping in an ironic reference to his favourite beverage, tea, as a certain destroyer of female beauty and virtue. In the next paper he composed an essay on a subject which was coming to obsess him, biography, noting that the narratives he found of greatest value were those 'in which the writer tells his own story', though no man, he reflected, could honestly be 'a hero to himself'. What was required was *another* man, sufficiently close, as he had been to Savage, and yet sufficiently detached to write from his own point of view; someone who would sit down, 'calmly and voluntarily to review his life for the admonition of posterity'. Silently he began to seek out such a man, or woman.[10]

He had struck into other veins of literary exploration, and quickly wrote laments for the current proliferation of books ('surely there ought to be some bounds to repetition') and calls for the end of slavery ('of black men the numbers are too great who are now repining under English cruelty').[11] He became involved in a controversy as to whether elliptical or semicircular arches were superior for the construction of the new Blackfriars Bridge and gave his opinion in a forthright manner, inviting those 'who may still doubt' which of the two designs were stronger 'to press an egg first on the ends, and then upon the sides'.[12] But the matter of biography preoccupied him, and he returned to it in his penultimate *Idler*. 'Few authors write their own lives,' he meditated; the author, 'however conspicuous, or however important', left his life 'to be related by his successors'.[13]

The hardships of the naval life, mentioned to Smollett when he begged that Francis Barber's 'delicate frame' might be spared, were cited in advertisements for *The World Displayed*, a compilation of voyages of discovery made before Columbus. In his introduction to the volume, Johnson went out of his way to comment on the barbarities of the Portuguese who 'murdered the negroes in wanton merriment', scarcely considering them 'as distinct from beasts'. Their attitude, he noted, 'however wicked and injurious, still continues to prevail. Interest and pride harden the heart, and it is vain to dispute against avarice and power.'[14] Barber's plight would not be lessened by efforts of the recently founded Marine Society to obtain 'a supply of two or three thousand mariners for the Navy', and Johnson's view of the naval life remained resolutely hostile: 'No man will be a sailor who has contrivance enough to get himself into a jail; for being in a ship is being in a jail, with the chance of being drowned.'

He wrote to George Hay, a lord of the Admiralty, petitioning him to discharge Frank Barber, a 'Negro Boy' whom he had treated 'with great tenderness'; 'as he is no seaman', he wrote, it all might be transacted 'with little injury to the King's Service'. But Barber, described in the Muster Books as 'L.M.' (Landman), remained in the navy for another six months and, when he was discharged, made it clear it was 'without any wish of his own'. Deprived of his assistance, Johnson made another move about this time, to Gray's Inn, where his slovenly habits were observed by a Mrs C— who, being a subscriber to his *Shakespeare*, wished to meet the author. She went accompanied by a Mr M—.

The parties accordingly arrived at Johnson's chambers in Gray's Inn about one o'clock; when, after thundering at the outer door for near a quarter of an hour, Mr M— at last peeped through the key-hole, and observed Johnson just issuing from his bed, in his shirt, without a night-cap . . . the *pot de chambre* in one hand and the key in the other. In this situation he unlocked the door, when, spying a lady, he gravely turned round, 'begged she would walk into another room, and he would have the pleasure of waiting on her immediately.'

As soon as ever Mrs C— had recovered her surprise, she observed to Mr M—, 'what a fortunate thing it was for her that Johnson's milliner had not cheated him of his linen as much *before* as she had *behind*.'[15]

Johnson's political attitudes were equally unkempt. Summoned by the publishers of the *British Magazine* to write a piece for their first number, he contributed an essay on 'The Bravery of the English Common Soldier' in which the word 'common' receives special attention. Johnson boasts of 'a kind of epidemick bravery' diffused through all the ranks of English soldiery, showing that a 'peasantry of heroes' may 'vie with that of their general'. Wars this common soldier fights in may be misconceived, but his valour cannot be faulted; the 'equality of English privileges' means he recognises few superiors, and thinks no better of 'his leader than of himself'. Born 'without a master' he seeks 'no protection from others', and those who, in peacetime, complain of his insolence should remember that 'insolence in peace is bravery in war'.[16] Shortly afterwards he wrote an equally eloquent tribute to the English common soldier's antagonist when asked to do so by Thomas Hollis from the Committee on French Prisoners. John Wesley had recently visited these prisoners at Bristol and seen 'above eleven hundred of them ... confined in that little place, without any thing to lie on but a little dirty straw, or anything to cover them but a few foul, thin rags'. The result was that 'they died, like rotten sheep'. Hollis was a republican, Wesley a Methodist, and the prisoners they commented on were mainly Catholics; what better defender could they have to write on their behalf than a Tory member of the Church of England? Johnson performed the task willingly and eloquently. 'For prisoners of war', he wrote,

> there is no legal provision; we see their distress, and are certain of its cause; we know that they are poor and naked, and poor and naked without a crime ... let animosity and hostility cease together; and no man be longer deemed an enemy, than while his sword is drawn against us.

It is testimony to his words that, two centuries later, they are reprinted, in French, in the official journal of the International Red Cross.[17]

Johnson, who received five guineas for the piece, was always prepared to defend Hollis, who 'would not have done harm to a man whom he knew to be of very opposite principles to his own'. The money must have been very welcome, and the idea of having shirts and greatcoats distributed to the prisoners may have seemed ironically appealing for, at the time, he himself was desperately poor. Murphy tells how one visitor to Johnson 'found an author by profession without pen, ink, or paper'; Johnson's notes of hand, indicating debts to Newbery of £30 and £40, suggest a man on the brink of destitution.[18] Frances Reynolds tells a story that she, her brother Joshua and Johnson called one day on Frances and Charlotte Cotterell, and that Johnson was the last to enter.

> When the servant maid, seeing this uncouth and dirty figure of a man, and not conceiving he could be one of the company . . . laid hold of his coat just as he was going up the stairs, and pulled him back again, saying, 'You, fellow, what is your business here? I suppose you intended to rob the house.'

Sir Joshua told another story of the visit which has much the same impact. The Misses Cotterell were engrossed in the company of the Duchess of Argyll, and neglected Johnson as 'low company of whom they were somewhat ashamed'. Johnson lowered himself to meet such callous condescension by addressing himself loudly to Reynolds and asking, 'How much do you think you and I could get in a week, if we were to *work as hard* as we could?' The role of the 'common man' – whether soldier or mechanic – was one Johnson greatly affected; first, because, being poor, he was not much above them; second because, being angry, he could understand their resentment; and third because being human he reached out to their sufferings. He could examine the bindings of a book and recollect it to be 'the work of his own hands' because he was one of the few, in the eighteenth century or now, who knew not only how to write but how to print and bind the books he treated so cavalierly. When the playwright Arthur Murphy first met Johnson, he found him 'all covered with soot like a chimney-sweeper, in a little room, with an intolerable heat and strange smell'.[19]

Johnson had first come to know Reynolds some four years earlier when having his portrait painted, and the two men had become close friends, despite the evident, and vast, difference in their incomes. Originally from Plympton, in Devon, Reynolds lived and had his studio at Leicester Square, from where he painted all the most fashionable people in society; but, though mixing with the aristocracy, Reynolds's own pleasures were quite plebeian and he was addicted to cards. If 'there was a Pharo table' in the room, a fellow artist remarked, Reynolds was sure to leave behind 'whatever money He had abt. him'. He dressed in a slovenly fashion and, what may have drawn Johnson to him particularly, was partially deaf, often, in later years, affecting a silver ear-trumpet. Under Reynolds's direction Johnson became a member of the Society of Arts, though often neglecting to pay his annual subscription. In 1760 the Society's first exhibition opened to crowds of people and its minutes ordered thanks to 'be returned to Mr. Johnson for his great assistance'. On George III's accession, Johnson wrote an 'Address' to the king from 'painters, sculptors and architects', but he found little pleasure in the visual arts.[20] Commenting on the second exhibition, he told Baretti that Reynolds, being 'without a rival', continued to add 'thousands to thousands' and the exhibition 'has filled the heads of Artists and lovers of art. Surely life, if it be not long, is tedious, since we are forced to call in the assistance of so many trifles to rid us of our time.' Visiting a friend in Twickenham, Johnson ran eagerly to the bookshelves 'intent on poring over the backs of books', observing which, Sir Joshua remarked that he had the advantage, for 'I can see much more of the pictures than he can of the books'. Johnson's interest in the sudden public enthusiasm for painting may simply have been recording a particular curiosity; more importantly, he was fascinated, trying to work out what it was that made people pay 'thousands' to Reynolds, 'which he deserves', he quickly added. All the same, it caused him to wonder that, having written the *Dictionary*, he now languished in debt, and his edition of Shakespeare might never see the light.[21]

Later that year he moved again, renting rooms at No. 1, Inner Temple Lane for an annual charge of fifteen or sixteen guineas, but the change of address brought no improvement in conditions. A Cambridge student, visiting Johnson to discuss Plutarch, described 'a dark and dingy looking old wainscotted ante-room, through which was the study'; the artist Ozias Humphry told how he had to cross 'three very dirty rooms' to come to one 'that looked like an old counting house' where Johnson was taking his breakfast – a little after noon – and noticed particularly Johnson's stockings, hanging down about his feet. But though his dress was slovenly, his conversation was quite the opposite; 'everything he says is as *correct* as a *"second edition"*.'[22] On his birthday he made himself a set of resolutions, among which was to 'Rise as early as I can' and to 'oppose laziness, by doing what is to be done', indicating he knew well enough what *ought* to be done and, by writing it down *three times*, made a show of doing it. He also resolved 'To apply to Study' and according to Thomas Birch was 'in treaty with certain booksellers' to produce 'three papers a week in the nature of essays like the *Rambler*, at the unusual rate (if my account be true) of three guineas a paper'. But Birch questioned 'whether even the temptation of so liberal a reward will awaken him from his natural indolence'. He was quite correct; Johnson may have toyed with the idea of producing more essays, just as he resolved 'To reclaim imagination' and 'To drink less strong liquours', but the reality was rather different. At least he had got Frank Barber back, though his appearance, to those not expecting to see him, was quite a shock. The Reverend Baptist Noel Turner called on him one day, to find Johnson had gone out: 'and when Francis Barber, his black servant, opened the door to tell me so, a group of his African countrymen were sitting around a fire in the gloomy ante-room; and on all turning their sooty faces at once to stare at me, they presented a curious spectacle.'

There were some twenty thousand black servants in London at the time, but whether they retained their original designation as slaves was hotly debated. 'No man is by nature the property of another,' Johnson declared in 1777, a judgement which the Somerset case, setting out a slave's legal rights to live alone and free without being sent back to slavery in the West Indies, would seem to bear out. Yet the *Gentleman's Magazine* still advertised a Negro boy for sale, for £32, in 1763, and 'a very agreeable negro girl' for thirty guineas five years later, right up until the date of that important case.[23]

'He who continues the same course of life in the same place, will have little to tell,' Johnson wrote in June to Baretti who, having sailed to Lisbon, was soon expected at Turin: 'One week and one year are very like another.'[24] But that was not entirely the case; little by little Johnson was becoming known, and he rather liked it. In October 'A Poetical Epistle to Samuel Johnson' appeared, written by Arthur Murphy, in which he was fulsomely celebrated:

> Whate'er you write, in ev'ry golden line
> Sublimity and Elegance combine.

Early the following year another poem appeared, entitled 'Anningait and Ajutt: A Greenland Tale', inscribed to him, in which his praises were sung even louder:

> O! Johnson, fam'd for Elegance and Sense,
> Whose Works, Instruction and Delight dispense . . .[25]

'Men will submit to any rule, by which they may be exempted from the tyranny of caprice and of chance,' Johnson continued to Baretti, disavowing any pleasure in these signs of public notice; 'I cannot but hope that a good life might end at last in a contented death.' To reconcile himself to living he went to the theatre 'more than in former seasons', going, he claimed, not in hopes of being entertained, but 'only to escape from myself'.[26] He saw Thomas Sheridan twice, once in *Cato*, once in *Richard III*, but thought the pleasure limited. Sheridan's voice lacked dignity and elegance; when strained, it was 'unpleasing, and when low is not always heard. He seems to think too much on the audience', Johnson wrote to Langton, 'and turns his face too often to the Galleries.' Sheridan, father to the playwright Richard Brinsley Sheridan, did not seriously disagree, wishing only to shift the blame: 'Acting is a poor thing in the present state of the stage,' he told Boswell, his attitude no doubt affected by an unacknowledged jealousy of Garrick; 'I don't value acting.' Mrs Thrale records Johnson arguing behind the theatre scenes one night while Garrick was playing Lear; asked at last to 'have done with all this Rattle' which destroyed 'his *Feelings*', Johnson replied he knew better. '*Punch* has no *feelings*,' he declared. Johnson also attended George Colman's *The Jealous Wife* which, though 'not written with much genius', was, he admitted, so well acted 'that it was crowded for near twenty nights'.[27]

In July 1761 Richardson died ('dead of an apoplexy') and Robert Levet, aged almost sixty, married 'not without much suspicion that he has been wretchedly cheated in his match'. The suspicions were largely accurate; the marriage ended shortly afterwards in separation from the woman, who was acquitted of a pick-pocketing charge, leaving Levet various debts.[28] In their place new people came into Johnson's life, amongst whom Thomas Percy and Oliver Goldsmith were the most notable. Percy, vicar of Easton Maudit in Northamptonshire, began his literary career publishing pieces from Chinese sources, but his main interest was in old English ballads; Goldsmith, an Irishman with what were unflatteringly described as 'monkey' features, had, like Johnson, undergone humiliation at Oxford where, a sizar at Trinity College, he had had to wait at the Fellows' table. Both were welcomed in by Johnson who advised Percy to publish his 'old ballads', reckoning he should get 'for the copy two pounds a sheet'. He followed up this bold pronouncement with a page of carefully worked-out calculations. The result of such lavish expectations was that Dodsley broke off all negotiations but, nothing daunted, Johnson continued his dealings with Andrew Millar. He reported back to Percy that Millar was 'well disposed' to the project and made 'no objection' to the price of 'an hundred guineas'. In May Percy arrived in London and together they conferred about the ballads, took tea with Miss Williams and met Charles Macklin the actor who, as Johnson related, had been '2 or 3 and 20 before he learnt to read'. Percy's letters and diaries of the visit mention many tactical preliminaries to renewed negotiations; 'held a council of war with Mr Johnson,' he reported back to his friend, the poet William Shenstone; 'bargained with Dodsley' and 'Called on Mr Millar', he noted, before finally, on Friday 22 March, 'Sold Dodsley my old ballads'. He told Shenstone that he and Johnson had talked of taking a journey to the Leasowes estate which Shenstone famously adorned, but warned him not to depend on it; 'he is no more formed for long journeys than a tortoise.'[29]

On the following Monday Percy, having completed his business, called on Goldsmith and together the two of them paid a visit to the exhibition of paintings at Spring Gardens. In return, Goldsmith invited Percy to ask Johnson to attend a dinner party at his home in Wine Office Court, for which Johnson dressed himself with great care, wearing a new suit and a new, well-powdered wig. Taxed by Percy on this sudden transformation, Johnson replied that he heard Goldsmith, 'who is a very great sloven', justified his neglect of cleanliness 'by quoting my practice'; he was desirous 'this night to show him a better example'. The day before, Goldsmith had visited Garrick, who was rehearsing *King Lear*, and picked up a subscription from John Orlebar of Bedfordshire for Johnson's edition of Shakespeare, which continued to accept such occasional contributions. Johnson received three more from Warton, who had them from John Ash the physician, and was able to comment, optimistically, to Baretti in July 1762, 'I intend that you shall soon receive Shakespeare.'[30]

That Easter he poured out the wretched feelings of loneliness that assailed him: 'I have led a life so dissipated and useless,' he prayed, 'my terrours and perplexities have so much encreased, that I am under great depression and discouragement.' He purposed 'steadfastly' to 'lead a new life' but his hopes, given the practice of recent years, cannot have been sanguine; in a letter to Baretti he confessed to living 'without the concurrence of my own judgment', ruled only by 'the tyranny of caprice'. One effect of this was a quick-tempered resentment at sudden fame, especially *literary* fame that anyone enjoyed; the much enlightened lady Miss Monkton greeted him one evening with an insistence that the first two volumes of Sterne's *Tristram Shandy* had greatly affected her. ' "Why," said Johnson, smiling and rolling himself about, "that is because, dearest, you're a dunce." ' Another thing which fascinated and a little discomposed him was the caprice which meant that his friend Reynolds should earn so much for, apparently, doing so little; his recurrent mention that he got 'six thousands a year' indicates a nagging feeling rather close to envy. Johnson's income for the same period was little more than £84, which must have left him always either borrowing or else in debt.

Such envy as he might have felt was briefly mollified by reading in the *St James's Chronicle* that Mr Garrick 'was willfully overturned in his Chair, as he was going to Drury-Lane Playhouse'. But, following the story further, his satisfaction would have abated; this 'outrage' was apparently committed by people desperate to see his *Lear* but 'who could not get in'. Such was Garrick's fame that, on the very day of the Coronation of George III, 'Hercules Vinegar' devoted his whole grumpy column in the *St James's Chronicle* to the actor's alleged appeal. 'Suppose Mr Garrick should some Evening stand forth and say "I am the best Actor the English Stage ever produced",' he remarked: 'though the Audience might be convinced of the Truth of the Assertion, do you not think he would stand a fair Chance to be handsomely pelted with Oranges and Apples?'[31]

Johnson thanked Percy for his invitation to Easton Maudit, but told him he was staying in London to be a witness to the 'great ceremony' of the coronation of George III. He had given serious thoughts to the staging of the ceremony in his pamphlet 'On the Coronation', which proposed a more extensive route for the royal procession in order that the monarch, not having 'crept to the temple through obscure passages', should be seen by as many people as possible accepting his role. 'Magnificence cannot be cheap,' he wrote; 'magnificence in obscurity is equally vain with *a Sun-dial in the Grave*.' He could not, however, neglect what he thought of as prudent economies, declaring that 'the excessive prices at which windows and tops of houses are now let, will be abated'. Excessive prices, though, were the order as the great day approached, even, or especially, within Westminster Abbey itself. The space of ground 'from the West-Gate to the Place where the Organ was fixed' was let out to have scaffolding built upon it 'for 2,500l'. *An Account of the Ceremonies observed in the Coronation of the Kings and Queens of England*, boasting of its '19 Cuts' or engraved illustrations, was offered for sale at the modest price of four guineas, and even warned potential readers to be very wary of cheap imitations. After the day of the coronation was over, a peeress advertised for the restitution of a much-bejewelled 'Drop of an Ear-Ring', which had been lost in all the excitement; she offered 'a reward of Fifty Guineas' to have it back. Johnson's pamphlet, priced at one shilling and sixpence (£7 in modern currency) may have been an example of his attempting, in a minor way, to cash in on the spectacle, yet sadly failing to gauge the true extent of human gullibility.

On Coronation Day, the number of carriages in the Strand 'was so great, that they extended without the least Intermission, from Parliament-street to Temple Bar' and 'it was not possible to cross the street in any Part'. A pregnant woman was so overcome that she fainted, but was immediately rescued 'by an Irish Drayman' who bore her up and 'carried her on his back to the first house he could find'. There she was delivered of a healthy boy and 'gave the Fellow a Guinea for his Trouble'. In New Palace-Yard a man ostensibly dressed for the occasion in 'a gold-laced Coat and Waistcoat' was attempting to pick a handkerchief from another man's pocket when he was detected, at which his potential victim 'delivered him over to the Mob, who carried him to the Thames' and there gave him 'a very severe Ducking'. Whether the organisers of the pageantry had read Johnson's pamphlet there is no way of knowing, but the procession was considerably longer and more glorious than on previous occasions. One hundred and twenty-four separate groups of people were listed, in their precise hierarchical order, as opposed to the 108 who had accompanied James II. Many of those who made up the procession were formal harbingers, like the king's herb-woman 'with her six maids', placed first in the long list of people, 'strewing sweet herbs, etc.'. The queen's position was number seventy-four in the list and the king himself was number eighty-one. The *St James's Chronicle* published a detailed list, with an illustration of how and where their lordships and ladyships ought to arrange themselves, in case they happened to forget.

Thirty cooks, with their assistants, toiled to produce the coronation feast and the offices of the Admiralty were illuminated with 250 lamps. Much of the ceremonial had begun earlier, when George had ascended the throne. The *Gentleman's Magazine* reported that 'upwards of three hundred prisoners from Ludgate, the two Compters and the Fleet were discharged at Guildhall by the Lord Mayor', and in June the numbers grew to 'near five hundred prisoners . . . discharged from the King's Bench prison, the New Gaol and Marshalsea' in October. Four hundred gold medals were specially minted for the king and the same number for the queen, 'one half to be thrown in the Abbey, the other in the Hall on the Day of the Coronation'; besides these, 'a greater Quantity of Silver ones are struck' to be tossed out 'amongst the Populace'. A courtier 'put on his armour' and 'tried a grey horse which his late Majesty' – that is, George II – 'rode at the battle of Dettingen' almost twenty years before, the last time a British monarch ever led his troops in battle. There were crowds of people throughout the city of Westminster, so that 'many persons who had places in the Hall, Abbey and scaffolding, were obliged to quit their coaches at Charing-cross, and press as well as they could through the crowd and dirt to their

Samuel Johnson by Joshua Reynolds, painted shortly after the publication of the *Dictionary* and disguising Johnson's many facial distortions. When William Hogarth first met Johnson he thought him 'an ideot . . . at that moment inspired.'

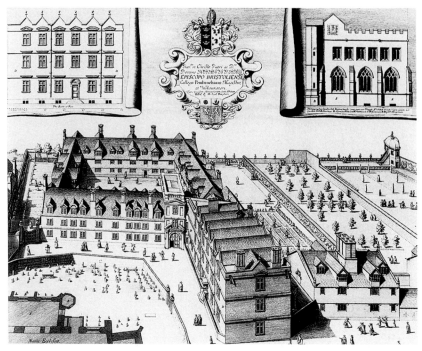

Pembroke College, Oxford, where Johnson was an undergraduate for just thirteen months in 1728–9, quitting for reasons of poverty.

Elizabeth 'Tetty' Porter who married Johnson in 1735. She was twenty years older than Samuel and their marriage was not particularly happy; but, as Johnson wrote, 'Marriage has many pains, but celibacy has no pleasures.'

Molly Aston, whom Johnson fell in love with in 1740. 'She was the loveliest creature I ever saw!!!'

THE

RAMBLER.

NUMB. I.   Price 2 *d.*

TUESDAY, *March* 20, 1749-50.

To be continued on TUESDAYS *and* SATURDAYS.

Cur tamen hoc libeat potiùs decurrere campo,
Per quem magnus equos Auruncæ flexit Alumnus,
Si vacat, et placidi rationem admittitis, edam.

                          Juv.

HE Difficulty of the firſt Addreſs, on any new Occaſion, is felt by every Man in his Tranſactions with the World, and confeſſed by the ſettled and regular Forms of Salutation, which Neceſſity has introduced into all Languages. Judgment was wearied with the inextricable Perplexity of being forced upon Choice, where there was often no Motive to Preference; and it was found convenient that ſome eaſy Method of Introduction ſhould be eſtabliſhed, which, if it wanted the Allurement of Novelty, might enjoy in its place the Security of Preſcription.

Perhaps few Authors have preſented themſelves before the Publick, without wiſhing that ſuch ceremonial Modes of

---

The *Rambler*, which Johnson wrote between 1750 and 1752, failed to achieve a large circulation, but satisfied his sense of the possibilities of journalism. His other works were wine and water but, he said, 'my *Rambler* is pure wine.'

A

DICTIONARY

OF THE

ENGLISH LANGUAGE:

IN WHICH

The WORDS are deduced from their ORIGINALS,

AND

ILLUSTRATED in their DIFFERENT SIGNIFICATIONS

BY

EXAMPLES from the best WRITERS.

TO WHICH ARE PREFIXED,

A HISTORY of the LANGUAGE,

AND

AN ENGLISH GRAMMAR.

BY SAMUEL JOHNSON, A. M.

IN TWO VOLUMES.

VOL. I.

Cum tabulis animum censoris sumet honesti;
Audebit quæcunque parum splendoris habebunt,
Et sine pondere erunt, et honore indigna ferentur,
Verba movere loco; quamvis invita recedant,
Et versentur adhuc intra penetralia Vestæ:
Obscurata diu populo bonus eruet, atque
Proferet in lucem speciosa vocabula rerum,
Quæ priscis memorata Catonibus atque Cethegis,
Nunc situs informis premit et deserta vetustas.   Hor.

LONDON,
Printed by W. STRAHAN,
For J. and P. KNAPTON; T. and T. LONGMAN; C. HITCH and L. HAWES;
A. MILLAR; and R. and J. DODSLEY.
MDCCLV.

Johnson's *Dictionary*, 1755; 'Dictionaries are like watches, the worst is better than none, and the best cannot be expected to go quite true.'

Charlotte Lennox, the young, ambitious American said 'unsubdu'd' she might 'control the world.' Johnson was one of many men who fell beneath her sway.

The house at Gough Square, London, where Johnson lived from 1746 and wrote the *Dictionary*.

David Garrick as Richard III: 'If Garrick really believed himself to be that monster, Richard the Third, he deserved to be hanged every time he performed it.' Garrick, one of the handful of pupils at Johnson's Edial school, journeyed with him to London in 1737.

Joshua Reynolds was Johnson's lifelong friend, though they differed in their favourite beverages: 'I did not count your glasses of wine,' said Johnson, 'why should you number up my cups of tea?'

Francis Barber, Johnson's servant, friend, and legatee. Granted his freedom in 1754, Barber lived almost his entire life as Johnson's servant, and was rewarded by being the principal beneficiary of his will.

Johnson (centre), Oliver Goldsmith, and Mrs. Thrale at Streatham; Johnson commented that when Goldsmith came into company he 'grows confused, and unable to talk.'

Johnson and Boswell, walking up Edinburgh High Street: 'I smell you in the dark!' The two men journeyed together through the Highlands of Scotland in 1773.

Mrs. Thrale and her daughter Queeney, 1781. Hester Thrale was the woman Johnson loved and broke with for ever when she married the Italian singer Piozzi. 'Oh poor Dr. Johnson!!!' she wrote on hearing of his death.

seats'. At Westminster Abbey sentries had been posted the previous week 'to prevent the Workmen being interrupted by the great Concourse of people' who pushed themselves forward for a glimpse of the place where the great ceremony was to take place. But the workmen, finding that they were thus 'deprived of what they called their Perquisites' by the fact that the sentries were 'taking the Money of those that were let in', stopped work, and said 'they would work no longer unless they were paid double Wages'. The authorities gave in, and double Wages were ordered 'till the Coronation Day'.

Despite the crowds it was generally reported that 'only three lives' were lost on the day; even convicted criminals had their executions delayed till after this time of 'great solemnity'. Thomas Daniel, found guilty on 16 September at the Old Bailey of murdering his wife, throwing her from a second-floor window on to the cobbles beneath, had his execution delayed until 2 October. Donald Campbell, once a lieutenant in the 42nd Highland regiment but subsequently fallen upon hard times, was found guilty of 'forging and counterfeiting a bill of exchange'; his poor education had let him down, for he had misspelt the names to whom the bills were payable. John Garnett of Ludgate Hill and John Ashworth were both acquitted of murder, but found guilty of manslaughter for having stabbed their victim 'in the belly, with a hay-fork'. Not all malefactors were so unfeeling, though; a certain Mr Lewis of Hammersmith was accosted by 'two Footpads' who rifled his pockets for 'a Moidore and six shillings', but then 'bad him good Night' and 'wished him well' before making off for Kensington. A man 'who plied about Newgate-Market' went into an alehouse in Bartholomew Close, 'called for a pint of beer, laid his head down upon the table, and expired immediately'. But generally the papers were more full of good than bad news. Horse-racing flourished up and down the country; at Lincoln the King's Plate 'of 100 guineas' was won 'by Mr Shaftoe's bay horse, Apollo' and on the same day, just a week before the coronation, there were also races at Derby, where £50 was won 'by Mr Simpson's bay filly, Pamela'. Not all horses fared so well; one, tethered to the railings by Covent Garden church, was stung so badly by flies it reared up, 'threw his head upon one of the iron spikes' and died 'in ten minutes'. Generally, though, the fates of lesser species, whether mammalian or reptilian, were a source of great merriment; twenty small boats eagerly 'pursued a Porpus' along the river Thames, starting below Greenwich and following 'a very diverting Chase' for a good two hours, before finally shooting him 'in one of his breathing Intervals above Water' and carrying him ashore 'in Triumph, to Rotherhithe'.

That August the *London Chronicle* praised Johnson, 'the best prose writer at present', but a skill for writing prose did not make for wealth. In the *Public Advertiser* Smollett might praise Johnson's 'Dignity, Strength and Variety of Stile', bewailing the fact that, not enjoying 'any share of the Royal Bounty', he remained 'exposed to all the Storms of Indigence, and all the Stings of Mortification'. But Johnson, for all the praise, remained desperately poor. Edmund Burke wrote in his review of *Rasselas* that he was appalled that the man who had improved British taste and whose life was employed 'in an astonishing work for the fixing the language of this nation' should have 'nothing' done for him by way of recompense.[32]

Johnson spent part of the winter revisiting Lichfield, where he had not been for twenty years, but the visit was intensely disappointing. 'I found the streets much narrower and shorter than I thought I had left them, inhabited by a new race of people, to whom I was very little known,' he wrote to Baretti:

> My play-fellows were grown old, and forced me to suspect, that I was no longer young. My only remaining friend has changed his principles, and was become the tool of the predominant faction. My daughter-in-law, from whom I expected most, and whom I met with sincere benevolence, has lost the beauty and gaiety of youth, without having gained much of the wisdom of age.

These feelings, recollected at a distance of months, still have the force of an overwhelming shock. It cannot be known exactly what thoughts he cherished in making this pilgrimage to his native city where the dear 'little Gipsy' lived to whom he had confided so much. But any tender thoughts were abruptly terminated. 'Miss Lucy is . . . a little dis-coloured by hoary virginity,' he wrote, some years later, to his then favourite, Hester Thrale. He left the city suddenly, after a mere five days, and returned to London where, if there were not much happiness to be found, 'there is at least such a diversity of good and evil, that slight vexations do not fix upon the heart'. He demanded of Baretti what had been his thoughts on first returning to his native country, and whether, 'when the first raptures of salutation were over, you did not find your thoughts confessed their disappointment'. His own feeling, in Lichfield, had been not only disappointment but radical shock to find the place, and people in it, so much older, and so *different* from the treasured memories he preserved. 'Nothing is little to him that feels it with great sensibility,' he wrote, trusting that a time would come when 'the present moment' would be no longer irksome, and 'we shall not borrow all our happiness from hope'.[33] In his prayer on the anniversary of Tetty's death, apart from listing the duties he *always* mentioned, but seldom achieved ('Labour diligently/ Rise early . . .'), there is self-laceration as he pleads 'that I may not be preserved to add wickedness to wickedness'.[34]

It was in this state that he was summoned to be amongst a group of sceptics examining a strange phenomenon hailed as the 'Cock Lane Ghost'. Johnson was undecided about the existence of ghosts, as Boswell mentions several times in the *Life*, giving Johnson's belief as being that while 'all argument is against it . . . all belief is for it'. Many celebrated people, including Horace Walpole and the Duke of York, saw and heard the story of the twelve-year-old girl who claimed to witness the knocks and tapping of poisoned 'Scratching Fanny', her medium. The newspapers were full of the story and the Lord Mayor of London gave directions that no expense was to be spared 'in detecting the Fraud, in order that due Punishment may be inflicted'. Stephen Aldrich and John Douglas (with whom Johnson had clashed over William Lauder) assembled with a dozen others to detect 'some enormous crime' and witnessed many strange events. One man was required to attend the spirit in the adjacent church of St John while women claimed to hear 'knocks and scratches' near the girl's bed. The girl herself declared she 'felt the spirit like a mouse upon her back'. But, on being required 'to hold her hands out of bed', the noises ceased and Johnson concluded that 'there is no agency of any higher cause'. He was satisfied it was a simple case of fraud, but his involvement in these events, and their notoriety, created a new public image for him. His long-standing antagonist Charles Churchill brought out a two-book poem, *The Ghost*, lampooning Johnson as 'Pomposo', 'Vain idol of a *scribbling* crowd':

> Who, proudly seiz'd of *Learning's* throne,
> Now damns all Learning but his own.[35]

Johnson remained very visible in the public prints; in March the *Universal Museum* had him leading forces against the powers of Dullness, in April *An Historical . . . Account . . . of the . . . Authors of Great Britain* believed the 'sagacity of his criticisms sufficiently proves his penetration', while in May the *Edinburgh Magazine* argued that 'the world has indeed been obliged to Mr. Johnson for many admirable instructions'. Such praise, though welcome, did not help him pay his bills. The April piece noted that 'though by no means in affluence, he is always ready to assist the indigent', and the *Edinburgh Magazine* lamented that his abilities were 'contracted by the necessity of writing for money'.[36]

The idea that he might gain a pension had already been largely canvassed in the press, with Smollett, Burke and the anonymous author of the *Edinburgh Magazine* all playing their part. The likelihood is, though, that a 'long and wordy anonymous letter' sent to the Earl of Bute in late 1761, lamenting that this 'truly great author' remained unpensioned, turned journalistic promptings into action. There may also have been a notion that granting a pension to the writer of *A Dictionary of the English Language* might help to put an end to the constant gibes against Bute's '*Scotch* pensioners'.[37] But acting upon such thoughts remained particularly difficult, given Johnson's own, very public, denunciation of a pension as '*pay given to a state hireling for treason to his country*'.

Arthur Murphy, chosen to sound out Johnson, went to his chambers 'which, in fact, were the abode of wretchedness' and disclosed the evolving plan to him. Johnson heard him patiently, asked 'if it was seriously intended?' and, on being assured that it was, said he would give his response the next day. Meanwhile he consulted Reynolds and was advised 'there could be no objection to his receiving from the King a reward for literary merit'. Whereupon he 'gave up all his scruples'. The following day Murphy '*got Johnson up, and dressed in due time*' to meet Lord Bute and thank him for the honour. In response to Johnson's query, 'What am I expected to do for this pension?' Bute assured him it was granted with no thought of political favours, present or to come, but 'for what you have done'. In writing to accept the pension of £300 a year Johnson once again insisted he had 'neither alliance nor interest' to earn royal favours, and that he had neither 'merited them by services' nor 'courted them by officiousness'. On Thursday came official word that 'His Majesty has been graciously pleased to settle a pension of 300£ per annum on Mr Samuel Johnson, a gentleman well known in the literary world'. He wrote that Saturday to Lucy up in Lichfield, in exultation that 'a pension was granted me of three hundred a year'.[38]

His immediate plan, no doubt dreamt up when he invited Reynolds's advice, was to join Sir Joshua on a long holiday tour of Devonshire and keep as far away as possible from any hostile criticism. Not that all comments were adverse; a friend of Charles Burney's wrote that he rejoiced 'at the prospect which the papers give us of Johnson's enjoying at last a decent independence'. Edward Blakeway told Thomas Percy he had not seen 'a piece of news that has given me so much pleasure'.[39] The *North Briton*, appearing just as Johnson and Reynolds made their final arrangements, merely mentioned that Johnson, '*a writer of reputation*', would have 'much to *unwrite*' at being 'thus nobly provided for'. It was not until the following week, by which time Johnson was travelling from Dorchester to Bridport, that the real criticism broke out. John Wilkes was contemptuous of Johnson's apostasy, which he presented as a 'steady attachment to the present Royal Family'.[40] He was answered on 2 September (by which time Johnson was at Plymouth, disputing with Mrs Mudge the rudeness of requesting an eighteenth cup of tea), by an anonymous letter in the *St James's Chronicle*, whose author, declaring 'solemnly' that he had not 'the least connection with' Johnson, suggested a note be added to the definition of *pension*, indicating 'a reward given to learned men for merit, worth, and genius'.[41] It was not until the end of September, when Johnson and Reynolds were travelling back to London, that the wittiest criticism of Johnson appeared in print: Churchill added a further book to *The Ghost* in which 'Pomposo' was attacked through ridicule:

How to all Principles untrue,
Nor fix'd to *old* Friends, nor to *New*,
He damns the *Pension* which he takes,
And loves the STUART he forsakes.

For good measure, Churchill made an additional point with a question which many people may have been asking:

He for *Subscribers* baits his hook
And takes their cash – but where's the Book?[42]

In later life Johnson made nothing of the protests that greeted his pension and said he wished that it 'were twice as large, that they might make twice as much noise'. Yet in the summer of 1762 he felt distinctly awkward, and was glad to be away from London. He would have felt yet more awkward had he known the pension came from a royal fund named 'Writers Political', his name being included in a list of 'Private Pensions, and Secret Service Money'.[43]

If the intention of the Devon journey was to escape the public uproar that greeted his pension, it also made him acquainted with parts of the country and people he had not previously known. Reynolds's notebook indicates the pair travelled via Winchester and Salisbury to Wilton, where they viewed a Reynolds portrait of Lord Pembroke; from Longford Castle and Blandford to Kingston Lacy, where they saw paintings by Lely and Van Dyck. Johnson was observed by Mr John Bankes, owner of the house at Kingston Hall where he and Reynolds stopped, making very strange manoeuvres,

> stretching out his legs alternately as far as he could possibly stretch; at the same time pressing his foot on the floor as heavily as he could possibly press, as if endeavouring to smooth the carpet, or rather perhaps to rumple it, and every now and then collecting all his force, apparently to effect a concussion of the floor.

Having observed him for some time, Mr Bankes assured him the floor would take his weight, whereupon Johnson immediately ceased his stretching.

From Dorchester Johnson and Reynolds travelled on past Bridport to Exeter and Torrington, where Reynolds had two sisters living, and on to Plymouth where they met John Mudge, a former schoolfellow, and stayed for the rest of the trip. Johnson formed a friendship with Zachariah Mudge, who preached a sermon in his church, St Andrew's, Plymouth, 'purposely that Johnson might hear him'; when Zachariah died, Johnson wrote his obituary for the *London Chronicle*. He also affected to be 'resolutely on the side of . . . the *established* town' in all disputes between Plymouth and the new Dock town of Devonport, two miles away. He talked 'warmly' of 'the *dockers*' as 'upstarts and aliens' and entered into local disputes over water supplies with great glee. 'No, no! I am against the *dockers*; I am a Plymouth-man. Rogues! let them die of thirst. They shall not have a drop.'[44]

It was on his trip to Devon that Johnson, luxuriating in the financial freedom which the pension gave him, became intoxicated for the first and only time that Reynolds ever saw. One night, after supper,

Johnson drank three bottles of wine, which affected his speech so much that he was unable to articulate a hard word which occurred in the course of conversation. He attempted it three times but failed, yet, at last accomplished it, and then said, 'well Sir Joshua I think it is now time to go to bed.'[45]

They sailed to the Eddystone lighthouse, but 'the weather was so tempestuous that they could not land'. On another occasion, walking in a garden, Johnson was asked if he was a botanist: 'No, Sir, (answered Johnson) I am not a botanist; and (alluding, no doubt, to his near sightedness) should I wish to become a botanist, I must first turn myself into a reptile.' The pair left Devon on 23 September and arrived back in London three days later, having been away precisely six weeks.

Johnson, having been somewhat lavish in his expenses during the Devon trip, was disappointed not to find the first instalment of his pension awaiting him on his return. He waited and, having received nothing by November, wrote to Lord Bute telling him the pension 'appointed to be paid me at Michaelmas' had not been received. Putting on his most obsequious act, he apologised profoundly for interrupting his lordship 'at a time like this with such petty difficulties' (on that day the preliminaries of the Peace of Paris, ending the Seven Years War, were signed); 'but . . . every man's affairs, however little, are important to himself. Every Man hopes that he shall escape neglect . . .' 'We all have good and evil', he wrote to Baretti the following month when, to judge by his sentiments, the pension had still not been paid; 'which we feel more sensibly than our petty part of public miscarriage or prosperity.' Not troubling himself with the matter of the war which 'extends itself to a very small part of domestic life', he comments on greatness ('negligent and contemptuous') and life at court, which 'is often languished away in ungratified expectation', comments which sound very like accusations of bad faith against Bute. 'Reynolds still continues to encrease in reputation and in riches,' he noted finally amid a number of gloomy comments ('Mr. Levet has married a street-walker . . . Bathurst went physician to the army, and died at the Havannah'). Baretti, writing back from Milan where he had heard about the pension but not about the difficulties involved in getting it, metaphorically shook his head. 'I am informed that you continue to live on in idleness', he wrote, 'and that you have not finished your Shakespeare. This, my Johnson, is blamable, very blamable.'[46]

Johnson, the pensioner, was now regularly mentioned in the press. The *St James's Chronicle* for January 1763 included a facetious piece listing various pensions, including 'Mr. Sheridan £200' and 'Mr. S. Johnson £300', lending validity to the story that on hearing of Sheridan's pension, Johnson declared: 'What, have they given *him* a pension? Then it is time for me to give up mine.' In the same paper, a fortnight later he was portrayed, in verse, as wanting just one art – 'the Art to hide/ Th' Emotions of scholastic Pride'.

> In general, his Diction's good,
> And generally understood:
> But sometimes five-feet Words offend
> Ears, which to Harmony attend;
> And readers of the softer Sex,
> With their enormous Length perplex.
> For instance now – Con-ca-te-na-tion
> Gives many a pretty Mouth Vexation.

He was mentioned in the *British Magazine*, the April number of the *North Briton* and in a copy of the *London Chronicle* that May, which linked Wilkes's animosity to the *Dictionary** to the definition it contained of a 'distiller' as 'one who makes and sells pernicious and inflammatory spirits'. Wilkes's father had been a distiller.[47]

* See Chapter Eight, p. 156.

Enter Boswell

genius n.s. *(Latin;* genie, *French.) A man endowed with superiour faculties.*

There is no little writer of Pindarick who is not mentioned as a prodigious *genius.*

Addison

'That I . . . am a wise man is an Axiom that I modestly presume cannot be contraverted,' wrote James Boswell to 'Dash' Erskine that July. It was the fourth letter he had written without receiving a reply, and he kept it brief, treating his non-correspondent 'as dead'. Which was decidedly depressing, for whom else might Boswell pester with accounts of his literary and amatory adventures, written in his best Roman style, other than his fellow member of the gloriously named Soaping Club in Edinburgh? 'Dash' had been his sounding-board; to 'Dash' he had told how in London he had plotted to become a Papist priest, and would have done so too, had not the pleasures of fornication risen up to foil his plans. To 'Dash' he had proclaimed, on reaching the age of twenty-one, that he believed himself 'one of the greatest geniuses in Europe'. And now, silence? 'I pronounced my Conclamatum est,' he wrote; it was all over.[1]

It was particularly galling as he had much news to pass on to his fellow Soaper. Since he had fallen in with parental wishes and agreed to study civil law (he had no plans *whatsoever* of practising it), life had been quite tolerable. His father had spent a lot refurbishing their mansion at Auchinleck (he insisted on pronouncing it, in the old style, as *Affleck*) and it was now pretty decent. If only it weren't so far from London, or from anywhere where people knew how to live. Ayrshire might just as well be Iceland. He longed to know the fate of their *Original Poems* by 'Scotch Gentlemen', and of his own *The Cub at Newmarket*, a fiction based partly on his own adventures, more importantly on his vivid imagination. In the absence of any other entertainment he had done what young men do, which had been why he wrote to his medical friend John Cairnie to 'concert a plan' about his 'little affair'. Peggy Doig was pretty enough, and he would do what he could to help her, financially. But 'Dash' hadn't, surely, believed 'the report of my marriage'? He burst out in rather awkward mirth. The whole thing just proved to him that he must go and let his genius shine and sparkle among those who would truly appreciate it.[2]

At last, after much pestering, his father did agree to let his son go down to London, provided he passed his examination in civil law, which Boswell promptly did; he even furnished him with an annual allowance of £200, which Alexander Boswell, eighth Laird of Auchinleck, considered truly munificent, but which Jamie Boswell regarded as mean in the extreme. Why, stockings and shoes cost him £40 a year – and that was in Edinburgh! In letters to 'Dash' he confessed to feeling an 'uncommon distaste' for rural life, longed for 'the variety and hurry of a town' and mused over the 'delicious prospects' of life in France or Italy. In a final letter before he left, Boswell confessed that he and 'Dash' were 'to be sure, somewhat vain'; he paused. 'We have some reason, too,' he said, delighting in the 'fine animated prospect of life' that 'now spreads before me'.[3]

He reached London on 19 November 1762, felt a sudden rush of 'life and joy', and repeated lines to himself from Addison's *Cato* that had been waiting for just such an occasion to be proclaimed and written down: 'It must be so – Plato, thou reasonest well.' Good fortune guided his steps. He was able to secure lodgings in Downing Street for £22 a year, knocked down from forty guineas, thanks to his personal skill. In his journal he noted this fact, and approved of it: 'I do think this a very strong proof of my being agreeable.' Meanwhile, in Scotland, his 'little affair' reached its term; his bastard Charles Boswell was born and baptised in early December; Charlie's mother too, he learned, was doing well.[4]

Which was just as he would have wished it though, at present, a new amour filled his head and heart; he was, he assured his journal, 'really in love'. So, while in Temple Lane Samuel Johnson, one of the London literary men Boswell longed to meet, was advising Baretti that 'love and marriage are different states', young James Boswell was happily lending two guineas to his new companion, Mrs Anne Lewis (known to his journal as 'Louisa'), an actress. He briefly wondered, as he kissed her, whether it might appear 'like demanding goods for my money'; but he did it, anyway. Throughout Christmas and new year, as Johnson applied himself to coach his printer's boy, George Strahan, by reading Cicero's *De officiis*, Boswell's amour proceeded at a most gratifying rate. On 8 December he talked of love 'very freely' with Louisa; the next day he drank tea with her and thought 'what delight' they should have together, and by the 30th he was talking of their love connection 'very freely'. There was then a postponement which only served to work him up more gloriously and filled his journal with thoughts on the science of '*l'amour*', on which, though only twenty-two, he considered himself an authority: 'Be sure always', he wrote, 'to make a woman better than her sex.' At last the night he had been waiting for arrived; they enjoyed the most gloriously prolonged climaxes together at Mr Hayward's establishment at the Black Lion, Fleet Street; narration of the details of their 'five episodes' of 'supreme rapture' occupied three whole pages of his journal. After which there was a certain coolness.[5]

A week later, while Johnson was wishing George Strahan would acquaint him with 'what [he was] doing', there came a sudden explosion of rage from Downing Street. Boswell was both astonished and enraged to find himself the victim of a vile conspiracy, for there before him were, too evidently, signs of a venereal disease contracted from Mrs Lewis ('Can corruption lodge beneath so fair a form?'). Immediately he demanded back his two guineas to pay for curing his affliction. 'I neither *paid* it for prostitution nor *gave* it in charity.' It was in a solemn mood that he addressed himself to his journal: 'What a cursed thing this is! What a miserable creature am I!' One of the greatest geniuses in Europe – reduced to this!'[6]

Some months later, having submitted to his cure and recovered his bodily strength, he wrote his memoranda for Monday 16 May: 'Breakfast neat today, toast, rolls, and butter, easily and not too laughable. Then [James] Love's and get money, or first finish journal . . .' About Love, the professional soubriquet of James Dance, an actor, he was being far too optimistic; love, with or without its capital letter, was certain to let him down; 'alas, a single guinea was all I could get.' He went on to drink tea 'at Davies's in Russell Street, and about seven came in the great Mr. Samuel Johnson'. Boswell had been waiting for just such a chance since first coming to London, but at this sudden encounter his confidence deserted him, or, at least, that is how he narrates it:

> As I knew his mortal antipathy at the Scotch, I cried to Davies, 'Don't tell him where I come from.' However, he said, 'From Scotland.' 'Mr. Johnson,' said I, 'indeed I come from Scotland, but I cannot help it.' 'Sir,' replied he, 'that, I find, is what a very great many of your countrymen cannot help.'[7]

It is one of those great meetings, like the meeting of Dr Livingstone and the explorer Henry Stanley ('Dr Livingstone, I presume?'), and, like that Victorian episode, the first recorded speech between them has achieved an emblematic, if apocryphal, quality. Boswell puts up his timid bait, and Johnson wolfs it down. Whether that was how it *really* was, who now can tell? From now on this biography accommodates not just one, but shortly a second biographer, each with a separate and utterly distinct agenda to perform.

12

Shakespeare

Huggermugger n.s. *(corrupted perhaps from* hug er morcker, *or hug in the dark.* Morcker *in* Danish *is darkness, whence our* murky. *It is written by Sir* Thomas More, hoker moker. Hoker, *in* Chaucer, *is* peevish, crossgrained, *of which* moker *may be only a ludicrous reduplication.* Hooke *is likewise in German a* corner, *and* moky *is in* English dark. *I know not how to determine.)*

'I shall mark what I remember of his conversation,' Boswell observes after that first meeting, yet his memory, though plausible, is highly deceptive. In total, Boswell spent just 426 days with Johnson during those last twenty-one years of Johnson's life, of which 101 were on their tour of the Hebrides in 1771; far less than Tetty had spent, or Frank Barber, or even Hester Thrale, all of whom might have given a very different sense of him. Now that the pension had secured him from poverty, Johnson had more time for writing letters. In the fifty-four years up to his letter of thanks to Lord Bute in 1762, some 180 of his letters survive; in the twenty-one years of his life after that date, there are thirteen hundred: one letter survives from his marriage, but there are 366 from his infatuation with Hester Thrale.

Differences crowded upon Johnson. No sooner had his own future been secured with the pension than he read of the death of his son-in-law, Jervis Porter, captain of HMS *Hercules*. He wrote to Lucy immediately, to offer comfort and to be informed 'in what condition your brother's death has left your fortune'. He wished to be magnanimous, now that it was in his power, and felt no little disappointment and shock to find Lucy had been left very well provided for indeed. He congratulated her on being rewarded 'with so large a fortune' and made plans to visit her, in Lichfield, that summer. He would, of course, bring Frank, his servant, and recommended Kitty to 'get a servant's bed at the three Crowns' (the inn next door in Breadmarket Street), enclosing £10 to pay for 'sheets and tablelinen and such things'. He was frankly astonished to learn, by the next post, that his plans were quite out of the question. He sought to make tactful reparations; he acknowledged that the fact there 'should not be room' for him at the house (*his* house, where he had been born) was 'some disappointment' to him, but he insisted, quite falsely, 'the matter is not very great'. More worrying, to him, was Lucy's plans to spend some of her £10,000 inheritance on building her own house. 'I am sorry you have had your head filled with building for many reasons', irritation getting the better of his syntax: 'You might have hired a house at half the interest of the money for which you build it. If your house cost you a thousand pounds. You might hire the palace' – the bishop's palace, in Lichfield, where Gilbert Walmesley used to live – 'for twenty pounds and make forty of your thousand pounds . . .' But it was useless. Lucy had money, and it was now beyond his power either to control her or advise. She built 'a stately house' with a 'handsome garden' which cost about a third of the money she inherited.[1]

The world was changing and, much as Johnson approved, in theory, of all such alterations, in practical details there were many things he disliked. Writing the dedication, to the king, of John Kennedy's *Chronology*, which established precise dates for the creation of the world, he declared, 'the validity of the sacred writings never can be denied', but human writings, or the lack of them, might be very daunting. 'You are not to imagine that my friendship is light enough to be blown away by the first cross blast,' he assured George Strahan, reminding him that 'in youth we are apt to be too rigorous in our expectations'.[2] That summer he was much preoccupied with the marital affairs of his old friend John Taylor of Ashbourne, whose wife had left him. Sympathising, and pointing out that 'unsuitable or unhappy marriages' happened 'every day to multitudes', he advised him to leave home for a while 'that you may not be a gazing Stock to idle people'. He particularly recommended that he be unyielding in any court proceedings: 'Nature has given women so much power that the

Law has very wisely given them little.'[3] The unusual degree of male prejudice one finds in these letters may have been influenced by the regular presence of Boswell as his boon companion that summer. Together, or in company with Goldsmith, they passed away evenings at the Mitre on Fleet Street, capping each other's witticisms. There is Johnson's attitude to Churchill's poetic gibes ('a tree that produces a great many crabs is better than a tree which produces only a few'), his view of Scottish ambitions ('the noblest prospect which a Scotchman ever sees, is the high road that leads him to England') and his notion of female religious eloquence ('a woman preaching is like a dog's walking on his hinder legs. It is not done well; but you are surprized to find it done at all').[4] These sayings, and many like them, have an authentic ring of quips the older Johnson may well have uttered in the convivial company of younger male companions, but can never be divorced from Boswell's preening sense of self-esteem at the company he kept. And they did nothing to prevent Boswell from celebrating the 'king's birth-night' three weeks earlier, in his own style, dressing down in 'dirty buckskin breeches and black stockings', wandering into St James's Park, picking up 'a low brimstone' and, in the guise of a barber, performing 'most manfully'. How much Boswell concealed of his nocturnal activities when in male company is difficult to judge. On 28 July Boswell records himself and Johnson walking 'along the Strand . . . arm-in-arm' when they were accosted by a 'woman of the town' in the 'usual enticing manner'. Johnson reproves her ('No, no, my girl . . . it won't do'), speaking without 'harshness'. He and Boswell then agree 'that much more misery than happiness, upon the whole, is produced by illicit commerce between the sexes'. This anecdote, appearing in the *Life of Johnson*, does not differ significantly from the version in the *London Journal*, except that the *Journal* mentions, almost as an afterthought, that some days later Boswell was 'tapped on the shoulder by a fine fresh lass' and 'could not resist indulging myself with the enjoyment of her'. Allowing that 'illicit love is always wrong', he argues 'the crime must be alleviated' since 'the woman is already depraved'. The result is that on the last day of his *Journal* Boswell sits heavily, his head nodding from lack of sleep, 'even in Mr. Johnson's company', while Johnson converses on the Convocation of the Church. While it would be wrong to find any *conscious* motivation in the presentation of their two characters on this final page, the accidental formulation is very revealing.[5]

At the end of the year Johnson wrote to Boswell 'à la Cour de l'Empereur, Utrecht', refusing to answer letters 'written only for the sake of writing', sending advice which intimates he had some sense of the seductive pleasures Boswell vaunted himself upon. 'Every desire is a Viper in the Bosom,' he warned; 'Depravity is not very easily overcome.' His letter concludes by counselling Boswell to study civil law 'as your father advises' and by asking for 'any books in the Frisick Language' and for information on 'how the poor are maintained' in the United Provinces (the Dutch Republic). If he thought his final request would tax his youthful admirer's powers, he was quite correct; writing the *Life* twenty-eight years later Boswell admits he still has not discovered any information on the subject.[6]

Johnson wrote to Lucy Porter wishing her well in her new house, sending some of her 'poor dear mamma's' books, and a diamond ring of which he hoped she would be 'very fond'. There is a degree of finality to the letter since, now he had the money to travel, he had nowhere to visit. His first journey after receiving news of the pension was not to Lichfield after all, but to Bennet Langton's place in Lincolnshire, which he made notable by one day climbing to the top of a steep hill and suddenly deciding 'to take a roll down'. He emptied his pockets, lay down 'parallel with the edge of the hill' and descended, 'turning himself over and over till he came to the bottom'. He had a constant love of shocking his more conservative friends with such demonstrations of physical pleasure; in Inverness he astonished a rather sober company by his imitation of a kangaroo, putting out his hands 'like feelers', gathering up the tails of his coat to resemble the animal's pouch, and making 'two or three vigorous bounds across the room!' In Oxford he had challenged Robert Vansittart, twenty years his junior, to climb over All Souls' wall, and even in his seventies the desire did not leave him. Searching out a wall in Lichfield 'he used to jump over when a boy', he gazed at it some time 'with a degree of rapture' and at last 'determined to try my skill and dexterity; I laid aside my hat and wig, pulled off my coat, and leapt over it, twice.'[7]

That year The Club was formed of Johnson, Reynolds, Burke, Goldsmith, Hawkins and others, meeting once a week at the Turk's Head in Gerrard Street, which he found a most welcome outlet. There had been nine members of the Ivy Lane Club and so, Hawkins writes, that number was chosen for the present group; Johnson 'looked upon nine as the most *clubable* number', which also included Anthony Chamier, the opera-loving statesman, Christopher Nugent, a physician, and two of Johnson's younger friends, Bennet Langton and Topham Beauclerk. In the summer he made his long-delayed trip to Easton Maudit to stay with Thomas Percy and with his help to 'strike a stroke' at Shakespeare, on whom he had been strangely silent for over two years. He travelled there with Anna Williams in a berlin, a 'coach of a particular form' as he defined it, and there may have been several occasions for them to perform entrances in the curious way observed by Fanny Reynolds at her brother Joshua's front door; Johnson took Miss Williams

> ... about on the steps as he whirled and twisted about to perform his gesticulations; and as soon as he had finish'd, he would give a sudden spring, and make an extensive stride over the threshold, as if he were trying for a wager how far he could stride, Mrs Williams standing groping about outside the door, unless the servant or the mistress of the House more commonly took hold of her hand to conduct her in . . .*

Over the course of the following two months he dined with Lords Halifax and Northampton and assisted in Percy's review of Grainger's poem 'Sugar-Cane'.[8] Whether he attended the Club meeting when Reynolds reduced the company to tears of laughter by reading from the poem, 'Now, Muse, Let's sing of *rats*', and another member mentioned the word had been changed from *mice* as 'more dignified', is uncertain. He was rather taken with the Club as a small, elite institution; when Garrick, hearing of the Club's existence, rather thought he should become a member, Johnson was most

---

* In the eighteenth century unmarried ladies acquired the title 'Mrs' when they reached mature years.

put out. '*He'll be of us*, (said Johnson) how does he know we will *permit* him.'[9]

Even such diversions, and the slow beginnings of serious work on his edition of Shakespeare, could not raise the mood of desolation which had settled on him after writing his last letter to Lucy, now so woefully interested in money and property. His new-year prayers had urged the Lord to make him 'avoid Idleness' and 'be diligent', with an additional plea to 'Deliver and preserve me from vain terrours'; but on Good Friday he recorded having made 'no reformation', having lived 'totally useless, more sensual in thought and more addicted to wine and meat'. He hoped 'To put my rooms in order' having found their disordered state 'one great cause of Idleness'. When Boswell was first shown around them he found several good books 'very dusty and in great confusion', the floor all 'strewed with manuscript leaves'. Johnson noted that his indolence, of which he constantly complained, had 'sunk into grosser sluggishness', his dissipation spread to 'wilder negligence' and his thoughts 'clouded with sensuality'. In partial defence he offered up a token of reformation: 'I have in some measure forborn excess of Strong Drink' (one notes the qualifying phrase 'in *some* measure'); how great his sacrifice had been may be judged by his confession that, for much of the past year 'a kind of strange oblivion has overspread me'. Clearly, this was not the life 'to which Heaven is promised'. He set down his 'Purpose', noting an intention 'to reject or expel sensual images, and idle thoughts'. What images these were that troubled him so much we cannot tell. At church next day he prayed 'in the presence of God, but *without a vow* (no doubt anticipating failure) to repel sinful thoughts'; in the evening he pleaded to be delivered 'from habitual wickedness, and idleness'. Presumably he indulged masturbatory fantasies, stimulated by his friendships for young people ('I love the young dogs of the age') and encouraged by many hours of indolent loneliness. He prayed five times to 'avoid idleness', pledging himself to rise early, and praying for Tetty, 'dear poor Tetty', his eyes full of tears. He noticed a 'poor girl' taking the sacrament along with him 'in a bedgown', and gave her 'privately' a crown, although her evangelical reading matter (Hart's hymns) upset him. He writes his thoughts impressionistically, a shilling to the church, a crown to the girl. 'I perceive an insensibility and heaviness upon me,' he notes; 'Against loose thoughts and idleness' he meditates, submitting to the very sins he prays to resist.[10] On his birthday he prayed again, making clear that for all the force of his Easter prayers, he had made 'few improvements'. He went to church and begged *'to be loosed from the chain of my sins'* for the time left to him (he was already fifty-six). There is the usual list of resolutions, though one of them 'as washing &c' indicates how far he had gone in neglecting personal hygiene. His last resolve, 'To morrow I purpose to regulate my room', shows how the positive purposes of Good Friday had failed.[11]

In the autumn he worked on Shakespeare, using it as an excuse to forgo another invitation from Reynolds's sister Frances and warning her that if she really *must* visit Italy, then she should go by land, not sea. 'I do not think the grossness of a Ship very suitable to a Lady,' he wrote, adding that her 'sudden folly' had quite disturbed him. He commended his former pupil, George Strahan, on election as a scholar of University College which, he noted with pride and a certain regret, was 'almost filled with my friends'.[12]

'It was on the Thursday of the Month of January 1765. that I first saw Mr. Johnson in a Room.' The writer is Mrs Thrale, and the room was in the Thrales' house in Southwark, close to their brewery in Dead-Man's Place. The shoemaker-poet James Woodhouse, a kind of 'wild beast from the country', was asked to dine as a temptation to him and, accordingly, 'Mr Murphy at four o'clock brought Mr. Johnson to dinner.'[13] Hester Thrale, née Salusbury, was then just days short of her twenty-fourth birthday, married for little more than a year, and mother to 'Queeney', her eldest daughter, who was just four months old. Her marriage to Henry Thrale had been transacted by her mother largely in order to secure her uncle Thomas's bond of £10,000, of which a mere £200 per annum came to the bride, but Hester gave every appearance of contentment. Her 'preference' for Thrale, she told her aunt, being 'not founded on Passion but on Reason' gave her 'some Right to expect some Happiness'. Nevertheless, she was still young and 'silly enough' to hope her husband's heart was to be won 'by the same empty Tricks that had pleased my Father & my Uncle'. She was to be sadly disappointed.

Henry Thrale had been introduced to Hester, by her uncle Thomas, as a *'real Sportsman'*; twelve years her senior, he had enjoyed himself at Oxford and in London, owned a brewery and had his eye on a parliamentary seat. He was, though, very dull. Years later Johnson, asked to name his qualities, replied that 'his conversation does not show the minute hand' but he could strike the hours 'very correctly'. The dinner was a success, and accordingly 'the next Thursday was appointed for the same Company to meet – exclusive of the Shoemaker'.[14]

Very soon Johnson grew familiar with the Thrales, becoming their 'constant Acquaintance, Visitor, Companion and Friend', finding in their Southwark house a welcome solace from the persistent sniping of the press, for whom his abjuration of his own definition of a pension was a constant goad. In November the *Gazetteer* ran a column on 'Mr *Independent* Johnson's Dictionary', attacking both him and Bute; in March the *Public Advertiser* listed a number of spoof book titles for the foregoing year in which 'The Charms of Independance, a Tale, by Sam. Johnson, Esq.' ranks alongside 'The Beauty of Innocence, a Tale' by the notorious courtesan Kitty Fisher.[15] In February he wrote the dedication, to the Countess of Northumberland, of Percy's *Reliques of Ancient English Poetry*, drawing attention to the poems as 'effusions of nature' which showed 'the first efforts of ancient genius'. More recent demonstrations of that English genius for nature were slow to appear. In May he wrote to Garrick soliciting his subscription for Shakespeare, much to Garrick's surprise, who replied that he had been 'one of the first' to subscribe, 'as soon as I had heard of your intention'. He mentioned others, like the Duke of Devonshire, that he had brought to the list, which Johnson acknowledged but, for whatever reason, chose not to believe. 'Garrick got me no subscriptions,' he remarked to Boswell, as they toured the Western Isles. That spring, conversing with Goldsmith and Boswell at the Mitre, he ordered for them a bottle of port, but abstained himself. Goldsmith remarked that he abstained likewise from the theatre, to which Johnson replied that 'the old man does not care for the young man's whore'. Boswell urged him to 'give us something in some other way' but Johnson replied, with irritation, that he was 'not obliged to do any more. No man is obliged to do as much as he can do. A man is to have part of his life to himself.'[16]

That summer he threatened John Taylor in Ashbourne with a visit, 'invited or uninvited', unless he was told he would be 'insupportably burthensome', but changed his mind upon receiving Hester Thrale's invitation to come down with them to Brighthelmstone (Brighton). He wrote back to her, bitterly regretting that work on Shakespeare meant that he could not do 'what I wish first', eagerly expressing his desire to be with them 'as soon as I can dismiss my work from my hands'. The task he was so eager to despatch was his Preface to the edition of the Complete Works, which he wrote last of all. Throughout the spring he and Hester had spent time translating extracts from the *De Consolatione Philosophiae* of Boethius, and to Johnson the labour was sweet. Hester translated:

> To him whom painful Tastes annoy
> Sweet honey yields a double Joy.

He responded in the same vein:

> And thus the Mind tormented long
> With wild Vicissitudes of Wrong,
> Contemns at length the treacherous toys
> And real Happiness enjoys.[17]

He rushed down to Brighton as soon as he had finished his work, only to find the Thrales had left the coast and were back in Southwark. A parliamentary member for the borough having died, Thrale was anxious to be on hand to announce his candidacy, which he did on 23 September. Four days later Mrs Thrale gave birth to a daughter, who was baptised and died within the following ten days. Johnson, unaware of any of this, felt suddenly neglected and wrote to her, hurt and angry to be disregarded in this way. He was, though, suitably mollified by her reply and 'from that time', Mrs Thrale wrote, 'his visits grew more frequent'.

In October, Johnson's *Shakespeare* was finally published. Of its eight volumes, the first six had been completed four years earlier; Strahan, the printer, made separate entries for the costs of volumes VII and VIII. 'My Shakespeare is now out of my hands,' Johnson wrote to Taylor, inviting himself to stay; 'I do not see what can hinder me any longer.' But many things arose to hinder him, and it was five years before he saw Ashbourne again. He wrote to Tonson, clearing up (he hoped) financial matters; to Warton, having 'taken care' of his copy – he apologised for doubting his subscription and thought he must actually 'have subscrib'd twice'; and to Charles Burney, thanking him for all the trouble he had taken in collecting subscriptions. He received 'no great comfort' from the conclusion of his work, he told Warton, yet was 'well enough pleased that the publick has no farther claim upon me'. In the nine years since he had signed the contract for Shakespeare he had received his pension, and now felt he had fulfilled his obligations.[18] Instead of such time-consuming work he received burdens in a new way, in the close attention of the press. The *St James's Chronicle* mentioned him 'in almost every issue until the end of the year'. Letters from 1736 were quoted, describing him and 'Davy Garrick' setting out, in poverty, from Lichfield, to find fortune with the works of Shakespeare:

> Lichfield – to thee a *double* Praise is due,
> Thou gav'st a Garrick – and a Johnson too!

Johnson rather resented the way his own work on Shakespeare was underestimated by comparison with Garrick's acting. 'I would not disgrace my page with a player,' he told Boswell; 'he cannot illustrate Shakespeare. He does not understand him.'[19] 'Detector' in the *Public Advertiser* attacked him as a 'Mercenary' selling his 'literary Talents' to 'the best Bidder', and the *Public Ledger* compared his present stance ('pompous and grave') to his role in the Cock Lane Ghost affair:

> And as he found no Witchcraft lurking there,
> He finds no heavenly fires, no magic here.[20]

In his own life too he felt divided tributes: the University of Dublin awarded him a Doctor's degree of LL.D, but Tonson was selling his Shakespeare edition 'for forty shillings' which was, he claimed in an irate letter, 'four shillings under the Subscription'. His irritation is clearly seen in his *over*-estimation of the correct price (two guineas, or forty-*two* shillings) by as much as Tonson undersold it. 'Demand for the Book has been such, as left yet no temptation to lower the price,' he snarled. He might have his pension, but he still knew the value of the work on which he had laboured. He was quite correct: the first thousand copies were sold out within the month, with a reprint following immediately. Such were the pains and pleasures of fame.[21]

In the Preface Johnson voiced his deepest reactions, not just to Shakespeare, but to literature generally, in passages of moving prose:

> Nothing can please many, and please long, but just representations of general nature . . . The irregular combinations of fanciful invention may delight a-while, by that novelty of which the common satiety of life sends us all in quest; but the pleasures of sudden wonder are soon exhausted, and the mind can only repose on the stability of truth.
>
> Shakespeare is above all writers, at least above all modern writers, the poet of nature . . . In the writings of other poets a character is too often an individual; in those of Shakespeare it is commonly a species.

These judgements on the generality of Shakespeare's appeal, creating characters who are not merely individuals but 'a species', recall earlier passages of his writing from *The Vanity of Human Wishes*, the *Rambler* and *Rasselas*; but gradually, in the Preface, he replaces general precepts with his own individual reactions to Shakespeare.[22] 'The allurements of emendation are scarcely resistible,' he writes, remembering his own *Miscellaneous Observations on . . . Macbeth*, published twenty years earlier; yet he had resolved 'to insert none of my own readings in the text'. He defends Shakespeare from criticism for neglecting the unities of time, place and action by making an appeal to Shakespeare as the 'poet of nature', in whose works 'oaks extend their branches, and pines tower in the air'. His story may require 'Romans or kings' but Shakespeare 'thinks only on men' and makes 'nature predominate over accident'; his tragedies and comedies may be too closely linked, but they are 'compositions of a distinct kind; exhibiting the real state of sublunary nature'. 'Nature', or 'the regular course of things' as he defines it in the *Dictionary*, becomes the characteristic of the Preface: 'there is always an appeal open from criticism to nature.' Even Shakespeare's love of quibbles is defended by a riot of imagery;

they are the 'luminous vapours' leading to 'the mire', the 'golden apple' forcing him to turn aside, the 'fatal Cleopatra for which he lost the world, and was content to lose it'.

The notes, written over the years since subscriptions had first been sought, supply various ideas, some first-rate and some eccentric, all resulting from close attention to the text. In the Preface Johnson preferred to pass over William Warburton's earlier edition, whose principal error was an 'acquiescence in his first thoughts'; but his Notes are rather more abrasive. In *Measure for Measure* Warburton had turned 'the flaws of her own youth' into 'the *flames* . . .' asking, 'Who does not see that the integrity of the metaphor' required the change. Johnson tersely, and accurately, replies, 'Who does not see that upon such principles there is no end of correction'. Some lines strike him particularly: 'When he speaks,/ The air, a charter'd libertine, is still', from *Henry V*, is 'exquisitely beautiful', as is the metaphor from *Measure for Measure*,

> Thou hast nor youth, nor age;
> But as it were an after-dinner's sleep,
> Dreaming on both.

In *The Winter's Tale* the metaphor

> How would he look, to see his work, so noble,
> Vilely bound up!

causes him to imagine it 'impossible for any man to rid his mind of his profession'. Thinking of his own works, Shakespeare's mind had 'passed naturally to the binder' and, risking a jest, Johnson ventures, 'I am glad he has no hint at an editor.' As in the *Dictionary* his own birthplace is not forgotten: in *Much Ado about Nothing* Dogberry mentions a 'bill' or weapon, which Johnson remarks 'is still carried by the watchmen at Lichfield'. Englishness is apparent in his comments on this English writer of both tragedy *and* comedy: 'I do not recollect among the Greeks or Romans a single writer who attempted both.' He remarks on the treatment of the French in *Henry V*: 'Throughout the whole scene there may be found *French* servility, and *French* vanity', and of Italians in *Romeo and Juliet*: 'It is observed that in *Italy* almost all assassinations are committed during the heat of summer.'[23]

His notes on characters such as Polonius in *Hamlet* or Falstaff in *Henry IV* carry the weight of his own experience of the world, while those on *Macbeth*, identical with those for his *Miscellaneous Observations*, at least exclude his former fondness for conjectural revisions. He merely notes, of Lady Macbeth's lines 'And pall thee in the dunnest smoak of hell . . .', that 'there is a long criticism in the *Rambler*'. Certain thoughts, though, show him still acutely conscious of his principal concerns. In Act IV of *Hamlet* occurs the line '*In hugger mugger to interr him*', which, he states, 'all the modern editions that I have consulted' give as 'In *private* to inter him'; he comments:

> That the words now replaced are better, I do not undertake to prove; it is sufficient that they are Shakespeare's: if phraseology is to be changed as words grow uncouth by disuse, or gross by vulgarity, the history of every language will be lost; we shall no longer have the words of any authour; and, as these alterations will be often unskilfully made, we shall in time have very little of his meaning.

Finally, his comments on the climax of *King Lear*, often wrenched from context, are a justly memorable conclusion to his thoughts on someone he celebrated as the 'poet of nature'. The Tate he mentions here is Nahum Tate, whose modified version of *King Lear* with the 'happy' ending (Cordelia lives and marries Edgar), first published in 1681, held the stage throughout the eighteenth century.

> A play in which the wicked prosper, and the virtuous miscarry, may doubtless be good, because it is a just representation of the common events of human life: but since all reasonable beings naturally love justice, I cannot easily be persuaded, that the observation of justice makes a play worse; or, that if other excellencies are equal, the audience will not always rise better pleased from the final triumph of persecuted virtue.
>
> In the present case the publick has decided. Cordelia, from the time of Tate, has always retired with victory and felicity. And, if my sensations could add any thing to the general suffrage, I might relate, that I was many years ago so shocked by Cordelia's death,

that I know not whether I ever endured to read again the last scenes of the play till I undertook to revise them as an editor.

This is the honest reaction of a man who, although he might no longer write a *Rambler* 168 modifying the language of *Macbeth*, could not withstand the horrors of the ending of *King Lear*. It is also recalls the behaviour of the boy who read *Hamlet* 'in his Father's Kitchen' and, coming to the ghost scene, 'hurried up Stairs to the Shop Door that he might see folks about him'.[24]

At the end of 1765 he wrote to one old friend, Edmund Hector, and one new, James Boswell. To Hector he complained, gently, that he had written 'business' to him (about obtaining Shakespeare), neglecting the role of friendship. 'My heart is much set upon seeing you all again,' he wrote, asking about his old friends, Warren, Paul and 'poor George Boylston', in a way that summons Justice Shallow to mind: 'And is old Double dead?' 'Perhaps no authour has ever in two plays afforded so much delight,' he wrote of *Henry IV* Parts I and II. But the sentiment was largely for the moment, and he passed through Birmingham in 1767 without stopping.[25] To Boswell he sent a wish 'to see you and to hear you, and hope that we shall not be so long separated again', reminding the young man of the value 'we learn to put on the friendship and tenderness of Parents and of friends'. The context was Boswell's father Lord Auchinleck's recent letter asking his son to come home from Paris because he was unwell, but the mention of 'friends' indicates Johnson's constant awareness of a potential biographer, less critical, more comprehensive than any recent journal.[26]

He wrote to Lucy to say that, although she had no further need of his house in Lichfield, 'I am unwilling to sell it, yet hardly know why'. He made various provisions to have it fitted out for letting, for Kitty to receive part of the rent, and several times apologised for troubling her to have the house surveyed. 'You must act by your own prudence,' he said; 'this whole affair is painful to me.' At his death he still owned the house, which was then sold and realised £235.[27]

Throughout the years he maintained a diary which, in its crabbed abbreviations, gives us a full awareness of his daily life. On 9 January 1765 he writes: '9 WEDN. At Mr Trails.', his way of noting the start of his acquaintance with the Thrales; only his brief comment 'Began this book' gives any indication of its potential importance to him. Reading these entries and attempting to interpret their brief laconic Anglo-Latin symbols becomes a challenge and many times, the editors confess, the abbreviations 'are uncertain'. 'M', we are told on editorial authority, is 'his symbol for defecation'; *why*, we are not informed. If, on the other hand, it is a symbol for masturbation, some difficulties may be more easily understood. Thus, on the morning of the 10th, the day *after* he had met Mrs Thrale, there is the symbol 'M 2'; on '13 SUND.' there is 'M with utmost difficulty' followed by the one word 'Ill'. The next day 'M. rose late' and on Monday 18 March 'Eheu! M. 3 in bed in the morning with little difficulty'. The editors say, 'Why Johnson begins the next day with "Alas!" is not easy to say'. The previous day, 17 March, he kept in memory of 'my dear departed Tetty' and having prayed for her and 'hoped to combat sin' he 'drank wine'. The following day he writes 'At 5 p.m. at Trail's'. The symbol, and his brief comments on it, make perfect sense.

He also notes a 'Lucy' – not Lucy Porter from Lichfield – to whom he gives 5s 3d on the 10th and again on the 14th, 'which makes 1 – 9 – 0', he calculates. 'This is some unknown recipient of his charity,' the editors comment, recollecting the crown he gave 'privately' to a girl 'at the Sacrament in a bedgown' the previous Easter. Occasional people who attracted his attention, and his money, are mentioned in his diary; for instance, the man whose 'pious behaviour' he had long witnessed, and to whom he offered wine on Easter Day, 'which he refused' leaving Johnson 'much disappointed'. Such potential charitable gifts are like the guinea he gave to 'Reid' (probably Joseph Reed) which, together with the 10s 6d he had previously given, were enough 'to free him from the Spunging house'. They were important solaces to his conscience, now he was no longer poor himself. He noted refunding '6 guineas' which he had borrowed from Mr Allen six years earlier to care for his mother's last decline.[28]

That Easter he prayed 'for repentance' and fasted all day, though he 'slept not well' and 'had flatulencies'; he was 'almost afraid' to renew his resolutions, knowing he had 'reformed no evil habit'. In this year's resolutions he prayed 'To avoid loose thought' and 'To rise at eight every morning', knowing how necessary it was 'to combat evil habits singly'. The purpose of early rising was to fight against a tendency, acquired in the past year, of lying in bed 'till two'. 'Forgive the days and years which I have passed in folly, idleness, and sin.' Throughout the year he fought hard, and often lost, a battle with himself to abstain from alcohol; on 19 March, after failing very badly the morning before (masturbating three times), he made a deliberate note that he 'drank tea' with Miss Williams and bought oranges for 6d. On 1 September there is a brief note 'In the morning M' but the final note for the evening reads 'Supped at Mr Allens. No wine.' The following year began with a struggle: 'Strongly tempted in a dream to M.,' he noted on 3 January. The following day he conceded defeat on two fronts: 'M. d. Rose at 10 . . . Drank wine for the first time this year.' He also kept a note on his ailments, from 'pain in face' on 1 January through 'Teeth bad' on Easter Day to 'rheumatism' in December.[29]

Over the winter months Johnson manoeuvred to extricate himself from expectations that he would work as a government spy, returning, in October, some papers connected with the peace negotiations to Charles Jenkinson, 'carefully preserved, and uncommunicated to any human Being'. He claimed he had hoped to make better use of them but was glad to pass them over to someone 'much more versed in publick affairs'. Jenkinson, a private secretary to Lord Bute, had sent the papers two years before, shortly after Johnson received his pension, with the implication that he was 'expected' to work on such things; equally clear is Johnson's resolute but silent refusal to do so. Among his prayers is one headed 'Engaging in Politicks with H—N', begging 'that no deceit may mislead me, nor temptation corrupt me', which makes his reservations clear.[30] There is an obvious, unstated dialogue in Johnson's 'delight' at returning the papers, 'carefully preserved', as there is in Jenkinson's request for their return 'if you have no further Use for them'. Any speculation regarding Johnson's work as a secret 'fact-gatherer', and hopes of a seat in parliament at this time, are unproven and highly unlikely.[31] Thrale was returned, unopposed, for the borough of Southwark just before Christmas and he thanked the electors for 'the unusual honour of an unanimous Election' in an address which Johnson penned; such was closest that he came to a parliamentary career.[32]

'O Lord let me not sink into total depravity,' he wrote on the first day of the new year 1766, resolving, amongst other things, to 'drink little wine'. This partial abstinence disturbed his sleep rhythms and, speculating on writing '*the History of Memory*', his brief diary entries are dominated by one word – 'sleepy'. He exulted to Langton that he had 'risen every morning since Newyears day at about eight', though conceding 'when I was up I have indeed done but little'. He wrote an advertisement for Anna Williams's *Miscellanies in Prose and Verse* which now appeared some sixteen years after the original Proposal; apologising for his tardiness, he hoped those who censured him 'may never learn from experience how slowly that is done, which is done gratuitously'. The slimness of the volume contributed to the delay. When finally it appeared, apart from the poems written or revised by him, it included pieces by Thomas Percy and Frances Reynolds. The 'Tale of the Fountains', ostensibly by Hester Thrale, was in reality by Johnson himself and written, as she confessed in a presentation copy, 'for the purpose of *filling up this Book*'.[33]

That summer he wrote a preface for Fordyce's *Sermons to Young Women* and dedications to Adams's *Treatise on the Globes* and Gwynn's *London and Westminster Improved*. 'To engage the heart, with a view to mend it' should prove the preacher's ambition, he wrote for Fordyce but, for himself, he still had desperate doubts. That Easter Saturday he had 'a doubt . . . of my State' but found his faith 'though weak, was yet Faith. O God strengthen it.' He had given up meat for Easter, dined 'sparingly' on fish, was equally sparing of tea ('I drank but one dish') and *almost* entirely abstained from wine, having just 'one glass on Sunday night' but found 'I bore this abstinence this day not well'. All through the Easter period he was troubled by 'scruples', which, though he fought against them, reading holy works, and praying earnestly, returned to perplex him every day.[34]

When, as in the spring and summer of 1766, he felt these scruples most strongly, he employed various nervous stratagems to soothe his mind, touching every post as he passed it, going back and starting again if he missed one out, adjusting his stride to reach a particular point with an odd, or even, number of paces. Frances Reynolds observed his behaviour while on his trip to Devonshire:

Sometimes he would with great earnestness place his feet in a particular position, sometimes making his heels to touch, sometimes his toes, as if he was endeavouring to form a triangle, at least the two sides of one, and after having finished he would beat his sides, or the skirts of his coat, repeatedly with his hands, as if for joy that he had done his duty . . .

Sir Joshua 'observed him to go a good way about, rather than cross a particular alley in Leicester-fields' and Boswell noted the various sounds he made with his mouth, 'chewing the cud', 'clucking like a hen', and how when he was 'a good deal exhausted' by the violence of his speech 'he used to blow out his breath like a Whale'.[35] Sometimes he attempted to calm his mind with chemical experiments, as he pictured 'Sober' doing, in a self-portrait from the *Idler*; sitting amongst his furnace and vessels, counting 'the drops as they come from his retort', forgetting that 'whilst a drop is falling, a moment flies away'.[36] More often it was writing that relieved his mental tensions. He wrote 'Considerations on Corn', the one piece of evidence that exists of a relationship between him and William Gerard Hamilton MP. Found amongst Hamilton's papers on his death and clearly written in Johnson's hand, the piece concerns the parliamentary bounty on exporting corn when harvests were bad and the miseries of the poor 'are such as cannot easily be born'.[37] Binding together a series of well-honed clichés, it was clearly designed for success, though whether its articulacy reached the heights of Burke, who, elected only at Christmas, had since made speeches which had 'filled the town with wonder', is rather doubtful.[38]

Johnson had 'maintained the newspapers these many weeks', he told Langton; the *St James's Chronicle* had been publishing a series of letters on textual cruces in Shakespeare since the previous November and continued to do so for three more years, alternating them with splashes of gossip. In January it reported 'whispers' that Johnson was hardly 'the properest Person in the world to compile a Dictionary of the English language' and in September lamented his 'mangled fame'. The *Gazetteer* went further, hinting at intimate encounters between Johnson and 'the celebrated and ingenious Mrs Lenox' in her *Remarks* on Shakespeare, 'an attack on the greatest poet the world ever produced'.[39] On Easter Day he was sorely troubled and prayed, took his prayer book with him to his breakfast tea, and 'I think prayed again'. He went to church but was unable to hear the sermon, his mind full of scruples which he mentions four times, once more even than 'Tetty, dear Tetty'.[40] After Easter the mental anguish continued until, one morning, the Thrales arrived

> ... and heard him, in the most pathetic terms, beg the prayers of Dr. Delap, who had left him as we came in, I felt excessively affected with grief, and well remember my husband involuntarily lifted up one hand to shut his mouth, from provocation at hearing a man so wildly proclaim what he could at last persuade no one to believe; and what, if true, would have been so very unfit to reveal.

What it was that Johnson proclaimed, 'so wildly' that it caused Henry Thrale physically to muzzle him, is unknown. Something he had read in Richard Baxter's book *Reliquiae Baxterianae*, setting down not certainties but doubts, called deeply to his 'scruples' which troubled him severely and, although he wrote down, in his diary for Easter Day, that 'the scruple itself was its own confutation', his doubts were resolved in words only, not in dreams. He set himself the task of reading 'the Gospels of St Matthew and St Mark in Greek' but the solace he needed was not intellectual, as Hester Thrale immediately realised. 'Mr. Thrale went away soon after, leaving me with him, and bidding me prevail on him to quit his close habitation in the court and come with us to Streatham, where I undertook the care of his health, and had the honour and happiness of contributing to its restoration.'[41]

In the fifty-six-year-old Johnson willingly giving up control of himself to the twenty-five-year-old Mrs Thrale, something important has happened. To Boswell he was always an elderly sage, conveying wisdom, though often in the wittiest form, but to Mrs Thrale he chose to appear helpless, an infant, needing to be cherished. Like Lear he knelt down, and asked of her 'forgiveness'; the two of them were alone and singing 'like birds i' the cage'.[42]

13

Club and Country

club n.s. (clwppa, *Welsh;* kluppel, *Dutch.*) *An assembly of good fellows, meeting under certain conditions.*

country n.s. (contrée, *Fr.;* contrata, *low Latin; supposed to be contracted from* conterrata.*) The place of one's birth; the native soil.*

> O, save my country, heav'n, shall be your last.
>
> Pope

Johnson remained at Streatham for more than three months, and when he returned to town not much seemed different. He still set himself rules to 'combat scruples' and 'rise at eight', but the context in which he prepared to meet these challenges had changed decisively. From now on he referred to Streatham as the place 'Mr Thrale allows me to call home', willingly accepted a deferential pose, addressed Mr Thrale as 'Master' and Mrs Thrale as 'Mistress'. Four years were to pass before he again mentioned Tetty in his formal prayers.[1] Uncomplainingly he became accustomed to wearing cleaner shirts and fresher wigs; at table he was content to follow Thrale's direction, even when he announced that 'we have had enough for one lecture, Dr Johnson'.[2]

'The little things which distinguish domestick characters are soon forgotten,' he wrote to Langton, recollecting thoughts upon 'the minute details of daily life' which he had so applauded in the *Rambler*.[3] He took special delight in the 'Children's Book' in which Mrs Thrale recorded memoranda of young Queeney's progress. On her second birthday she was 'just 34 Inches high', spoke 'the Pater Noster', telling 'all her Letters' and her numbers, though 'none beyond a hundred'. He was soon regarded as 'a regular Inmate' at both Streatham and Southwark, where 'Mr Thrale fitted him up an Apartment over the Counting House Two Pair of Stairs high – & called it the *Round Tower*'. Johnson reciprocated and drew notable people to dine with the brewer and his wife; Baretti and Burke, Goldsmith and Reynolds, who first noted an engagement on 2 September.[4] Bad things were far away; Johnson wrote to William Drummond of Perthshire, deploring the 'practice of the Planters of America', meaning slave-holding; they were 'a Race of Mortals whom I suppose no other Man wishes to resemble'. He wrote to Boswell, now a qualified advocate, recommending hard work, since the 'unexpected inconveniencies' of his profession were luxury 'compared with the incessant cravings of Vacancy'. He briefly visited Robert Chambers in Oxford, where he had at last been elected Vinerian Professor of Law.[5]

In London he strove to recall dim memories from childhood, of his mother who 'one Sunday between Church and supper lay with the children on the bed'. There is a strange impersonality to his phrase 'the children'; he still cannot recall Nathaniel by name. Some years before, when writing the *Life of Roger Ascham*, he had wondered aloud 'who can hope, that any progeny more than one shall deserve to be mentioned?' What exactly did he mean by that? Did he, but not Nathaniel, deserve to be mentioned? 'Mother after my Fathers death', he recalled, and then 'Lucy – There are six days in the week'.[6] This Lucy was a servant who busied herself about the handsome new quarters of his home in Johnson's Court, Fleet Street, with Miss Williams on the ground floor, Mr Levet in the garret and Francis Barber attending, but the name recalled her namesake in Lichfield. 'It is now too late in the year to repair the poor old house,' he wrote to Lucy Porter; 'the days are now grown short, and a long Journey will be uncomfortable.' Had he travelled on from Oxford to Lichfield when he first got her letter, weeks earlier, this would not have been the case, but for some reason he had not cared to do so. 'Let me know how you go on in your new house,' he concluded.[7]

Having secured the Vinerian professorship, Chambers panicked and produced no lectures for the Michaelmas term, for which he was fined

£2 for every lecture missed. 'Come up to town, and lock yourself up from all but me,' Johnson wrote to him; 'I doubt not but Lectures will be produced. You must not miss another term.' Together in December 1766 they embarked, in utter secrecy, on a collaboration to produce the lectures. 'Sit very close', Johnson counselled him six weeks later, and 'there will be no danger.'[8] It filled him with pride to be writing, albeit secretly, lectures for the university from which he had had to withdraw. That pride was massively increased a few weeks later when, in February 1767, ensconced studying books at the library in Buckingham House to which Barnard, the royal librarian, gave him access, he was interrupted by King George himself. Boswell, who loved the episode, published an eight-page version of their 'Conversation' in 1790, as a preparation for the *Life of Johnson*. In it we learn that, having begun with a discussion of libraries at Oxford and Cambridge (the Bodleian, Johnson believed, was the largest), they ranged over Warburton's learning, Lyttelton's history and the *Journal des Savans* before George concluded their conversation by expressing 'a desire to have the literary biography of this country ably executed, and proposed to Dr. Johnson to undertake it'. Johnson 'signified his readiness' to accede. He 'loved to relate' all the circumstances of this fortuitous meeting, Boswell insisted, whenever asked to do so by friends, which 'gratified his monarchical enthusiasm' no end.

To find the king himself admired his work, to the extent of enquiring 'if he was then writing any thing', was both flattering and daunting; Johnson answered that 'he was not, for he had pretty well told the world what he knew'. The law lectures on which he was currently engaged remained a covert enterprise. 'I am not obliged to do any more,' he told Boswell; 'A man is to have part of his life to himself.' 'The King's information of what is going on . . . is much more Extensive than is Generally imagined,' he told Sir James Caldwell, before reminding him of a party 'at the Mitre next Tuesday' and threatening him with 'Tea with Mrs Williams'.[9] He sent an anxious note to Hester Salusbury, mother to Hester Thrale and a woman for whom he did not care, enquiring after her daughter; he did not write to Mrs Thrale, he explained, lest his letter might 'give her trouble at an inconvenient time'. The inconvenience was soon over when Henry, the Thrales' first boy child, was born the next day and within weeks he was apologising to Mrs Thrale for being in Oxford ('I will come as soon as I can') and being thus unable to decide about 'my dear little Girl's bathing'. It is noteworthy that, even in so intimate a matter as little Queeney's bathing, Hester applied for Johnson's advice; he referred her to Daniel Sutton, who had just inoculated her against smallpox: 'I think you must trust him.'

From Oxford, where he spent more time attending to the Vinerian lectures, he did go on this year to Lichfield where Kitty (Catherine Chambers), who minded his house for him, was dangerously ill. Liking to demonstrate how he had risen in status since he had left Lichfield, he wrote not once but twice to Thomas Lawrence MD, President of the Royal College of Physicians, begging 'the favour of your advice for an old Friend' whose symptoms he described in detail. Still in Lichfield a month later, his affections developed from a tenderness for Lucy Porter to flirtatious feelings for Hester Thrale, who is treated to a worldlier, more metropolitan regard. Everything he sees at Lichfield 'recals to my remembrance years in which I purposed what, I am afraid, I have not done', but why should he 'depress your hopes by my lamentations? I suppose it is the condition of humanity to design what never will be done.'[10]

Three months later, still in Lichfield, he wrote again, feeling all around him the heaviness of 'the shackles of destiny'. Hester would have spent an agreeable summer enjoying herself at Brighton, but for him 'there has not been one day of pleasure'. 'Ill-health', he told George Colman, the playwright, 'has crusted me into inactivity.' He asked Chambers how soon they would have to meet: 'If I cannot immediately go with you to Oxford, you must be content to stay a little while in London.' It gave him a faint flush of pleasure to address the Vinerian Professor, a man who had just been offered, and refused, the attorney general's post in Jamaica, in this way.[11] His journal confirms continuing ill health, though he bravely abstained from wine and insisted on taking purges. 'I have been disturbed and unsettled for a long time,' he noted on 2 August, adding that his disorder left him 'without resolution to apply to study or to business'. It also left his mind to wander strangely; earlier that year he had noted that if his mother 'had lived till March she would have been eighty nine', whereas the truth was that his mother, who died over eight years earlier, had *then* been eighty-nine. Perhaps the 'ease' he felt at precisely '5.24 p.m.' might be 'such a sudden relief as I once had by a good night's rest in Fetter Lane', he suddenly says, musing on a period that was twenty years ago in London. Alone, in the house in which he had dreamt of future lives, he was forced to face up to what his real life had become. 'Abstinence is not easily practiced in another's house,' he wrote, mentally refusing to accept that the house in which he wrote the thought *was* his own; 'the shortness of time' which 'the common order of nature' allowed him to anticipate was 'very frequently upon my mind'. This mental confusion appears to have stayed with him for a fortnight at least, but then 'by several purges taken successively and by abstinence from wine' it cleared, and he found a 'freedom of mind' he had not known 'for all this year'. He wrote sacraments 'preparatory to her death' for Kitty Chambers, and, in the presence of Lucy, kissed her. 'Kitty is, I think going to Heaven,' he wrote. But it was a further two months before she took her leave and Johnson, having said he would not quit Lichfield until she died, filled in his days as best he could. To Langton he confessed regretting his 'long stay' away, hoping to see him soon, in town; to Hester he called his time in Lichfield an 'exile'.[12] At last, on 17 October, Kitty Chambers, who had 'buried my Father, my Brother, and my Mother', died. 'She is now fifty eight years old,' he wrote, which must have affected him; he was fifty-eight himself. On the last day he prayed for her, and kissed her 'with swelled eyes and great emotion of tenderness'. She said she hoped they would 'meet again in a better place', and he agreed.

Once she had died, anywhere would be a better place than Lichfield. 'I returned this week from the country, after an absence of near six months,' he wrote to William Drummond a week later. From the security of Fleet Street he wrote to Edmund Hector to apologise for not stopping in Birmingham, and to thank him for the teaboard he had sent; he also wrote to Elizabeth Aston of Lichfield, with advice to mingle more in society. 'Solitude excludes pleasure, and does not always secure peace.'[13] While away from London he found he had been attacked in print for requiring 'a pot of convivial Burton ale' to ease his 'terrible gripe', but not accused of amorous misadventures.

The writer of *The Sale of Authors* had caught him where he was most vulnerable: 'He has lost that which procured him his pension. He has lost all his *powers*.' Even the *St James's Chronicle*, usually a loyal defender, published a letter from 'Tim Trimmer' suggesting affinities between Johnson's dislike of Shakespeare and his own experiences as author of the 'unfortunate *Irene*'. Trimmer's main barb was his final comment, that Johnson had opened himself to censure by 'raising Expectations in the Publick, which he has not answered'.[14]

Actually he was very busy, writing a substantial quantity of the sixteen Vinerian lectures which Chambers was to give that year; but since responsibility for these was confidential, he made what noise he could of other work. Writing from New Inn Hall in Oxford, where Chambers was principal, he told Hester that he would 'write another advertisement' for Thrale, who was campaigning once again for his Southwark seat, 'lest you might suspect that my complaisance had more of idleness than sincerity'. He enclosed an election address which was immediately signed by Thrale and printed in the London press, and wrote to Richard Penneck 'soliciting your Vote and Interest' on Thrale's behalf. 'If I can be of any use I will come directly to London,' he wrote a week later. Evidently there was some nervousness in the Thrale household, where both Henry and Hester were expectant. Johnson asked 'to be immediately informed' of the results and was told, on 23 March, that Henry was returned at the head of the poll. Anna Maria was born just eight days afterwards.[15]

Jackson's Oxford Journal announced the Vinerian lectures for March and in his journal for 9 April Johnson noted, 'I returned from helping Chambers at Oxford', before scoring it through as part of his agreement to keep silent on the whole affair.[16] Sixteen lectures were delivered that year on the theme of English Public Law and Johnson's style is evident throughout, nowhere more than at the outset where, considering 'The law of nature, the revealed law, and the law of nations', he pens some trenchant passages. 'Professors like princes are exposed to censure not only by their own defects, but by the virtues of their predecessors,' he writes, making clear both his fidelity to Blackstone, the first Vinerian Professor, and his attempt to surpass him. He argues that society 'implies . . . a pursuit of the highest degree of happiness that can be obtained and enjoyed by any number', suggesting an affinity with Thomas Jefferson who wrote, nine years later in the Declaration of Independence of the United States, that 'Life, Liberty and the pursuit of Happiness' were the 'unalienable rights' of men. Certain verbal habits, like beginning sentences with a universal negative, are noticeable: 'Nothing is more evident from daily experience . . .' 'No man, however diligent could ever understand . . .' 'No human law was ever perfect.'[17] Some sentences come, almost unaltered, from earlier works: 'Nations, like individuals, have their infancy,' he wrote in his Preface to his edition of *Shakespeare*; here it becomes, in the second lecture of his series on 'The Public Law', 'Nations as well as individuals have their childhood'.[18]

He became ill that spring while still at Oxford, and wrote a prayer in his diary to remember 'that *the night cometh when no man can work*'. Informed by Lucy Porter that her aunt had died, he let out tearful commiseration. 'My Dear Dear Love,' his letter begins, as if mentally travelling back some twenty years to when their correspondence had been an illicit pleasure; 'such is the condition of our nature, that as we live on we must see those whom we love drop successively, and find our circle of relation grow less and less.' He begged her, 'my dear darling', not to forget him in her prayers, indicating that he had been 'very poorly'. To Hester too he wrote that he had been 'very much disordered', but congratulates himself that at least he was 'not at Streatham' where he would have been 'troublesome to you'. His letter, though, sent a day afterwards to Lucy, asks to be read by contraries; really he *did* wish he were at Streatham, being cared for by Hester, instead of which he lay rolling 'the weak eye of helpless anguish', seeing nothing 'on any side but cold indifference'. He tried not to complain: 'These reflections', he insisted, 'do not grow out of any discontent at C[hambers]'s behaviour'; but, in his illness, he felt like an infant, and longed to be cared for by an indulgent mamma. 'I design to love little Miss Nanny very well', he wrote, 'but you must let us have a Bessy some other time', indicating his wish for another Elizabeth, a 'Tetty', upon whom he could lavish special affection.[19]

'I count the friendship of your house among the felicities of life,' he wrote to Hester the following month, when he was back in London.

While in Oxford, Boswell had made a special trip to see him, remonstrating (tactfully) against criticism of his *Account of Corsica* which Johnson had scribbled in a brief note to him in Scotland. He must have visited him when he was well, for he cites, among Johnsonian aphorisms, the contrast between Richardson and Fielding being that between 'a man who knew how a watch was made, and a man who could tell the hour by looking on the dial-plate'. Boswell also notes Johnson indicating the kind of bond between the two of them: 'Nay, Sir, when I am dead, you may do as you will.'[20] Such was the public interest in his affairs that the London newspapers got hold of his ill health as a choice item, with the *Gazetteer* noting that 'Dr Samuel Johnson, the celebrated author of the Rambler, we are told, is at present in a declining situation'.[21]

Johnson's gradually developing reputation as a national fount of wisdom was called upon when Barnard approached him for advice on how and where to import books of interest for the king's library; Johnson replied that he was venturing into regions of the world divided 'between bigotry and atheism'. He kept up his regular correspondence with Lucy Porter, whom he addressed as 'My Dearest' or 'My Love', going to immense trouble to ensure that the reading glass which she entrusted to him to be altered was as pretty and proper as could be. He commiserated with her on the deaths of friends – 'Every day Somebody dies, and it must soon be our turn' – and told her he designed to go to the seaside 'next month'. In August the *Public Advertiser* warned its readers that he lay 'dangerously ill at Brighthelmstone' but a week later issued a correction, describing the previous news as 'without foundation'. Whether the correction covered his location, his condition or both, it is impossible to say. On his birthday, which he noted as his sixtieth (though actually his fifty-ninth), he was in Kent, at the home of an attorney, where he had been taken by the Thrales for the benefit of his health. 'How the last year has past I am unwilling to terrify myself with thinking,' he writes, though he finds solace in reading 'which I therefore intend to practice when I am able'. It came into his head 'to write the history of my melancholy', but, as with so many other schemes, nothing resulted. He prayed, 'Heal my body, strengthen my mind. Compose my distraction, calm my inquietude, and relieve my terrours', and read 'a great part of Pascal's Life' which seemed to soothe him.[22] He wished Hester's mother, Mrs Salusbury, well when she was ill in November, wanting 'no pleasure at the expence of one to whom you have so much greater reason to be attentive', assuring her he was 'not, I thank God, worse than when I went'. His work with Chambers still continued, though his enthusiasm for it had waned; 'Chambers has no heart,' he grumbled, making himself ready to go to Oxford and instil some courage in him.[23]

'How the last has past', Johnson wrote on the first morning of the new year 1769, it would perhaps be 'not prudent too solicitously to recollect'. He did not feel himself to be in a state to form resolutions, but one plea, offered in prayer, is notable; he begged that he might 'become less desirous of sinful pleasures'. He was clearly thinking of those heinous bottles of wine, though a deeper dread lay in his mind which he had divulged to Hester Thrale. She wrote, somewhat proudly, that 'no Man can live his Life quite thro', without being at *some* period of it under the Dominion of *some* Woman – Wife, Mistress or Friend'. Johnson, she said, had 'trusted me about the year 1767 or 1768 – I know not which just now – with a Secret far dearer to him than his Life'. What that secret was she does not say, but congratulated herself on trustworthiness: 'I sincerely believe he has never since that Day regretted his Confidence.' It is possible this secret was a masochistic desire to be enslaved by his 'Mistress' of which there are many later hints; more probably here it is the fear of madness, with measures, including padlocks and a chain, that he entrusted her to take to make sure he should never be a burden, or a spectacle.[24]

'I know you want to be forgetting me,' he writes, quite blithely, to Hester in May, threatening he will write her letters, 'like *Presto's*', that is, like Swift's *Journal to Stella*, telling her what he says and thinks and does at every moment. Aware that her fifth pregnancy had almost come to term, he begged to be informed 'that your trouble is over'. Lucy Elizabeth was born on 22 June and he wrote to congratulate her on this 'pretty little Miss'; 'surely', he said, on becoming her godfather, he would be 'very fond of her'.[25] Greatly touched by the names the Thrales had given her, he wrote, on a quick visit to Lichfield, that he had taken care 'to tell Miss Porter, that I have got another Lucy'.

Following them to Brighton, he was out of town when Boswell called, anxious for Johnson's advice about the marriage on which he was about to venture. In a letter Johnson wished him well, but did not promise a speedy return to London: 'I shall perhaps stay a fortnight longer and a fortnight is a long time to a lover absent from his Mistress.'[26] He was determined *not* to be present at the Shakespeare Jubilee, with Garrick as its Steward, which took place in Stratford in September 1769, and was chiefly memorable for the sudden floods which ruined its tableaux. The newspapers were keen to link Johnson and Garrick as modern champions of Shakespeare: the *Gazetteer* published a tale featuring adventures of the 'two Staffordshire swains', while the *Public Advertiser* described a 'Shakespeare Ribband' on sale in Stratford, advertised with lines of Johnson's verse. Johnson, though, was never happy that Garrick's portrayal of Shakespeare's heroes, strutting and fretting their hours on stage, could gain so much more than his own adjudication of their lines. 'Many of Shakespeare's plays are the worse for being acted,' he told Boswell, words which in the Preface to his edition he states defiantly: 'Familiar comedy is often more powerful in the theatre, than on the page; imperial tragedy is always less.'[27] Back in London at the end of September, he saw Boswell, though less often than the guileful presentation of conversations in the *Life* would make appear. However, his judgement on London ('there is more learning and science within the circumference of ten miles from where we now sit, than in all the rest of the kingdom') sounds accurate, as does his triumphant comment on an evening when he had 'tossed and gored' many people.

When in the mood for disputation it is the case that there was 'no arguing with Johnson', or, as Goldsmith put it, 'when his pistol misses fire, he knocks you down with the butt end of it.' Though he found most solace with Hester Thrale, his personality blossomed beside men of wit with whom he entered instinctively into bouts of competitive repartee. Boswell records many such occasions of which one, a meeting of the Literary Club, is typical. It began with Johnson, Boswell and Topham Beauclerk seated together, discussing travel books on Europe, while the waiters rushed around them, taking orders. Johnson cited Addison quoting (from the original Italian) *'Stavo bene; per star meglio, sto qui'* ('I was well, I would be better, I took physic, and dyed') while legs of pork, boiled till they dropped from the bone, and veal pies made with plums and sugar were set before the company. He offered his opinion that the first thing the Italians should do on their revival of learning was 'to collect all that the Roman authours have said of their country', while Charles Swinden, who kept the house, fussed round, ensuring there was plenty of good red wine. He had earlier been harangued for serving claret 'so weak' that Johnson would, had he been a drinker, have drowned in it before it made him drunk. Johnson shook his head; it was 'poor stuff', he said, but since he confined himself to the juice of Seville oranges, and as no one else complained, he did not grumble. Claret, he pronounced, was 'liquor for boys'; port was the drink of men, but he who aspires to be a hero, he looked around the table, smiling, must drink – 'Brandy!' the rest of them roared back, having heard Johnson's monologue on liquor many times before.

In a discussion of the Erse poem 'Ossian' Johnson opined the Highland Scots 'wrote their native language', to which Beauclerk readily assented; why, the ballad 'Lillibulero', once 'in the mouths' of all Britons (there was, briefly, a chorus, to prove that what he said was true), was now quite forgotten. Thomas Percy, engaged in writing a history of the wolf, perked up to say that if the poem had been ancient it would surely have mentioned wolves. There was general agreement to that, which carried Johnson to broach the theme of wild animals, specifically bears; he persisted with his chosen topic, despite the meeting having, for the moment, broken into two, with Reynolds and Bennet Langton engaged upon a different, rather more amusing topic. He was 'dull of hearing', explains Boswell in the *Life*, apologising for the situation in which Johnson sat repeating '*Bear*' ('like a word in a catch,' said Beauclerk) increasingly loudly, seeming to those unfamiliar with him (who could be very few) like a man in ursine disguise. The rest of the Club's members 'could hardly stifle laughter' but came to order to hear Johnson opine that the black bear was apparently innocent, but he 'should not like to trust myself with him'. Quick as a flash Edward Gibbon muttered, just loud enough for those at his end of the table to hear, that he 'should not like to trust myself with *you*'. It was fortunate that Swinden reappeared, to see if the gentlemen required anything else, at that moment.

Patriotism then became their topic. Johnson gave his well-known epigram that patriotism was 'the last refuge of a scoundrel', which Boswell eagerly noted down before going on to argue that of course 'he did not mean' it. Finally the conversation turned to actresses, specifically Hannah Pritchard on whom, having watched her play the part of Irene (he had not *quite* forgotten the episode of the strangulation), Johnson had firm opinions. It was 'wonderful', he thought, 'how little *mind* she had'. She prided herself on never reading more of a tragedy than her own lines (he mentioned *Macbeth* lest they thought he had in mind *Irene*) and thought no more of the play from which her part came 'than a shoemaker thinks of the skin, out of which the piece of leather, of which he is making a pair of shoes, is cut'. There was general agreement and some applause at that, after which the Club broke up, its members going their separate ways; Reynolds to Leicester Fields, Gibbon to Bentinck Street, Johnson to Johnson's Court, off Fleet Street.[28]

In October Baretti killed a man in a Soho brawl, requiring Johnson, Reynolds and Garrick to testify on his behalf. Baretti had been propositioned by a whore and, when he declined, she grabbed him, painfully, by the testicles. He struck her in the face; she screamed and suddenly three men emerged from the shadows and descended on Baretti who, in his hurry to escape, began to flash his pocket knife. As the *Independent Chronicle* reported it, 'intimidated by the suddenness of the attack, and the darkness of the night, the shops all shut, and no refuge at hand . . . at last he drew his knife (an instrument which almost every foreigner carries about . . .)'. Unfortunately one man died from a slash with this blade. Baretti was arrested, taken to Newgate and charged with murder. While he was there another Italian came to him 'to desire a letter of recommendation for the teaching of his scholars, when he . . . should be hanged'. Baretti flew into a rage and threatened to kick him down the stairs. The witnesses he had to speak up for him at the Old Bailey, a fortnight later, were most distinguished;[29] Garrick insisted 'that every one abroad carried such a knife, for in foreign inns only forks were provided'. Asked about Baretti's eyesight, Johnson replied, diplomatically: 'He does not see me now, nor I do not [*sic*] see him.' 'After a hearing of four hours', reported the

Independent Chronicle, 'the verdict brought in by the jury was *self-defence*'. Johnson generalised to Boswell: 'Why there's Baretti, who is to be tried for his life to-morrow' with all his friends rallied round; but 'if he should be hanged, none of them will eat a slice of plumb-pudding the less'. He had a characteristic tendency to get at what he considered the heart of any problem, not worrying overmuch about the subtleties. One day, outside the church in Harwich, he and Boswell disputed Berkeley's 'ingenious sophistry to prove the non-existence of matter'. Boswell observed that though both of them were satisfied 'his doctrine is not true, it is impossible to refute it'. Johnson replied, with great alacrity, 'striking his foot with mighty force against a large stone, till he rebounded from it, "I refute it *thus*." '[30]

For someone whose appearances in the London press were regular, Johnson had written little for over a year. Dedications to Payne's *Introduction to Geometry* and to Hoole's *Cyrus* and *Metastasio*, plus an obituary for Zachariah Mudge, were all of which he could boast. Yet still *Lloyd's Evening Post* reckoned him 'at the head of the present press' and he was about to justify the judgement.[31] In early January 1770, 'between eight o'clock on Wednesday night and twelve o'clock on Thursday night', Johnson wrote *The False Alarm*, a pamphlet on the activities of John Wilkes, agitation on whose behalf was threatening to become a parliamentary farce. Between 1768 and 1770 Wilkes had been elected four times to sit for Middlesex, but each time his election had been set aside and Henry Luttrel, who gained 296 votes (as opposed to Wilkes, who polled 1,143), was declared the winner, since he was a *qualified* candidate. Wilkes, who had outstanding charges of seditious libel and obscenity against him, was ruled ineligible but Boswell, travelling down to London from Oxford, was mesmerised by people 'roaring with "Wilkes and Liberty", which, with "No. 45", was chalked on every coach and chaise'. Modern readers, siding with Wilkes in a dispute which takes its place in the history of struggles to enlarge the electorate, have viewed Johnson's position as at best misguided, at worst as a travesty of electoral justice. Yet Johnson, who said he thought *The False Alarm* the 'best' of his political writings, had reasons for writing as he did, mainly his loyalty to his friends the Thrales. 'We read [*The False Alarm*] to Mr Thrale when he came very late home from the House of

Commons,' reported Hester Thrale, indicating the extent of the worries she felt for her homes and family.[32] Johnson wrote the pamphlet quickly, exploiting a rich vein of scorn, as here, where he reckons up the ways of getting signatures on a petition for a Bill of Rights:

> Names are easily collected. One man signs because he hates the papists; another because he has vowed destruction to the turnpikes; one because it will vex the parson; another because he owes his landlord nothing; one because he is rich; another because he is poor; one to shew that he is not afraid, and another to shew that he can write.

Of Wilkes the individual he makes it clear he will not speak, though there is a certain satisfaction in noting that 'the man' he writes of is not only 'expelled the House of Commons' but 'confined in jail as being legally convicted of sedition and impiety'.[33]

However, when *The False Alarm* was published he realised how acute, and politically charged, the situation was. The *Public Advertiser* immediately reported a 'well-known RAMBLER' was to receive an additional £100 for writing it; this was immediately contradicted by the *Middlesex Journal*, which assured its readers that Dr S. Johnson 'had had no addition made to his pension'. 'Intelligence Extraordinary' in the *Independent Chronicle* announced a forthcoming duel between Wilkes and Johnson, who would fight 'at *single rapier*, for the *good of their country* in *St George's fields*' on the day 'after the Patriot's release' in a battle to decide 'Literature, writing and HONOUR'.[34] Johnson tried to be unaffected by such press attention, warning Henry Bright, at Eton, to examine a dim pupil carefully, preferably in his father's presence. Hester Thrale knew both the father and the son: 'I asked [him] who succeeded Romulus – and Johnson said I might as well enquire who phlebotomized Romulus.' But the Wilkes controversy rumbled on and, while Wilkes was deprived of the Middlesex seat, the newspapers carried many stories about Luttrell, his qualified opponent. Apparently, several years before, Luttrell had been involved with a Miss Bolton whom he had allegedly infected with venereal disease. Suddenly *The Memoirs of Miss Arabella Bolton* had a very great sale, describing as it did, in graphic detail, the 'barbarous treatment' Miss Bolton had received from 'the honourable Colonel L—l'. Johnson preferred to concentrate on paying for Frank Barber's education at Bishop's Stortford, where he had been for two years now. 'Be a good Boy,' he wrote, though Frank, now twenty-five, could hardly be considered a boy and whether he were 'good' or not depends very much upon interpretation.[35]

Johnson's judgements, not only in the case of Wilkes but generally, seem somewhat antique when faced with contemporary political issues. Relying on axioms drawn from Greece and Rome, or on modern instances 'from China to Peru', his universalising instincts were somewhat awkward and inflexible when faced with situations that were local and specific. Five years later he wrote to support a political edifice which, even as he was composing his patrician thoughts, was crumbling. To Boswell he confided his intention 'to write about the Americans', swearing the younger man to silence: 'but mum, – it is a secret'.[36] Lord North had intimated to him, through Strahan, that a pamphlet on the American situation, where the Thirteen Colonies had bound themselves together at the Congress at Philadelphia, would be most welcome. Johnson complied but was far from happy, not with the substance of what he wrote but with official reactions to it. 'I am sorry to see that all the alterations proposed are evidence of timidity,' he told Strahan; 'I do [not] wish to publish, what those for whom I write do not like to have published.' Reading through the proofs a couple of days later, he made the same point: 'why should I in defense of the ministry provoke those, whom in their own defense they dare not provoke.' Wondering whether such men were 'fit to be the governours of kingdoms' he asked to have half a dozen copies printed up 'in the original state' for his own benefit; 'the changes', he said, 'are not for the better.' No such offprints have ever been discovered; instead, Johnson received the degree of Doctor in Civil Law from Oxford, of which North just happened to be Chancellor. Pleased with the award, he was still frustrated at being required to pen pamphlets which his political masters could alter to suit their current mood. Even Boswell was dismayed on his behalf: 'How humiliating to the great Johnson!' he wrote originally, in the *Life*, before prudently omitting the comment. Johnson complained to Gerard Hamilton that his pension, granted for literary merit, was being used to exert political pressure on him and 'declared his resolution' to resign it; Hamilton effectively argued him out of renunciation, but the point was made. *Taxation no Tyranny* was the last political pamphlet that Johnson wrote.[37]

The pamphlet, re-edited in conformity with North's latest position, appeared in March and was several times reprinted. Taking a firm tone, it viewed its opponents as 'croakers of calamity' who sought 'to infect the people of England with the contagion of disloyalty'. The arguments are posed between the 'mother-country' England and her unruly brood of thirteen American colonies. 'In sovereignty there are no gradations,' he argues; 'all government is ultimately and essentially absolute.' The power vested in governments 'is not infallible, for it may do wrong; but it is irresistible'. Life, liberty and the pursuit of happiness may appear as worthwhile goals, but 'Government is necessary to man, and where obedience is not compelled, there is no government.' Johnson developed his reasoning impressively; Coleridge liked his political pamphlets 'better than any other parts of his work – particularly his *Taxation No Tyranny*'; but in the end, it is an offhand remark that memorably sums up his position. 'If slavery be thus fatally contagious', he responds to an argument that has been put against him, 'how is it that we hear the loudest yelps for liberty among the drivers of negroes?' Once again, Francis Barber's presence had a real effect in shaping the attitude that Johnson – a natural conservative – adopted towards the slavery of one race by another.[38] It is this crucial moral quality that makes his ideas relevant, even when subsequent history threatens to label them reactionary. Listening to Johnson dictate arguments in favour of a 'negro' claiming liberty in Scotland, Boswell recalled his 'zealous' dislike of slavery 'in every form'; specifically his radical toast among some 'very grave men' at Oxford: 'Here's to the next insurrection of the negroes in the West Indies.'[39]

Boswell, with thoughts of the *Life* he would write uppermost in his mind, was keen to see his subject in all situations, and was bent upon promoting an encounter between him and Wilkes, with whom, Boswell liked to boast, he himself lived 'in habits of friendship'. Six years after *The False Alarm* he discovered an opportunity, though his method of inveigling Johnson into accepting an invitation to dine at the home of Edward and Charles Dilly, booksellers in the Poultry, with some 'patriotick friends' was almost wrong-footed. Johnson had his counter-thrust prepared, 'forgetting' the invitation and ordering his dinner 'at home with Mrs Williams'. Boswell was forced to go to Mrs Williams (whom he described as 'peevish'), begging her to release Johnson from the arrangement he had just made: 'I shall be quite disgraced if the Doctor is not there.' The episode is an interesting illustration of Johnson's reactions to an attempt by Boswell to trap him into a situation in which his behaviour was to be observed.

In the event the dinner passed off perfectly agreeably. Wilkes was assiduous in helping Johnson to his food ('Some fat, Sir – A little of the stuffing – Some gravy – Let me have the pleasure of giving you some butter'); they disputed, in a friendly manner, the claims of Garrick, whom Johnson praised for giving away 'more money than any man in England'; and they agreed in a judgement of Scottish settlers in a barren part of America: 'The *Scotch*', said Johnson, 'would not know it to be barren.' 'What should he be doing?' he wrote, in the third person, to Hester Thrale, still in Bath, to whom this was his third unanswered letter; why, 'he is breaking jokes with Jack Wilkes upon the Scots'. Boswell was travelling home, he wrote to her a few days later, 'with no great inclination', carrying with him 'two or three good resolutions; I hope they will not mould upon the road.'[40]

14

Strawberries and Fetters

strawberry n.s. *(* fragaria, *Latin.)* *A plant.*

Strawberries, by their fragrant smell, seem to be cordial; the seeds obtained by shaking the ripe fruit in Winter, are an excellent remedy against the stone.

Arbuthnot on Diet

fetter n.s. *It is commonly used in the plural* fetters. *(from* feet; fettere, *Saxon.) Chains for the feet; chains by which walking is hindered.*

Pleasure arose in those very parts of his leg that just before had been so much pained by the *fetter.*

Addison.

'Mitigate the diseases of my body, and compose the disorders of my mind,' Johnson prayed on New Year's Day 1770, following the dictates of habit, rather than any particular distress. Actually he was feeling better about himself than he had for some time. He had lived for sixty years, and was still enjoying life. He was written about in the newspapers; he went swimming in the sea; he had appeared as an important witness at the Old Bailey and had pronounced as a professor of law (albeit in covert guise) in Oxford; he had a town house in Fleet Street, a regular weekend retreat at Streatham and a country property at Lichfield. 'Let not pleasure seduce me,' he wrote, noting his appointments ('Dined with the Academy. Went to Mrs. Salusbury & to Club') and remarking, the next day, an interesting piece of gossip: 'Mrs Lucy Southwel got a thousand pounds in the Lottery.' He felt, for the first time, quite content with himself.[1]

Under pressure from the Thrales, Johnson took some notice of his appearance, and found his own body unappealing; 'I have grown fat too fast,' he noted, indicating that the unlimited largess he enjoyed at Streatham, which had already made him change his shirt more often, was having an unfortunate effect upon his body. He set himself to 'live on Milk' but found it a miserable diet: 'I grew worse', he commented, 'with forbearance of solid food.' He ended the year with yet more honours, being appointed Professor of Ancient Literature to the Royal Academy, a grand title, but entirely honorary, there being neither salary nor duties annexed to the post. He felt no diminution of past anxieties at these new glories ('The perturbation of my nights is very distressful,' he registered, striking a by now conventional note); really he was quite content.[2]

He went to Oxford for a few days to help out Chambers, with nothing but rheumatic pains as a disincentive, but still found the press hounding him. The *London Evening-Post* published a fantasy in which Johnson's *'amiable consort'* became pregnant, 'the old lady's bulk' not arising from 'the *Stamina of his arbor vitae*' but from a surfeit of cabbages sent to her 'as a present from *Kew-Gardens*'. She swelled up until relieved 'by an abortion *backwards . . .*' which was, he remarked, a quite ludicrous fancy, for while he frequently commented on the pleasures he experienced at Ranelagh, he had never even been to Kew.[3] He received disturbing news of John Taylor at Ashbourne, before leaving London for what was becoming a regular feature of his life, time spent in Lichfield. 'I reckon to go next week,' he told Hester in the first of a regular series of twice-weekly bulletins in which he mentioned strawberries, children and break-ins all in one hectic rush. 'I have passed one day at Birmingham with my old Friend Hector – there's a name – and his Sister, an old Love,' he wrote; 'My Mistress is grown much older than my friend'. He found much to interest him in the book of the local apothecary, listing families who paid the parish levies a century ago: 'Many families that paid the parish rates are now extinct like the race of Hercules', he mused, confessing he would mourn 'when old names vanish away'. He paid daily visits to Mrs Aston and approved a local bull but was very pleased to hear from her that 'you want me home'; 'nothing goes well when I am from you.'

On the anniversary of his wife's death, 28 March, he made a special mention of his 'poor dear Tetty . . . I have recalled her to my mind of late less frequently'; not speculating on why that should be, he made an interesting mental leap: 'When I saw the sea at Brighthelmston I wished for her to have seen it with me.' Now he was to repeat the experience, for another seaside excursion was promised. 'The Journey to Brighthelmston makes no part of my felicity,' he told Hester, and he went only because 'I love those with whom I go'. While he had been away, the newspapers had changed from commenting on what he wrote to how he appeared. The *Gazetteer*'s 'Cosmophilus' commented that while passing a print-shop, he had seen a print 'inscribed *Samuel Johnson*' taken from a portrait by Sir Joshua Reynolds, and hastened to enquire, 'Pray Sir, can you inform me whether he is blind . . . it seems to represent him so.'[4]

At Easter Johnson was ill, with pains of 'Lumbago, or Rheumatism' affecting his loins and belly. At night he lay, 'wrapped in Flannel with a very great fire near my bed'; the next night, being no better, he 'took opium' and felt the spasms in his stomach decrease. He used his illness to excuse non-attendance at church that Friday, yet worried about doing so, wondering in his diary whether it were 'rather an excuse made to myself'. He spent 'a very tedious and painful night' at the Thrales', and had recourse once more to opium, finding the relief it brought 'very cheaply purchased'. At home on Easter Day he followed his own prescribed ritual of prayers and resolutions, but suffered distraction at church as he went forward to take Communion: 'Some vain thoughts stole upon me while I stood near the table' but 'I hope I ejected them effectually.' The principal vanities which might have affected him concerned Hester Thrale, but such thoughts, however 'thrown' into his mind, must needs be 'ejected'. 'I hope God has heard me,' he prayed, his mind still haunted by flashbacks from his opium-inspired dreams.[5] Before leaving for his month in Lichfield he wrote down a 'thought' in his diary, significant in that he almost never did so: 'Every man naturally persuades himself that he can keep his resolutions,' he wrote; 'nor is he convinced of his own imbecility but by the length of time, and frequency of experiment.' He had been reading back through pages of resolutions, so solemnly made but equally quickly abandoned. 'He who may live as he will, seldom lives long in the observation of his own rules,' he concluded, having, as the exception to prove the rule, the memory of Mrs Harriots of Trysull, who had provided the money for him to go to Oxford, but between whom and his father there had never been much kindness.

He was occupied for much of the year in revising his edition of *Shakespeare* with the help of Richard Farmer and George Steevens. In September he wrote to Joseph Warton, recalling he had 'misrepresented your opinion of Lear' and offering him the opportunity to change it; whether Warton replied is unknown, but the paragraph in the edition of 1773 is unaltered from that of 1765. 'I have done very little to the book,' he confessed to Farmer, hoping that amongst them all 'Shakespeare will be better understood'.[6] Otherwise his life resumed its familiar pattern, with the Club on Mondays and Streatham at weekends. On his way, walking home from the club, waylaid by beggars, he would give them all his loose change. 'He loved the poor,' said Mrs Thrale, remarking on his 'earnest desire to make them happy'. If it were objected that any money given was wasted since they would 'only lay it out in gin or tobacco', he would reply, 'And why should they be denied such sweeteners of their existence?' He wrote to Frank Barber advising him to read more ('You can never be wise unless you love reading') for only then would he appreciate that he, as much as Johnson, was becoming a regular feature in the press. In May the *General Evening Post* carried a 'Literary Anecdote' featuring an alleged conversation between him and Goldsmith on the subject of 'his little lacquey', Frank Barber. Asked by Dr G[oldsmith] whether he intended bringing 'the lacquey' up 'a scholar', Dr J[ohnson] nods; 'scholar enough to write a *bailiff scene* in a Comedy', an allusion to Johnson's recent rescue of Goldsmith from arrest for debt by his landlady. This anecdote on Barber's claimed ambitions became something of a favourite, with other papers keen to point out that the 'little lacquey' was in fact a 'young Negro'.[7]

'I have at length got out my paper,' Johnson wrote to Langton in March the following year, referring to his *Thoughts on the Late Transactions Respecting Falkland's Islands*. But sales were immediately stopped by Lord North until an unflattering reference to George

Grenville ('if he could have got the money, he could have counted it') was softened. But, Johnson smiled, 'a sufficient number were dispersed to do all the mischief, though perhaps not to make all the sport that might be expected from it'. It is unlike Johnson's normal reactions to his work to speak of 'mischief' and 'sport', and the pamphlet is one of his happiest attempts at writing political prose.[8] His description of the islands, though bleak, is accurate enough: 'a few spots of earth, which, in the deserts of the ocean, had almost escaped human notice', of which 'the soil was nothing but a bog, with no better prospect than that of barren mountains'. And this, he quotes Captain John Macbride as saying, 'is summer'. 'That such a settlement may be of use in war, no man that considers its situation will deny. But war is not the whole business of life.' War was, however, an important preoccupation of William Pitt (now Earl of Chatham), whose fulminations in the House of Lords were bellicose in the extreme: 'I . . . never met with an instance of candour or dignity in [the Spaniards'] proceedings; nothing but low cunning, trick, and artifice.'[9] Against such growing clamours for war, Johnson offered these sober reflections:

> The life of a modern soldier is ill represented by heroick fiction. War has means of destruction more formidable than the cannon and the sword. Of the thousands and ten thousands that perished in our late contests with France and Spain, a very small part ever felt the stroke of an enemy; the rest languished in tents and ships, amidst damps and putrefaction; pale, torpid, spiritless, and helpless; gasping and groaning, unpitied among men made obdurate by long continuance of hopeless misery.

Lord North held firm, never giving up the British claim to sovereignty yet doing nothing to push the Spanish into war: 'The real crime of the ministry is, that they have found the means of avoiding their own ruin,' Johnson commented and received, as means for his own ruin, press rumours about himself and Mrs Thrale, disguised as references to Swift's entanglement with Hester Vanhomrigh. 'Literary Intelligence' in the *Gazetteer* remarked that a '*certain lexicographer*' had '*rambled* into the luxurious regions of *love-poetry*' at the command of a certain '*Vanessa* no less remarkable for learning than malt', where the mention of '*Vanessa's*' widowhood does not disguise a clear innuendo towards her and her 'cruel *Cadenus*'.[10] 'Dr Percy has written a long Ballad', he told Langton of Percy's new ballad 'in many *Fits*', 'The Hermit of Warkworth'. The poem ('pretty enough') evidently greatly amused him and provoked him to produce not one but three brief parodies, of which one is best known from Wordsworth's later ridicule of it in his Preface to *Lyrical Ballads*:

> I put my hat upon my head
>   And walk'd into the Strand,
> And there I met another man
>   Who's hat was in his hand.[11]

Langton's elder sister, Elizabeth, had fallen ill that spring and Johnson sent best wishes: 'To preserve health is a moral and religious duty,' he wrote; 'for health is the basis of all social virtues.' Unfortunately, he began his letter with 'Madam', which, he told Hester Thrale, surprised Miss Langton 'as if an old friend newly meeting her, had thrown a glass of cold water in her face'. If she threatened to ignore his letters, Boswell was just the opposite; Johnson wrote, masking irritation with apologies, admitted that nature '*abhors a vacuum*', and promised to 'climb the Highlands' and be 'tost among the Hebrides' according to Boswell's wish; the only question was *when*.[12]

The letters he sent to Hester, three times a week, from his summer trip to Lichfield in 1771 are brief, allusive and intimate, trying to make witty adventures out of the most trivial, domestic details. As he had remarked the year before, 'what is nearest us, touches us most.' Miss Turton's spectacles and Miss Porter's dogs and cats were mentioned, but it was a third subject, the Thrales' unborn seventh infant, that carried the day. 'A new Being is born that shall in time write such letters as this,' he writes in June, and by July hopes 'the dangers of this year' are over and that she is 'safe in Bed with a pretty little Stranger in the cradle'. Delay made for anxiety ('This naughty Baby stays so long that I am afraid it will be a Giant like King Richard') and he attempted to make her smile: 'I suppose I shall be able to tell it, "Teeth hadst thou in thy head when thou wert born".' His fears were real enough: 'I wish your pains and your danger over.' He bitterly regretted the adjective 'indifferent' he had used of his feelings for her: 'Indifference is indeed a strange word in a Letter from me to you,' he said, assuring her such feelings would be a 'contradiction from my own thoughts'. 'Dearest Madam,' he began the letter, ending with the same superlative of affection.[13]

The intensity of Johnson's feelings for Hester Thrale, thirty years his junior and married, is difficult to decipher; but there are hints, of which one should be aware, that nothing of an overtly amorous nature can be admitted. His use of '*Dearest* Madam' in the opening of his letter was very understandable, but still a blunder, as ill-judged as his use of 'Madam' in his letter to Elizabeth Langton. 'Madam' – like a shocking drench of cold water – was clearly the form they decided on, yet, amongst the trivia of frequent letters, there was *something* which meant rather more to both of them. The previous summer he had written, 'For your strawberries, however, I have no care. Mrs Cobb has strawberries, and will give me as long as they last', which had evidently been turned into a jest between them. This year he fairly swamped her with references to Mrs Cobb's strawberries, and cream too. 'I have never wanted Strawberries and cream,' he wrote on 3 July, followed by 'Strawberries and cream every day', 'Toûjours strawberries and Cream', 'This day we had no strawberries', and 'To Strawberries and cream which still continue' on 20 July. The pair of them were being referred to as Cadenus and Vanessa in the *Gazetteer*, the most notorious element in whose correspondence was Swift's frequent references to coffee ('riches are nine parts in ten of all that is good in life, and health is the tenth; drinking coffee comes long after, and yet it is the eleventh'). Johnson's frequent references to strawberries have much the same ambiguous appeal.[14]

On 10 July, the baby still having not appeared, he applauded her use of opium, though regretted the need for it: 'I am sorry that opium is necessary, and sincerely wish your pain and your danger happily at an end.' He attempted to cheer her by speculating on chemical experiments they would perform together in the furnace Henry was having built for them on 'the pump side in the kitchen Garden'; a chymist is 'very like a Lover', he confessed, before going on with details of iron, copper and lead. 'One of our swans is sick,' he wrote, a few days later;

life, evidently 'is chequerwork', he said, misquoting Congreve; four days later the swan was dead 'without an elegy either by himself or his Friends'. 'The other swan swims about solitary, as Mr Thrale, and I, and others should do, if we lost our Mistress.' He turned from this dangerously agitated tone to playful criticism of Queeney, who 'might have written to me' but hadn't. This little game, repeated with several variations, kept them both amused till Sophia at last was born, in late July; he left Lichfield in August. Hester wrote, apologetically, that 'Queeney has at last squeezed out a kind word',[15] to which he replied, addressing her as 'My sweet, dear, pretty, little Miss', saying she had 'got my heart, and will keep it'. His attempts to leave Lichfield were delayed only by Lucy Porter ('a very peremptory Maiden'): 'if I had gone without permission, I am not very sure that I might have been welcome at another time.' His game of seeking permissions of a younger, wealthier woman was now quite sophisticated. 'Lucy is a Philosopher,' he wrote, a fortnight earlier, who considered him 'as one of the external and accidental things that are to be taken and left without emotion. If I could learn of Lucy would it be better? Will you teach me?' In his last letter that summer to Hester, he bids her consider: 'Do you think, that after all this roving you shall be able to manage me again?'[16]

On receiving the sacrament at Easter he prayed for 'such a sense of my Wickedness as may produce true contrition' for 'I have committed many crimes'. At the end of a long page of prayers in English, he wrote a phrase in Latin: '*De pedicis et manicis insana cogitatio*' ('mad thoughts on manacles and shackles'). These thoughts, the threat of madness and a consequent chaining up, come from nowhere, and yet proceed from his overwhelming desire to confess his 'crimes'.[17] In August, after his return from Lichfield, he writes a list of rituals, noting attendance at church, additions to devotions and reading his Greek Testament 'regularly'. On the negative side he confesses, 'I have M. once by accident' and 'I have used more corporal action'. 'M' has not been noted for five years, since he struggled to give up alcohol; but 'corporal action' is significant. In the *Dictionary* he glossed *corporal* as meaning 'relating to the body' with a quotation from Atterbury: 'Beasts enjoy greater sensual pleasures, and feel fewer *corporal* pains, and are utter strangers to all those anxious and tormenting thoughts which perpetually haunt and disquiet mankind.' Coupled here to his mad Latin thoughts of manacles and shackles, after a summer of letters in which he gave himself up to the management and governance of younger women, this suggests that the 'Secret far dearer to him than his life' was indeed a deep masochism. The fact that, in making her comment, Hester Thrale adds, 'Pope & Swift, were softened by the Smiles of Patty Blount & Stella; & our stern Philosopher Johnson trusted me', indicates her sense of her importance to him. She goes on: 'Johnson is more a Hero to me than to any one – & I have been more to him for Intimacy, than ever was any Man's Valet de Chambre.' For his part, Johnson replied, 'I do certainly love you better [tha]n any human Being I ever saw.'[18]

Back in London it was not long before he was busy. 'I am engaging in a very great work,' he told Langton in August 1771; 'the revision of my Dictionary from which I know not at present how to get loose'. Thrale frequently teased him on the subject, claiming there were 'three or four' flaws in it, to which Johnson replied that there were 'four or five *hundred*'; but Hester claimed that when the booksellers asked him to revise it, 'he went cheerfully to the business, said he was well paid, and that they deserved to have it done carefully'. 'If you have observed or been told any errors or omissions, you will do me a great favour by letting me know them,' he begged Langton.[19] Actually Johnson already had several notebooks filled with rejected manuscript material from the first edition, on which he and his assistants, Macbean and Peyton, had worked. Examining these, some of Johnson's important, though unacknowledged, criteria become evident. An amanuensis had listed, under *blow*, 'To blow nails: a proverbial expression for poor Comfort, akin to that in Scotland *He blaws a cald coal*.' This is crossed through by Johnson, as is another Scottish example where the amanuensis had noted: 'Baby (Babée) In Scotland denotes a half-penny, as alluding to the Head impressed on the copper coin.' All such examples of Scotticisms were struck through by Johnson, who made it clear he wished to create an *English* dictionary; to that end he was content to rule out any regional or dialect variations. For *baldrick* the amanuensis had surmised it was 'very probably derived from the inventor or first wearer of this belt, who was called Balderic, baldric'; Johnson did not so surmise, and ruled it out. For *barbarlie* he went further, omitting completely an indelicate reference taken from some lines of Thomas Tusser ('I dare assure,/ cast dust in his arse'), blacking them out on the paper slip and leaving the entry out of the *Dictionary* entirely; it is 'the only case . . . of such assiduous blacking-out' that exists.[20] He used Alexander Cruden's *Concordance to the Holy Scriptures* to help him provide more orthodox definitions for this fourth edition, except when the sense of guilt prevented him. Under 'Chaseth' in Cruden's *Concordance* there is the quotation 'He *chaseth* away his mother', from Proverbs. This was one that Johnson knew well and in his definition of the word *chase* he inserted the whole sentence: 'He that *chaseth* away his mother, is a son that causeth shame.' It was a biblical text that haunted him.[21]

Towards the end of September, when he was deeply involved in making these revisions, he felt his mind 'less encumbered' and 'less interrupted in mental employment'. It was some years since he had given himself wholly to work in this fashion, and he liked it. 'I have gone voluntarily to Church on the weekdays but few times in my Life,' he wrote, having come home from the Thrales' 'that I might be more master of my hours'. 'I think to mend,' he noted, before going out 'with Macbean to dine' and to discuss further revisions. He was so deeply involved in the work that interruptions came badly, particularly if the person introducing them, like Garrick, was one with whom he experienced a deep sense of unacknowledged envy. Garrick had written to him with a draft of his epitaph for William Hogarth, who had died earlier that year, asking for Johnson's comments. 'Of your three stanzas, the third is utterly unworthy of you,' he wrote back, dropping instantly into his schoolmaster's tone. 'Hogarth would not be distinguished from any other man of intellectual eminence.' He made several more abrupt criticisms ('*Art* and *Nature* have been seen together too often') before throwing the epitaph back with the comment 'When you have reviewed it, let me see it again'. Garrick was gracious in reply, admitting he was 'tired' of the task.[22] In March Boswell returned to London to appear in a schoolmaster's appeal to the House of Lords against being stripped of office for having been 'somewhat severe in the chastisement of his scholars'; an ejection Johnson judged 'very cruel, unreasonable, and oppressive' without hearing a word of the case. He insisted that

Mrs Thrale, Miss Williams, Beattie and himself all loved Boswell, which may have stretched a point; as Boswell wrote in a letter to Mrs Thrale about his first encounter with her, 'I told you, Madam, that you and I were rivals for that great man.'[23]

That Easter he noted 'an unpleasing incident', almost certain 'to hinder my rest', and told John Taylor he no longer ventured upon night-time company in which there might be 'anything disagreeable, lest something should fasten upon my imagination, and hinder me from sleep'. He noted the date as 'the death of Tetty', but memories of Tetty were, like those of his mother, only occasional guilty recollections. Among the rules he gave himself in 1772 was a new one: 'To appropriate something to charity.' On Good Friday he remembered he had honoured it by paying Peyton 'without requiring work'. Returning, he found Boswell waiting for him and together they discussed style. Boswell mentioned Garrick's complaint that the Preface to *Shakespeare* reflected on him as a collector of rare editions which he was rather selective about lending. Johnson countered that Garrick wished to be 'courted for them'. The truth was that Johnson's own 'slovenly and careless' practice with books was well known and Garrick, like several other people, hesitated to put their own volumes forward to be mauled.[24]

In August he wrote to John Taylor of the recent bankruptcy of Alexander Fordyce, a leading London banker: 'Such a general distrust and timidity has been diffused', he said, 'that credit has been almost extinguished.' The *Gentleman's Magazine* reported that 'An universal bankruptcy was expected . . .'[25] Yet this was the context for Henry Thrale's choosing to risk his entire enterprise in a scheme of Humphrey Jackson's for brewing without the expense of malt and hops. The experiment failed, unsurprisingly, leaving Thrale facing utter ruin; where previously he had been a ruthless buccaneer in business, he now felt utterly crushed, leaving it all to Hester, assisted by Johnson, to rescue his enterprise. Money was borrowed from Hester's mother, Mrs Salusbury; it was begged for from many others, and bankruptcy was, at last, avoided, but the brewery was left with over £100,000 of debts. Mrs Thrale's ruthless endeavours caused her more personal anguish; her latest child, Penelope, born on 15 September, lived less than a single day. 'Poor little Maid!' she wrote in her Children's Book; 'one cannot grieve after her much, and I have just now other things to think of.'[26]

Johnson offered what advice he could; as Miss Williams wrote, he was 'constantly at Streatham'. Even later in the year, going to Lichfield, which was now part of his annual routine, his letters to Hester are not the teasing missives of earlier years but anxious bulletins. 'Malt is five and sixpence a strike, or two pounds four shillings a quarter,' he wrote in October: 'Wheat is nine and six pence a bushel. These are prices which are almost descriptive of a famine.' A week later he wrote again: 'The price of malt has risen again. It is now two pounds eight shillings the quarter. Ale is sold in the publick houses, at sixpence a quart, a price which I never heard of before.' It is clear he has taken on the Thrales', or rather *Hester's*, problems as his own from the ease with which he slips into using the first person plural: 'The first consequence of our late trouble ought to be, an endeavour to brew at a cheaper rate . . . Unless this can be done nothing can help us, and if this can be done, we shall not want help.'[27]

Johnson endeavoured to 'encrease the general cheerfulness of Life' by recommending 'a little apparatus for chimistry' to John Taylor, which might 'offer you some diversion'. Earlier he had been part of a company of 'persons of the first distinction' who had witnessed a demonstration of fireworks at Ranelagh, which was, the *Gazetteer* enthused, 'universally allowed to be one of the most capital exhibitions ever seen in this kingdom'. His trip to Lichfield had been delayed, partly by the sudden brewery crisis, partly by his revisions to the *Dictionary*. 'I am now within a few hours of being able to send the whole dictionary to the press,' he wrote to Taylor in October, confessing his work on it had been 'sluggish' and that he was not 'much delighted at the conclusion'. 'Some superfluities I have expunged, and some faults I have corrected, and here and there have scattered a remark; but the main fabrick of the work remains as it was.' There is more Milton and less James Thomson in it but, looking back on the work the following year from the solemn perspective of his prayers, he acknowledged he had seldom been withheld from doing it 'but by my own unwillingness'.[28]

From Lichfield he wrote to Hester, bidding her thank her mother for the gift of a chair covered by Hester herself 'when she was a good little Girl and minded her Book and her Needle'. Initially he had not cared for Mrs Salusbury, a feeling heightened when her dog devoured his toast while he was talking to her daughter, but with the years his attitude had mellowed. Now he wrote from Lichfield, hoping that 'dear Mrs Salusbury is easy'. 'Do not be dejected,' he told Hester; 'send for me, if I can do you either service or pleasure.' At the start of November a major property move was forced upon the Thrales through financial problems and illness: Mrs Salusbury, who was suffering badly with cancer, gave up her house in Dean Street, Soho and moved to Streatham, whereupon the Thrales decamped to their Southwark house, which Hester loathed. She told Johnson she and her mother had formed a resolution 'to contend who shall live the cheapest'; he replied he was 'inwardly pleased however I may pretend to pity you'. Since Thrale had withdrawn his attention from running either the brewery or his house, Johnson had risen to assume a more dominant role, though always in a pose of deference. In one letter he refers to her 'injudicious' correspondence; she responds in kind, writing a fortnight later of Thrale's refusal to stir himself to 'speak a kind word to a Customer when he knows it would save him a house – You see this is a *private Letter*.' For his part, Johnson could not refuse himself 'the gratification of writing again to my Mistress', giving Hester her special title which, for whatever reason, had been dropped from more recent letters. He instructed her to 'bustle in the Brewhouse' as her mother urged, and wrote to Queeney, his 'Dear Sweeting', to acquaint her that Lucy Porter's 'fine black Cat' was no more. 'So things come and go. Generations, as Homer says, are but like leases.'[29] He was glad Hester exerted 'your new resolution with so much vigour' and calculated that, continuing in the same way, she would 'annually add to your fortune three thousand pounds', pay off all their loans and begin 'annually to lay up almost five thousand'. All of this, he believed 'is in your power'. If he hurried back to Southwark, he wished to know, 'will you promise not to spoil me? I do not much trust yet to your new character.' In his next letter he promised he would come if required, but Dr Taylor, with whom he was staying at Ashbourne, became 'moody' if he talked of leaving. 'If I am wanted at the Borough I will immediately come.' He confessed the pleasure of writing, regularly, when in reality 'there is nothing to be said', one of the secret delights of being in love. Hester told him the round tower was kept aired for his return, but he remained elusive, keeping his brain active with arithmetic, estimating that 'every two thousand pounds saves an hundred pound interest, and therefore as we gain more we pay less . . . Continue to be a housewife, and be as frolicksome with your tongue as you please.' He visited Chatsworth, where he wished she had been, for 'we should have gained something new to talk on'. He begged that 'I may not be flattered' and risked calling her his private name, 'Pray keep strictly to your character of governess', where his choice of adverb, *strictly*, indicates how he saw her. A year before, with Lucy, the 'very peremptory Maiden', insisting he remain, while Hester, his 'Mistress' and 'Governess', urged him to return, he had inhabited a masochistic state of bliss. In December he returned to Lichfield and made plans to visit Oxford first and then come back to London: 'Do not be depressed. Scarce years will not last forever,' he wrote; 'hope, you know was left in the box of Prometheus.' He made up verses on the subject of love, and told her that Lucy, who 'seldom wheedles', was 'wheedling for another week'; but, since he 'had not promised her' he was 'not distressed by your summons'. By the end of the week he hoped to lie 'in my old habitation, under your government'.[30]

He began 1773 praying that nothing should 'encrease my guilt', but many others, particularly in the press, thought his guilt should be more widely known. Boswell came down to London in April and Goldsmith showed him in a newspaper 'how an eminent Brewer was very jealous of a certain Authour in Folio, and perceived a strong resemblance to him in his eldest son'.[31] Hester Thrale, busily working with John Perkins, the brewery clerk, to rescue the enterprise, wrote in frustration to Johnson of her 'tyger hearted' husband's coldness: 'You saw the Leave we took, & He has never sent me a Scrap since to ask or tell me anything.' Johnson took a cool view of such scurrilous gossip, and advised her to do likewise: 'Why should Mr Thrale suppose that what I took the liberty of suggesting was concerted with you? He does not know how much I revolve his affairs, and how honestly I desire his prosperity'. Thrale, who made no secret of his own affairs with Polly Hart and others, was also the subject of gossip. In March, the *Westminster Magazine*'s 'Court of Cupid' section ran the 'Memoirs of Miss H—t', in which she described falling for the Southwark brewer 'more famed for his amours than celebrated for his beer'. In June it narrated the tale of 'Mrs. D—n', tempted from the taproom of her haunt by St Clement's church by 'Mr. Th—le' who came for her, not 'in the machine of his occupation, a dray, but in a chariot'. 'Great pleasures', however, 'too often pall and cloy' and Mr Th—le, the *Magazine* informed its readers, 'had procured him a new favourite, the celebrated Mrs. R—'.[32]

Hester meanwhile was throwing herself into the brewery business, assisted by Johnson, who is noted several times in her memorandum book: 'I went to Mr Johnson yesterday: he approved of all I had done.' Perkins warned that 'while Jackson possesses Mr. T's heart nothing but ruin can be hoped'. Hester talked everything over with Johnson, especially Humphrey Jackson's latest scheme, to build coppers in East Smithfield, 'the very Metal of which cost 2000£ . . . to make Experiments & conjure some curious Stuff which should preserve Ships' Bottoms from the Worm'.[33]

At home in Fleet Street Johnson made small efforts at doing good, aware that 'the gloomy and the resentful are always found among those who have nothing to do'. He found a lawyer for Poll Carmichael, 'a Scotch Wench', said Hester, 'who has her Case as a Pauper depending in some of the Law Courts', and settled the work of epitomising Chambers's *Cyclopaedia* on John Calder. Frank Barber had recently married, carrying 'the empire of Cupid farther than many men', Johnson confided to Hester Thrale; together with his wife, Elizabeth Ball, they lived, not very harmoniously, beneath Johnson's roof. He took advantage of a lawyer embarking home to Philadelphia to write to several 'American Friends', noting he had received a copy of an American edition of *Rasselas* to place alongside its translations into Italian, French, German and Dutch.[34] But chiefly he maintained a bantering relationship with Hester: 'You live upon Mock turtle, and stewed Rumps of Beef,' he wrote, whereas he 'dined upon crumpets. You sit with parish officers, caressing and caressed, the idol of the table, and wonder of the day. I pine in the solitude of sickness.' Between them a relationship had developed of mutual obligations. Invited to dine with Joshua Reynolds on Tuesday, his normal day of dining with the Thrales, Johnson asked Hester whether he might accept; asked by Hester how to treat the chemist, Alexander, who threatened to sue Thrale for fraud, Johnson advised her to be firm. 'Your advice was precisely right,' she gushed; 'upon my talking in a higher and more fearless Tone my friend Alexander was much disconcerted.' Johnson advised remedies for Mrs Salusbury's afflictions ('Dear Lady, how I love her now'), including 'a poultice of rasped carrots' to abate 'any offensive smell'. But, above all, he urged Hester to be optimistic. 'Mr Perkins says that the customers are much pleased with their beer. That is good news, and Perkins is always a credible witness.' That kind of optimism struck her with great force as she struggled with a dying mother, a lecherous husband and a brewery just regaining its buoyancy. 'Your Letter is like yourself, so wise, so good, so kind,' she wrote: 'I have read it twenty Times.' The following month, with things at Southwark no better, she concluded a long lamentation: 'Oh My Dear Mr. Johnson! And is it really possible that a mind like yours can by the mere impulse of friendship be made to take interest in such trumpery stuff.' Johnson replied she must allow Thrale to enjoy himself as he wished, which, at present was in schemes for building; 'My Master must gratify himself a little, now he is at liberty, else how will Liberty be enjoyed.'[35]

By this time Boswell was accorded semi-official recognition as Johnson's biographer, though he was much criticised in the role; 'I hope you shall know a great deal more of me', Johnson said to him, 'before you write my Life.' He had disapproved of Boswell's attendance at Duff House where the first masquerade *ever* in Scotland took place: 'What says your Synod to such innovations?' But he reassured him that he continued 'to stand very high in the favour of Mrs Thrale'. Among the literary gossip he relayed to her was the tale that Murphy was 'preparing a whole pamphlet' against Garrick, who could be relied upon to reply. 'No wonder, Sir, that he is vain', he pronounced a month later, 'a man who is perpetually flattered.'[36] That spring he learnt Spanish from Baretti, dined variously with Goldsmith, Boswell,

General Paoli and Beauclerk and proposed Boswell's membership of the Club, which was agreed. 'They knew that if they refused you, they'd probably never have got in another.' At his Easter devotions, where Boswell insisted upon accompanying him, he prayed for Mrs Salusbury 'and I think the Thrales'. The sense of uncertainty comes with a slight change of tone between them. At the end of March 1773 he wrote to Hester: 'Do not let vexation come near your heart', confident of their intimacy, but by early May this had changed. 'What we shall tell each other I know not,' he writes, inviting himself for 'tea and business' and hoping 'we shall say nothing that can make us have less respect or kindness for one another than we have'. In preparing their letters for publication in 1788, Mrs Thrale decided to omit this one, feeling they had gone too far in confiding their secret feelings to each other. Johnson outwardly concurred; they must do what they could to silence 'any remains of suspicion' and settle themselves 'as we were before in the publick opinion'. On Easter Sunday, Johnson prayed for 'my Wife again, by herself'.[37]

Boswell returned to Edinburgh having noted down Johnson's swathe of abbreviations: 'Beauclerk, Beau; Boswell, Bozzy; Langton, Lanky; Murphy, Mur; Sheridan, Sherry.' More importantly he obtained a near promise to explore the Highlands later in the year. Immediately Johnson's relations with Hester improved. She had spent much of the spring dealing with the elopement of Thrale's fifteen-year-old niece with a distiller's son from Tooting, much against her father's wishes; Thrale was applied to for a resolution but 'I have not seen Mr Thrale this Week, & if he knew all I suppose we should not see him for a fortnight'. Johnson offered to intervene, although his opinion was generally against the young couple: 'Conscience cannot dictate obedience to the wicked, or compliance with the foolish.'[38] He began a little badinage with her on the subject of flattery until, by the end of the month, he was forced to confess, 'My eye is yet so dark that I could not read your note . . . I wish you could fetch me on Wednesday. I long to be in my own room.' Somewhat reluctantly Mrs Thrale sent a coach for him to come to Streatham, where Baretti believed there was a great risk of Johnson losing his sight; but that is not the chief reason why his stay at Streatham is remembered.[39]

Sometime during his time at Streatham, having recovered his sight, he wrote a letter to Hester, in French, asking where and with what freedom he was allowed to wander in the house. With her mother at the point of death, Hester's nerves were exhausted; still Johnson asked for her attention, while ostensibly denying it. He found himself, he wrote. '*dans une solitude profonde*' ('profoundly alone') and sought only to know if he might wander where he would, '*a plein abandon*' ('with full freedom'), or whether he too was to be confined '*dans des bornes prescrites*' ('within prescribed boundaries'). Reading the letter it is impossible not to feel a strong plea to be constrained within limits whose only law comes from her will; his desire is to be thought worthy ('*digne*') of '*protection d'une ame si aimable par sa douceur*' ('protection from a sweet and lovable soul'), all the more apparent by her firm dictation '*de ce que m'est permis, et que m'est interdit*' ('of what is permitted, and what forbidden to me'). She has only '*la peine de tourner le clef dans la porte, deux fois par jour. It faut agir tout a fait en Maîtresse, afin que vôtre jugement et vôtre vigilance viennent a secours de ma faiblesse*' ('the pain of locking me up, twice a day. You must assume your role as Mistress, if your judgement and vigilance are to assist me in my frailty'). In his final paragraph, he pleaded for a state of happy slavery ('*esclavage*') to his '*patronne*', his '*maîtresse*', a term used four times in this brief, fawning letter, written in a foreign language for fear it should fall under servants' eyes:

> Is it too much to ask of such a soul as yours that, mistress of others as well as itself, it may triumph over the inconstancy that has too often overtaken it, making it neglect to follow its own laws, forget its own promises, and condemning me so frequently to reiterate my pleas that the recollection fills me with dread. You must either accede to my request, or refuse it, remembering always what it is to which you have acceded. I beg of you, my mistress, that I may always be sensible of your strict control and that you hold me in the slavery which you know so well to make truly blissful.[40]

In his blind dependence, Johnson wished to give up everything, to become entirely subject to her will; he left it to her to lock him up, prescribe his food and tell him where he could, or could not, wander;

anything, so that he would have her attention. That is the tale that lies behind the padlock put up for auction with the rest of Mrs Thrale's possessions in 1823, with her brief handwritten note attached: 'Johnson's padlock, committed to my care in the year 1768', and of a terse footnote to her journal for 1779: 'the Fetters & Padlocks will tell Posterity the Truth.' Johnson's note, in French, a language for which he had contempt but which made his message both more clandestine and sensual, was a direct call for her aid.

At the time she appeared to have turned his darker meanings aside, replying only to his overt message, in English:

> What Care can I promise my dear Mr: Johnson that I have not already taken? What Tenderness which he has not already experienced? . . . You were saying but on Sunday that of all the unhappy you was the happiest, in consequence of my Attention to your Complaint; and today I have been reproached by you for neglect.

In the letter that has survived, she takes the secrecy and loneliness, for which he had pleaded, and apologises for it, urging him to 'shake off these uneasy Weights, heavier to the Mind by far than Fetters to the Body':

> Let not your fancy dwell thus upon Confinement and severity. I am sorry you are obliged to be so much alone; I foresaw some Ill Consequences of your being here while my Mother was dying thus; yet could not resist the temptation of having you near me, but if you find this irksome and dangerous Idea fasten upon your fancy, leave me to struggle with the loss of one Friend, and let me not put to hazard what I esteem beyond Kingdoms, and value beyond the possession of them.

The unspoken 'dangerous Idea' which had fastened on Johnson's fancy was one she chose not to articulate or, it seems, to act upon. 'Mr. Boswell will be at last your best Physician,' she wrote, anxious for the needs of this invalid to be catered for in another country.[41]

'At our age,' Johnson wrote to John Taylor, they could not easily find any 'that will interest themselves in our health or sickness', proud to inform his near contemporary that he had been blooded 'very copiously' twice and purged some thirteen times. He wrote to Boswell in July to tell him he was at last coming north, with Robert Chambers as a companion, at least as far as Newcastle. After the success of 'his' Vinerian lectures, Chambers had been appointed as a judge in Bengal 'with six thousand a year' and was taking leave of his relations. Before he left for Scotland, Johnson took his leave of Mrs Salusbury, who died on 18 June. The day before he had kissed her hand, and she had 'pressed my hand between her two hands, which she probably intended as the parting caress'. Mrs Thrale took the death badly: 'Mr. Thrale & Mr. Johnson are the mere Acquisitions of Chance,' she confided to a notebook; 'One solid Good I had & that is gone – my Mother!'[42] Johnson's original writing for publication had dwindled to a bare minimum; in February he wrote a brief dedication to Payne's *Elements of Trigonometry*, and in June a preface to the *Geography* which Alexander Macbean had produced. The *Geography*, he argued, was fine, but hinted, 'it is seldom used otherwise than as a Dictionary'. In July 1773 he was looking through old papers and 'perceived a resolution to rise early always occurring. I think I was ashamed.' He offered his decrepitude as a partial excuse. 'My memory has been for a long time very much confused. Names, and Persons, and Events, slide away strangely from me.'[43] He seemed to hesitate before embarking upon the Hebrides adventure, and Boswell wrote at last to Thrale to '*launch* him from London'. It had the required effect, and Johnson set out for Scotland on 6 August. 'What I shall see, I know not', he wrote to Taylor, 'but hope to have entertainment for my curiosity.'[44]

PART FOUR

The Biographer

15

'A Wide Sail'

anchor n.s. *(anchora, Lat.) It is used, by a metaphor, for any thing which confers stability or security.*

Which hope we have as an *anchor* of the soul, both sure
and stedfast, and which entereth not into that within
the veil.

Bible Hebrews, vi. 19.

'I am a kind of ship with a wide sail, and without an anchor.'

16 November 1775

'He was', says Boswell, 'at bottom much of a *John Bull*; much of a blunt *true-born Englishman.*' He writes this in part to differentiate Johnson from himself ('I am, I flatter myself, completely a citizen of the world'), in part to indicate that the tone of his own *Journal of a Tour to the Hebrides*, published in 1785, ten years *after* Johnson's death, will be very different from Johnson's *Journey to the Western Islands*. He correctly picked up a hint that Johnson did not relish a *Supplement* to his *Journey*; 'between ourselves', he wrote to Temple, 'he is not apt to encourage one to *share* reputation with himself.'[1] Johnson had not begun his Scottish tour with any thoughts of writing his *Journey*; at most he intended to provide Hester with a series of letters to entertain them both with accounts of a region of Britain still in its primitive state. In Newcastle he had misgivings about his trip. 'I am afraid travel will end . . . in disappointment. One town, one country is very like another.' He risked a joke on the drawbridge standing over the River Wear, at Durham, 'to be raised at night lest the Scots should pass it'. It was not until he and Boswell reached Anoch, a fortnight into their trip, that 'I first conceived the thought' of writing the *Journey*, and there the inspirational setting was very apt. The day was 'calm', the air 'soft', all 'was rudeness, silence, and solitude'; Wordsworth himself could hardly have conceived a more appealing spot.

Johnson realised the appropriateness of a certain pastoral tone: 'I sat down on a bank, such as a writer of romance might have delighted to feign.'[2] Yet anything *less* like pastoral would be difficult to conceive. 'I measured two apartment[s] of which the walls were entire and found them 27 feet long and 23 broad,' he writes to Hester. He is describing the dimensions of the old fort he encountered at Inch Keith. Such bald measurements are not included in the *Journey*, but many others are. Loch Ness 'is about twenty-four miles long, and from one mile to two miles broad'; alongside it Johnson finds 'four shucks' (i.e. shocks of cereal) each containing 'twelve sheaves of barley'. He judges the length of Raasay island to be 'by computation, fifteen miles, and the breadth two', though he acknowledges that 'computation by miles is negligent and arbitrary'. At Inch Kenneth, off the Isle of Mull, he measures a cave in detail: the breadth starts at 'about forty-five feet', the height 'about thirty feet', but penetrating further, down 'a narrow passage, perhaps not more than six feet wide' they reach 'a second cave, in breadth twenty-five feet'. Measuring their way back 'we found it more than a hundred and sixty yards, the eleventh part of a mile'. He gives it as his opinion that 'no man should travel unprovided with instruments for taking heights and distances'.[3]

Measuring in this way gave him a sense of *doing* something purposeful. In Oxford, all those years before, he had set down a page of numbers, from ten to 14,400, calculating how many lines of Latin he could memorise per day, per week or per month; he did that just a fortnight before he left the place for good. At Anoch, Johnson made a present of a book to the girl who made their tea which, upon enquiry, was found to be *Cocker's Arithmetick*: 'if you are to have but one book with you upon a journey, let it be a book of science,' he said, claiming they were 'inexhaustible'. Surveying the places that he came to was just one of the ways that Johnson retained a sense of Englishness while travelling in the Highlands. Another was his use of the English language. On Skye he smelt, but did not drink, their whisky, which 'was free from empyreumatick taste or smell'; speaking of their harvest songs, he mentions the 'ancient proceleusmatick song by which the rowers of gallies were animated', and in remarking their methods of making necessary items, like bridles and whips, he commends their 'succedaneous means for many common purposes'.[4] By using this precise, patrician vocabulary and by quantifying everything, Johnson endeavoured to isolate himself from the subject he investigated.

The third element by which he invoked a sense of distance between the reality he saw before him and a mythic world of dreams was his use of classical comparisons. Before thinking of his narrative he viewed hills which 'may be called with Homer's Ida "abundant in springs"', deserving the epithet 'which he bestows upon Pelion by "waving their leaves"'. The Highlanders were 'like the Greeks in their unpolished state, described by Thucydides', and in Raasay, 'if I could have found an Ulysses, I had fancied a Phaeacia'.[5]

It was Boswell who broke down this solemn façade, allowing Johnson to be seen as an irritable but very human subject; nowhere more so than at the start. At Boyd's inn in Edinburgh, Boswell rescued him from nursing a sense of Scottish dirtiness. Asked to have his lemonade made sweeter, 'the waiter, with his greasy fingers, lifted a lump of sugar' and put it in his glass; Johnson promptly 'threw it out of the window'. Later, walking with Boswell 'arm-in-arm up the High-street', Johnson was 'assailed by the evening effluvia of Edinburgh' or, in other words, the contents of a chamber-pot. 'As we marched slowly along, he grumbled in my ear. "I smell you in the dark."' With Johnson dead, there was no one to say these incidents did not occur exactly as Boswell relates them; they place the *two* of them, arm in arm, as the Laurel and Hardy of a joint comic enterprise.

As they travelled along the Firth of Forth, Boswell suggested that it was 'the finest prospect in Europe' apart, perhaps, from those from Naples, or Constantinople. Johnson capped this ('Water is the same everywhere') but had noted something of greater significance. 'From the banks of the Tweed to St Andrews I had never seen a single tree . . . A tree might be a show in Scotland as a horse in Venice.' It was a complaint he repeated to Hester Thrale from Skye, saying that 'in all this journey' he had not seen 'five trees fit for the Carpenter'.[6] He thereby set the tone for their journey, neatly recaptured in their two antiphonal narratives. Johnson is lofty, irascible and just a little pompous; Boswell is his oleaginous companion, attempting to bridge the gap between this quintessential Englishman and his Highland setting, and almost, but not quite managing it. In St Andrews, Johnson's *Journey* gives a sober narrative of the decline and fall of a once noble university and cathedral city. 'St Andrews indeed has formerly suffered more atrocious ravages and more extensive destruction, but recent evils affect with greater force. We were reconciled to the sight of archiepiscopal ruins.' But in Boswell's *Journal* he reminisces of the old days in Lichfield, when decent people 'got drunk every night, and were not the worse thought of'.[7]

At Banff Johnson expressed elegant thoughts on the inelegant habits of the natives with regard to windows. The 'necessity of ventilating' homes had 'not yet been found by our northern neighbours', he declared. Even in houses 'well built and elegantly furnished' a stranger might often 'wish for fresher air'. He hesitated before communicating such thoughts: 'These diminutive observations seem to take away something from the dignity of writing,' he remarked, before adding that life 'consists not of a series of illustrious actions, or elegant enjoyments' but rather 'in compliance with necessities, in the performance of daily duties, in the removal of small inconveniencies, in the procurement of petty pleasures'. His conclusion was a well-worn homily, rendered newly apposite: 'The true state of every nation is the state of common life.' Boswell, reading these comments, very much 'regretted that [Johnson] did not allow me to read over his book before it was printed'. The windows, he conceded 'had no pullies' but believed it most unfair to deduce from this 'wretched defect' a general lack of civilised life north of the border.[8]

Differences between their two accounts may be seen in their descriptions of 'an old woman, boiling goats-flesh' whom they encountered on the shores of Loch Ness. Johnson begins with an accurate depiction of her hut ('no floor but the naked earth') and the wall ('commonly about six feet high, declines from the perpendicular'), introducing her in six factual sentences, full of numbers and all beginning 'She': 'She spoke little English . . . She has five children . . . She is mistress of sixty goats . . .' By contrast, Boswell gives her a name (Fraser), a husband ('He was a man of eighty') and a manner of speaking, translated from Erse by one of their guides. 'She answered with a tone of emotion, saying . . . she was afraid we wanted to go to bed to her.' It is clear that Boswell, writing ten years later, gives a livelier, more humane, though not necessarily more accurate, sense of the encounter.[9]

That Johnson had no love for rural beauty was rather an inconvenience. Boswell claimed to have 'very little' himself but tried, and failed, to tease Johnson into an appreciation of the landscape they travelled through. At Glenshiel he pointed out an 'immense' mountain; Johnson replied that it was 'no more than a considerable protuberance'. Often deaf, unable to speak the native tongue, with no circles of like-minded learned literati to spark his wit, he frequently became sullen and silent. Many times Boswell noted that their resting-place, which but yesterday had been 'a hospitable house', was turned overnight into 'a prison'. There was not 'enough of intellectual entertainment for him', he explained. Johnson admitted as much; 'I long to be again in civilized life,' he said. At times Boswell, at great trouble to make Johnson's tour agreeable, wished Johnson would take a little more trouble himself to be acceptable, less 'narrow-minded'. On rare occasions when in company, Johnson's temper sometimes got the better of him. Asked by Lady MacLeod whether man was naturally good, he replied so firmly, 'No more than a wolf', that the lady was quite startled. She whispered, 'This is worse than Swift.'[10]

At Kingsburgh, they were introduced to Flora Macdonald, who played such an important part in the flight of Charles Stuart from Skye. Johnson slept the night in the bed that Charles Stuart had used, which caused Boswell quite a flurry of emotion: 'To see Dr. Samuel Johnson lying in that bed . . . struck me with such a group of ideas as it is not easy for words to describe.' Johnson was less moved: 'I have had no ambitious thoughts in it.' He was discreet whenever the subjects of Culloden or the '45 rebellion occurred and wrote approvingly to Hester Thrale of an elderly man they met who 'had been *out* as they call it, in forty five, and still retained his old opinions'. On Raasay he spoke of the late laird leading out 'one hundred men upon a military expedition' and mentioned the unfortunate effects of post-Culloden laws, leaving 'the whole nation dejected and intimidated'. But his conclusion has the sense of realism: 'Their case is undoubtedly hard, but in political regulations, good cannot be complete, it can only be predominant.' He did, though, fear that emigration, which followed the ending of Jacobite dreams, might have a sad effect and wrote that the peoples of the Scottish Highlands 'are not happy as a nation, for they are a nation no longer . . . Once none went away but the useless and poor; in some parts there is now reason to fear, that none will stay but those who are too poor to remove themselves.'[11]

'I have now the pleasure of going where nobody goes', he wrote to Hester from Skye, 'and of seeing what nobody sees.' His gloom was undisguised, and only thoughts of her, 'my honoured Mistress', kept him sane. A week later he was cold, wet, 'miserably deaf' and consequently 'troublesome' to Lady MacLeod; 'I force her to speak loud, but she will seldom speak loud enough.' Offered an island of his own by Lord MacLeod, he could only say it 'would be pleasanter than Brighthelmston'. He was deeply annoyed when Boswell, with his 'troublesome kindness', not only remembered his birthday but informed the MacLeods of the fact. 'I can now look back upon . . . a life diversified by misery, spent part in the sluggishness of penury, and part under the violence of pain,' he wrote to Hester. 'I find my memory uncertain . . . My Nights are still disturbed by flatulencies,' he noted in his diary. To distract himself, having no Erse, he composed several odes in Latin, but though the language varied, the sentiments were still the same:

> *Pervagor gentes, hominum ferorum*
> *Vita ubi nullo decorata cultu*
> *Squallet informis, tugurique fumis*
> *Foeda latescit.*

('I am wandering through clans where the life of wild men, enhanced by no culture, is marred by squalor and skulks in ugliness behind the smoke of a hovel.')[12]

By now he had grown weary of the dreary sameness of the Highlands, their people and their weather. 'There is little variety in universal barrenness,' he wrote to Hester, finding the Highlanders 'a very coarse tribe, ignorant of any language but Earse'. To Boswell he confessed, 'I cannot bear low life', grumbling at a landlord's preparation of mutton chops 'which we could not eat', his lady leaving them to pick up lumps of sugar with their fingers, and a bed which, certain that if he lay *in* it he would '*catch something*', Johnson lay *upon*, with a pile of hay beneath him, huddled in his great coat. 'I am now content with knowing that by a Scrambling up a rock, I shall only see other rocks, and a wider circuit of barren desolation,' he reported, ending his letter, 'We are this morning trying to get out of Skie.'[13] His next letter, dated three days later, begins, 'I am Still in Skie'; the misery that this entails was, he judged, best left unspoken.

> Ev'ry Island is a prison
> Strongly guarded by the sea . . .

were lines which summed up his gloomy mood as the weather became worse, though as conditions deteriorated his reception grew better, which made him feel guilty about acknowledging such sentiments. 'The hospitality of this remote region is like that of the golden age,' he wrote to Hester from Dunvegan, wondering how she herself was occupied;

> *Seu viri curas, pia nupta, mulcet,*
> *Seu fovet mater subolem benigna . . .*

('Whether as a devoted wife she soothes the worries of her husband, or whether as a loving mother she looks after her child'); but he consigned these thoughts to classic verse:

> *Quot modis mecum, quid agat, requiro,*
> *Thralia dulcis?*

('In how many ways do I ask myself what sweet Thrale is doing?')

At Dunvegan they were the guests of the MacLeods and found themselves 'treated at every house as if we came to confer a benefit'. He joined in an entertainment of Erse songs, with a lady on his knee, who kissed him to the huge merriment of all the company; but simultaneously he spoke to Boswell 'of hastening away to London, without stopping much at Edinburgh'. 'It would require great resignation to live in one of these islands,' he remarked candidly on Coll, noting to Hester that there was 'literally no tree upon the Island'. 'We are hastening home as fast as we can,' he wrote to Robert Chambers.[14]

At last, at the start of October, the wind changed and it seemed possible to make his 'Escape from this Island'. 'I long to be again at home,' he confessed to Hester, summing up his sense of the Hebrideans he had met over the past five weeks: 'They are a Nation just rising from barbarity.' He dreamt fondly of having made the journey 'with great pleasure' had only 'you and Master, and Queeney been in the party'; as it was, his mind was 'too much at home'.[15] Landing at last at Oban, on the mainland, and staying at a tolerable inn, he found the newspapers were much of his opinion. In the *Glasgow Journal* he read that, confined on Skye by 'tempestuous weather', Dr Johnson, the philosopher, resembled 'a whale left upon the strand'. He felt cheered by the unflattering simile, delighted to be back on terra firma, and in a spirit of recklessness actually took a gill of whisky at Inveraray to discover 'what it is that makes a Scotchman happy!' He declined, though, to take up Boswell's proposal of a toast to Mrs Thrale. He remembered that she was 'near a dangerous time' having been pregnant, for the ninth time, when he left; 'I hope the danger is quite over.'[16]

As soon as he was back on the mainland he began to think again of London matters, writing to ask Thrale to send ten pounds to Mrs Williams to tide her over until he returned. He was so relieved to be back on the mainland that, treated as an honoured guest by the Duke and Duchess of Argyll at Inveraray, Boswell had never seen him 'so gentle and complaisant'. At Glasgow he received six letters from London which had been waiting for him for anything up to two months. He cheerfully replied, rejoicing that the Thrales' Welsh estate contained 'fifteen thousand trees', having been in a land, he said, 'where trees and diamonds are equal rarities'. He assured Hester he had not 'willingly left off' his powers of 'scrambling', informing her he was 'too well acquainted' with mire and rocks to fear 'a Welsh journey', of which they had already spoken. Boswell speaks of Johnson developing 'a weakness in his knees' which made walking difficult, but Johnson himself, always unwilling to admit restrictions, refused assistance to disembark and sprang 'into the sea and wade[d] vigorously out'. With Boswell, while his attitude was always cordial, there was little real warmth of affection. Johnson confided he was 'very convenient to travel with' since 'there is no house where he is not received with kindness and respect', which, though definitely praise, lacks the sense of genuine enthusiasm and makes a Scottish virtue of his rather English necessity.[17]

A subject on which his opinion was constantly sought as he travelled through the Highlands was James Macpherson's *Fingal*. This poem, supposedly an ancient Gaelic work by Ossian, son of Fingal, had been modernised and published in London the year before the tour began. Johnson's view of it was very simple; it was a deceit: 'a man might write such stuff for ever, if he would *abandon* his mind to it'; it was merely 'unconnected rhapsody'. Throughout his journey he met several individuals, such as Donald Macqueen, reputedly 'the most intelligent man in Sky', Sir Adolphus Oughton and Mr Tytler, who all championed Macpherson's claims, but he remained consistent. *Fingal* was 'as gross an imposition as ever the world was troubled with'. In the *Journey* Johnson goes further, claiming to hear Macpherson, 'the father of Ossian', boasted 'of two chests more of ancient poetry' which he suppressed only 'because they are too good for the English'. Such insolent audacity, he wrote, 'is the last refuge of guilt', yet he found a rationale for the widespread acceptance of the fraud in the Scots' 'fondness for their supposed ancestors. A Scotchman must be a very sturdy moralist, who does not love Scotland better than truth.'[18]

Johnson was quite light-hearted about Macpherson's crimes and, in the first days of the tour, he and Boswell came to Nairn, a royal burgh but 'a miserable place'. Over the room where they sat a girl span wool on a spinning machine, accompanying herself by singing a song in Erse. ' "I'll warrant you," (said Dr Johnson) "one of the songs of Ossian." '[19]

It was the start of November when Johnson arrived at Boswell's ancestral home, Auchinleck. Here he was advised by Boswell, and agreed to abide by his instruction, to avoid three topics which might only lead to disagreement with Boswell's father; namely Whiggism, Presbyterianism and – Sir John Pringle. And for three days he succeeded. Then, riled by the local Presbyterian minister's description of 'fat bishops and drowsy deans' in the Church of England, he exploded, telling him he knew no more of the Anglican church 'than a Hottentot'. This led to a violent difference of opinion between himself and Boswell's father on 'Charles the First, and Toryism'. They left two days later, Johnson having absolutely refused to join in Sunday worship at the local parish church. They were both now 'in another, and a higher, state of existence,' commented Boswell in 1785, remarking that in heaven 'there is no room for *Whiggism*'.

For much of the tour Johnson was afflicted by deafness although, like many other ailments, the symptoms of it lessened as he found himself on solid ground; 'My deafness went away by degrees,' he noted, answering Hester's query. In Edinburgh he took time to visit a 'philosophical curiosity' which 'no other city has to shew', namely a college for the deaf and dumb. His *Journey* ends with a naive but optimistic picture of the scholars 'waiting for their master, whom they are said to receive at his entrance with smiling countenances and sparkling eyes, delighted with the hope of new ideas'. It is a curious but hopeful note on which to end his *Journey*, asking, 'after having seen the deaf taught arithmetick, who could be afraid to cultivate the Hebrides?'[20]

After Johnson's death, Boswell would allow himself to luxuriate in the thought that it was he who attracted Johnson northwards: 'Had it not been for me, I am persuaded Dr. Johnson never would have undertaken such a journey.' But already, in November, Johnson's thoughts were on the south, writing from Edinburgh to comfort Hester for the death of her uncle, Sir Thomas Salusbury, and of any hopes she might have had of his will. 'Be alone as little as you can,' he counselled, assuring her in his next letter that 'while You are reading it, I shall be coming home'. He was pleased with himself at having an Italian *Rasselas* to give Queeney, and uttered fervent hopes for his godchild, Lucy, to recover from a recent ear infection. Worries on her behalf may partly explain the closing pages of his *Journey*, but he was also realistic, dropping the hint that he would 'love another god-child'. 'I long to be at home, and have taken place in the Coach for Monday,' he wrote: 'Please to let Mrs Williams know.' Lucy died on 22 November, just four days before Johnson arrived home; he was not asked to be a godfather to Hester's new infant, Ralph.[21]

In January 1775, a little over a year later, Johnson's *Journey to the Western Islands of Scotland* appeared, investigating a kind of primitive Britishness on the verge of disappearance. Empty of emotion, it measures dwellings, counts flocks and calculates the means of survival for the Highlanders who remain. Johnson mentions their tales and legends, but impersonally, always keen to stress they are a people devoid of written memorials; he is implicitly proud of himself for having ventured so far into the north-west at the age of sixty-four, and investigated what remains of their story. Occasionally he mentions Boswell, but his role is like a cameraman's on a natural history film, necessary but not part of what is being created. The tour of the Highlands clearly developed Johnson's love of travel. 'I shall go to Oxford on Monday,' he wrote to Boswell as soon as he reached London, telling Chambers he was 'no more weary than if I had not moved from the same place'.

Johnson began seriously to discuss with Thrale the notion of a trip to Rome. 'I have seen a new region,' he boasted to John Taylor in Ashbourne, saying how, with 'very little ill health' and bearing wind and rain 'tolerably well', he had 'traversed the east coast of Scotland' from Edinburgh to Inverness, and the west coast 'from the Highland to Glasgow'. On New Year's Day, at almost two in the morning, he confessed to God that he had taken 'a journey to the Hebrides' but wondered if his mind had been 'not free from perturbation'; his deficiency was still 'a life immethodical, and unsettled' which left 'too much leisure to imagination'. At much the same time Hester Thrale was writing in her 'Children's Book' a poignant adieu to the year: 'So Farewell to all I formerly loved – to my Mother, my House in Hertfordshire, my lovely Lucy – and to this accursed Year 1773.'[22]

Johnson 'pretended to be very angry' at finding the bookseller Tom Davies had taken advantage of his absence to publish two volumes of *Miscellaneous and Fugitive Pieces* by 'the Authour of the Rambler', but, finding Davies was struggling for money, he let the matter go; 'I believe the dog loves me dearly.' In February he told Boswell he was staying at Mrs Thrale's 'that I might be taken care of', having developed a bad cold and cough. 'How happy it was that neither of us were ill in the Hebrides,' he wrote, enquiring if it were 'practicable' to send a cask of porter to Dunvegan, Raasay and Coll; 'I would not wish to be thought forgetful of civilities.' The fact that, at the same time, he was also able to formulate proposals setting out an author's interest in the matter of literary copyright indicates that neither travel nor ill health had blunted his mental acuity. He also managed to dissuade Boswell from coming to London to celebrate Easter at St Paul's; it would be, he said, like 'going up to Jerusalem at the feast of the Passover'. He cheerfully used Mrs Boswell as his handy assistant: 'Life cannot subsist in society but by reciprocal concessions. She permitted you to ramble last year, you must permit her now to keep you at home.'[23]

At the end of March he took a final leave of Chambers, who carried Johnson's fulsome letter to Warren Hastings with him, as well as unbound sheets of Jones's *Persian Grammar*. There had been so much delay about arranging this last meeting that Johnson began to suspect a private grievance, but it was only Chambers's habitual dilatoriness. He recommended the old Quaker Thomas Cumming to move from Tottenham Green to Clerkenwell, where Levet and Mrs Williams could attend him with 'proper food'; but his letter came too late; Cumming, who acquired the nickname 'the fighting Quaker' for having defeated the French in Senegal, declared that 'the pain of an anonymous letter' had 'fastened on his heart' and died within a few days. Meanwhile Johnson worked at producing his *Journey*, telling Boswell the first sheets, including an elegant tribute to him, were already in the press. 'I have stipulated twenty-five for you to give in your own name,' he wrote, asking for a list of those in Scotland who should receive a copy. Apart from these duties his time was largely at the Thrales' disposal; he took them to visit John Scott's 'Dryads and Fairies' in his estate at Amwell and advised Hester to get the children 'into Habits of loving a Book by every possible means', for, he remarked with injudicious candour, 'You do not know but it may one Day save them from Suicide.'[24]

The trip to Rome had to be forgone, but at the start of July he set out with the Thrales, his Master, Mistress and nine-year-old Queeney, on a journey to Wales. They headed for Bach-y-Graig, near Caernarvon, 'to take possession of at least five hundred a year' fallen to Hester by her uncle's death.[25] About to leave, he wrote to Boswell telling what he knew of Goldsmith, who had died three months before. 'His debts began to be heavy', he said, 'and all his resources were exhausted. Sir Joshua is of opinion that he owed not less than two thousand pounds. Was ever poet so trusted before?' To Langton he wrote simply, 'He was a very great Man.'

Johnson and Hester both kept diaries of their three-month tour, Johnson because he had become acclimatised to the practice by his tour of Scotland, Hester because she kept notes on everything she did. Boswell was strangely innocent of both journals, and dismissed the jaunt as not 'discursive' in the manner of their Hebridean tour, but actually these journals offer interesting comparisons with Boswell's and Johnson's own accounts of their Scottish trip. Setting out from Streatham on 5 July, the party enjoyed 'a good cold dinner' at Barnet and proceeded on to Dunstable with the price of their four horses, Johnson noted, snapping up these unconsidered trifles, '2s a mile'. He himself read Cicero's *Epistles* throughout the journey, alternating it with Martial. The next day they travelled eighty-three miles to the Swan Inn at Lichfield, arriving a little before midnight. Johnson, whose poor eyesight gave him no enjoyment of scenery, observed 'how much pleasanter it was travelling by night than by day'.

The next morning he was anxious to show them round his native city but, finding Mrs Thrale's costume ('a morning night gown and close cap') unbecoming, made her 'alter it entirely before he would stir a step with us about the town'. She noted that he said the 'most satirical things' concerning her appearance 'in a riding-habit'. They paid visits to Richard Greene's museum ('much admired'), to the cathedral, to Lucy Porter and to Elizabeth Aston, sister of Molly, enjoying themselves to such an extent that 'she was sorry to part'.[26] They visited Erasmus Darwin and Anna Seward, to whom, Hester complained, Johnson 'would not suffer me to speak', and took breakfast with David Garrick's brother, Peter. From there it was on to John Taylor's home at Ashbourne, whence they visited Ilam ('less pleased . . . than when I saw it first') and Chatsworth ('not struck with the house'). The only creature which gained Johnson's admiration at Chatsworth was Atlas, the famous racehorse, '15 hands inch and half'. Hester agreed with him; 'Dr. Taylor took us to Chatsworth, where I was pleased with scarcely anything,' she wrote. They also agreed the inn they stopped at, in Edensor, was poor, only differing in the terms of their disapprobation; Johnson said it was 'bad', Hester 'wretched'. Things got worse, not better; in Oakover chapel the wood of the pews was 'grossly painted' and at Dovedale the place 'did not answer my expectation'. Johnson was pleased to note that 'Capability' Brown was similarly 'disappointed'. He fell back on his standby of measuring: the cave called 'Reynard's hall' went backwards 'several yards'; 'he that has seen Dovedale', he concluded, 'has no need to visit the Highlands.'[27]

They spent the rest of July touring Buxton, Macclesfield, Congleton and Combermere, taking part in the newly fashionable vogue for sightseeing. At Kedleston, recently built by Robert Adam for Lord Scarsdale, Johnson found 'more cost than judgement' while at Shavington Hall, Lord Kilmorey showed the place 'with too much exultation'. Johnson gradually allowed his own tastes to be influenced by Hester, who made censorious remarks on Kilmorey for attempting to unite 'the bluster of an Officer to the haughtiness of a Nobleman newly come to his estate'. At Hawkstone Park, seat of Sir Rowland Hill, Johnson became uncharacteristically effusive, rhapsodising on 'the awfulness of its shades, the horrors of its precipices, the verdure of its hollows and the loftiness of its rocks . . . The Ideas which it forces upon the mind are the sublime, the dreadful, and the vast.' Such picturesque writing, quite unlike Johnson's normal tone, has puzzled many. 'It looks more like a burlesque of Johnson's style than his own travelling notes,' John Croker writes, questioning the authenticity of the remarks and Johnson's sensitivity towards external nature. Mrs Thrale observed him saying, of the different shades of verdure, that 'a blade of grass is always a blade of grass, whether in one country or another'. At Chester they visited the cathedral ('not of the first rank') and city walls, where they had a disagreement which Johnson remembered ever afterwards. He was anxious for Queeney to 'walk on the wall' and kept her up after dark, which Mrs Thrale, apprehending 'some accident to her – perhaps to him', very much disliked. At last, on the twenty-eighth, they entered Wales.[28]

Bach-y-Graig was, frankly, a disappointment. 'The floors have been stolen; the windows are stopped. The house', Johnson said, 'was less than I seemed to expect.' Mrs Thrale, conscious of her Welsh-ness, put up a certain resistance. Llewenny struck her as 'of no small dignity' and the house at Bach-y-Graig had 'three excellent rooms'; the place 'might really be made delightful if one pleased'. Johnson scorned the whole country and, she thought, 'wanted *me* to scorn it' too but attempted to aid her efforts to save the woods from felling. Thrale refused their pleas and warned her against setting 'your old Bull Dog [Johnson] upon me'. The woods were cut down and Thrale was £4,000 richer. Next day they went to St Asaph amid signs of making up. The cathedral, though 'not large', with a cross aisle 'very short' and with 'scarcely any monuments', had yet 'something of dignity and Grandeur', thought Johnson; it was presided over by a bishop who was 'very civil'. Hester took up the theme; the bishop's wife 'pressed us to stay dinner, and was as civil as she knew how'.[29]

Tremeirchion church in Bach-y-Graig was in 'a dismal condition' but, riding away, Johnson noted another instance of nature which pleased him: 'The way lay through pleasant lanes, and overlooked a region beautifully diversified with trees and grass.' Whether he felt quite as gratified by the reaction of one foolish clerk who, upon seeing Mrs Thrale, declared with joy that 'he was now willing to die' is not recorded. The clerk was rewarded with a crown, something, she noted, he 'had probably never seen . . . before'.[30] Travelling on in the coach to Holywell, Johnson and Hester discussed flattery, with her being 'saucy' and saying she 'was obliged to be civil for *two* – meaning himself and me'. But by the time Fanny Burney heard the story numbers had swelled and to Johnson's query why she was 'so indiscriminately lavish of praise', Hester said that when she was 'with you, and Mr. Thrale, and Queeny, I am obliged to be civil for four!' At St Winifred's Well at Holywell he was somewhat disturbed to witness a woman bathing 'while we all looked on' but the town's iron and copper works engaged a different kind of attention, having 'several strong fires with melting pots'. 'I have enlarged my notions,' he commented, giving a shilling for the privilege.[31]

Johnson no doubt thought himself, and was regarded as being, generous and learned. A fortnight later, at Bodvil, he met a simple Welsh parson who had heard of him as 'the greatest man living'. Yet he maintained a clear sense of the relative values of money. At Anoch in the Highlands he had been pleased to distribute his shilling among the soldiery and to be saluted with shouts of 'my lord' by all of them.

'He is really generous, loves influence, and has the way of gaining it,' commented Boswell, noting Johnson pronouncing that he was 'quite feudal'. A shilling was similarly quite generous to the men at the iron works, but next day, when Mrs Thrale expressed great uneasiness at losing her purse, Johnson thought the sum involved must be 'very great'; when he heard it was only a matter of 'seven guineas' he was greatly relieved. The difference of status between those, like the peasant woman at Auchnashiel, to whom 'a shilling was high payment' and those, like Mrs Thrale, to whom the loss of *only* seven guineas was merely an inconvenience is something necessary to grasp when examining the life of one who came to London in 1737 with twopence halfpenny in his pocket, and became great friends with Joshua Reynolds, who regularly made £5,000 a year.[32]

At Bodryddan, he 'teased' the owner, Mrs Cotton, about her 'cascade' so much ('I trudged unwillingly, and was not sorry to find it dry') that 'she was ready to cry'. The following days, with John Myddelton of Gwaynynog, who had never 'had so great a man under his roof' before, Johnson spent correcting sheets of the *Journey* which had found their way to him. A week later they came to Conway on race day and 'the town was so full of company, that no money could purchase lodging'. They travelled on a further fourteen miles, past Penmaen Mawr ('with some anxiety') in increasing darkness, and came, at last, to Bangor, where they could only find 'a very mean Inn'. The 'woman of the house' proposed that the whole party of them should sleep together, all 'stuffed in one filthy room': Johnson records 'I had a flatulent night'. He sent a letter to Robert Levet, telling him that Wales was 'very beautiful and rich', a considerable exaggeration on the details he recorded in his journal. Mrs Thrale longed for letters from London, but none came, forcing her to 'come into my own room to cry'. Mrs Cotton, she reflected, loved her children 'as well as I do' yet would never have cried just to hear from them: 'Why does every body . . . perpetually do better than I can?' She felt for the loss of her mother most acutely. 'My present Companions have too much philosophy for me. One cannot disburthen one's mind to people who are watchful to cavil, or acute to contradict before the sentence is finished.' They met General Paoli with Sir Thomas Wynn, who invited them to dine: 'The Dinner mean, Sir T. civil. His Lady nothing. Poali [*sic*] civil,' commented Johnson. Mrs Thrale went considerably further, describing Wynn's wife, Lady Catharine Perceval, as 'an empty woman of quality, insolent, ignorant, and ill bred', who 'set a vile dinner before us, and on such linen as shocked one'. Afterwards Johnson remarked, tactfully, that he had 'not been very well'.[33]

Some days afterwards they visited Bodvil, where Mrs Thrale had been born. 'I saw the place which I first saw, and looked at the pond with pleasure.' Johnson, watching her hazily recalling moments from her childhood, noted that such memories were 'always melancholy'. The sycamore walk was 'cut down'; the pond 'was dry': 'Nothing was better' though the present owners of the house were 'very civil'. They went on to Cefn Amwlch and found a man there who, Mrs Thrale recalls, 'gave us the first melon we have seen since we came from home'. From there it was the homeward journey, dining again with Myddleton, whose subsequent erection of an urn 'to your Memory', as Johnson grimly quipped to Hester, 'looks like an intention to bury me alive'. Back in England, they stopped at Hagley, where Mrs Thrale was pressed by the ladies there to play at cards not once but twice, 'notwithstanding all my excuses, with an ill-bred but irresistible importunity'. At Leasowes Johnson thought of 'Poor Shenstone' who 'never tasted his pension' and 'died of misery', and at Blenheim he announced with great authority that 'the park contains 2500 Acres about four square miles'. At Oxford they dined in Hall at University College where, Mrs Thrale reports, she was greatly honoured; 'I sat in the seat of honour as Locum Tenens forsooth'.[34] That was on 24 September. A week later they arrived home and found a mood of great excitement; parliament had been dissolved and there was much talk of things to do. That night Thrale held a political dinner with several friends, which turned exceedingly drunken; his wife commented in her diary: 'I thought how I had spent three months from home among dunces of all ranks and sorts, but had never seen a man drunk till I came among the Wits.'[35]

Wales was 'so little different from England' that it offered 'nothing to the speculation of the traveller', Johnson wrote to Boswell as soon as he returned. While he had been away Boswell had sought urgent help in a case of sheep-stealing but, failing to reach him, the sheep-stealer had been hanged. Johnson wrote to clear himself of any hint of negligence. He now purposed 'to drive the book [i.e. the *Journey*] forward', assuring John Taylor that it would be out 'in a Month' and would be 'a pretty book'. Before then he had to pen election material for Thrale, draft press announcements ('Votes, Interest, and Support on the Day of Election') and write the *Patriot*, a party pamphlet. Using his broadest brush, Johnson painted Thrale's opponents, including Wilkes, as 'rabble'; 'Patriotism', he declared once more, was 'the last refuge of a scoundrel'. He denounced the recent furore over the Falkland Islands ('for a barren rock under a stormy sky, we might have now been fighting and dying') but reserved his greatest contempt for those who supported 'the ridiculous claims of American usurpation'. In 1773 the 'Boston Tea Party' had led to the closure of Boston harbour and a rise in temperature between Britain and its colonies, 'which were settled under English protection; were constituted by an English charter; and have been defended by English arms'. Johnson's opinion, writing for Thrale, was clear: 'We have always protected the Americans; we may therefore subject them to government.'[36]

The election was fiercely contested and, at first, it seemed that Thrale might lose. 'We lead a wild Life', Hester wrote to Johnson, 'but it will be over tomorrow seven-night; the Election will be carried, but not so triumphantly as I hoped for.' She warned him to stay away 'till the Storm is over', penning her message 'surrounded by people making a noise & scarce know what I say but that I am very busy'. Thrale was returned to parliament, though only second on the poll: 'The truth is', Hester noted with self-admiration, 'I have been indefatigable'. Even this amount of pride was dangerous; she instantly fell from her horse and believed her life was over. More soberly, Johnson reported, she would soon be well, and had not miscarried. Less positive news came from the *London Chronicle*, which reported the drowning of nine people between Mull and Ulva, including Maclean of Col. Reminding Boswell that they too 'were once drowned', Johnson hoped it was a journalistic error. He wrote again, a month later, having just 'corrected the last page' of the *Journey* and hoping, again without much optimism, that 'they might be given before they are bought'. But, he reflected, 'trade is as diligent as courtesy'. The work was published in January 1775 with just three copies being sent out in December, for the king, for Hester Thrale and for Warren Hastings in Bengal.[37]

Johnson's principal endeavours at the time were all benevolent: petitioning to gain a charitable grant for Mrs Williams, cancelling a possibly offensive leaf in his *Journey*, recommending a play ('I have no doubt of its success') and seeking advice from John Taylor for help for their old schoolfellow Charles Congreve, Archdeacon of Armagh, who was sadly sunk in drunkenness. He also wrote to one cousin to ascertain whether another cousin, Thomas Johnson, was mad, or bad, or simply insatiable, for he had, in a little over sixteen months, 'consumed forty' of Johnson's pounds, 'and then writes for more'. He sent Hester a letter recommending someone keep a public house ('He seems to have a Genius for an alehouse'), but she, recovering from her fall, was full of misery. She wrote in her diary, 'what shall I do? Johnson & Baretti try to comfort me, they only plague me.' If her accident didn't kill her, *or* her unborn child, 'sure we are made of Iron'. His new year letter, bubbling over with excitement, must surely have tried her patience, for it told how the king was so taken with his *Journey* that he read bits aloud to Queen Charlotte and she, besotted with desire to hear the rest, borrowed the copy from the king's library. 'Of the two Queens', he asked, alluding to Queen*ey* Thrale, now ten years old, 'who has the better tast?'[38]

When the *Journey* was published, in January 1775, James Macpherson tried to get Johnson either to change his text or to apologise for it; finally he challenged him to fight a duel over Ossian's authenticity. All he succeeded in was drawing from Johnson his famous letter of response:

> Whatever insult is offered me I will do my best to repel, and what I cannot do for myself the law will do for me. I will not desist from detecting what I think a cheat, from any fear of the menaces of a Ruffian . . .
>
> You may print this if you will.

Johnson told Macpherson he thought his book 'an imposture from the beginning', seeming invigorated by the possibility of a literary confrontation. 'Macpherson is very furious,' he wrote to Boswell; 'can you give me any more intelligence about him, or his Fingal?' To Hector he confided, 'the King says, I must go into that country no more.'[39] There were, he told Boswell defiantly, 'no Erse manuscripts', begging him to be less credulous: 'you know how little a Highlander can be trusted'; but he took prudent defensive measures. He provided himself with an enormous oaken staff, six feet long, tapering from one inch thick at its lower end to three at its tip, to arm himself against any Scottish conspiracy of 'national falsehood'. 'Do not censure the expression,' he warned Boswell; 'you know it to be true.' Worse was to come when he discovered he had erroneously given the house of Dunvegan superiority over that of Raasay. 'If they could come hither, they would be as fierce as the Americans,' he confided to Hester. He wrote back to John Macleod, promising to apologise in the press, having a reverence 'for truth'.[40]

He was now very much a public figure, whose ventures into literary controversy brought him a prominence he both loved and hated. 'The patriots pelt me with answers,' he told John Taylor: 'Four pamflets I think, already, besides newspapers and reviews'. 'I have not been attacked enough for it,' Boswell records him observing: 'I never think I have hit hard, unless it rebounds.' He applauded the 'full tide of human existence' which passed him 'at Charing-cross' and laughed heartily when in company 'like a rhinoceros'.[41] But his letters, from this time almost daily, reveal a man more concerned with smaller, more intimate matters: the gift of china the Hectors designed for Mrs Thrale, suggestions for rheumatic remedies for Langton, personal flattery to Charlotte Lennox. He was particularly keen to keep up old acquaintanceships, with Hector, with Taylor, even with Charles Congreve who drank 'a bottle a day'. But the steady rhythm of his life relied especially upon the deep sense of intimacy he gained from Hester and the Thrales. 'I wish to live under your care and protection,' he wrote in March, followed by 'I am, Dearest of all dear Ladies, Your servant and slave'. He was unhappy not to hear from her, or see her, almost every day. 'I have wished to hear from you every post, and am uneasy,' he wrote to her from Oxford on 6 March, followed by an abject apology ('I . . . did not know but you were angry') two days later, upon receiving *two* letters. Mrs Thrale, pregnant at this time, presented her tenth baby, Frances Ann, on 4 May. That Easter Johnson confided there had been, perhaps, some 'diminution' of his knowledge: 'Much time I have not left.' He settled down to a book after evening prayers that Easter Eve, 'but found reading uneasy'.[42]

After Boswell left for Scotland at the end of May, bearing with him Johnson's praises for Scotch politeness, hospitality, beauty and 'everything Scotch, but Scotch oat-cakes and Scotch prejudices', Johnson was minded also to go northwards, to Lichfield and Ashbourne; but something, anything, prevented him. The queen of Denmark, sister to the king, died, leaving him uncertain about mourning clothes, 'which you have', he wrote to Hester, 'in the chest'. For some days he dithered, having 'no great mind to go'; he discussed Boswell's written but unpublished 'Journal' of their Scottish trip, which she had read: 'Is it not a merry piece?' he asked. 'There is much in it about poor me.' At last, he fancied he would go, and 'I fancy I shall not wish to stay long away', but once in Oxford, a panic seemed to strike him, having not heard from her for *three* days. It caused him the kind of trepidation that English could not contain: '*Trois jours sont passéz sans que [je] reçoive une lettre . . . Un silence si rare, que veut il?*' ('Three days have passed since I received a letter . . . What means this unaccustomed silence?') His consternation grew for two more days ('What can be the reason that I hear nothing from you?') until he *did* hear and turned immediately to worrying about the cost of travelling on to Lichfield, 'Frank and I in a postchaise'.[43]

At Lichfield nothing was new, just a little older and less hopeful than before. Lucy Porter had gout so badly she no longer dressed herself; Miss Turton grew old, Miss Vyse had been ill, but Mrs Aston, Miss Adey and Mrs Cobb were as before. They all remembered the Thrales well; 'you left a good impression behind you.' Almost as soon as he was there, Johnson was fabricating measures to escape. In Oxford, when he had not heard from her, he wondered 'whether it would not be proper to come back, and look for you'; after only a week in Lichfield, he 'would fain flatter myself that you begin to wish me home'. Subjects for discussion seemed rather tired and repetitive; Boswell is 'a favourite' but less so since Johnson has revealed 'that he is married'. One would think, he writes, 'the Man had been hired to be a spy upon me', having 'found my faults, and laid them up to reproach me'. Hester's venture to attend the first regatta ever held in England was their subject for several letters, particularly since Queeney appeared greatly to enjoy her 'first excursion into the regions of pleasure'. The outlook for little Ralph, aged eighteen months, was far bleaker, and he died at Brighton of a brain condition, putting Johnson's own ailment, a distressing deafness, into perspective.[44]

At Ashbourne Johnson wrote that it was only she who prevented him from going 'to Cairo', sailing 'down the Red Sea to Bengal' and taking 'a ramble' into India; but, in reality he knew, the thought was just a pose: 'I was, I am afraid, weary of being at home', he told Boswell, 'and weary of being abroad. Is not this the state of life?' Hester's desperation at her infant son Ralph's fatal condition drove her into agonies of self-critical despair: 'has the flattery of my Friends made me too proud of my own Brains?' she demanded of Johnson; '& must these poor Children suffer for my crime?' In her present state, the least thing could throw her into despair: 'If Hetty tells me that her head achs, I am more shocked than if I heard she had broken her Leg.'[45] Away in Ashbourne, Johnson sent what comfort he could, insisting that worries about her 'other Babies' were 'superfluous. Miss and Harry are as safe as ourselves'; if he had 'the prolixity of an emperour', he assured her, 'it should be all at your service'. Still, his talk of taking 'a ramble' into India alarmed her; 'I lost a child last Time you were at a distance,' she wrote. In despair, she lashed out at all in her vicinity, including Baretti who, she claimed, usurped her authority at the Streatham estate, acting as arbiter in disputes between herself and her servants, who would besiege him with their appeals. Johnson attempted to assuage her irritation, urging her not to quarrel with 'Poor B[arett]i', who was only trying to be 'frank, and manly, and independent'. By her next letter she acknowledged she was 'sorry I was so peevish with him' and Johnson, regaling her with Staffordshire tales of Polish oats and Siberian barley, let her know that 'if I thought you wanted me' he would immediately return. 'You have not all the misery in the world to yourself,' he said, attempting to lighten the tone; 'I was last night almost convulsed with flatulence.'[46]

The news that reached him from America, where the battle of Lexington had been followed up by the disaster of Bunker Hill, was decidedly gloomy: 'I suppose nothing told in the papers is true.'

Instead, he buried himself in family thoughts, thanking Queeney for her letter ('I hope the Peacock will recover'), claiming Susy as 'always [his] little girl' and paying special attention to Lucy Porter from whom 'fits of tenderness', such as he had recently received, were 'not common'. 'Are we to go to Brighthelmston this autumn?' he asked, amid pleas to her to send 'a few strawberries or currants' to Mrs Williams who, he heard, was ill. Mrs Thrale did better than that, and actually visited the invalid, to whom, as Johnson heard, she 'behaved lovely'. Yet, though he kept up this cheerful badinage, he wanted her to know that, inside, he was lonely: 'Here sit poor I, with nothing but my own solitary individuality; doing little, and suffering no more than I have often suffered'. He hoped she kept his letters, which would be 'the records of a pure and blameless friendship' and might 'in some hours of languour and sadness' revive 'the memory of more cheerful times'. Her letters back, though equally blameless, had the frantic tone of a mother watching as her children died before her eyes. In August she wrote of the 'agonies' she suffered as Sophie complained of pains in her head: 'I concluded Sentence was already past, and that She was about to follow her Brother and Sisters, so I fairly sate me down to cry.' Actually, this was an over-reaction; within hours the girl was up, eating 'a good Dinner', and went on to live another fifty years, but the danger was always there.[47] Johnson did what he could to rally her spirits, telling Boswell she so enjoyed his *Journal* of their Scottish trip that 'she almost read herself blind'. He complimented her by a reminder that she was 'but five and twenty' when they first met, which might have had more effect had it been either more accurate or more to her advantage; actually, she had been twenty-*three*. He was marginally more tactful in his poem 'To Mrs Thrale on her Thirty-fifth Birthday', which he gave her when she was thirty-six, though the final couplet, 'And those who wisely wish to wive,/ Must look on Thrale at Thirty-five', may have seemed just a little presumptive.[48]

Johnson returned to London in mid-August, in time to write a brief preface to Baretti's *Easy Phraseology*, a book designed 'for the use of young ladies' intending to learn colloquial Italian, which had grown out of his lessons to Queeney. It was a work of 'trifles' certainly, but 'life is made of trifles', and it ended with some lines which Johnson delighted to turn into an elegant compliment to Queeney's mother:

> Always young and always pretty;
> Long may live my lovely Hetty!'

He remained on excellent terms with both Baretti and Mrs Thrale for the start of their next excursion, which was not, as he had imagined, to Brighton, but to France.

The four of them, led by Henry Thrale and accompanied by Queeney, crossed from Dover to Calais on 17 September; 'The Weather was lovely – the Ship all our own, the Sea smooth,' Hester wrote in her journal; '*A Calais / Trop de frais*,' Johnson wrote in his, but seemed genuinely excited to be venturing abroad. 'I will try to speak a little French,' he wrote back to Robert Levet; 'I tried hitherto but little, but I spoke sometimes.' It was an experiment which did not succeed. 'When Johnson was in France, he was generally very resolute in speaking Latin,' Boswell records; 'It was a maxim with him that a man should not let himself down, by speaking a language which he speaks imperfectly.'[49]

His journal for the start of their journey has been lost, leaving only rhymes on towns they travelled through; at St Omer '*Tout est cher*' and at Arras '*Helas!*' At Rouen, speaking Latin, he entered into 'a most ingenious Argument' with the abbé concerning 'the demolition of the Jesuits', which Mrs Thrale could hardly follow, but soon enough she managed to make herself understood, having 'a good Deal of Literary Chat' with gentlemen they met, 'sometimes in English, sometimes in French, sometimes in Latin, sometimes in Italian; we all made Mistakes & those Mistakes made us laugh.' In October at Paris they visited widely, having a general recommendation from David Murray, the English ambassador. At François Racine de Monville's house Johnson noted 'small apartments furnished with effeminate and minute elegance', but Mrs Thrale was quite affronted by its decorations, 'contrived merely for the purposes of disgusting Lewdness', with ornaments which were 'all obscene'. Johnson was particularly interested in drawing unfavourable contrasts between French customs and those in England; he noted that the French had 'no laws for the maintenance of their poor', that as many people were 'killed' at Paris (by which he meant met violent deaths) 'as there are days in the year', that there was 'no middle rank' in France and that nobody 'but mean people' ever *walked* in Paris. He noted the inadequacy of French roads, and the French military's way of dealing with sexual misdeeds ('Five soldiers – Woman – Soldiers estraped') rather than have the soldiers hanged: 'The Colonel would not lose five men for the death of one woman.' While he visited the Palais de Justice, Mrs Thrale viewed the Palais Royal and Tuileries gardens and was astonished by the gross manners she encountered: 'The Youngest and prettiest Ladies of the Court will hawk and spit straight before them without the least Attention to Delicacy.' Even the shopkeepers were unpleasant: 'The Shops here at Paris are particularly mean & the Trades-people surly & disagreeable.' Both agreed that French cookery was vastly inferior to English. 'Their meals are gross,' was Johnson's remark; she commented that 'Onions & Cheese prevail in all the Dishes, & overpower the natural Tast of the Animal excepting only when it stinks indeed, which is not infrequently the Case'. They were mildly excited, when going to watch 'the King and Queen at dinner' ('like two people stuffed with straw', noted Hester); the queen was 'so impressed' by Queeney that she 'sent one of the gentlemen to enquire who she was'.[50]

The party visited Versailles ('a mean town') and were suitably disenchanted: 'Mean shops against the wall,' Johnson noted, being chiefly interested not in the palace ('of great extent') but its menagerie. He saw a rhinoceros with a broken horn, a young elephant whose tusks were just appearing, two camels, one lion and a tame brown bear which 'put out his paws'. In the playhouse ('very large') Mrs Thrale asked him what play he would wish to see there, suggesting Samuel Foote's *Englishman in Paris*. The answer came directly; 'No indeed, says he, – we will act Harry the fifth.' He made a note of the money he had distributed that day: in the menagerie '3 livres'; elsewhere '6 Livres'. Two days later, at the Bastille, he met Santerre, a brewer, who told him that beer sold 'retail at 6d. a bottle', that he himself brewed '4,000 barrels a year' and that of the seventeen brewers in Paris, none brewed more than he did. Johnson worked out this meant that 'they make 51,000 a year', which pleased himself and Mrs Thrale greatly. Three years later they were desperately endeavouring to make Mr Thrale promise 'that he would never more brew a larger Quantity of Beer in one Winter than eighty Thousand Barrels', more than half as much again as all the breweries of Paris.[51]

Johnson's tone in his journal of the visit to France is mainly hostile and depreciating, yet there were things he enjoyed. In the exhibition of paintings at the Palais Royal he thought 'the pictures of Raphael fine', despite the fact he had little time for paintings. He realised, as he wandered alone around palaces and great buildings, that, having no one with whom to discuss them, their images would be fleeting: 'As I entred my Wife was in my mind. She would have been pleased; having now nobody to please I am little pleased.' In all their tour of France the evening he liked best was when, Mrs Thrale being unwell, they stayed behind while Sir Harry Gough, Henry Keene and Captain Kilpatrick joined the rest of Thrale's party for an evening at the theatre. 'Mr. Johnson sat at home by me, & we criticized & talked & were happy in one another – he in huffing me, & I in being huff'd,' she wrote. By the start of November they were on their way home and suddenly Johnson approved of everything they saw. At Compiègne the church was 'very elegant and splendid'; at Noyon the cathedral was 'very beautiful' and Cambrai cathedral was not only 'very beautiful' but had a 'splendid' choir, a 'very high and grand' nave and 'very splendid' vestments. His journal breaks off in this paean of praise, leaving Mrs Thrale to comment on the grisaille paintings by Geeraerts at the Benedictines' Church. This was on 5 November; six days later they were back in England.[52]

Immediately Johnson sent at least four letters to various friends, telling them of his travels. Paris was 'very different' from the Hebrides, he told Boswell, but 'not so fertile of novelty', which in the *Life* became 'France is worse than Scotland in every thing but climate'. He mentioned to Hector the French queen's enquiring after Queeney, and sent Lucy Porter the snuffbox he had purchased at the *palais marchand*. To John Taylor he reminisced, old codger style, their friendship having lasted so long 'that it is valuable for its antiquity'. His was a life 'turned upside down', he thought; having been 'fixed to a spot' when he was young, he was now 'roving the world. I am wholly unsettled,' he wrote. 'I am a kind of ship with a wide sail, and without an anchor.'[53]

16

Biographer of the Poets

poet n.s. *(*poete, *Fr.* Poeta, *Lat.* ποιητης.*) An inventor; an author of fiction; a writer of poems; one who
writes in measure.*

Johnson remained for some weeks at Streatham following their
return, politely but resolutely declining Boswell's suggestion for a
written narrative of their tour of France: 'I cannot pretend to tell the
publick any thing of a place better known to many of my readers than
to myself.' He tried, unsuccessfully, to wriggle out of offering his opinion of the increasingly acrimonious dispute between Boswell and his
father over entailing family estates to male heirs only, writing that he
was unsure whether he was 'quite equal to it'. Boswell would not be
shaken free, however, and so eventually Johnson, not entirely approv-
ing 'either your design or your father's', gave a Delphic judgement
inclining rather to the father's position, which, he noted, 'excludes
nobody'. More worryingly, he had received no acknowledgement from
Lucy Porter of the snuffbox he had sent, and wrote again, at
Christmas, entreating her to send him a few words, if necessary using
an amanuensis: 'Do, my dear Love, write to me, and do not let us forget each other. This is the season of good wishes . . .' Boswell, not giving up, sent a more favourable opinion of his side of the entail
question from Lord Hailes, but Johnson now found the whole dispute
vexatious and Hailes's judgement 'something . . . like superstition'.
'Get it off your hands and out of your head as fast as you can,' he wrote
to John Taylor, who likewise wrote to him begging informal legal
advice; 'Your health is of more consequence.' Another former
schoolfellow of theirs, Caleb Harding, had died: 'At Lichfield there are
none but Harry Jackson and Sedgwick,' sighed Johnson, 'and
Sedgwick when I left him, had a dropsy.'[1]

His melancholy tone may have been affected by the death of Frances Ann, the baby of the Thrale family, aged just seven months. In January 1776 he thanked God for allowing him to see 'the beginning of another year'. 'At least light your candle,' he counselled John Taylor; 'a man is perhaps never so much harrassed by his own mind in the light as in the dark.' For his writing, he turned from light to sound, publishing a dedication to the queen of Charles Burney's *History of Music*. 'The science of musical sounds' might justly be enjoyed as an art which 'gratifies sense, without weakening reason'. What he, personally, *felt* about music would be less easily stated, though Burney's *History* of the subject brought Johnson as close as possible to an appreciation. Listening to some sentences read from the preface before printing, he see-sawed on his chair exclaiming: 'All animated nature loves music – except myself!'

Plans for the same group as had visited Paris to take a trip to Italy were well advanced, and Baretti negotiated with friends to ensure a painless journey. Boswell, it seemed, was feeling 'melancholy', for which his best remedy was a visit to Johnson. 'Mr. Thrale will take me to Italy', Johnson warned, 'on the first of April', so if he must come 'you must come very quickly'. Privately he rather hoped Boswell would stay away, and alerted him to his wish to 'scour the country', visiting Oxford and Lichfield, before leaving 'on this long journey', from which, the implication was, he might never return.[2] He wrote to his oldest friends, Edmund Hector and John Taylor, of Charles Congreve whose morose drunkenness was most dispiriting; neither glad nor sorry to see him, Congreve answered everything 'with mono-syllables'. Johnson anticipated his forthcoming visit to Lichfield with low spirits: 'I see the old places, but find nobody that enjoyed them with me.' At least Peyton, his old amanuensis on the *Dictionary*, was 'not worse this morning', he wrote to Hester Thrale, taking his leave of her: '*Sunt lacrymae rerum.*'[3]

Boswell's arrival at Johnson's latest home in Bolt Court, a little way further along Fleet Street, raised both their spirits, and Boswell wittily recorded their principal adventures. There was the episode of Johnson assisting a drunken gentlewoman to cross Fleet Street, 'upon which she offered me a shilling, supposing me to be the watchman'.

At Oxford, Johnson reminisced about John Fludyer, of his college, who 'had been a scoundrel all along'. 'Did he cheat at draughts?' demanded Boswell at which Johnson affected to be appalled. 'Sir, we never played for *money*.' Dining at an inn, Johnson expatiated 'on the felicity of England in its taverns and inns', asserting that '*a tavern chair was the throne of human felicity*'. At Birmingham the two met Hector and his sister, Mrs Careless, 'the first woman', Johnson remarked, 'with whom I was in love'. When they reached Lichfield, Boswell was introduced to Lucy Porter, Peter Garrick and Harry Jackson, and lodged with Johnson at the Three Crowns inn, 'the very next house' to that where he was born. Johnson held forth on the inhabitants of Lichfield as 'the most sober, decent people in England', who spoke 'the purest English', a detail which Boswell queried, recalling David Garrick's caricature of Johnson 'squeezing a lemon into a punch-bowl, with uncouth gesticulations, looking round the company, and calling out, "Who's for *poonsh*?" '4

In a little over a week Boswell had been introduced to most of the people, and many of the places, that Johnson loved; Johnson was endeavouring to ensure that whatever he wrote of him should at least have the merit of accuracy: 'They only who live with a man can write his life with any genuine exactness and discrimination.' Johnson had written to John Taylor that he was at Lichfield and was awaiting his visit when he received a letter 'which seemed to agitate him very much'. 'One of the most dreadful things that has happened in my time,' he exclaimed, by which Boswell assumed he meant a public event such as the assassination of the king or another gunpowder plot: 'Mr. Thrale has lost his only son!'5 Boswell's private comment that, though regrettable, this affliction was 'comparatively small' says much about his jealousy of Mrs Thrale. 'I could wish he had been independent,' he said, arguing Johnson 'would have had more dignity'. For her part, Mrs Thrale could be equally tart, congratulating Johnson, the following year, at having Boswell by him; 'nothing that you say for this Week at least will be lost to Posterity.'6

The letter informing him of Harry's death had been sent by John Perkins and concluded, 'I need not say how much they wish to see you in London.' Johnson wrote immediately to Hester Thrale, promising to come immediately: 'the tears are in my eyes.' Making their excuses to John Taylor at Ashbourne, he and Boswell set off for London, but arrived just as Mrs Thrale, Queeney and Baretti were setting out for Bath. 'Do not indulge your sorrow, try to drive it away by either pleasure or pain,' he wrote to her, relieved that at least the boy had not perished while they had been en route to Rome: 'You would have believed that he died by neglect, and that your presence would have saved him.' The sense of death was all around him; that very day, he heard that 'Poor Peyton expired this morning'. Henry Thrale, unable to bear company in grief, sent Johnson away and did not call on him for days, until Good Friday when he came 'for comfort' and sat with him 'till seven when we all went to Church'. The 'all' he mentions there included Boswell, who had 'interrupted' his solitary devotions; of him 'I could have rid myself', he writes, impatiently, had not Thrale's presence made that impossible. The three of them, goaded by Boswell, talked of many things, including gaming, upon which Johnson pronounced there were 'not six instances' of men ruined by it 'in an age'.[7]

Mr Thrale, having wavered for a few days, now pronounced: the trip to Rome was off. Johnson, though disappointed, did not dispute the decision, which was, he wrote to Hester, not 'weakness of resolution' but 'a wise man's compliance with the change of things'. He did not 'grieve at the effect' but only 'at the cause'. Mrs Thrale wrote back that, should he write 'about Streatham and Croydon, the book would be as good to me as a journey to Rome'. But Baretti did not take this change in the family's plans with anything like the same philosophical demeanour. He was openly angry at his wasted months of careful planning and arrangements, until his anger was abated with the present of a hundred guineas by Thrale. That evening Johnson dined at the Thrales', where Hester had just returned. Boswell also was present to record a painful conversation, on children, in which Johnson claimed he 'should not have had much fondness for a child' of his own, to which Mrs Thrale reacted with some horror. Johnson modified his remark to 'I never wished to have a child'. The Thrales had lost three children within less than a year, two boys, Ralph and Henry, and baby Frances. 'Mr. Thrale has seen your letter', Hester told Johnson, '& shed Tears over reading it – they are the first he has shed.'[8]

Johnson joined the Thrales at their lodgings in Bath, which Queeney, a precocious eleven-year-old, did not much care for, pronouncing the Pump Rooms 'very like the *South Sea house*' and the company which frequented them 'very like *the Clerks*'. Johnson's principal activity was attempting to shake off Boswell, who wrote to him from London complaining of neglect. He was rapidly tiring of 'peevish' Mrs Williams, who, being blind, would eat in a manner which 'could not but offend the delicacy of persons of nice sensations'. 'Why do you talk of neglect,' Johnson demanded. 'When did I neglect you?' He invited Boswell to Bath, but gave him 'business' to transact in London which would delay his arrival for some days. 'Make my compliments to all our Friends round the world', he wrote, 'and to Mrs. Williams at home.' When the party moved from Bath to Bristol, they were accommodated at a less than pleasing hotel, which Boswell was all for getting them to describe. Johnson leapt to the challenge. 'Describe it, Sir? – Why, it was so bad that Boswell wished to be in Scotland!'[9]

The sense that Johnson wished to keep Boswell, his acknowledged biographer, at a distance is evident. In part this was on account of Mrs Thrale, who never ceased to ridicule him, but even in London Boswell was less welcome than he liked to depict. In the *Life* he mentions that he 'occasionally slept' in Johnson's house, 'in the room that had been assigned to me', but his *Journal* offers a rather cooler sense of welcome: 'Johnson would give no hint for me to stay the night. I did, and lay there.' Boswell having made the decision to stay, Johnson rallied, gave him his hand and said, 'Glad to have you here.' But he also wrote to Hester a week later, assuring her that 'Boswell goes away on Thursday'.[10] Before then Boswell narrates a conversation in which he and Johnson were joined by Reynolds and Sir William Forbes at the Crown and Anchor tavern, debating the pros and cons of drinking; meanwhile all (except Johnson) drank heartily. Reynolds maintained 'a moderate glass' enlivened the mind, allowing people to talk more volubly, but Johnson disagreed, arguing that Reynolds confused genial hilarity for noisy tumults. 'Cock-fighting, or bear-baiting, will raise the spirits,' he contended, but would not improve the conversation. Sir William suggested that possibly a man might be 'warmed' with a little wine 'like a bottle . . . set before the fire' and Johnson was about to crush his argument but, mindful of the time when he himself had been drunk in Sir Joshua's company, he sat back and laughed, uneasily.[11]

For much of the summer Johnson was hobbled by gout which permitted him only to 'creep' to the end of his court and 'climb' with much effort into a coach; he could 'go up stairs pretty well', he told John Taylor, but 'am yet aukward in coming down'. Hester, coming home from Bath and stricken with a form of cholera, urged him not to visit: 'What should we do together if both want nursing?' she wrote. 'If you have any pity for me do not come home till I have got my house a little to rights.' The house in Streatham was without servants, and she asked his help finding 'a *Butler* or a *Footman* or a *Maid*'; he, in his lame condition, made only the facetious suggestion of a 'running Footman'.[12] She also hinted she was in an interesting condition, and he immediately congratulated her that she was 'going to be immediately a mother'. 'Mrs. Thrale . . . fancies she carries a boy,' he wrote to Boswell, which was 'necessary to the continuance of Thrale's fortune; for what can misses do with a brewhouse?' In this she was to be disappointed; the child, her eleventh, was born in February 1777 and was a girl, Cecilia.[13]

In July Baretti stormed out of the Thrales' house, after an explosion of the undercurrent of ill humour that had been evident since the cancellation of the Rome trip. 'Mrs Thrale did not like Baretti', Johnson remarked to Boswell, 'nor Baretti her. But he was the best teacher of Italian that she could have for her daughter.' Their antagonism was exacerbated over a dispute in Bath about some 'tin pills' she gave Queeney for her stomach, but which Baretti protested against. He was also annoyed at the *Monthly Review*'s article on his *Easy Phraseology*, which remarked the book was 'not the most contemptible' of its kind, but objected to 'the Author's vanity, which breaks out continually'. At almost the same point Johnson had a falling-out with Boswell over the length of his letters, his continual complaints about his 'black fits', but mainly over his failure even to open a box of books that Johnson had sent to him. Such neglect, he remarked, was 'very offensive'; he was, he confessed, 'very angry that you manage yourself so ill'. With Johnson, though, fits of anger, or of melancholy, seldom lasted long. Four days later he wrote again: 'Now, my dear Bozzy, let us have done with quarrels and with censure. Let me know whether I have not sent you a pretty library', confirming what he had told Boswell a year before; 'I look upon *myself* as a good humoured fellow.' In November he was still attempting to patch things up: 'Let us not throw any of our days away upon useless resentment,' he wrote. It is always wisest to stay on good terms with your biographer.[14]

He spent October in Brighton, with the Thrales, but did not venture into the sea until almost the end of their stay; he was rather sceptical, he told Robert Levet, whether bathing 'does me any good'. Johnson was a strong swimmer, but mainly when something other than his health was at stake. Swimming in the river, near Oxford, he was cautioned against a pool which was thought to be 'particularly danger-ous'; upon which 'Johnson directly swam into it'. To entertain himself he wrote down the various sums he had borrowed from Mr Thrale, which came to seven guineas, and the amounts he had expended, which, including £1 18s 'given away', 2s 'purloined by Mr T' and £1 19s 'in my pocket', came to seven guineas and fourpence. Back in London he wrote to Boswell of Baretti's leaving the Thrale household 'in some whimsical fit of disgust or ill-nature'; 'to live at variance at all', he wrote, alluding to Boswell's recent reconciliation with his father, 'is uncom-fortable . . . Let it now be all over.' Hester Thrale, devoid of male children, found fault with her girls; there was 'something strangely perverse' in Queeney's temper; she was 'full of Bitterness and Aversion to all who instruct her'. She found fault even with her husband, who, if she died, would 'treat me with a Monument' and promptly marry again; it was 'Poor Mr. Johnson', she thought, who would feel 'the greatest Loss of me'.[15]

The new year commenced with prayers to be delivered 'from the intrusion of evil thoughts' and bad nights, when he could scarcely breathe. A surgeon came and bled him, twelve ounces, but when he found himself no better he contrived to bleed himself again, with the help of Frank Barber and Robert Levet. To no avail: 'the difficulty of breathing allowed no rest.' When Hester came to hear of it, she was most alarmed; 'pray don't be bleeding yourself & doing yourself harm – my Master [Mr Thrale] is very angry.' Johnson was rather proud of his own resilience, filling his letters for the next month to Hester, John Taylor and Boswell with details of how he lost 'as was computed, six-and-thirty ounces of blood in a few days'.[16] To Boswell he recalled their Hebridean expedition as 'the most pleasant journey that I ever made'; in April he remembered spending a night of 'such sweet uninterrupted sleep, as I have not known since I slept at Fort Augustus', remembering it the following year as the best night's sleep he had had for twenty years. In February he received a letter informing him that a gentleman had planted 'above fifty million of trees' on ground at Monimusk. Though probably both stories are exaggerations, they indicate that, five years on, memories of his tour of the Highlands were acquiring the pleasing patina of nostalgia.[17]

He wrote to Elizabeth Aston in the spring, having heard worrying rumours of her health: 'Gayety is a duty', he informed this sprightly sixty-nine-year-old, 'when health requires it.' He used the same word ('you are all young and gay and easy') to Mrs Thrale, drawing a melancholy contrast with himself ('I have miserable nights, and know not how to make them better'). Mrs Thrale was being presented at court, an honour which, in Johnson's view, 'was delayed too long'. 'The Ceremony was trifling, but I am glad it's over,' she replied; 'one is now upon the footing one wishes to be', dropping rather awkwardly into what she took for courtly speech. He mentioned meeting 'you all' at Dr Burney's the next day, where Fanny Burney had her first sight of him. 'He is, indeed, very ill-favoured,' she wrote to her father's friend and adviser, Samuel Crisp; 'tall and stout; but stoops terribly; he is almost bent double. His mouth is almost [continually opening and shutting], as if he was chewing.'[18]

During the spring Johnson proposed Sheridan's membership of the Literary Club and Mrs Thrale went to see a *School for Scandal* which, she claimed, knowingly, was '*a Thing* it seems'. Johnson was concerned in writing a prologue for a benefit performance of *A Word to the Wise*, having been not particularly friendly with Hugh Kelly, the author, but, he protested, 'what can a man do?'

> To wit, reviving from its author's dust,
> Be kind, ye judges, or at least be just . . .

Johnson, being partially deaf, did not often frequent playhouses, which may have been a good thing. Boswell narrates an anecdote of Garrick's (both of whom were liable to exaggeration) concerning Johnson's behaviour at the theatre in Lichfield when, having vacated his chair 'between the side-scenes' for a moment, he returned to find it occupied by a gentleman who 'refused to give it up', upon which 'Johnson laid hold of it, and tossed him and the chair into the pit'.[19] He wrote a dedication 'To the King' for the late Bishop Pearce's commentary on the *Four Evangelists*, in which the author exhibited 'Qualities, which may be imitated by the highest and the humblest of mankind'. But apart from such occasional puffs, the ever-lengthening entries in his diary and obsessive letters to Hester Thrale, he had virtually ceased to write – until, that is, the end of March when he was visited by three members of the book trade, Thomas Cadell, Thomas Davies and William Strahan, representing the interests of over forty publishers, who invited him to write prefaces to an edition of English poets. 'I am engaged to write little Lives, and little Prefaces, to a little edition of the English Poets,' he wrote to Boswell, asking if he could get him 'some information' on Thomson. The meeting with the publishers was important enough for him to include it in his diary for Easter Eve: 'I treated with booksellers on a bargain.'[20]

Told that his 'literary strength lay in writing biography', Johnson could not disagree; but he was now sixty-seven and, surveying his life, 'I discover nothing but a barren waste of time with some disorders of body, and disturbances of the mind very near to madness.' He was torn between the man who had declared 'the publick has no farther claim upon me' and the one who had written in his diary, on his sixty-second birthday, that 'perhaps Providence has yet some use for the remnant of my life'. But had he left it too late? 'Days and months pass in a dream,' he wrote, a week later; 'I am afraid that my memory grows less tenacious, and my observation less attentive. If I am decaying it is time to make haste.'[21] The press was suddenly full of news of the death of Henry Thrale; he wrote immediately to John Perkins, the brewery manager, believing this to be the chatter of a 'foolish newspaper' but anxious, nevertheless. This rumour was false, but on his journey to the Midlands that summer he found Mrs Aston sick ('She is old') and Mrs Roebuck dead; at Lichfield, Harry Jackson and Miss Turton were both dead; '*De spe decidi*,' he wrote, 'fallen from hope.' Hope had always been his watchword and when, within the week, he found press announcements that *The English Poets* with a *Preface, Biographical and Critical* by *Samuel Johnson, LL.D* was 'In the Press, and speedily will be published' he felt again a surge of hope which brought 'sweet uninterrupted sleep'.[22] The London booksellers were acting promptly in efforts to prevent the Scottish publisher John Bell from flooding the English market with his edition of *Poets of Great Britain Complete from Chaucer to Churchill* in over a hundred volumes. This 'little trifling edition', as the bookseller Edward Dilly described it to Boswell, with print so small that 'many persons could not read them' and 'conspicuous' inaccuracies, was the principal reason for the urgency of the London consortium, who left it 'entirely to the Doctor' to name the fee. He 'mentioned two hundred guineas' and 'it was immediately agreed to'. The word 'immediately' there is noteworthy. Edward Malone expressed astonishment at the agreement. 'Had he asked one thousand guineas, or even fifteen hundred guineas, the booksellers, who knew the value of his name, would doubtless have readily given it,' he said, estimating the booksellers stood to make 'five thousand guineas' from the volumes. They agreed to offer him a 'farther compliment' once the work was completed, but Johnson did not feel underpaid: 'The fact is, not that they have paid me too little, but that I have written too much.' He made some few alterations to what they proposed, recommending the inclusion of John Pomfret, Thomas Yalden and Isaac Watts and the exclusion of Charles Churchill, as a punishment for a lifetime of ridiculing him. Mrs Thrale remarked that this last was 'the only unjust or resentful Thing I ever knew him to do'.[23]

He was suddenly concerned about the Reverend William Dodd, a well-known preacher and chaplain to the king, who dressed in the smartest fashion, wore diamond rings and had a 'well-disposed *bouquet*'. Dodd had been convicted of forging the Earl of Chesterfield's signature on a bond for £4,200 which was 'a thing almost without example for a Clergyman of his rank to stand at the bar for a capital breach of morality'. Johnson was sympathetic: 'I am afraid he will suffer.' He had briefly met Dodd years before, when the clergyman found Johnson spoke 'good sense', but in a manner 'so obstinate, ungenteel, and boorish, as renders it disagreeable and dissatisfactory'.

Lady Harrington besought Johnson's aid on Dodd's behalf, and he wrote several petitions, sermons and letters for him, including a letter to the king, which he sent, enjoining Dodd 'not to let it be at all known that I have written this Letter'. There was a petition with 1,256 signatures begging for clemency, and a very great deal of support, but there were some things of which Dodd could not bear to accuse himself. In the 'Last Solemn Declaration' which Johnson wrote for him on 25 June 1777 he changed the bald phrase 'My life has been hypocritical' to the more oleaginous 'My life for some few unhappy years past has been dreadfully erroneous'. Johnson commented in the margin, 'With this he said he could not charge himself.' Two days later, all the petitions having failed, and 'in opposition to the recommendation of the jury – the petition of the city of London – and a subsequent petition signed by three-and-twenty thousand hands', Dodd was hanged. 'Surely the voice of the publick, when it calls so loudly, and calls only for mercy, ought to be heard', was Johnson's comment, having wished Dodd's sentence might have been changed to transportation. Five years later, though, he took a slightly different view, remarking that, although he had campaigned to have Dodd's death sentence commuted, 'I did not wish he should be made a saint'.[24]

Mrs Thrale had recently become 'such a Gadder' that he claimed she cared 'not . . . a peny [sic]' for him; he sought to obtain a ticket for her to a fête at Devonshire House, but the fête was 'deferred to another Year'. She and Queeney went to Ranelagh instead, but Johnson could match even that: he spent his evening with the prominent bluestocking hostess Elizabeth Vesey and had his Prologue for A Word to the Wise praised by all the ladies – 'you can't think'. Unfortunately Mrs Kelly fared less well; 'Only fifty pounds.' 'Can we not meet at Manchester?' he asked Boswell, planning his summer travels, and reminding him 'Mrs. Williams is, I fear, declining . . . We must all die.' Before he died he must do something to dignify the business of writing authors' lives. He wrote to his friend Richard Farmer at Cambridge to enquire whether there were any manuscripts or other relevant materials in the university; if so, 'I will come down.' He had previously experienced the 'civilities of Cambridge' and welcomed another visit. Boswell expressed the conviction that Johnson was supremely well equipped for writing the *Lives*; he had 'little more to do than to put his thoughts upon paper'.[25]

Actually he had rather a lot to do, for as he explained in the case of Isaac Watts, though 'his name' had long been held by him 'in *veneration*', of his life 'I know very little'. He went to Oxford, 'picked up some little information for my Lives at the library', then on to Birmingham and Lichfield. 'At Birmingham I heard of the death of an old friend, and at Lichfield of the death of another,' he wrote to Hester Thrale, keeping up his mournful threnody: 'One was a little older, the other a little younger than myself.' 'My nights are very tedious,' he wrote, keeping a careful diary of his night thoughts. 'Hope – Mother – never thought till Lately' came into his mind, as he lay where she had lain; 'K. William could not breathe but in a Room many feet high,' he noted, as he felt the walls close in upon him. 'Miss Turton, and Harry Jackson are dead. Mrs Aston is, I am afraid, in great danger,' he wrote; 'I have been very faint and breathless since I came hither.' 'The tears each other sheds' he pondered on that night, his mind already churning over his forthcoming life of Pope. Already he was thinking far beyond the 'lives' printed in the French Miscellanies 'containing a few dates and a general character'. He did not feel that 'the life of any literary man in England had been well written'; it was up to him to change that.[26]

Mrs Thrale wrote of a dinner at Reynolds's house in Richmond, which the Garricks, Mr Langton and his two 'elegant Creatures' of four years old attended. The infants were 'very troublesome . . . with their Prattle, every word of which their Papa repeated in order to explain'. Garrick, pleading a sickness in his stomach, 'desired a Table to himself' but their mother 'directed them to go to Mr. Garrick's Table, and *eat fair*. He was sick before, and I actually saw him change Colour at their approach . . .' Johnson stayed in Lichfield for race week, though many left town 'to escape the cost of entertaining company', and was in Ashbourne by the start of September, to greet Boswell. He wrote to Hester that he supposed she was 'pretty diligent at the Thraliana, and a very curious collection posterity will find it'. To have not one but two avowed annalists noting his every move gave Johnson a certain pride and, conscious of his status as a biograph*er* as much as a biograph*é*, he laid down a few guidelines. 'Chronology you know is the eye of history; and every Man's life is of importance to himself. Do not omit painful casualties or unpleasing passages, they make the variegation of existence.' Above all, he warned that 'every day' had 'something to be noted'.[27]

While he waited for Boswell he filled his days with preaching optimism to his correspondents; it was 'the business of a wise man to be happy', he counselled Boswell in a letter he directed to be left at Carlisle; 'all sickness is a summons,' he told Elizabeth Aston at Lichfield. To Hester he confided that Boswell, shrinking from his own idea of a voyage to the Baltic, spoke instead of Wales; but, he said, conscious that he wrote to a Welshwoman, 'what is there in Wales?' His nights he devoted to reading; Norden's *Travels in Egypt and Nubia* was his current favourite, in which he spoke of crocodiles 'in upper Egypt, one he thought fifty feet long'. His sixty-eighth birthday brought less joy than ever ('Age is a very stubborn Disease') but the final arrival of Boswell caused him pleasure. He 'plays his part with his usual vivacity', he reported to Hester, bringing a change from John Taylor, whose 'uniformity of life' he found more than a little wearisome. Boswell, surprised to learn that the *Lives* Johnson was to write were 'not an undertaking directed by him', nevertheless joined him in debating whether he should be candid in publishing men's vices. If he mentioned 'that Addison and Parnell drank too freely' would his readers more easily indulge in drink themselves? Of Rochester the question was how best to 'castrate' him; Johnson wittily observed that Gilbert Burnet had produced 'a good *Death*' for the poet, emphasising in his *Passages* of Rochester's *Life and Death* his (not undisputed) repentance; but 'there is not much *Life*'.[28]

Together they toured the Derby china works and Islam gardens, at both of which Boswell spent far more than the prudent Johnson had expected, leading him to 'beg' Mr Thrale for a loan. But Boswell obtained what most he sought, conversation and, particularly, quotations. Of Dr Dodd's misfortune Johnson declared; 'Depend upon it, Sir, when a man knows he is to be hanged in a fortnight, it concentrates his mind wonderfully', and, while discussing Boswell's constant desire to reside in London, he memorably observed that 'when a man is tired of London, he is tired of life; for there is in London all that life can afford'.[29]

With Boswell gone, Johnson begged Hester to send the *Biographia Britannica* to his London home, where he expected imminently to go. But Taylor had other plans; Johnson remained at Ashbourne, writing four sermons for his friend in payment for his accommodation, but also writing for himself. On 11 October his diary has the entry 'Finished the life of Cowley', followed two days later by 'Finished the life of Denham'. He was clearly in a mood for serious intellectual endeavours; between these two dates he noted, in Latin, shaving his arms in order to discover 'how much time would restore the hairs'. He wrote to Mrs Thrale at Brighton, hoping to come and begging to be informed of every little difficulty that the family had encountered in their lodgings: 'Let me hear the whole series of misery, for as Dr Young says, *I love horrour*'. 'Could not you do some of them for me,' he adds, setting out the list of thirteen authors in two columns, from Milton at the head of the first to Broome and Fenton at the foot of the second. 'I wish I were with you,' he writes, noting a quotation from Dryden indicating that he too was in his thoughts. 'You know, I have some work to do,' he wrote a week later, imagining coming up to London 'with nothing done'. Now at least he had 'stop[ped] their mouths', having finished Cowley; but, looking at the lives ahead, he sensed a lessening of his enthusiasm. John Bell had already pushed ahead with twenty volumes of *Poets of Great Britain* but, six months after signing the contract, Cowley was all that Johnson had to offer. 'Life has upon the whole fallen short, very short, of my early expectations,' he wrote, having only the Thrales to counteract his melancholy disposition.[30]

The Thrales were accustoming themselves to Brighton society, including John Wilkes, who, said Mrs Thrale, 'professed himself a Lyar and an Infidel'. Johnson had moved to Lichfield and could provide little to mitigate the news of the elopement of Elizabeth, daughter of Mrs Charles Burney by her former marriage, to an 'undesirable young man' named Samuel Meeke. 'Every avenue of pain is invaded at once,' he said: 'Whither will the poor Lady run from herself.' He had only 'a collection of Misery' to offer up in compensation: 'Mrs. Aston paralytick, Mrs. Walmsley lame, Mrs. Hervey blind, and I think another Lady deaf. Ev'n such is life.' 'In a Man's letters you know', he wrote a few days later, 'his soul lies naked', which was rather a formal aphorism for their correspondence. His letters to Mrs Thrale vary in tone from intimate consolation to jocose familiarity, but he was always conscious 'how small a part of our minds' they wrote down; usually he manages to avoid both cliché ('None but the Brave deserve the Fair') and quotation, though sometimes he entertains her with odd lines from Shakespeare, Dryden or Pope. In Lichfield he made careful lists of his expenditure ('o-10-6' to his barber; 'o-1-o' to a 'Woman at door') which were very detailed though not necessarily accurate; on 27 October he noted 'Lucy Porter is this day sixty-three' when she was actually a year younger. Arriving back in London, he was summoned down to Brighton, where the fashionable company had practically all gone, 'through storms and cold and dirt and all the hardships of wintry journeys'. 'We have a *lame* Lord left, a *deaf* Gentleman, and Mr. Palmer who *squints*,' Hester informed him. He looked forward to seeing her dressed not in a wig ('We will burn it') but in her own hair, which must be combed, he warned her, 'at least once in three months, on the quarter day'.[31]

Arriving in Brighton on 14 November, he travelled back with the Thrales to London four days later and spent December making odd experiments, such as finding that, dried, an ounce of green laurel leaves weighed only 139 and a half grains, and writing the *Lives* of various poets. He was annoyed, and said so, that Boswell had repeated an untrue anecdote about his attitude to Henry Hervey 'in such a strain of cowardly caution as gave me no pleasure' but, switching tone abruptly after administering this sharp reproof, he hinted to him that Mrs Thrale was 'in hopes of a young brewer'. These hopes, however, proved illusory; Henrietta Sophia was born in June, but died aged only four. Meanwhile the brewery flourished and Thrale's avowed wish 'of an hundred thousand barrels' was very nearly achieved. When, the following January, Boswell wrote that his wife had been showing 'alarming symptoms' for the past three months, Johnson offered her the use of his own rooms; 'London is a good air for ladies,' he said.[32]

The first *Lives* he wrote, of Cowley and Denham, set the standard high. 'I have been drawn to a great length,' he explained, because neither poet had 'any critical examination before'. Johnson made clear that, in his roles both as biographer and critic, he would be fearless in passing judgements. Cowley's 'wish for retirement' in the 1650s he believed was quite 'undissembled', yet judged that 'if his activity was virtue, his retreat was cowardice'. This agreed with his earlier criticism, in the *Rambler*, of Cowley's 'cowardly' wish for a 'scheme of happiness to which the imagination of a girl, upon the loss of her first lover, could have scarcely given way'. He notes that Cowley abandoned thoughts of seeking shelter in America in the 1660s, 'wisely' leaving 'the bustle of life' only so far that 'he might easily find his way back, when solitude should grow tedious'. The chief value of this *Life*, however, and the reason he considered it 'the best', was for observations he set down, in a few trenchant paragraphs, on the poets he referred to as metaphysical:

> The metaphysical poets were men of learning, and to shew their learning was their whole endeavour; but, unluckily resolving to shew it in rhyme, instead of writing poetry, they wrote verses, and very often such verses as stood the trial of the finger better than of the ear; for the modulation was so imperfect, that they were only found to be verses by counting the syllables.
> ... Their thoughts are often new, but seldom natural; they are not obvious, but neither are they just; and the reader, far from wondering that he missed them, wonders more frequently by what perverseness of industry they were ever found ... The most heterogeneous ideas are yoked by violence together; nature and art are ransacked for illustrations, comparisons, and allusions; their learning instructs, and their subtilty surprises; but the reader commonly thinks his improvement dearly bought, and, though he sometimes admires, is seldom pleased.

These sentences have been worried over by critics, particularly in the twentieth century when metaphysical poetry came to dominate the writing of verse. T. S. Eliot's notion that 'A thought to Donne was an experience; it modified his sensibility' was, in reality, a reworking of Johnson's sense of 'heterogeneous ideas' yoked violently together in the poems of the previous century. Johnson's critical axioms were invariable, and 'great thoughts are always general' reformulates his observation that 'nothing can please many, and please long, but just representations of general nature', made of Shakespeare fifteen years before. He notes that Cowley's 'fault', and that, perhaps, of 'all the writers of the metaphysical race', was that he pursued his thoughts 'to their last ramifications, by which he loses the grandeur of generality'.[33] Negative judgements of particular poems are both severe and specific: 'Nothing can be more disgusting than a narrative spangled with conceits,' he writes of Cowley's unfinished epic, *Davideis*: 'Nothing', he declares, risking a tautology, 'is less exhilarating than the ludicrousness of Denham.' But his concluding judgement, that Denham was an author whom 'we ought' to read 'with gratitude' though 'he left much to do', puts both his subject *and* his reader under a stern pedagogic gaze.

He wrote to Saunders Welch, once justice of the peace for Westminster, now at the 'English Coffee-House' in Rome, that he felt 'the hand of time, or of disease' lie heavily upon him; but he realised his hopes of taking coffee in Rome were now almost entirely gone. He must speed up the rate of production of the *Lives*, and yet that winter he felt particularly ill. 'I am very poorly,' he wrote to Lucy Porter in late February 1778, while still struggling to grind out the lives of Waller and of Butler. The *Morning Post* reported him on his deathbed, 'without the smallest hopes' of recovering, but he did revive sufficiently to prevail on Sheridan to stage Congreve's *Way of the World* for Tom Davies's benefit, who might otherwise be forced to sell his 'household stuff'.[34]

In mid-March Boswell came down to London and attended Johnson as much as Johnson tolerated, alone, with the Thrales or at dinner parties. He was on hand at dinner with Thomas Percy when tempers ran high over the merits of Thomas Pennant, a man of whom Johnson approved but who had been 'disrespectful' of the earls of Northumberland. Boswell was available to smooth their ruffled plumage and to show Johnson how inseparable he had become from his later reputation. 'I could perceive', he writes, 'he was secretly pleased to find so much of the fruit of his mind preserved.' At a meeting of the Club attended by Burke and Reynolds, Gibbon and Sheridan, Johnson was, however, keen to keep him in his place. At one point Boswell articulated the valuable powers of application, which had been rewarded by a monarch with a bushel of barley. He must have been 'a King of Scotland', Johnson promptly replied, 'where barley is scarce'. Another day they discussed (apparently the only time they did) the nature of sexual attraction; much of it, according to Johnson, was owing to imagination. 'Were it not for imagination', he declared, 'a man would be as happy in the arms of a chambermaid as of a Duchess', which Boswell frequently had been. But imagination, as he wrote in his *Life of Butler*, was 'useless without knowledge'. 'The great source of pleasure is variety . . . We love to expect; and, when expectation is disappointed or gratified, we want to be again expecting.'

Towards the end of May Boswell at last departed, having brought Johnson as close to rage as was possible. He had, in his self-important manner, acquainted Lord Marchmont with the fact that Johnson was writing a *Life of Pope* and prevailed on him to call and 'communicate all he knows about Pope'. Whereupon Johnson declared that he would 'not be in town to-morrow' to greet his lordship and did not 'care to know about Pope' anyway. Rallied by Mrs Thrale, he allegedly declared that 'if it rained knowledge' he would 'hold out his hand' but had no wish to go in search of it. Even after he had gone Boswell's letters continued to press him with urgent requests. 'You must not tye your friends to such punctual correspondence,' Johnson wrote back, in exasperation; 'happiness, such as life admits, may be had at other places as well as London.'[35]

In May he wrote the Dedication to Reynolds's *Seven Discourses*, which he had mentioned, thinking it 'necessary' to write, but yet not writing. On Easter Day he dedicated himself, once more, to God's care. 'Contemplative piety, or the intercourse between God and the human soul, cannot be poetical,' he judged, rereading the *Sacred Poems* of Waller: 'Poetry loses its lustre and its power, because it is applied to the decoration of something more excellent than itself.' Reviewing his time since the previous Easter he found a 'shameful blank; so little has been done', though, he acknowledged, 'I have written a little of the lives of the poets'. Mainly he thought on Tetty, now dead for a quarter-century; 'whatever were our faults and failings, we loved each other . . . Couldest thou have lived—' He ends with that thought left in the air.[36]

He continued to work on the *Lives* throughout the summer, taking a little opium 'which though it never gives me sleep, frees my breast from spasms', interrupting progress with occasional cultural excursions. He visited the studio of Nollekens with Mrs Thrale, whom the sculptor, unaware of her presence, described as 'sharp . . . one of the blue-stocking people'. He dined at Dr Burney's house with both the Thrales when the company was entertained by an Italian singer, Gabriel Piozzi. 'I am very far advanced in *Dryden*,' he wrote to the printer and writer John Nichols, asking him to bind up a proof volume of the *Lives* of Cowley, Denham, Butler and Waller which he could 'show to my Friends, as soon as may be'. In his months of writing the *Lives*, and reading the works of their subjects, his aim had shifted from writing the 'little' lives he had first embarked upon; he was now attempting something longer. Dryden, he acknowledged, 'will be long' or, as he wrote, submitting it, 'very long'; so would be 'the next great life' he would attempt, '*Milton's*'. Meanwhile he received desperate letters from Hester Thrale, begging for his intervention with her depressed and irritable husband: 'Conjure him not to fret so . . . he is woeful cross,' she wrote; 'glad at heart shall I be to have you with us – for we *grind* sadly else.'[37]

That summer all the talk was of the novel *Evelina*, the more so when it was learnt the author was none other than Dr Burney's twenty-six-year-old daughter, Fanny. Johnson declared it contained 'passages in it which might do *honour* to Richardson', which sentiments, freely offered, quite 'crazed' Fanny Burney's mind. 'Dr. Johnson's approbation!' she wrote, astonished and amazed. It gave her such 'a flight of spirits' she danced a jig. Throughout the summer he enchanted her, kissing her hand, enticing her to eat cake or make jokes about 'the Scotch'. He was always 'in high spirits, and full of mirth and sport', though at night he took musk, and later valerian, to help him sleep: 'The first night I thought myself better but the next it did me no good.' He visited his friend Langton for a few days, where he was a captain at camp in Essex, and told him that Boswell wished to come to town, but this year he was able to dissuade him. He presented Fanny Burney with his *Life of Cowley*, and Mrs Thrale with that of Waller. 'They are now printed', Burney noted, 'though they will not be published for some time.'[38]

He sat for his portrait to Joshua Reynolds ('he seems to like his own performance') and the portrait, finished by the end of October, seemed 'to please every body'; he wished to 'see how it pleases you', he wrote to Hester Thrale who, having 'done' Tunbridge Wells, was now at Brighton. 'I hope he will soon shake off the black dog', he wrote, consolingly, of Henry Thrale, 'and come home as light as a feather.' Henry did shake off his black mood, but not quite as Hester had intended. Her last entry in the Children's Book, for the last day of the year, is: 'Mr. Thrale is once more happy in his Mind, & at leisure to be so in Love with S:S: that it is comical'. 'S:S:' was Sophia Streatfeild, whom Hester had described as 'very lovely' in a letter to Johnson in late October. In her postscript to her entry in the Children's Book, Hester wrote: 'I will not fret about this Rival this S.S. no I wont.'[39]

In October Thomas Cadell wrote demanding some account of how work on the *Lives* was progressing. Johnson apologised, but explained that he had taken 'a course very different from what I originally thought on . . . my apology to the partners'. Three days later an advertisement appeared in the *London Chronicle* and *Gazetteer*, assuring the public the 'WHOLE WORKS' of the poets were 'entirely printed' and awaited only Dr Johnson's 'LIVES of the POETS' to be published, which would be done, for the first twenty volumes at least, by 'CHRISTMAS NEXT'. Through autumn and early winter Johnson wrote while all about him were squabbles. 'We have tolerable concord at home, but no love', he told Hester in November 1778: 'Williams hates every body. Levet hates Desmoulins and does not love Williams. Desmoulins hates them both. Poll loves none of them.' Hodge, his cat, alone had fared well, with Johnson going out himself to buy oysters from fear, if he left it to the servants, they 'should take a dislike to the poor creature'. Edmund Hector 'looked in', he said, in London to see his niece 'who is ill of a cancer'; in reporting this, as in relaying the deaths of two clerical friends, there is nothing of the funerary drama he had formerly reserved for such events. Now, aged sixty-nine, with thirty-five more *Lives* to write, he could not afford such indulgences. Curiosity he did still have ('Is it true that Mrs. Davenant is enceinte?'), but most of all he loved to see her, and told her so, repeatedly.[40]

'Excite me to amend my life,' he prayed to God on the first morning of 1779, though the *Lives* he had so often promised went on 'but slowly': 'I hope we shall be able to publish a good many Volumes soon,' Strahan told Boswell. At last, as the weeks went by, the proprietors decided to publish the works of the fifty-six authors they had already printed without waiting for Johnson to complete his *Prefaces*; they would appear as a separate publication, available *solely* to purchasers of the works. At some point, over the winter, Johnson lost a note on Duke, and urgently requested 'another list of our authhours', uncertain how many he was required to do. But at last, in mid-February, he told Frances Reynolds he had 'about a week's work to do' before he could come to Dover Street and 'talk things over' with her about her deteriorating relationship with her brother Joshua. By the start of March he had completed, and sent to the booksellers, twenty-two of the *Lives* he was contracted to write. Sending Lucy Porter two barrels of oysters, he told her, 'I shall have some little books to send You soon.'[41]

It had taken a tremendous effort to get these *Lives*, among them two further long lives, of Dryden and Milton, done, if not to deadline, at least within a few months of it. He complained to Elizabeth Aston of 'old complaints' hanging heavily upon him; his nights were 'very uncomfortable and unquiet', he said, but, as he wrote in *Milton*, 'Our powers owe much of their energy to our hopes.' Milton, as a republican, was a poet with whom he had little sympathy, but he had paid dearly for attempts to diminish Milton's poetic originality in his involvement with the fraudster Lauder. Here he states, as a fact beyond equivocation, 'his literature was unquestionably great'. *Paradise Lost* may 'with respect to design . . . claim the first place' and 'with respect to performance the second, among the productions of the human mind'. Johnson deplored Milton's republicanism, which was 'I am afraid, founded in an envious hatred of greatness', and noted a natural tendency to admire *Paradise Lost* but, on laying it down, to forget to take it up again; but his final judgement was clear: 'his work is not the greatest of heroick poems, only because it is not the first.'[42] Of Dryden, a most versatile poet who 'enriched his language' with an unprecedented 'variety of models', it is his prose that most strikes Johnson's ears. 'Dryden', he writes, 'may be properly considered as the father of English criticism', and, making a comparative assessment, states that whereas Rymer's criticism has 'the ferocity of a tyrant', Dryden's has 'the majesty of a queen'.[43]

Three years earlier, having thoroughly refurbished the Drury Lane theatre, David Garrick retired, announcing to his brother that 'no culprit at a jail delivery' could be happier than he at shaking off his chains; 'I really feel the joy I used to do when I was a boy at a breaking up.' Now, in the winter of 1779 this old pupil, antagonist and friend died and Johnson paused from his remaining *Lives* to send a brief note to his widow, wishing 'that any endeavour of his could enable her support a loss which the world cannot repair'. Into the life of Edmund Smith, which he was writing at the time, he inserted these words, which pay a deep tribute to Garrick, the more genuine because totally unexpected: 'What are the hopes of man! I am disappointed by that stroke of death, which has eclipsed the gaiety of nations, and impoverished the public stock of harmless pleasure.' Boswell once accosted him on his frequent criticisms of Garrick, having observed 'that you attack Garrick yourself, but will suffer nobody else to do it'. Johnson, smiling, replied: 'Why, Sir, that is true.' But when Boswell attempted to break in on Johnson's mood, reminding him, by letter, how 'pleasing' it had been 'when I received a letter from him at Inverary', Johnson was distinctly irritated. Boswell had presumed to write to Mrs Thrale saying he was 'negligent' and to Francis Barber, telling him 'to do what is so very unnecessary', namely preserve 'the M.S. and Proof sheets' of his recently completed *Prefaces*. He wrote to tell him so, but his letter was too late and crossed with Boswell coming down to London, arriving on 15 March and interrupting a tea-time conversation Johnson was enjoying with a clergyman who wrote poems. 'I gave Boswel Les Pensées de Pascal', Johnson wrote in his diary for Good Friday, 'that he might not interrupt me.'[44]

Johnson disliked the sense that Boswell was hounding him. As his biographer he could acknowledge, and even applaud, the rigour with which he sought to preserve his papers; but as a man *living* the life which would be the other's raw material, he felt inhibited by Boswell's looming shadow following him everywhere, even to church. 'I am now in my seventieth year,' he wrote; 'what can be done ought not to be delayed.' He repeated the thought next day: 'I am almost seventy years old, and have no time to lose.' Despondency was in the air; 'I am not conscious that I have gained any good, or quitted any evil habit.' He shook off Boswell as much as Boswell could be shaken off, and Boswell covered it up, speaking of being 'unaccountably negligent' during this visit. Three days after he arrived Johnson took to opium, and 'was blooded'. There was an awkward dispute with the booksellers over the poor sheepskin binding of the *Lives* he was granted to distribute to his friends. He reminded Cadell that he was 'bred a Bookseller, and have not forgotten my trade' and urged him to supply him 'with what I think it proper to distribute among my friends. Let us not dispute about it,' he wrote; 'I think myself not well used.'[45]

Henry Thrale spent the spring 'in high good humour' in London, no doubt with Sophy Streatfeild, leaving Hester and Fanny Burney together, concocting a weekly paper called the *Flasher* – 'we have a Hack Phrase here at Streatham of calling ev'ry thing *Flash* which we want other folks to call *Wit*.' Johnson remained at Bolt Court, waiting for notices of the *Prefaces*, expecting 'to be attacked'; but 'Benevolus' in the *London Evening Post* lived up to his pseudonym. He advised Bell to concede victory, since this new edition 'under the direction of Dr. Johnson' must have a 'consequence which no costly embellishments can reach'. The principal complaint of potential readers was that the *Prefaces* were 'not to be bought unless you buy *also* a *perfect litter* of poets'. Horace Walpole enquired 'if I could buy the *Lives* separately' and was told 'no, the whole are sixty volumes'. In his diary Johnson noted that 'Last week I published the lives of the poets written I hope in such a manner, as may tend to the promotion of Piety'; he also noted he had 'tried opium' to help him sleep, but found it 'counter ballanced with great disturbance'.[46]

He felt a certain pleasure at receiving Boswell's melancholy note which informed him of his immobility owing to an 'inflamed foot' and visited him immediately, sending him back to Edinburgh with an introduction to John Wesley. To friends in Lichfield he sent copies of the *Prefaces*, bulletins of his health (nights 'very troublesome', breath 'short') and news that he would shortly visit them. 'Eddies of life' which carried Hester Thrale southward called him northward: 'When shall we meet again?' In Lichfield he visited Green Hill bower, which he had not seen 'perhaps for fifty years', with Dr Taylor and Mrs Cobb; but it was 'much degenerated. Every thing grows old'. A fortnight later he wrote again, to say that Lucy had bad feet ('she cannot walk to church') and Mrs Aston bad digestion; then apologised for writing seldom but 'I have very little to say'.

This changed, though, when, a few days later, Henry Thrale had a sudden stroke. 'Oh Lord have mercy on us!' cried Mrs Thrale, annoyed that Johnson should again be from her, 'down at Lichfield or Derby , or God knows where, something always happens when *he is away*'. Johnson wrote back to her from Ashbourne, assuring her the seizure was 'hysterical' and 'not dangerous to life', but she was not satisfied, and said so. He wrote several letters, to herself or Thrale, indicating his willingness to come, and sending £100 for Thrale to invest, so certain was he of his recovery. 'There is nobody left for me to care about but you and my Master,' he wrote to her, attempting to pacify her irritation. He also wrote to Boswell: 'What can possibly have happened, that keeps us two such strangers to each other?' He had had a shock and realised he could not *permanently* abuse the affection of those he felt closest to and expect no retaliation.[47]

His pacification worked; soon Hester was writing in her diary that, should she die of a miscarriage, 'Johnson would have a serious Loss of me'. He spent the summer teaching Queeney and Fanny Burney Latin, which Thrale cynically reckoned was worth 'a Thousand Pounds added to their Fortune'. 'Dr Johnson was as brilliant as I have ever known him', Fanny Burney wrote, 'and that's saying something.' When he left Streatham, he said to Hester, 'there hung over you a cloud of discontent . . . Drive it away as fast as You can.' Unfortunately it drove itself away, for a week later she suffered a miscarriage; 'a Boy', she noted in her diary, 'quite formed & perfect'. Johnson spent part of the summer conducting the same shaving experiments on his arm that he had done the previous year, adding to the sense that his memory would occasionally fail him. He spent his birthday at the home of the MP Anthony Chamier, content that nobody there knew of it, but, saying his prayers, he hesitated, unable to 'perfectly recollect the prayer'. 'Desertions of memory', he noted quickly, 'I have always had'; but now they came more frequently. 'I slept ill.'[48]

Boswell wrote back to him, a salutary letter, saying he had 'often suffered severely from long intervals of silence on your part' and been 'chid' for expressing his uneasiness. Johnson, though he read the message, did not take it in. 'Are you playing the same trick again, and trying who can keep silence longest?' he wrote: 'Remember that all tricks are either knavish or childish.' Boswell replied immediately, suggesting they exchange 'a sheet once a week?' There was no more said on the matter of neglected correspondence. Less than a month later Boswell arrived in person and, finding Johnson still in bed, was greeted with coffee and breakfast '*in splendour*'. Mrs Thrale was in Brighton with Fanny Burney, where they attended raffles and reported that 'the chief object for the Raffles at present is Dr. Johnson's Lives of the Poets. Bowen, a Bookseller just set up here, says they sell extremely well.' Johnson, suffering from gout in his toes, resolved to turn his pains to epistolary pleasures for Mrs Thrale, leading her 'jolly life' by the sea, but the effort lasted little more than a week. Everybody told him 'how well I look', which, he thought, sounded very ominous. 'Why should you importune me so earnestly to write?' he demanded of Boswell, claiming he could make 'new friends faster' than he wanted. The truth was rather different. 'I live here in stark solitude,' he wrote to Hester in November; 'nobody has called upon me this livelong day'. He wrote letters filled with anything and nothing, from the gout in his toes to his fears of a French invasion: 'All trade is dead', he wrote to Elizabeth Aston at Stow Hill, 'and pleasure is scarce alive'.[49]

He looked forward to the Thrales' return with impatience; they would frolic, make a feast, 'drink his health and have a noble day'. But, on their way back to London, Thrale suffered a second stroke. They all rallied, though, a week later, for a game of animal charades in which Fanny Burney was an antelope, Sophy Streatfeild a dove, Mrs Thrale a rattlesnake and Johnson an elephant. 'Poor Mr. Thrale!' she wrote, 'to be inamour'd of a Pigeon & coupled to a Serpent'.[50]

'Let me be no longer idle,' Johnson prayed on New Year's morning, conscious of the number of poets' lives he still had to do. He wrote to John Nichols, his principal assistant, asking him to procure 'some volumes' of Matthew Prior, about whom he was keen to launch his 'next attempt'; he followed this request with others, for the works of Hughes and Addison, Collins and Thomson. In March Boswell wrote that 'the state of [his] affairs' did not admit of his coming to London that year, which, to Johnson, was a welcome relief. He replied, applauding the decision, but being very careful *not* to offer unwelcome advice involving 'prudence' or 'frugality': 'Among the uncertainties of the human state', he wrote in the *Life* of Addison, 'we are doomed to number the instability of friendship.' Friendships conducted by letter, rather than in person, seemed to minimise the danger. War with France which had been in place for eighteen months was having a dire effect on beer production; Mrs Thrale noted that 'the Year before last we brew'd 96,000 Barrels', but last year it was 'only 76,000' and this year 'we shall scarce turn 60,000. So horribly is the Consumption lessened by the War.' Johnson wrote to comfort Thomas Lawrence on the death of his wife, though the understanding he evinced was hardly comforting; he that outlives his wife 'sees himself disjoined from the only Mind that had the same hopes and fears, and interest', he said. 'The continuity of being is lacerated.'[51]

In March 1780 Mrs Thrale went to Bath, taking Fanny Burney as her companion, and, once there, set up at first in competition, later in company with Mrs Elizabeth Montagu as leaders of fashionable society. It was not company of which Johnson approved, having long observed the way that Mrs Montagu shunned him, though naturally in the most hospitable manner. Horace Walpole caught exactly their styles of competitive industry when he observed, at a soirée of Lady Lucan's, 'Mrs Montagu kept aloof from Johnson like the West from the East' and that the two of them 'kept at different ends of the chamber, and set up altar against altar'. Johnson forced himself to say something about the men of Bath, 'of whom I know nothing but their verses, and sometimes very little of them'. Addison he did know, for Addison's father had been Dean of Lichfield, and his early career allowed a mention of Andrew Corbet, a man Johnson had known 'when I was a boy'. Yet, because he knew him, and had been much influenced by the *Spectator*, he felt the burden of his biographical duties particularly acutely. The 'necessity' of 'sparing persons', he wrote, was the 'great impediment of biography'; he felt himself '*walking upon ashes under which the fire is not extinguished*', feeling it proper rather to say '*nothing that is false, than all that is true*'. He does say Addison was vain and 'drank too much wine', solving tactfully the problem he had raised three years before, and cites his ambitious but ill-chosen marriage which 'made no addition to his happiness'. But he ends with a glowing tribute: 'Whoever wishes to attain an English style, familiar but not coarse, and elegant but not ostentatious, must give his days and nights to the volumes of Addison.' He was delighted, shortly afterwards, to report to Hester that Nichols 'holds that Addison is the most *taking* of all that I have done'.[52]

In May he wrote again to say that 'Addison, Prior, Rowe, Granville, Sheffield, Collins, Pit, and almost Fenton' were all done, and that he intended to take on Congreve next. Hester worried over the forthcoming parliamentary election, but Johnson had a simple notion to get round their problems: 'Mr. Perkins is to imitate Mr. Thrale's hand.' This, his only known recommendation of an illegal act, indicates his love of Hester Thrale, his feelings of obligation to her husband and his relatively low estimate of the House of Commons to which they all proclaimed their loyalty. (Perkins was evidently a coming man, something confirmed by his activities during the Gordon riots when he stopped the mob from burning down the brewery by keeping them supplied 'with Meat & Drink & Huzzaes'. Mrs Thrale presented him with 'two hundred Guineas, and a Silver Urn for his *Lady*' for his efforts.) Meanwhile she canvassed the borough for her husband, having been solicited to do so by Johnson who advised her to 'be brisk, and be splendid and be publick'. Mr Thrale 'will be elected and not pleased,' she said, whereas 'I shall be fatigued and never thanked – no matter'.[53]

Working hard and in poor health, Johnson still found time to slip occasional teasing tricks into his letters. He took exception to Hester's habit of never dating her letters, which became a fetish for a while; he was fascinated by Fanny Burney ('what a Gypsey it is') and lamented, in mock-despair, her failure to correspond with him: 'She no more minds me', he wrote, 'than if I were a Brangton', naming unappealing characters from *Evelina*. He made a play of disliking 'petticoat

Government', but wrote to Queeney, in all seriousness, recommending the delights of novelty and stating that 'our earliest years are commonly our happiest'. Meanwhile he composed his *Life* of Congreve, candidly confessing that he could not 'speak distinctly' of his plays, for 'since I inspected them many years have passed'. The reader feels 'what he remembers to have felt before'; critical sentiments which served Johnson well. Writing of Gray's 'Elegy' he remarks that the 'four stanzas beginning *Yet even these bones*, are to me original . . . yet he that reads them here, persuades himself that he has always felt them'. Both reactions have the feeling of honest and original thoughts, the more so as with Congreve he couples the sense of *not* having read the plays recently with a feeling of having given them a most rigorous inspection when he did.[54]

He continued dining in the homes of ladies who were delighted to attract so grand a name; one week it was Mrs Southwell, Mrs Ord and Miss Monkton; the next it was Lady Craven and Lady Lucan: 'Thus I scramble, when you do not quite shut me up,' he told Hester. He felt a certain irritation at her presiding, together with Mrs Montagu, over a 'petticoat' set at Bath, and was forced to compete. 'Nothing finer [was] said of you than was said last Saturday night of Burke and Me,' he told her. 'We were at the Bishop of St Asaph's, a Bishop little better than *your* Bishop, and towards twelve we fell into talk to which the Ladies listened just as they do to You.' Used to finding London the hub of his world, he was disconcerted to find Bath and even *Brighton* set themselves up not merely as alternative milieux but as 'Blue Stocking' centres where the ladies not only listened but *argued*. He attended the annual Royal Academy exhibition at Somerset House, decided it was 'eminently splendid' and sent this judgement to Mrs Thrale, conveying an implication of the importance of *London* events.[55]

Mrs Thrale returned to Southwark, electioneering 'like a Tigress' for a week in May, and Johnson happily completed his *Life* of Congreve which, he thought, was 'one of the best of the little lives' because 'I had your conversation'. But then she went away and a lady sent him a vial of essence of roses. 'What am I come to?' he asked, uncertain whether to be flattered or affronted. He wrote the preface to 'the model and the master-piece' of classical drama, *Oedipus Tyrannus*, in the free translation of Thomas Maurice, and told her that he had 'as many invitations to the Country as You'. He was bluffing: a fortnight later he confessed he had 'no invitations' and should dearly like to move 'when every body is moving' but he would stay 'till the work is done, which I take little care to do. *Sic labitur aetas.*' The fanatically Protestant Gordon riots, opposing government legislation to relieve Catholics from penalties, caused a week of consternation, but he assured her that as far as her properties were concerned 'the harm is only a few buts of beer'. The rioting was 'without any modern example', as was the fact that the rioters' attempt to burn down the Bank of England was driven off by 'Jack Wilkes'! 'My Lives go on but slowly,' he confessed, telling her he was unwell and using an opiate to sleep, though simultaneously admitting in his diary to a remission of the convulsions 'which had distressed me for more than twenty years'. 'I have not seen or done much since I had the misfortune of seeing You go away,' he wrote, wistfully, but Hester received rather different information from Fanny Burney, who told her Johnson 'was in high spirits and good humour . . . I never saw him more sweet.'[56]

Mr Thrale 'is eating *him*self into an Apoplexy, spite of Friends, Physicians, & common Sense', Hester wrote, noting also that she and Johnson had been 'uncomfortably parted this year' for the first time since they first met; but, 'such is my Tenderness for Johnson . . . I always keep his Books about me'. Soon she would have 'two little volumes' more, though in his loneliness he felt a terrible ennui. He stayed at home and worked, but 'not . . . diligently'; he wished the 'work was over, and I was at liberty', and yet, 'what would I do if I was at Liberty?' Fanny Burney read his latest volumes and declared, 'Oh what a writer he is!' Addison she thought 'equal to any of the former batch', though she believed him rather hard on Prior and Gay. Mrs Thrale wrote how 'frolicksome' Johnson could be with some verses of congratulation to Sir John Lade, but also noted that 'Piozzi is become a prodigious Favourite with me'.[57]

In the absence of the Thrales, Johnson cast a wider net; lamenting the death of one of the Prowse family in Somerset, he asked if they ever heard of 'one Johnson, who more than forty years ago was for a short time, a Bookbinder or Stationer in that town'. Dreams of his brother Nathaniel still haunted him. 'When do You think of coming home?' he asked Hester, tired of reading through the works of Pope and Swift he had ordered from Nichols. Her daughters had enjoyed a fine summer and it was a comfort, he said, without irony, 'to think that somebody is happy'. He made what he could of his surroundings and commended Mr Levet who, at eighty, had just returned from a stroll to Hampstead and back; 'eight miles, in August'. His females though (meaning Desmoulins and Williams) were both ill, took physic and barely had strength to argue. 'When I have no letter from Brighthelmston, think how I fret,' he protested; 'write oftener . . . I really live but a sorry life.' In desperation he wrote to Boswell, complaining of his taciturn agenda of resolving 'not to write till you are written to'; for himself, Johnson lamented he had spent the summer 'thinking to write the Lives' without actually writing them.[58]

Parliament was dissolved and the Thrales came back to London for Henry to canvass, much as Hester had been dreading. Illness, she wrote in her diary, 'made him look a perfect Corpse in the full View of an Immense Congregation assembled to see the Gentlemen who wished to represent them'. Thrale had had many warnings; just a fortnight before, Johnson had counselled Mrs Thrale that 'slight phlebotomies' were useless, they were mere 'popgun batteries'; he needed to be bled properly and fed on a diet of peas. But it was all of no use; Thrale lost his seat, coming in a lowly third in the poll.[59]

Writing his birthday prayer for his seventy-second year Johnson believed himself to have 'more strength of body and greater vigour of mind than, I think, is common' at his age. Before him were two more mountains yet to climb: 'I have Swift and Pope yet to write', and Swift was 'just begun'. He laid these tasks before God, wishing for at least time to end them. 'Perhaps God', he thought, 'may grant me now to begin a wiser and a better life.' He travelled down to Brighton with the Thrales in late October 1780 but, before he went, sent a quick letter to Boswell; he did not much like the place, but would go 'and stay while my stay is desired'. He was reunited with the Thrales, but yet, how different! Henry was very ill, and no longer a member of parliament. Hester believed 'his Death' was 'too probable'; Johnson himself was old and weighed down with his last few *Lives*. 'I love you so much,' Johnson wrote to him, as if he felt the touch of death upon him.[60]

Johnson enjoyed the journey; he 'doats on a Coach', Mrs Thrale wrote in her diary; in the life of Swift, which then engaged him, he noted how much 'the love of ease is always gaining upon age'. But he registered a dislike of the Irish satirist who from small things, like his abiding 'love of a shilling', to great, such as his misanthropic loathing of mankind, manifested a deeply repugnant nature. He focused particularly on Swift's schemes to help the poor, lending them small sums, from five shillings to £5, asking no interest but setting a specific day for repayment. 'A severe and punctilious temper is ill qualified for transactions with the poor,' he wrote, noting that 'the day was often broken', the loan not repaid and the debtors consequently sued. Yet Johnson was fascinated that, rather than hating Swift, the poor of Ireland came to love him: 'they reverenced him as a guardian', he wrote, 'and obeyed him as a dictator.'[61]

They stayed in a largely deserted Brighton for less than a month. Shortly after their return he received a letter from Mary Prowse in Somerset, who had made strenuous but fruitless efforts to discover anything she could about the Johnson who had lived at Frome. Johnson was touched by her reply and the obvious trouble she had taken. He wrote back, thanking her, saying the 'adventurer' he enquired about, who 'came in 36 and went away in 37', would certainly have attracted notice 'as a lively noisy man, that loved company'. He might well be still remembered 'in some favourite alehouse' but, after so many years, there was probably 'no man left that remembers him'. Yet, having given so much information about Nathaniel, and his confused feelings for him, he would not say how close they were: 'He was my near relation,' he writes, the word 'brother' feeling too intimate to utter. His need *not* to own up to a close family connection, which had kept him from Lichfield during all the years his mother lived, was manifested in Streatham now, as Henry Thrale grew increasingly ill. Mrs Thrale noted Johnson's 'aversion' to the liberties exacted by the sick; 'it is so difficult says he for a sick Man not *to be a Scoundrel*.'[62]

In January Thrale took a house in Grosvenor Square, where his wife began to strike a figure in fashionable society. The *Morning Herald* described her appearance at one gathering 'in a striped satin Otaheite pattern, trimmed with crape, gold lace, and foil'; at her *conversazione* a little later, she told Fanny Burney, 'Mrs Montagu was brilliant in diamonds . . . Sophy smiled, Piozzi sung . . . Johnson was good-humoured.' 'My master', she noted, was 'not asleep.' Henry's principal vice was over-eating; 'everything was most splendid and magnificent,' reported Samuel Crisp, a long-time friend of Charles, and later Fanny, Burney, 'two courses of 21 Dishes each, besides Removes . . . I never saw such at any Nobleman's.' As he gorged himself to somnolence his wife shone, but still remembered Johnson, giving a room of the Grosvenor Square house over to his use. Johnson was troubled by his 'old disease of mind' and, most unusually, at night took wine to help him sleep, but to no avail; he 'did not sleep well'. He had, though, only one more *Life*, that of Pope, to write: 'I will not despair,' he wrote.[63]

The section of Pope's life on which most care seems expended is the section where Johnson explains Pope's physical condition; like 'a spider', he said of himself, 'protuberant behind and before'.

When he rose, he was invested in boddice made of stiff canvass, being scarce able to hold himself erect till they were laced, and then put on a flannel waistcoat. One side was contracted. His legs were so slender, that he enlarged their bulk with three pair of stockings, which were drawn on and off by the maid; for he was not able to dress or undress himself, and neither went to bed nor rose without help. His weakness made it very difficult for him to be clean.

After this frank exposure of Pope's frailties, and the simple statement that he was so small 'that to bring him to a level with common tables, it was necessary to raise his seat', Johnson proceeds to enumerate the splendours and failings of Pope's verse. The section is not consciously inserted to make readers feel more kindly towards Pope, or even towards Johnson: he exposes Pope's fussy and repeated demands of servants; his niggardly concern to use *both* sides of his letters or translations 'by which perhaps in five years five shillings were saved'; his voracious appetite leading, by many accounts, to his death from 'a silver saucepan, in which it was his delight to heat potted lampreys'. Yet the image of a puny Pope, so frail 'as to stand in perpetual need of female attendance', remains with us: 'Self-confidence is the first requisite to great undertakings,' Johnson writes, giving the flimsy physical base upon which Pope's self-confidence was erected.[64]

In writing this, his last substantial piece of work, there is a sense that Johnson looks backwards over *his* career, putting himself up to be judged, as well as Pope, his ostensible subject. 'Indolence, interruption, business, and pleasure, all take their turns of retardation,' he writes, self-consciously. 'Perhaps no extensive and multifarious performance was ever effected within the term originally fixed in the undertaker's mind.' Listing particular traits of Pope's character, there is a tendency to dwell on features he shares; speaking of Pope's love of his grotto, he remarks that it is often seen 'of the studious and speculative' that 'their amusements seem frivolous and childish'; writing of Pope's subscription difficulties with the *Iliad*, he states that 'He that wants money will rather be thought angry than poor'; recording Pope's 'exemplary' filial piety he says that life offers 'few things better . . . than such a son'. Praise of the poems, while fulsome, appears almost incidental; the 'Essay on Criticism', written when Pope was just twenty, exhibits 'every mode of excellence'; 'Eloisa to Abelard' is 'one of the most happy productions of human wit'; even the 'Essay on Man', which 'tells us much that every man knows', does so with 'the dazzling splendour of imagery' and 'the seductive powers of eloquence'. Though he acknowledges his 'partial fondness' for the memory of Dryden, the antithetical balance with which he measures these two Augustan satirists is finely weighed, culminating in the judgement that 'Dryden is read with frequent astonishment, and Pope with perpetual delight'.[65]

'Having now done my lives,' he wrote to Strahan on 5 March, 'I shall have money to receive.' He was happy to have successfully completed this last commission and asked payment for it, as well as what remained due to him from the *Journey to the Western Islands* and occasional political pamphlets. 'You cannot charge [me] with grasping very rapaciously,' he boasted, proud to have brought the *Lives* to a culmination. Privately he was less confident of what he had achieved; he wrote among his prayers for Good Friday that he had finished the *Lives of the Poets* 'which I wrote in my usual way, dilatorily and hastily,

unwilling to work, and working with vigour, and haste'. How fortunate he was to have completed them can be gauged from the entry
immediately before this one: 'I forgot my Prayer and resolution till two
days ago I found this paper.' Memory was becoming an increasing
problem for him.[66] Mrs Thrale correctly judged how well Johnson,
with his formidable grasp of literary history, was suited to the writing
of the *Lives*. 'He knew every adventure of every book you could name
almost,' she said; 'and was exceedingly pleased with the opportunity
which writing the Poets' Lives gave him to display it.' She went on:
'He loved to be set to work, and was sorry when he came to the end of
the business he was about.' Johnson's sorrow was not the foremost
thought on her mind at present, though. Early on the morning of
Wednesday 4 April, Henry Thrale died.[67]

17

'The Town Is My Element'

health n.s. (*from* heel, *Saxon.*) *1. Freedom from bodily pain or sickness.*

Our father is in good *health*, he is yet alive.
Bible *Gen. Xliii. 28*

3. Salvation spiritual and temporal.

My God, my God, why hast thou forsaken me, and art so far from my *health*, and from the words of my complaint?
Bible *Ps.*

Both Hester and Johnson had seen Henry Thrale's death coming for some time, though Johnson especially had attempted to ward off the blow. Thrale had had 'many strokes of an apoplexy', he wrote to Lucy Porter in March, was 'very feeble', but 'I think in no immediate danger'. Mrs Thrale heard her husband talk of Italy again and wondered 'how shall we drag him thither?', being barely awake for four hours at a stretch and scarcely able to 'retain the Faeces & c.' Johnson would be able to console himself 'by learning *how it is* to travel with a Corpse'. Watching him eat '*so* voraciously' both had thought 'such eating is little better than Suicide' and had 'pressed forbearance upon him' but without success. 'I felt almost the last flutter of his pulse,' Johnson recorded, noting that he had known Thrale 'for almost a fourth part of my life'.[1]

Mrs Thrale's first instinct was to flee, hurrying away with Queeney to Brighton even before the funeral. Johnson remained and, though absenting himself from the Club on the evening of Thrale's death ('Mr Thrale died this morning,' he wrote to Joshua Reynolds), he stayed in London to supervise the winding up of Thrale's affairs and prove the will for which he was an executor. 'Why should I not tell You that You have five hundred pounds for your immediate expences', he wrote to her, 'and two thousand pounds a year with both the houses and all the goods?' Though clearly upset by Thrale's death, the idea of running a brewery appealed to him, as Hester realised on her return; he was 'but too happy with his present Employment', she noted, indicating the relish with which they 'jointly or separately sign Notes Draughts &c. for 3 or 4 Thousand Pounds'. While she was away in Brighton, he wrote to her every other day, assuring her of his friendship 'be it worth more or less', and wishing her well with her bathing. John Perkins was keen on a partnership, and Johnson thought business 'the best remedy for grief' as soon as she was ready for it. If the brewery were sold, Henry Thrale's will stipulated that she would receive £30,000 outright, with the rest of the proceeds held in trust for her daughters. Johnson loved the 'dirty Delight of seeing his Name in a new Character flaming away at the bottom of Bonds & Leases', said Hester. In March he wrote to Boswell, who had announced his imminent arrival, and criticised his 'hypocrisy of misery' and 'affectation of distress'; yet, when Boswell arrived and Johnson was busy in the brewhouse, his tone was utterly different. Boswell recorded a day with him in April as 'one of the happiest days that I remember to have enjoyed in the whole course of my life'.[2]

'Consult only your own inclination,' Johnson wrote to Hester in Brighton, which is exactly what she did. After barely a month of the counting house she wished to 'defecate my mind' of it, and sold the brewhouse to Perkins and Robert Barclay for £135,000, exchanging what Johnson called the 'potentiality of growing rich, beyond the dreams of avarice' for the security of cash. She wrote to a female friend of having lost the 'Golden Millstone' from around her neck; even Johnson seemed quite impressed, informing Lucy Porter and Langton of the exact amount, and borrowing a mere £30 from Perkins to fund his customary trip to Lichfield. He was quite blithe about it all; Fanny Burney records him becoming 'gayer and gayer daily'; Boswell had no trouble having him and John Wilkes dine together without preliminary negotiation.[3]

The reasons for such light-heartedness are not difficult to discern. On the day after Thrale's funeral Boswell, with appalling tactlessness, composed an ode 'by Samuel Johnson to Mrs Thrale upon their supposed approaching nuptials'. Fanny Burney wrote to Hester of verses she had seen 'about you & Dr. Johnson! such as you foretold'. A few days later Boswell went further, noting that 'Scott and I agreed that it was possible Mrs. Thrale might marry Dr. Johnson, and we both wished it much'. Johnson never confessed to such a desire, and was no doubt irritated that Boswell should treat the subject with so much levity; Horace Walpole referred to Boswell as 'that quintessence of busybodies' and Fanny Burney called him 'a caricature . . . of all other of Dr. Johnson's admirers'. Johnson might well have enjoyed living his last years in the company of a woman he had known, and loved, for so long; such a partnership would have prolonged the friendship he had shared with Henry Thrale. Whether as a married couple, or loving friends, he wished their relationship to remain essentially the same, with Hester being the one person with whom he shared his most intimate secrets.[4]

What such calculations did not allow for was Hester's own predilections. Even before Thrale died, in the final days when her life was agony, the Italian singer Gabriel Piozzi sought to comfort her, singing little arias to her to keep up her spirits. 'I suppose', said Mrs Byron, who heard him, 'that you *Know* that Man is in Love with You.' Hester replied she was 'too miserable to care *who* is in Love wth me', but gradually a slight distance grew up between the eligible, wealthy young widow of forty and Johnson. She lent money to Perkins on the understanding that Johnson should know nothing of it; she corresponded secretly with Piozzi, who had returned to Italy, but did not speak of it to Johnson. Fanny Burney came gradually to occupy the place which Hester Thrale had once filled in Johnson's mind as the witty, bookish, attractive young female. 'He really likes not I should be absent from him half a minute,' Fanny Burney confided to her diary in June 1781.[5]

In October he left for Lichfield where Mrs Aston would greet him, though, old and paralytic as she was, he thought it would be a 'melancholy errand'. 'The motives of my journey I hardly know,' he wrote in his diary. 'Why am I here?' he asked Hester, recollecting he had left Mrs Aston '*skinny and lean*', recovering from a bad bout of ergotism or

St Anthony's Fire. Lucy Porter was 'kinder than ever', a 'valetudinary' whose last illness left her 'very deaf'; his own 'Gravedo', or cold in the head, remained; 'my nights have commonly been bad.' By November Mrs Aston had become a 'paralytic crawler', Lucy was 'unable or unwilling to move', Dr Taylor of Ashbourne 'lives on Milk'. Hester herself was to blame for neglecting his advice and not consuming 'full meals in a warm room'. 'All here is gloomy,' he commented, quite unnecessarily. At some point he went down to the river by Stowe Mill and recollected, in Latin verse, his father teaching him to swim:

> *Hic delusa rudi frustrabar brachia motu,*
> *Sum docuit blanda voce natare pater . . .*

('Here I would vainly thrash my arms, which got nowhere with their inexpert movement, while my father with his calm voice taught me to swim'). As Johnson recalls his own frustrated efforts and his father's patient care, it is as though a flash of sunlight catches a happy moment in the past, which is now gone forever:

> *Nunc veteres duris periere securibus umbrae,*
> *Longinquisque oculis nuda lavacra patent.*

('Now the shadows of old have fallen victim to cruel axes, and the bathing place lies exposed to distant eyes.')[6]

'Piozzi, I find, is coming,' he wrote at the end of November; 'and when *he* comes and *I* come, you will have two about you that love you.' There is only the faintest hint of annoyance at the presumption of the Italian singer to return, though Johnson may already have sensed a slight difference in Hester's feelings. In August he noted in his diary his purpose 'to employ the next six weeks upon the Italian language for my settled study'. He wondered why she told him nothing of her own health, worrying instead over that of Perkins who looked, she said, 'like a Man that would not live two years'. Mrs Thrale was secretly celebrating: 'I have got my Piozzi home at last, he looks thin & battered, but always kindly upon me.' Piozzi had brought for her an Italian sonnet which she instantly translated and he ('prudent Creature') insisted upon her burning the original, lest it should 'get about the Town'. 'When we meet', said Johnson, still in Lichfield in

December, 'we can compare some passages. Pray contrive a multitude of good things for us to do when we meet, something that may *hold all together*.' 'Nobody will ever love you better,' he wrote from Birmingham, but, when he at last reached Streatham, he was tired and tense. 'My fear is lest he should grow paralytick,' Mrs Thrale wrote in her diary; 'there are really some Symptoms already discoverable I think, about the Mouth particularly.' Between Piozzi, her own age and alive with charming attentions, and Johnson, who at seventy-two was a man of interesting but often melancholy reminiscences, there was little to debate.[7]

Mrs Thrale began the new year of 1782 as she meant it to continue, in a 'new Character' which she intended to wear 'decently yet lightly'. She would not be 'wild', yet in a long *If* section of her diary she weighed up her prospects: what *if* 'Dear Mr Johnson' were taken from her, or *if* Piozzi should 'pick him up a Wife'? Or how would it be *if* she chose *not* to marry again? She took a house in Harley Street for three months knowing 'the World' would stare at her, thinking she came husband-hunting 'for myself or my fair Daughter': but would the world be right? Johnson began the year in 'tottering' health as he wrote to Boswell, yet sufficiently in command of his mental forces to address his doctor confidently in Latin, to be blooded of sixteen ounces and to need 'frequent' opiates to help him rest. Robert Levet, 'a very useful, and very blameless man', was less fortunate and died, aged seventy-seven; buried three days later, he was celebrated by Johnson in a nine-stanza poem which demonstrated clearly that his poetic skills were still at their very best.

> Condemn'd to hope's delusive mine,
>   As on we toil from day to day,
> By sudden blasts, or slow decline,
>   Our social comforts drop away.
>
> Well tried through many a varying year,
>   See Levet to the grave descend;
> Officious, innocent, sincere,
>   Of ev'ry friendless name the friend.

> Yet still he fills affection's eye
>> Obscurely wise, and coarsely kind;
> Nor, letter'd arrogance, deny
>> Thy praise to merit unrefin'd.

It is entirely appropriate that this, Johnson's finest poem, should be in honour of a man whose unlettered healing went to cure or alleviate the sufferings of those whose poverty put 'real' physicians beyond their reach. It is also fitting that Hester Thrale should memorialise Levet's death with a sudden burst of irritation against Johnson's sense of charity. 'He lived with Johnson as a sort of *necessary Man*, or Surgeon to the wretched Household he held in Bolt Court,' she fumed; 'where Blind Mrs Williams, Dropsical Mrs Desmoulines, Black Francis & his White Wife's Bastard with a wretched Mrs White, and a Thing that he called Poll; shared his Bounty, & increased his Dirt.'[8]

Johnson developed a habit of sending short letters, to almost anyone, itemising details of his health: he told Hester of his cough, but 'my hearing is restored'; to Perkins and Hester Chapone he was 'ill' or 'very ill'; and to Margaret Strahan, wife of his publisher, he said the house he lived in was 'but a melancholy place, clouded with the gloom of disease and death'. 'What shall we do for him?' Hester Thrale rhetorically enquired. From March he began, in his diary, to keep a daily record of his health and other matters, using the Greek letters $o\acute{v}$ to indicate urination (which, he noted, at night was 'wonderfully frequent'), determined that, though his time was unemployed, it should not be unaccounted for. From these brief entries an interesting landscape of Johnson's mind emerges, from a childlike sense of wonder ('When I waked I saw the penthouses covered with snow') to deep feelings of remorse on the anniversary of Tetty's death: 'She was I think very penitent.'[9]

At the beginning of March, after a year of mourning, Hester began hosting assemblies; soon the *Morning Herald* was reporting on the 'present state of literary parties – Mrs. Thrale for *Variety*; Dr. Johnson for *Charity*; Mrs. Ord for *Brilliancy*; Mrs. Montagu for *Universality*'. She wrote to Fanny Burney that she feared 'the world' would be shocked at her 'dissipation' and assume she was in 'haste to be married'. She joked of it to Johnson, saying perhaps the man did not exist 'who would do me honour by marrying me'. Meanwhile Johnson wrote to Boswell agreeing to a postponement of his next visit to London, owing to financial considerations: 'Poverty, my dear friend, is so great an evil', he wrote, 'I cannot but earnestly enjoin you to avoid it.' Writing to him in June 1782 he confessed he had 'scarcely been well for a single week' in the meantime, but planned a brief visit to Oxford that month. Mrs Thrale wrote saying Johnson appeared to be gaining strength and received immediate, wholehearted thanks; 'I kissed the subscription H. L. Thrale with fervency,' Boswell replied, adding hopes for a glimpse of her reminiscences of their 'illustrious Imlac'. The biographers were already closing in.[10]

Johnson was now so frequently unwell that Mrs Thrale began to fear for his life. He 'got so very ill', she wrote in May, 'that I thought I should never get him home alive'. Hannah More, the blue-stocking writer, said that 'Poor Johnson is in a bad state of health; I fear his constitution is broken up.' He now regularly took opium to help him sleep, but 'I begin to be afraid of it' since it subjected him to 'the tyranny of vain imaginations'. In his poor state of health he took badly to jests at his expense; he was *not* going to Oxford 'to frisk', he told Mrs Thrale, taking exception to her 'unfeeling irony'; he went in the hope, however vain, 'to catch at . . . better health'. When he returned it seemed to him that everything in the world was worse than it had been. 'Almost all news is bad,' he remarked to John Taylor at Ashbourne, 'Perhaps no nation not absolutely conquered has declined so much in so short a time.' He made provisional arrangements to see Boswell in the autumn, at Ashbourne or in London, but both were unavailing, as Boswell's father died at the end of August.[11]

At the end of that month he had an important conversation with Hester in which she acquainted him that expenses at Streatham were 'more than my Income will answer'; she must 'go abroad & save Money'. Amazingly, he did not disagree; indeed, he 'thought well of the Project', wishing her to 'put it early in Execution'. She was quite upset by such reasonableness. For eighteen years she had 'so fondled and waited on him in Sickness & in Health' (echoes of the marriage ceremony are clearly not an accident) but now he 'feels nothing in parting with me, nothing in the least'. Johnson, sharp enough to recognise Mrs Thrale's current infatuation with Piozzi, to whom she refers on the same page of her *Thraliana* as 'an Angel', clearly thought a period in Italy with him might be necessary to clear her mind of its delusion. In September the 'dear discerning Creature Fanny Burney' gave her opinion that Hester was 'in love with Piozzi – very likely!' she expostulates, but then spends two pages of *Thraliana* debating the matter, resolving she will 'resolve on nothing'. On 6 October Johnson attended the Streatham church for the last time, 'bade the church farewell with a kiss' and dined 'moderately' at the house 'in no joyful mood . . . that I might not at the last fall into the sin of intemperance . . . When shall I see Streatham again?' He composed a prayer, remembering 'the comforts and conveniences which I have enjoyed at this place'. He then packed his bundles ready, the next morning, to accompany Mrs Thrale and her daughters to Brighton, that hated seaside resort.[12]

As soon as they arrived, their travelling ensemble provoked gossip, with the *Morning Post* describing the marriage which, it announced, was 'on tap' between them. Johnson was hardly the typical groom. His breathing was obstructed for most of the month, he coughed persistently and, in his diary, kept a note of his defecation and urination, in Latin. He was deaf, at church could hear nothing and walked very unsteadily, resting every so often. At the start of November he gave in, took two grains of opium and for once enjoyed a full night's sleep (*'Nox placida'*). Fanny Burney, who came to join them in late October, was quite shocked by the alarm his moods could cause. Only one of their group, Mr Metcalf, was *voluntarily* willing to communicate with him: 'He has been in a terrible severe humour of late', she wrote, 'and has really frightened all the people, till they almost ran from him.' Metcalf took him on a brief tour of west Sussex, including Arundel ('My breath would not carry me to the old castle'), Chichester Cathedral ('beautiful'), Cowdray and Petworth, leaving Mrs Thrale free to declare to Fanny Burney 'the Strength of my Passion for Piozzi, the Impracticability of my living without him'. Burney heard her out, declared that Mrs Thrale's interests were directly opposed to the marriage, but cried herself 'half blind' over Hester's dilemma. 'My mind tolerably calm,' Johnson noted as the little group headed back to London, with all but he gloomily aware of the situation; he read Dutch as they travelled home, always keen to lose himself in fresh mental challenges.[13]

'He that lives, must grow old,' he wrote to Boswell on his return, somewhat annoyed he had received no letter from him since he had become 'head of your house'. He wrote separately to Mrs Boswell, acknowledging her kind invitation to Auchinleck and saying he was 'not without hope' of fulfilling it. Mrs Thrale had taken a house in Argyll Street which she aimed at making the height of fashionable London: 'no Parties are thought highly of, except Mrs. Thrale makes one of them,' she crowed in *Thraliana*: 'my Wit, & even my Beauty – God help me! is celebrated.' She had settled a lawsuit outstanding against her by Lady Salusbury with a 'Compromise for 7500£' which meant that she and her three daughters must find a more economical means of living, ideally, she thought, in Italy. 'Sickness concentrates a man's attentions so much in himself, that he thinks little upon the affairs of others,' wrote Johnson, not wishing to be involved. Mrs Thrale's expenses only turned 'uncoined silver into silver coined', he told her, tartly. His life was unsettled between the consternation at Argyll Street and the ruinous conditions of Bolt Court; he was physically disabled and now took frequent doses of opium. He still made efforts to keep up his old routine, attending a meeting of the Club in December and attempting manfully to keep up a discussion of Mrs Siddons: 'Can You', he asked Mrs Thrale, pathetically, 'talk skilfully of Mrs. Siddons?' Occasionally he could spark back to life, as when, the day after Christmas, he complimented Fanny Burney's new novel, *Cecilia*, as being 'far superior to Fielding's', but such moments were increasingly rare. On the last night of the year he reported a 'tolerable night without opium', which was at least one optimistic note.[14]

The new year gave fresh evidence of Johnson's extreme helplessness; he begged Perkins for more coal to put upon his fire, and told Hester he had moved downstairs at Bolt Court to help with his breathlessness. She herself bid a fond 'Adieu to all that's dear' in *Thraliana*. 'I am parted from my Life, my Soul! my Piozzi,' she wrote.

Queeney had communicated her dislike of Piozzi to others, who had treated her mother insolently and him 'very strangely'. Fanny Burney told Hester that, for her reputation's sake, she must 'marry him instantly, or give him up'. 'I actually groaned with Anguish,' Hester reported, throwing herself on the bed 'in an Agony'. Faced by intolerable pressures, she yielded up her passion for Piozzi and he returned her letters and promises of marriage. She felt she must leave England, or at least London, and Boswell arrived, on 21 March, just in time. She had been 'uneasy to leave Dr. Johnson till I came', she told him. Johnson, who was very ill, said she had been 'driven . . . out of London' by ceaseless insolent attacks upon her reputation by the press. On 5 April 1783 Johnson 'took leave of Mrs. Thrale. I was much moved. I had some expostulations with her. She said that she was likewise affected. I commended the Thrales with great good will to God; may my petition have been heard.' Next day she flew 'to my Dearest loveliest Friend my Fanny Burney, & poured all my Sorrows into her tender Bosom', and within the week had fled to Bath. Though neither of them knew it, Johnson had taken his last leave of Mrs Thrale.[15]

For some time Johnson's letters had been short, factual affairs but, writing to Robert Chambers in Bengal, he gave himself more space though no increase of optimism. 'I have lost many friends,' he wrote, and 'am now either afflicted or threatened by many diseases'. Afflictions came on all sides; having just arrived in Bath, Mrs Thrale was forced to return on hearing that her daughters Sophia (Harriet) and Cecilia were dangerously ill. A few days later Harriet died, and Cecilia seemed in great danger: 'My Children my Income (of course) and my health are coming to an end,' she wrote to him, though not, she added, 'my vexations'. Even Piozzi had ceased to sing, having apparently 'four Ulcers' in his throat, which had been lanced. Had he 'cut his own Throat?' Queeney enquired, ironically. Johnson wrote to Hester Thrale, sympathising with the loss of 'the dear, pretty, little girl. I loved her', for, he said with a slight emphasis, 'she was Thrale's and your's . . . I love You all.' To Queeney he wrote, recommending the 'pleasure of arithmetick', for counting, as he told Boswell, 'brings every thing to a certainty'. 'God protect my best beloved, my Piozzi!' cried Mrs Thrale, having decided that although he had ostensibly abandoned her (or rather, she him), Piozzi remained her one hope of happiness.[16]

Johnson wrote twice more to Queeney, having decided that nineteen was old enough to hear how he had been 'driven to opium'; but really it was not her he wished to hear from: 'Let me know', he begged, 'how my Mistress goes on.' In June he wrote to Mrs Thrale directly: 'Why do You write so seldom?' he asked. 'Do not please yourself with show-ing me that You can forget me, who do not forget You.' She replied, speaking of her 'placid acquiescence' to life at Bath, which affected him so much that he immediately had a minor stroke that deprived him, if only for a day, of the power of speech. He attributed this phenomenon to God's pleasure and inevitably his only thoughts of relief were very painful, questioning whether 'a vomit, vigorous and rough' might rouse his 'organs of speech'. Tom Davies told Mrs Thrale the news, saying Johnson was 'much to be pitied. He has no female friend in his House that can do him any service of this occasion . . . I would not ask—' but Hester made no move to come to him. It was a 'dreadful Event . . . poor Fellow!' she wrote in *Thraliana*, but was glad the pre-sent danger was over. Johnson's doctors, William Heberden and Richard Brocklesby, attended him ('God bless them'); soon he was repeating the Lord's Prayer 'with no very imperfect articulation', but it is obvious he wished for Hester to be there beside him. He wrote, in a lengthy letter to her, that his condition would 'have affected you with tenderness and sorrow', but now 'You will perhaps pass over . . . with the careless glance of frigid indifference.' No doubt she had 'reasons which I cannot know' for staying away from him. He neither knew, nor *wished* to know, the exact status of her feelings for Piozzi, but there is a clear sense of jealousy here. 'How this will be received by You, I know not,' he writes, thinking of Swift's cynical 'Verses on the Death of Dr Swift' and turning, by accident or not, the phrase 'Is he gone?' to 'Is he dumb?' 'I have loved you with virtuous affection,' he says, placing this emotionally charged statement not as a gift but as a virtue, demanding reciprocation. But it did not come: she made it clear she had 'no Desire that he should come to Bath'.[17]

The newspapers carried news of his stroke, though assuring readers that 'from his great Strength of Constitution' he had hopes of a much longer life. Apologising for his letter, Johnson decided instead to send 'a regular diary' to Mrs Thrale in which the 'gross images' of his disease might allow him to torture her; presenting 'Cantharides' and 'vesicatories' (two blistering devices), 'fauces' and 'prolapsus' which are 'very properly flayed'. His savage bulletins had their desired effect; within the week he was thanking her for her letter. 'Your offer, dear Madam, of coming to me is charmingly kind', he wrote back, 'but I will lay up for future use, and then let it not be considered as obsolete', the tone of which alters depending on the reading of his adverb 'charmingly'. He wished very much to forgive her, but was well aware of the presence of Piozzi. 'Write to me very often,' he signed off, his 'very' being very noticeable. Regular letters conveying 'cool reciprocations of esteem' were what he desired, not 'hyperbolical praise'. She mentioned the 'black dog' affecting his mood, as it had once affected Thrale's, but, with the recent deaths of all his neighbours (and he recounted them), how should he 'exclude the black dog from a habitation like this?' 'If I were a little richer', he speculated, though how seriously one cannot say, 'I would perhaps take some cheerful Female into the House.' In the absence of this cheerful female he made what compromise was possible; in his diary increasingly one finds 'prayed with Francis' as a regular entry. It gave him great pleasure to announce he had *not* joined John Cator in requiring Hester to return to Streatham, currently being overrun by highway robbers and footpads. He gave details of his stroke to Boswell, to help with his biography of Samuel Johnson, by which, now that he had no other biographies to write, he became morbidly fascinated. 'How near is the Evening,' he wrote to Hester Thrale; 'None can tell.' 'The world passes away', he wrote to Lucy Porter, 'and we are passing with it.'[18]

That summer he spent a fortnight on the Medway, staying with Langton who was there with his regiment. Both men had spoken of the visit so often that neither knew how to refuse, though 'eight children in a small house will probably make a chorus not very diverting'. In the event the visit passed off pleasantly, its high point being a short Medway voyage 'with four misses and their maid' who were all 'very quiet'. He would not positively declare that his 'short rustication' had done him good, but certainly he was 'not worse', he told Hester. Back home he sent a flurry of letters, to each of the young Thrales, advising them to be 'busy upon trifles', and he accepted William Bowles's invitation to spend the latter part of the summer at Salisbury, an acceptance several times delayed while he suffered an operation to remove a hydrocele on his testicles. The tumour was removed, but without the hoped-for benefits; 'I have suffered little, and gained little,' he told Bowles. To Hester Thrale he was more emphatic: 'I am now broken with disease', he wrote, 'without the alleviation of familiar friendship, or domestick society'; hearing nothing from her, he wrote again, a week later, to where she was holidaying at Weymouth, saying that Mrs Williams was on the verge of death: 'At home I see almost all my companions dead or dying,' he indited mournfully, making even the honour of having his portrait painted by Frances Reynolds into a chore; 'I sat near three hours, with the patience of *Mortal born to bear.*'[19]

Mrs Thrale's thoughts were on a different subject and, though she responded to Johnson's letters, she evaded their tone, part begging and part hectoring. 'Six Months have this Day elapsed since I suffered the inexpressible Agony of telling my Piozzi that we must absolutely part,' she wrote on 27 July. While Johnson spent his time weighing dried vine leaves or composing final prayers for Anna Williams, who might die before his return from Salisbury, Hester bemoaned her situation, in love against her daughters' interests and forbidden to marry by their will. Although Salisbury was no great distance from Weymouth, Johnson, having received no invitation, made no move to see her. Mrs Williams did die, and was buried, giving rise to some sudden and inaccurate arithmetical calculations in his diary. 'Nothing amuses more harmlessly than computation,' he had written to Sophia Thrale two months before; even when *not* correct, he might have added. Bolt Court, when he returned, seemed very solitary. Not well enough to walk far, he did not share the craze for air-balloons which Mrs Thrale had caught, but wrote a sober, technical letter to her describing how they functioned, finishing by pointing out to her they could not 'possibly be of any use'. He concluded his letter saying there was 'a danger of a gangrene' if his testicles were not immediately excised and wrote again next day, enclosing his surgeon's recommendation. He had 'loved You much, and loved you long', he said and she took the hint. 'Johnson is dying,' she wrote in *Thraliana*; 'poor Soul! I shall be very sorry.'[20]

Johnson did not die. Through the skill of his surgeon a discharge was obtained which lessened the tension of the tumour and diminished his inflammation. Not that he was by any means fit. He told Queeney he was in a state 'to be pitied', having, apart from his punctured sarcocele, a raging fit of gout, which reduced him to hobbling with the aid of a pair of sticks, and an agonising toothache. He sent mournful letters, itemising his ailments, across town to Frances Reynolds and round the globe to Robert Chambers. To Hester Thrale, a week later, he was 'no longer crawling upon two sticks' but sat shoeless, with his feet 'upon a pillow'. In such a state he was liable to snap at unwelcome suggestions, such as her notion that his now regular doses of opium might have contributed to his illness. 'I am as I was,' he said, ticking her off for the 'instability of attention' her last letter betrayed, and then apologising; 'what did I care, if I did not love you?' he wrote. 'I am very solitary.'[21]

Ill and alone, with little to occupy him, his letters to Hester were the highlight of his day. Sometimes what he wrote was sharp as he felt the sting of her neglect; at other times he wrote with the tenderness of half her lifetime's love; 'a friendship of twenty years', he whispered, 'is interwoven with the texture of life', and, just as an '*old Friend*' never could be found, he 'cannot easily be lost'. Yet, even as she read these words, a new disaster struck Hester Thrale in the sudden unprovoked fits of her daughter, Sophy. 'Oh spare my Sophia, my Darling, oh spare her gracious heaven,' she wrote in *Thraliana*; '– & take in Exchange the life of her wretched Mother!' Seeing the terrible effect that Sophy's crisis had on her mother's condition, Queeney at last gave in. The doctors were consulted and agreed that a letter should be sent to Italy inviting Piozzi to return. A fortnight later Johnson wrote to Hester, returning thanks to 'the great Giver of existence' that 'dear, sweet, pretty, lovely, delicious Miss Sophy' was safe, and he invited the little one to return to 'her arithmetick', a science suited to her 'ease of mind'. But he wrote in ignorance of the revolutions occurring in Thrale family affairs which put Hester's mind into a tumult of contradictory passions. One moment she was ready to think her confidante, Fanny Burney, was treacherous; at another she feared that Piozzi, safely installed with the Prince de Belgioioso, would be 'too happy there to think very much of me'. Johnson wrote to her of a dinner he had had with old friends, the first for thirty years, and boasted that 'no mention had been made among us of the air ballon'. 'Do you not wish for the flying coach?' he wickedly enquired.[22]

That winter Johnson thought he was back to his old self and helped establish a new dining club in Essex Street, including Boswell, Arthur Murphy and John Nichols among its members. But his own attendance at it was sporadic, made impossible by his obstructed breathing. Dr Brocklesby, who attended him, came every day 'to see if I were alive'. His nights were sleepless, interrupted by spasms for which, reluctantly, he took opiates, and felt 'very heavily crushed', as he related to Queeney. He had a horror of opium, he told her mother, and when, *in extremis*, he took some, 'durst not go to bed' for fear of the dreams which oppressed him. He felt lonely, even though many people called in to see him: 'Visitors are no proper companions in the chamber of sickness,' he wrote wearily; what he liked, and missed, were 'familiar and domestick companions', such as he had had 'with Levet and Williams, such as I had where—' he stopped, implicitly asking her to complete the vacant sentence.[23]

'The first talk of the Sick is commonly of themselves,' he wrote to Hester again a fortnight later, recognising that such letters were duties, not pleasures to answer, but not realising exactly how his former 'Mistress's' mind was taken up. 'Sophia has written to Piozzi to invite him back to England', is a January entry in *Thraliana*: 'Oh how grateful, how kind that was in her.' Johnson, for eight weeks incarcerated in Bolt Court, with opiates to dull his senses, broke out in irritation against those who cared for him: 'Opium dismisses pain but does not always bring quiet,' he wrote to Bowles, while Mrs Thrale marked the 'dreadfullest of all Days to me!', the anniversary of the day she had been forced to send for Piozzi '& tell him we must part'. Johnson wrote to Boswell, asking for suggestions of a warmer climate; Ramsay had done well in Italy though Fielding had died in Lisbon.

'Think for me what I can do.' In apology for his ill humour he recommended Bowles for membership of the Club, which he doubted he would ever see again. Suddenly, in February, he passed full twenty pints of urine and experienced much relief. 'I am', he said, expressing himself to Hester Thrale in the language of his surgeon, 'amazingly better'; asking her no longer to send him letters about '*dying with a grace*', he wondered, longingly, whether they would ever again 'exchange confidences by the fireside'.[24]

In Bath Mrs Thrale contented herself reading the 'English & Roman Histories, the Bible; – not Extracts, but the whole from End to End,' while in Italy Piozzi still delayed. 'Younger Men die daily about me,' Johnson noted, though for himself even standing 'carelessly at an open window' had become a dangerous act, requiring opium to allay the cough it brought on. He had not stepped outside his house for five months, and feelings of stagnation were growing; writing to Susanna Thrale he might enthuse over wonders of the universe revealed by Herschel's telescope, but most of his letters were weary catalogues of colds and coughs, asthma, dropsy and opium. 'My Life is very solitary and very cheerless,' he wrote to John Taylor, having been forbidden by his physicians to attend church for the Easter sacrament. Writing to Hester to thank her for a 'magnificent Fish', he told her that after being confined for 129 days he had just been to St Clement's church to thank God for his recovery, which was 'indeed wonderful'. That Saturday he visited an exhibition of paintings, going up all the stairs 'without stopping to rest or to breathe'; he was like 'the Doge of Genoa at Paris' admiring nothing but himself.[25]

The following week Boswell came to town, and the two resumed their banter, with the faithful biographer noting down Johnson's sayings on the Empress of Russia or the three women (Hannah More, Fanny Burney and Mrs Carter) who had dined at the Essex-Head. When they were alone, the subject of Mrs Thrale came up and Johnson blurted out that she had 'done every thing wrong' since Thrale's death. As always, the authenticity of Boswell's narrative must be treated with care, but the words attributed to Johnson are appropriate. It was a year since Johnson and Hester had met, despite his frequent hints of coming to her and, though Piozzi's name was never mentioned, he was the principal cause of their separation. Mrs Thrale returned to London briefly in mid-May, making arrangements for her future married life. She stayed in a Mortimer Street apartment and was visited by Fanny Burney who said that she 'saw nobody else'. It has been argued that Johnson did see her, and that the start of his letter of 31 May ('Why you expected me to be better than I am I cannot imagine') would seem to confirm it. The question cannot finally be decided, but if he *did* see her it can only have been very briefly, secretly (Boswell knew nothing of it) and with a conversation alluding to none of the reasons that had brought her to town. 'I am better than any that saw me in my illness ever expected to have seen me again,' he wrote, implying Mrs Thrale *has* seen him and been shocked by the sight: 'Think of me, if You can, with tenderness . . .'[26]

By this stage Mrs Thrale was concerned only for her own priorities, talking over 'my intended – (& I hope – approaching Nuptials)', worrying that 'Nobody likes my settling at Milan'. Might that 'Nobody' include Johnson, who might have been told the location, if not the status, of her removal abroad? Either way, both became suspicious; she regretted confidences she had placed in Fanny Burney and he became restless to leave London for Oxford, something which Boswell, knowing of his four-month incarceration in Bolt Court, could not understand: 'He was impatient and fretful to-night because I did not at once agree to go with him on Thursday.' Boswell did at last agree to accompany him to Oxford, but came back to London for the weekend, to attend a musical tribute to Handel. 'What I shall do next I know not,' Johnson wrote to Hester Thrale a fortnight later, when he had returned to London: 'Let me know, dear Madam, your destination.' For some weeks he had been considering Italy himself, where the milder climate might ease his asthma, and the notion of his removal was so well known that 'his arrival was anxiously expected throughout Italy'. At a meeting of the Club he 'looked ill' and Boswell began, secretly, to canvass opinion among his friends as to the practicality of sending him abroad. Money was a problem; his pension was paid irregularly and he recently told Queeney that having not received it for 'near a year' he was 'very poor'. Boswell checked with Sir Joshua Reynolds and wrote to Lord Chancellor Thurlow who gave his blessing, only querying 'the sum it will be proper to ask'. When

Johnson learnt of the plan he was quite overwhelmed by his friends' kindness; 'tears started into his eyes, and he exclaimed with fervent emotion, 'GOD bless you all'.[27]

The following Saturday, 26 June, he wrote again to Hester, telling her that his old friend Macbean had died: 'He was one of those who, as Swift says, *stood as a Screen between me and death.*' Boswell left London early on 1 July, the day on which Johnson received Mrs Thrale's devastating letter. It was one of a number sent by her to the executors of Thrale's will, notifying them of her intention to remarry. The letter to Johnson enclosed a special section in which she apologised profusely for having concealed from him her plans; she had done so 'only to spare us both needless pain; I could not have borne to reject that Counsel it would have killed me to take.' Dread of his disapprobation, she went on, 'has given me many an anxious moment . . . I feel as if I was acting without a parent's Consent . . .' Whether or not that veiled reference to the gap in age incensed him, it was as a *parent*, to Queeney, who had moved with her sisters to the family home in Brighton, that he first wrote. 'You have hitherto done rightly,' he told her. 'You have not left your Mother, but your Mother has left You.' Only then did he reply to Mrs Thrale:

> Madam:
>
> If I interpret your letter right, You are ignominiously married, if it is yet undone, let us once talk together. If You have abandoned your children and your religion, God forgive your wickedness; if you have forfeited your Fame, and your country, may your folly do no further mischief.
>
> If the last act is yet to do, I, who have loved you, esteemed you, reverenced you, and served you, I who long thought you the first of humankind, entreat that before your fate is irrevocable, I may once more see You. I was, I once was, Madam, most truly yours,
>
> SAM. JOHNSON
>
> I will come down if you permit it.

Johnson had interpreted correctly Hester's refusal to sign her letter, not wishing to confess to her yet unmarried state. His letter is an explosion of pent-up resentments but, more than that, in the second paragraph he holds out the hope of repentance. Reading her references to the decisiveness of his advice he recognised why, for over a year, she had refused to see him. Yet, even as he wrote, she was celebrating 'The happiest Day of my whole Life . . . my Piozzi came home Yesterday . . . Tis all over now.' 'What I think of your Mothers conduct', Johnson wrote to Queeney, 'I cannot express, but by words which I cannot prevail upon myself to use'. What Hester thought of *his* conduct in writing her his 'rough' letter came the next day in a letter which desired 'the conclusion of a Correspondence which I can bear to continue no longer'. Piozzi's birth, she asserted, was 'not meaner' than Thrale's; it was 'want of Fortune then that is *ignominious*', she ripostes, catching Johnson, as she knew, on a sensitive point. Her fame, she closed the letter by asserting, was 'as unsullied as Snow'. She *may* have believed that to be the case, but was soon to be disabused.[28]

Johnson, in despair, wrote his *Aegri Ephemeris* or 'Sick Man's Journal' in his diary, chronicling the daily symptoms, in Latin, of his last few months: '*Crura et femora tument*,' he began, his shins and thighs were swelling. He told Lucy Porter he would bring his 'poor, broken, unwieldy body' once more to see her and informed Reynolds that any money the chancellor might obtain for him should not be 'upon false pretences'. Finally he wrote again to Hester Thrale, urging her not to allow the 'phantoms of imagination' to 'seduce you to Italy'. He drew an elaborate, and historically inaccurate, parallel between her and Mary, Queen of Scots; determined to find a refuge south of the 'irremeable Stream' in England, the queen pushed forward while the desperate Archbishop of St Andrews 'pressed her to return'. 'The Queen went forward. – If the parallel reaches thus far; may it go no further. The tears stand in my eyes'. In her conciliatory reply, dated 15 July, Hester told him to have 'no *real* Fears' for her since 'my Piozzi' would need little persuasion 'to settle in a Country where he has succeeded so well'. A week later she was married in a Catholic ceremony in London, followed by an Anglican ceremony at Bath. 'What a noble Heart has the Man to whom I was this day united!' she wrote to Queeney, but, if this was her opinion, it was not at all shared. Mrs Montagu spoke for blue-stocking opinion when she said she felt 'the worst kind of sorrow, that which is blended with shame' at the news; she was convinced 'the poor Woman is mad'. In August the *Morning Herald* reported that 'Mrs Thrale, in consequence of her marriage with Piozzi, has the children taken away from her. This the guardians insisted on. The new married couple mean to pass the next winter abroad.' In November Johnson wrote to Fanny Burney, 'I drive her quite from my mind. If I meet with one of her letters, I burn it instantly'.[29]

Johnson sent a sheaf of letters informing people of his plans to set out immediately for Lichfield; he wrote to William Bowles, to William Adams, to Bennet Langton, to Thomas Bagshaw, to John Ryland and lastly to Boswell, conceding that, at last he had 'my consent to settle in London' provided that 'your expence never exceeds your annual income'. He thus fulfilled two purposes; primarily he knew he must be somewhere *else* when the Piozzi marriage ceremony took place; secondly, he was at last agreeing to have his biographer on hand to see him, daily, during his last few months or years. He arrived in Lichfield in mid-July and found a new person, Dr Brocklesby, with whom he might correspond on a regular basis, in place of Hester Thrale. Over the next four months he sent Brocklesby a total of nineteen letters, but their subject was bleak – his health, or rather, lack of it. In his first he grumbles at Lichfield itself; being 'unable to walk' it gave him 'no great pleasure', he wrote, adding that the weather was benign 'but how low is he sunk whose strength depends upon the weather?' In his last, in mid-November, he declared, 'My Spirits are extremely low'; he had 'supported myself with opiates'.[30]

Of the Piozzi marriage he said nothing, but Hawkins published a scrap of correspondence in which, allegedly, he grumbled that Mrs Thrale was now become 'a subject for her enemies to exult over, and for her friends, if she has any left, to forget or pity'. He moved to Ashbourne from where he wrote to Boswell, finding the town bleak and Taylor's house in it 'half built' with renovations. Why a septuagenarian should condemn himself to live 'among ruins and rubbish' he could not imagine. He wrote to Lucy Porter complaining that 'the pleasures of the sick are not great nor many' and told Brocklesby that his chief distress was 'want of sleep'. As a remedy for this he took opium regularly, one grain or two per evening to quiet his mind and still his body. Warned by Brocklesby of the dangers of addiction, he shook his head. Sometimes he was 'gloomy and depressed', he wrote, and found opium 'useful'. 'Wherever I turn', he wrote to Charles Burney, 'the dead or the dying meet my notice.' In mid-August he received a letter from Queeney Thrale which gave rise to a truly dreadful night ('*Nox insomnis, suffocatio gravis*'); next day he replied to her that he 'would not have You forget me, nor imagine that I forget you'. But forgetfulness was soothing and he took extra opium to regain his calm. 'O Lord,' he prayed, 'enable me to drive from me all such unquiet and perplexing thoughts as may mislead or hinder me.'[31]

'Of company I am in great want,' he wrote to Lucy; 'Dr Taylor is at his farm, and I sit at home. Let me hear from You again'. Mortality rose up against him wherever he went, he wrote to Joshua Reynolds, having just learnt that Allan Ramsey, whose decision to winter in Italy he had approved, had died – at Dover, upon his return. 'I left three old friends at Lichfield, when I was last there, and now found them all dead.' Opium gave him his only relief from gloom and depression, though he assured Brocklesby that it was only 'seldom' he took more than a single grain; yet still, whenever his thoughts turned, by solitude or darkness, on his past life, 'I shrink with multiplicity of horrour'. At last he heard that his application for funds to pay for a Continental expedition had been turned down, a refusal which, coming as a surprise, raised his ironic skills to renewed heights. Writing to acknowledge the chancellor's unavailing efforts, he made clear that though the application was made 'without my knowledge' he 'did not expect to hear of a refusal. Yet as I had little time to form hopes, and have not rioted in imaginary opulence, the cold reception has been scarce a disappointment.'[32]

His letters at this time, of which there are many – sometimes as many as four in a day – are further bleak rehearsals of his illnesses, taking a kind of mournful pleasure in the frequent rehearsals of every detail of his purges, asthma and dropsy. He replied to Queeney's letters, reiterating stoic lessons first recommended 'in our pretty lecture room at Streatham'; but the memory of it was too much, and he needed another grain of opium to sleep. 'Enable me O Lord to repent truly of my Sins,' he wrote that Sunday, going on with his daily measurement of his urine, or occasionally inserting a note ('*urina non constat*') that he had neglected to measure it. At the start of September he felt rather better, travelling with Dr Taylor to Chatsworth; the duchess privately reported that he 'look'd ill', but Johnson reported that he was 'wonderfully recover'd'. He found again 'an inclination to walk for amusement', something he had not done for months, returning 'neither breathless nor fatigued'. To Lucy Porter he wrote that he would return from Ashbourne to Lichfield 'within a fortnight'. He celebrated his seventy-fifth birthday by writing a prayer to God, asking to be made 'truly thankful' for the call to 'Repentance' and by sending a letter to Reynolds to say the *three* letters he had received that day, all telling him of Lunardi's successful balloon flight, were more than sufficient: 'I could have been content with one,' he wrote. 'Do not write about the balloon, whatever else You may think proper to say.'[33]

From Lichfield he wrote to Brocklesby, complaining of a newspaper notice about himself at Chatsworth; it was, he said, 'like a trick of Boswel's'; he would 'hardly have suspected any body else'. This is a brief, but telling illustration of how far Boswell went in order to get good 'copy' not just for Johnson, but for his own biography. Johnson does not deplore the snippet ('It did no harm, but what was the good?'); but it reminded him of those waiting, patiently, for his death. As if in response to such expectations, the rest of his letter is full of unsavoury medical details ('The faeces in the Rectum have concreted to such hardness . . .'). It was appropriate he should recall 'Rochefoucault, or Swift' in this context, but equally revealing that, though recalling them, he should dismiss the notion that their cynical view of human pleasure was 'all of it'. He was bored with the talk of balloon flights and though applauding Reynolds's achievement of the post of the King's Painter, he liked his pointing out the position was neither of a dignity or profit to rival 'His Majesty's rat catcher'.[34]

His brief period of better health was quickly over; he made a jest to Dr Scott that his legs 'would not carry me far, if my breath would last' and that his 'breath would not last if my legs would carry me'. 'I have rather gone backwards these three weeks,' he declared in late October, though not in regard of correspondence: he wrote six letters in a single day and found, amid his talk of dropsy, asthma and castor oil, a place to hope for 'new topicks of merriment'. A letter from John

Taylor, telling him 'recovery [was] in my power', angered him: 'This indeed I should be glad to hear, if I could once believe it.' He made ready to return to London and became sentimental at the thought: 'The town is my element,' he told Brocklesby; 'there are my friends, there are my books to which I have not yet bidden farewell . . .' Gradually he felt his health decline and cared not 'to think on my own state'; even to Fanny Burney he could write only 'one melancholy truth, that I am very ill'. To Boswell he recognised he had 'lost ground very much', sought letters to relieve him and wondered why none came: 'Are you sick, or are you sullen?' Among his prayers he wrote a 'Repertorium' of book titles, followed by 'Preces' which went from 'Against the incursion of wicked thoughts' to 'Under dread of Death'. Prayers were too often 'performed and forgotten – without any effect on the following day'.[35]

'I am, at this time very much dejected,' he wrote to John Ryland: 'My Spirits are extremely low,' he told Brocklesby: 'I am relapsing into the dropsy very fast', is Hawkins's version. He set out on his homeward journey, reached Bolt Court on 16 November and sent friendly greetings to the Burneys, but more truthful sentiments to Edmund Hector, his oldest living friend, with whom he had broken his journey in Birmingham: 'We have all lived long, and must soon depart.' Away in Milan Mrs Thrale, or Piozzi as she now was, received a copy of Johnson's picture and confessed she did love him dearly, still. 'Poor Johnson did not ever *mean* to use me ill,' she wrote in *Thraliana*; 'he only grew upon Indulgence, till Patience could endure no further.'[36]

His last days were spent in Bolt Court, preparing for the end. He caused a parcel of all his major works to be sent to Dr Adams at Pembroke College, spent an evening with Bennet Langton supervising the publication of his poems in Latin, and wrote epitaphs for his father, mother and brother to be engraved on 'deep, massy and hard' stone and placed in the middle aisle of St Michael's Church, Lichfield. He begged that 'all possible haste' might be made about this last task, 'for I wish to have it done while I am yet alive'. To Lucy Porter he sent a notice, by the same post, of the inscription of the stone that he had laid upon her mother's, his Tetty's, grave, in

Bromley. In Milan Mrs Piozzi toyed with the notion of translating 'Johnson's Lives into Italian,' fearing she had 'neither Language enough yet, nor Time enough', while in London Johnson wrote three times, on 29 November, 7 and 10 December, to William Strahan to have as much of his pension as was due to him. He acknowledged receipts of £88 5s on 10 December and £75 on the 13th, which may have been the last thing he ever wrote.[37]

Ever since the deaths of Tetty and his mother, Johnson's life had been a preparation for death, but that last fortnight, back in his own element, London, it was as if he were following a timetable. On 5 December he composed his final prayer, in which he begged God to 'have mercy upon me and pardon the multitude of my offences'. On the 8th and 9th he finally made his will, urged to do so by Hawkins, leaving all of his residual estate 'to the use of Francis Barber, my manservant, a negro'. The amount of his bequest was handsome, amounting to 'little short of fifteen hundred pounds, including an annuity of seventy pounds'. Hawkins grumbled at such 'ostentatious bounty and favour to negroes', but Johnson's mind was clear; he rewarded Frank with £20 a year *more* than a nobleman would bequeath to his most faithful servant as a deliberate sign that he, Johnson, was *nobilissimus*. In his last weeks he had many visitors, including John Nichols, to whom he confessed that, of all his writings, only the parliamentary *Debates* 'gave him any compunction'; they had been written, as he then had boasted, 'from very slender materials, and often from none at all'. Burke and Reynolds, Langton and Hawkins, Brocklesby, Hoole, Windham and Warren all came to spend time with him. Some days before the end he asked Brocklesby directly whether he could recover and was told not 'without a miracle'. Johnson took the judgement kindly and from then on gave up all medicines, even opiates; 'I have prayed', he said, 'that I may render up my soul to GOD unclouded.' He spent his last days in a state of perfect resignation, seldom fretful or ill-tempered. On 13 December Miss Morris, daughter to a friend of his, called and asked Frank Barber to be permitted to seek Johnson's blessing. He 'went into his room, followed by the young lady, and delivered the message. The

Doctor turned himself in the bed, and said, "GOD bless you, my dear!" These were the last words he spoke.' He died that day, 'about seven o'clock in the evening'. Two days afterwards his body was taken, on a cart, from Bolt Court to Windmill Street where, at Hunter's School of Anatomy, all of his physicians, Heberden, Brocklesby, Wilson and Cruikshank, were waiting to cut him open. It was observed that his heart was 'exceedingly strong and large'.[38]

Epilogue

epilogue n.s. *(*epilogus, *Latin.) The poem or speech at the end of a play.*

If it be true that good wine needs no bush, 'tis true that a good play needs no *epilogue*; yet to good wine they do use good bushes, and good plays prove the better by the help of good *epilogues*.

Shakespeare's As you like it.

Are you mad, you dog?
I am to rise and speak the *epilogue*.

Dryden's Tyran. Love.

Johnson was buried in Westminster Abbey the following week, but it was hardly an impressive interment. Sir John Hawkins, still fretting over the lamentable bequest of all of Johnson's estate to the Negro Barber, determined it should be done in 'the cheapest manner'. No organ was played, no burial service was sung, there was only Dr Taylor reading out the service over the grave, beside the final resting place of David Garrick. Nothing, however, could diminish the public recognition that Johnson received. Nine coaches bore Johnson's closest friends; in the last, because, as chief beneficiary of Johnson's will he could not be excluded, much as Hawkins might have wished it, sat Frank Barber. Behind these came fifteen coaches bearing Johnson's gentry admirers, and many other people who came on foot.[1]

Away in Edinburgh, Boswell heard of Johnson's death only when it was too late to travel down for the funeral. More worryingly, there were already rumours of at least half a dozen biographies in preparation, notably one by Hawkins, who had not only been acquainted with

Johnson for the longest time but who, as an executor of his will, had access to all his personal papers. When the will was published, a week later, Boswell was deeply hurt to find no mention of himself; there were bequests of books to Bennet Langton, Drs Heberden and Brocklesby, even to the Reverend Mr Strahan of Islington; but not to him. He had been overlooked. The publication of the Will caused great consternation, not for the various small bequests of books, but for the large amount bequeathed to the manservant Frank Barber, a black man who had been a slave.

> All the rest, residue, and remainder, of my estate and effects, I give and bequeath to my said Executors, in trust for the said Francis Barber, his Executors and Administrators. Witness my hand and seal this ninth day of December, 1784.

That Johnson had favoured this Negro, had paid for his education and treated him as a friend was widely known; but to leave him 'an annuity of seventy pounds' was scandalous. Yet it provided Boswell with an opportunity. There had been ill feeling, he learned, about a diary volume which had found its way into Hawkins's pocket in the last few days of Johnson's life. It was alleged Hawkins meant to preserve it from someone who 'might find and make an ill use' of it, by which it was clear he meant Frank Barber. When Johnson heard of the affair he became greatly agitated and 'warmly insisted on the book being delivered up'.[2] On his visit to London the following spring, Boswell made it his business to befriend Frank Barber and gain from him custodianship of the diary. Barber, accustomed to ill-treatment from that 'basest of mortals', as he referred to Hawkins, was only too glad to assist: 'I am happy to find there is still remaining a friend who has the memory of my late good master at heart,' he wrote. Under Boswell's direction, Barber wrote to each of the executors, Sir John Hawkins, Sir Joshua Reynolds and Dr William Scott, demanding the return of all Johnson's papers.[3]

Boswell found that Barber was a good fellow, full of tender affection for his dead master and willing to do almost anything to have his memory respected. As his money declined (he seemed to have no way of hanging on to it), Boswell purchased odd items of Johnsoniana from him; thus a letter Mrs Thrale had written in April 1780 appears in the *Life*, about which, when she discovered it, she was imperiously conde- scending: 'This is the famous letter with which Boswell threatened us all so; He bought it of Francis the Black for half a crown to have a little Teizing in his Power.' Tetty Johnson's wedding ring, which had been so carefully kept in its wooden box, Frank Barber offered to her daughter, Lucy; but when she declined it, he had it enamelled 'as a mourning ring for his old master' and gave it to his own wife, Elizabeth Barber.[4]

Mrs Piozzi's book appeared first; *Anecdotes of the Late Samuel Johnson* was published in March 1786 and sold out on the first day of publication. Three more editions of the eminently readable book were published that year, proving that Mrs Piozzi could put together a witty, saleable version of the man she had known so well. 'Oh poor Dr. Johnson!!!' she had written when news of his death first reached her, taking refuge in punctuation rather than in words to convey her emotional reaction. Three years later her book *Letters to and from the Late Samuel Johnson* placed on record her version of the intimacy they had shared; furthermore, she declared that she had been informed that Johnson 'burned many letters in the last week'. That may have been true, but from his careful work of collection, Boswell was amassing an impressive number of those that remained.[5]

Between Piozzi's two books, Hawkins published his *Life of Samuel Johnson* in March 1787, which, though accurate in terms of facts, was laborious to read; a reviewer joked that there were plans for it to be *'translated into English'*. More seriously, it took a rigidly censorious attitude to many of Johnson's most well-known characteristics, his slovenliness in dress, his compassion to the poor, his odd outbursts of mirth. In his own *Life of Johnson*, Boswell noted that the greater part of it had been written while Hawkins was still alive, specifically to make him feel 'some compunction for his illiberal treatment of Dr. Johnson'. On 16 May 1791, twenty-eight years to the day since their first meeting in Tom Davies's bookshop, Boswell's *Life of Samuel Johnson* appeared, selling twelve hundred copies in the first three months.[6]

Two centuries later, Boswell's *Johnson* is still what most people know of Johnson, because it contains so much of what he said, as fresh now as when he *might* have said it. I use the subjunctive mood deliberately, for there have been many reservations about Boswell's means of presenting biographical facts, from Mrs Piozzi down to Donald Greene, who has suggested Boswell's *Life of Johnson* might more accurately be renamed 'Memoirs of James Boswell, concerning his acquaintance with Samuel Johnson'. But while Boswell's desire to make his name in celebrating the life of his mentor must be conceded, so also must his closing judgement; the more we think on Johnson, 'the more he will be regarded . . . with admiration and reverence'.[7]

The last words should go to Johnson, who struggled constantly to ensure that an individual's works were seen in the context of the turmoils of his life. 'Life', he wrote to Mrs Thrale, 'to be worthy of a rational being, must be always in progression; we must always purpose to do more or better than in time past.' Biography to him was special. 'No species of writing' was more 'worthy of cultivation . . . I have often thought that there has rarely passed a life of which a judicious and faithful narrative would not be useful.' He once declared that it was the 'biographical part' of literature that he most loved; I trust that, in writing this account, I may not wholly have disappointed that hope.[8]

Johnson's works

The Yale Edition of the Works of Samuel Johnson, presently 15 vols, not consecutive (New Haven: Yale University Press, 1958 onwards):

Diaries, Prayers, and Annals, ed. E. L. McAdam Jr. with Donald and Mary Hyde, vol. I (1958)

The Idler and The Adventurer (ed. W. J. Bate, John M. Bullitt and L. F. Powell), in Works, vol. II (1963)

The Rambler, ed. W. J. Bate and Albrecht B. Strauss, vols III–V (1969)

Poems, ed. E. L. McAdam Jr. with George Milne, vol. VI (1964)

Johnson on Shakespeare, ed. Arthur Sherbo (with an introduction by Bertrand A. Bronson), vols VII and VIII (1968)

A Journey to the Western Islands of Scotland, ed. Mary Lascelles, vol. IX (1971)

Political Writings, ed. Donald Greene, vol. X. (1977)

Sermons, ed. Jean Hagstrum and James Gray, vol. XIV (1978)

Voyage to Abyssinia, ed. Joel J. Gold, vol. XV (1985)

Rasselas and Other Tales, ed. Gwin J. Kolb, vol. XVI (1990)

Johnson on the English Language, ed. Gwin J. Kolb and Robert DeMaria Jr., vol. XVIII (1990)

A Commentary on Mr Pope's Principles of Morality, or Essay on Man (a Translation from the French), ed. O M Brack, vol. XVII (2005)

The Works of Samuel Johnson, ed. Arthur Murphy, 12 vols, London: J. Johnson, 1806.

The Works of Samuel Johnson, Oxford English Classics, 9 vols, London and Oxford: William Pickering, and Talboys and Wheeler, 1825. The Dictionary of the English Language (1st edn, 1755)

The Works of Samuel Johnson, L. L. D. (with life), ed. John Hawkins (15 vols, 1787–9)

The Dictionary of the English Language (1st edn, 1755)

The Dictionary of the English Language (4th edn, 1773)

Chapman, R. W. (ed.), The Letters of Samuel Johnson (3 vols, 1952)

Fleeman, J. D. (ed.), The Complete English Poems (1971)

Fleeman, J. D. (ed.), Journey to the Western Islands of Scotland (1985)

Fleeman, J. D. (ed.), Early Biographical Writings of Dr. Johnson, Gregg International Publishers, 1973

Hazen, A. T. (ed.), Samuel Johnson's Prefaces and Dedications (1937)

Lonsdale, Roger (ed.), *The Lives of the Most Eminent English Poets* (4 vols) Oxford: Clarendon Press, 2006

Redford, Bruce (ed.), *The Letters of Samuel Johnson* (5 vols, 1992–4)

Rudd, Niall (trans. and ed.) *Samuel Johnson, The Latin Poems*, Lewisburg, Bucknell University Press, 2005

Notes

List of Abbreviations

Anecdotes Hester Lynch Piozzi, *Anecdotes of the late Samuel Johnson*, ed. Arthur
Sherbo (Oxford University Press, 1974)

Gleanings Aleyn Lyell Reade, *Johnsonian Gleanings* (11 vols, privately printed,
1909–52)

Letters *The Letters of Samuel Johnson*, ed. Bruce Redford (5 vols, Clarendon Press,
Oxford, 1992)

Life James Boswell, *Life of Johnson*, ed. Birkbeck Hill, revised L. F. Powell
(6 vols, Clarendon Press, Oxford, 1934)

Lives Samuel Johnson, *The Lives of the Poets*, ed. Roger Lonsdale (4 vols,
Clarendon Press, Oxford, 2006)

London Journal James Boswell, *London Journal* (1762–3), ed. Frederick A. Pottle
(London, 1950)

Notebook Boswell, James, *Boswell's Notebook* (1776–7), ed. R. W. Chapman
(London, 1925)

Poems Samuel Johnson, *The Complete English Poems*, ed. J. D. Fleeman
(Harmondsworth, 1971)

Thraliana *Thraliana: The Diary of Mrs Hester Lynch Thrale*, ed. K. C. Balderston
(2 vols, Clarendon Press, Oxford, 1942)

Yale *The Yale Edition of the Works of Samuel Johnson* (at present 15 vols, Yale
University Press, New Haven, 1958–)

Prelude

1. *Life*, I, 58, 271–2.
2. *Letters*, I, 8997.
3. The 'Short Scheme' is dated, in Johnson's hand, 30 April 1746. See *The
   R. B. Adam Library Relating to Samuel Johnson* (London, 1929); *Life*, II, 161.
4. *The World* 100 and 101 (28 November and 5 December 1754); *Yale*, V, 317.
5. *Letters*, I, 94–7; *Life*, I, 471.
6. *Life*, I, 264–5. See Catherine Dille, 'The *Dictionary* in abstract', in *Anniversary
   Essays on Johnson's Dictionary*, ed. Jack Lynch and Anne McDermott
   (Cambridge, 2005), 198–211.

7. *Letters*, I,
8. *Life*, I, 146–7.
9. *Letters*, I, 106–8.

1 Lichfield

1. James L. Clifford, *Young Samuel Johnson* (London, 1955), 3.
2. Amongst later persons commemorated with plaques are Erasmus Darwin (1731–1802) and Anna Seward (1742–1809).
3. *Life*, II, 261. In the Churchwarden's Accounts for St Mary's, Lichfield he is assessed, in Tamworth Street, for 3d, the next smallest amount of the 246 people assessed. The name 'Johnson' reappears in the assessment in 1679, when 'Widd Johnson' is assessed for 6d at 'Bird and Sandforde streete'. MS record, compiled by Percy Laithwaite (1950), Staffordshire and Stoke on Trent Archive Service, 6.
4. ibid., 9; The Warden's Account for 1671, presented on 8 December, records £3 paid out to 'William Johnson's Boy' for 'training, schooling and indenturing him', and in 1672 notes 'Michael, ye son of William Johnson Deceased, 04. 00. 00.' We also find '12 April, 1673: pd Mrs Johnson widow Toward placcing her sonne Michael Johnson Apprentice to Mr Richd Simpson: Stationer of London for 8 years from 11 April 1673 – £3 10s & for carrying him up to London & charges in his Journy 10s: all 04. 00. 00.' Laithwaite, MS record, 11.
5. In 1682 Michael Johnson was charged £8 for his property in Sadler Street while 'Widd Johnson' paid £2 for her place in Bird Street. Michael's name appears every year until his death in 1731, paying a rate 'four or five times what was formerly paid by his parents'. Laithwaite, MS record, 9; '*The Touchstone of Medicines, etc.* By Sir John Floyer of the City of Litchfield, Kt., M.D', 1687.
6. Copies of fifteen letters, which cover only the period from October 1684 to August 1685, are in the William Salt Library in Stafford and are described by A. L. Reade (*Times Literary Supplement*, 17 June 1949, 404).
7. 'Recd of Michael Johnson for a seat 01.00'. Laithwaite, MS record, 18 and *Gleanings* (1922), III, 11; 10 January 1691/2, 'Rec'd of Mr Mich Johnson for his mother's grave 00. 3. 4.'; 1695, 'To Mr Johnson for a skin of parchment 00. 01. 02'. Laithwaite, MS record, 16, 20, 24; *Gleanings*, III, 13; *TLS*, 1949, 404; *Gleanings*, IX, 9.
8. Laithwaite, MS record, 22: Article of agreement between Michael Johnson, Cornelius Ford, Richard Pyott and Joseph Ford concerning the proposed marriage between Michael Johnson and Sarah Ford, 11 June 1706. Birthplace Museum, MS 1. The marriage took place on 19 June.

9. Indenture drawn up 24 June 1708. Birthplace Museum, MS 34; Assignment, 31 July 1707. Birthplace Museum, MS 2001.75.17.

10. *Yale*, I, 3–4.

11. The nurse's son 'had the same distemper, and was likewise short-sighted', writes Johnson. Reade reports that 'as an adult he was unable to earn a living'. *Yale*, I, 5; *Gleanings*, X, 22.

12. Richard Wright, who first published the *Annals* in his *Account of the Life of Dr Samuel Johnson* in May 1805, gives the date of composition as 'January, 1765', but offers no evidence for this assertion. Later portions of the *Annals* suggest dates of around 1772. See *Yale*, I, xv; *Life*, I, 146–7.

13. *Yale*, I, 134; *Gleanings*, III, 180.

14. *Yale*, I, 7.

15. *Gleanings*, III, 47; *Yale*, I, 7–8.

16. 'For the Execution of the Late Dr Fowke, Feb ye 5th 1710', Birthplace Museum, MS 2001.70.2; Percival Stockdale, *Memoirs* (London, 1809), II, 102; *Gleanings*, III, 93; Birthplace Museum, MS 2001.75.3.

17. *Thraliana*, I, 160.

18. *Yale*, I, 9–10.

19. *Thraliana*, I, 181

20. *Notebook*, 12; *Life*, I, 39; *Gleanings*, I, 31; III, 79–80.

21. *Yale*, I, 10, 17; *Anecdotes*, 27; *Weekly Journal or British Gazetteer*, Saturday 14 April 1716.

22. *Gleanings*, III, 12.

23. *Yale*, I, 13, 19; probably Uncle Nathaniel, from Sutton Coldfield, whose wife had given evidence of her 'good-natured, coarse' manner. *Gleanings*, III, 115.

24. *Life*, I, 71; *Thraliana*, 161; *Notebook*, 19; Birthplace Museum, Lichfield. There are four examples of it in two sentences; *Yale*, I, 20.

25. '*Bonae leges ex malis moribus proveniunt*' ('Good laws spring from evil conduct'). Bodleian Library, MS Eng. Lett. c.275, f.30; *Handlist*, no. 2; c.275, f.29: *Handlist*, no. 4. I am indebted to O M Brack for bringing these manuscripts to my attention.

26. *Life*, I, 44, 46.

27. *Anecdotes*, 154; *Gleanings*, III, 115; *Life*, I, 48. The anecdote can be found, with variants, in John Hawkins, *The Life of Samuel Johnson, LL.D* (London, 1787), 7–8; *Life*, I, 47–8; *Notebook*, 4.

28. The first three entries to the *Annales* are as follows: NOVRIS. 10MO 1734 / A.D. 1709 SEPTRIS. 7MO / Samuel Johnson Lichfeldiae natus est. / 1725. MENSIBUS AUTUMNAL. S.J. ad se vocavit C.F. a quo, anno proxime insequenti, Pentescostes feriis, Lichfieldiam rediit. / 1728 / NOVRIS 1Mo. / S.J. Oxonium se contulit. Clifford, *Young Samuel Johnson*, 80; *Yale*, VI, 4; *Poems*, 25.

29. *Thraliana*, 171; *Yale*, VI, 10–12; *Poems*, 37.

30. *Anecdotes*, 155.

31. Bishop Percy to Edmond Malone, 17 October 1786, *The Percy Letters*, ed. David Nichol Smith and Cleanth Brooks (Baton Rouge, 1944), 43; *The Private Papers of James Boswell from Malahide Castle*, ed. Geoffrey Scott and Frederick A. Pottle (18 vols, privately printed, 1928–34), IX, 257; *Life*, I, 50. See also *Gleanings*, III, 155–6.

32. *Yale*, VI, 4–27. The comment to Boswell is contained in *Notebook*, 19. There are eleven poems printed, in a transcription by James Ross, in the order which Boswell gave them.

33. *Yale*, VI, 15–17; *Poems*, 47.

34. *London Journal*, 301; *Gleanings*, III, 14–17.

35. Laithwaite, MS record, 30–1; *Gleanings*, III, 180; Birthplace Museum, 2001. MS 13.

36. Stebbing Shaw, *The History and Antiquities of Staffordshire* (2 vols, London, J. Robson, 1798–1801), I, 324; *Life*, I, 441; William Shaw, *Memoirs . . . of Dr Samuel Johnson* (1785), 14–15.

37. Nichol Smith, *The Post Boy*, 4 June 1713.

38. Some of the bills for stationery and journals are at Pembroke College, Oxford. See also *Gleanings*, III, 171–2; *Lives*, II, 179.

39. See John Nichols, *Illustrations* (1822), VII, 323, 343; *Life*, V, 386.

2   Oxford

1. *Life*, I, 58. Johnson post-dated his arrival at Oxford by a single day, as the caution book of Pembroke College acknowledges. 'Octob:31, 1728. Recd. then of Mr Samuel Johnson Comr. Of Pemb: Coll. ye sum of Seven Pounds for his Caution . . . Recd. By me, John Ratcliff, Bursar.'

2. *Life*, I, 78. Croker states that 'an examination of the college books proves that Johnson, who entered on the 31st October, 1728, remained there, even during the vacations, to the 12th December, 1729, when he personally left the college, and never returned – though his *name* remained on the books till 8th October, 1731.'

3. Hawkins, 9; *Life*, I, 60, 74.

4. *Life*, I, 76, 59. One of four surviving exercises which Johnson undertook at school takes its heading from the *Saturnalia* of Macrobius, 3.17.10, Bodleian Library, MS Eng. Lett. c.275, f.29; *Anecdotes*, 70, 72.

5. William Windham, *Diary of William Windham* (1866), 17; *Anecdotes*, 30; *Johnsonian Miscellanies*, ed. G. B. Hill (2 vols, Oxford, 1897), I, 165.

6. Pembroke College Library, 62/1/53.

7. Pembroke College Library, 62/1/53/1. '*Carmina vis nostri scribant meliora Poetae/ Ingenium jubeas purior haustas alat.*' Johnson misspells *munificentissimus* as *munifentissimus*, and erroneously gives *facit* not *faciat* ('*Poema licet non magni*

faci[*a*]*t*', 'the poem may not amount to much') where *licet* requires the subjunctive. Croker suggests that it was well-known the college beer 'was at this time indifferent' (1831 *Life*, I, 44).

8. *Gleanings*, V, 129–39, where a caricature of Jones, and further insults on him, are reproduced.

9. *Life*, I, 70. For the full catalogue of eighty-six items, and a description of them, see *Gleanings*, V, 214–29. See also James Northcote, *The Life of Sir Joshua Reynolds* (1813), I, 236.

10. For the members of Pembroke in residence in 1729 see *Life*, I, 63.

11. *Life*, I, 272–4; III, 304; IV, 94.

12. 'The buttery books . . . prove that Johnson batelled in College from Nov. 1, 1728, till Dec. 12, 1729.' Douglas Macleane, *A History of Pembroke College* (Oxford, 1897), 340. For a discussion of the problems of reading the college buttery books, see *Gleanings*, V, Appendix H.

13. *Life*, I, 60–1.

14. *Notebook*, 9; *Johnsonian Miscellanies*, II, 312; Hawkins, 13.

15. *Yale*, I, 26; *Life*, I, 72.

16. *Yale*, I, 27.

17. In 1994 J. C. D. Clark's book *Samuel Johnson; Literature, religion and English cultural politics from the Restoration to Romanticism* (Cambridge University Press) argued that Johnson had left because 'he could not, however, graduate, for that would require the oath of allegiance; still less could he take a fellowship, for that would call for the oath of abjuration comprehensively disowning the exiled dynasty' (96–7). However, Johnson would well have known the stipulations regarding the administration of the oaths of allegiance, supremacy and abjuration before ever he entered Pembroke College. In addition, his father, Michael was a loyal Tory, but also a prominent member of Lichfield Corporation. As such he was required to swear oaths of allegiance and abjuration both as mayor and as a magistrate. Copies of his oaths may be found for April 1710, July 1712 and October 1726 (*Gleanings*, III, 67, 165; IV, 201–3; Percy Laithwaite, *History of the Lichfield Conduit Lands Trust* (Lichfield, 1947), 29). Clark argues that while many Tories, including evidently Michael Johnson, were prepared to 'prophane such an oath' Samuel Johnson never did; 'he never took it' (99). In reply to this and similar arguments which Clark adduces to support the thesis that Johnson was a lifelong Jacobite, a special edition (No. 7, 1996) of *The Age of Johnson* was produced by Howard D. Weinbrot entitled 'Johnson, Jacobitism, and the Historiography of Nostalgia' which should be consulted. I shall cite only those arguments which have most weight with me.

18. *Life*, I, 77, 73.

19. ibid., 73, 79. There are eight subsequent entries against his name: 7d on 19 December 1729; 5d on 26 December 1729, 2 January, 30 January, 27 March and

15 May 1730 and 4s 7d on 13 March and 18 September 1730. The last time his name appears is for 1 October 1731. *Life*, I, 78.

20. *Life*, I, 68.

21. *Correspondence and Other Papers of James Boswell Relating to the Making of the Life of Johnson*, ed. Marshall Waingrow (New York, 1969), 49 n. 9. The poem is printed in *Life*, I, 54–5 and, in its later form, *Yale*, VI, 72–3.

22. *Yale*, I, 28; see the Vulgate Genesis 43 : 14 for the word *orbatus* used in the story of Joseph and Benjamin.

23. Clifford, *Young Samuel Johnson*, 128.

24. *Gleanings*, III, 98–100; Laithwaite, *History*, 69.

25. *Life*, I, 57, 445; Shaw, *Memoirs*, 14–15; *Life*, IV, 373.

26. *Anecdotes*, 62.

27. *Life*, I, 63–5.

28. ibid., 66.

29. A. L. Reade, 'A New Admirer for Dr Johnson', *London Mercury* 21 (January 1930), 247. The remark is reportedly third-hand.

30. The burial register of St Michael's, Lichfield states: '1731, Dec.7. Buried Mr. Michael Johnson, a Magistrate of the City.' *Yale*, I, 28.

31. *Life*, II, 459–61.

32. *Yale*, VI, 79–80; *Anecdotes*, 71; *Life*, I, 92–4.

33. *Life*, I, 83, 93–4.

34. *Yale*, VI, 39–40; *Life*, III, 197.

35. *Letters*, I, 3. This is the first of Johnson's surviving letters. For further comment on Johnson's refusal of Hickman's invitation, see *Gleanings*, V, 66.

36. For further examples of Sir Wolstan's bizarre behaviour see S. Hopewell, *The Book of Bosworth School* (1950), 52–3; Adam MS ed. Abraham Hayward, *Autobiography of Mrs Piozzi* (2nd edn, 2 vols, 1861), II, 103–4; *Gleanings*, V, 77–8.

37. *Life*, I, 84–5.

38. *Yale*, I, 29–30; the translation is Hawkins's, apart from the final sentence which, as E. L. McAdam notes, is 'omitted by both biographers'. Boswell offers a more florid translation (I, 80) of Johnson's note which is in Latin.

39. *Yale*, I, 29–31. 'Leading to Heaven'; the book, bearing the inscription 'Sam: Johnson', the date 13 July 1732 and a list of erroneous Latin words, is in the Rothschild collection. It seems unlikely that he would have used, or encountered, such a work at Market Bosworth.

40. *Letters*, I, 4; see *Gleanings*, V, 89.

3 Marriage

1. 'The only known copy is for May 21, 1733 (now in the office of the *Birmingham Post*)': Clifford, *Young Samuel Johnson*, 330. Unfortunately this is no longer the case. In the reorganisation of the *Birmingham Post*'s and the City Council's

offices this sole copy of the *Birmingham Journal* was apparently lost.
Quotations are taken from a reproduction which is still available.

2. *Yale*, I, 31.

3. *Life*, I, 86.

4. Clifford follows Hawkins in assuming that Hector borrowed the book.
However, no copy of the work is ever listed as having belonged to Pembroke
College library and 'it is probable that the work was secured from a private
source' (*Young Samuel Johnson*, I, 330). Boswell's *Life* says that Johnson himself
'borrowed it of Pembroke College' (I, 86).

5. In the copy of the work which Johnson gave to Hector, there is the note 'Sl.
Johnson, Translator, 24 yrs.' and Hector's inscription: 'Donat Amici S. J.
Authoris ad Ed. Hector 1734.' J. D. Fleeman's note quoted in *Yale*, XV
(ed. Joel J. Gold), xxv. *Life*, I, 87.

6. *Yale*, XV, 3–4; my italics.

7. ibid., 91, 88, li–lv.

8. Private letter from Adam Phillips, 2004. For details of the extent of Johnson's
'errors' in translating French numbers, see *Yale*, XV, xlix.

9. *Life*, I, 87.

10. *Yale*, XV, 167.

11. 'AUGUSTI 5to 1734. Conditiones edendi Politiani Poemata emisi.' *Yale*, I, 32;
see also *Gleanings*, V, 99.

12. The library register has the following note: 'June 15, 1734. Borrow'd of Mr.
Meek, Librarian, Angeli Politiani Opera, by ye Revd. Mr. Robt. Boyse *for ye
Use of Mr. Johnson*. Witness. J. Ratcliff. A. Blackford.' 'The words italicised
were entered by another hand. After the entry the words "never returned"
were written and erased' (*Life*, I, 90).

13. *Life*, I, 90; *Letters*, I, 5; Hawkins, 27.

14. For the original Latin and Greek of this notation see *Yale*, I, 33.

15. *Anecdotes*, 110.

16. *Life*, I, 94–5. Johnson's alleged love for Lucy Porter is presented by Anna
Seward's *Letters* (Edinburgh, 1811), I, 44–5 and discussed in *Gleanings*, V,
102–3; X, 99.

17. *Anecdotes*, 110; *Life*, I, 99.

18. Shaw, *Memoirs*, 25, 111.

19. *London Journal*, 304–5; Shaw, *Memoirs*, 28–9.

20. Walter Jackson Bate, *Samuel Johnson* (London, 1984), 145; Shaw, *Memoirs*,
25–6; and *Gleanings*, VI, 32, which clears up the ambiguity about whose
brother, Tetty's or Harry Porter's, made the offer.

21. Seward, I, 44–5. There is no evidence that Johnson had an uncle hanged, as he
is alleged to claim in this exchange.

22. *Letters*, I, 5–7.

23. *Gleanings*, V, 108–18.
24. *Letters*, I, 9–11.
25. *Life*, I, 96; *Thraliana*, I, 178.
26. Act IV, sc. v, *Yale*, VII, 351.
27. Letter at Pembroke College, Oxford, *Gleanings*, VI, 29–30.
28. *Life*, I, 99–100; *Letters*, I, 11–12.
29. Different estimates of numbers at Edial come from *Life*, I, 97; Thomas Davies, *Memoirs of the Life of David Garrick* (2 vols, 1780), I, 8; Hawkins, 36; *Gleanings*, VI, 44–5.
30. *Life*, I, 99, 531. 'Malone in a marginal note to his copy of Mrs Piozzi's *Anec.* (p. 148) writes of the dialogue in question: "This was a dialogue between Mrs J. when in bed, & J^n in his shirt, the lady thinking he delayed too long to come to bed. Garrick made it entertaining, but doubtless it was all invention." '
31. *Yale*, I, 35–6; *Life*, I, 97.
32. Birthplace Museum, 2001.71.57.
33. *Gleanings*, VI, 44, 104; *The Private Correspondence of David Garrick*, ed. James Boaden (London, 1831), I, 1–2.
34. Clifford, *Young Samuel Johnson*, 164; *Gleanings*, I, 1; *Life*, I, 101.
35. *Gleanings*, I, 1; *Yale*, II, 182.

4   London

1. *Daily Journal*, 22 February 1736/7.
2. Philip Dormer Stanhope, fourth Earl of Chesterfield, *Miscellaneous Works* (1777), I, 228 ff.
3. *Life*, I, 103.
4. Yale Boswell Papers; see *Gleanings*, VI, 65.
5. Hawkins, 43; John Nicholls, *Literary Anecdotes of the 18th Century* (9 vols, London, 1812–15), VIII, 416.
6. *Life*, I, 106.
7. Petition to the King in Council, 21 July 1737, Coram Foundation Library, reproduced in full in R. H. Nichols and F. A. Wray, *The History of the Foundling Hospital* (London, Cambridge University Press, 1935), 16–17 and Ruth McClure, *Coram's Children* (Yale, 1981); *A Trip to Vaux-Hall: Or, a General SATYR on the Times of 1737*, quoted by David Coke, *The Muse's Bower: Vauxhall Gardens 1728–1786* (Sudbury, 1978). For the other details of London's daily events, see *Read's Weekly Journal*, the *Daily Post* and *Daily Gazetteer*.
8. They met at the Fountain Tavern in the Strand. When in 1776 Boswell heard the story in Lichfield, Joseph Porter, being of the company, declared the Fountain was a 'notorious bawdy-house'. *Notebook*, 11–12.

9. *Life*, I, 106; *Letters*, I, 12–13. Clifford believes it 'reasonable to suppose' that Johnson came to a vague agreement with Cave (*Young Samuel Johnson*, 176); Thomas Kaminski believes Cave rejected him (*Early Career of Samuel Johnson* (New York, 1987), 9).

10. *Life*, I, 110; *Daily Advertiser*, 8 December 1743.

11. It succeeded, staying in business till 1922 and providing 'more in quantity, and greater variety, than any Book of the kind and price' (*The Grubstreet Journal*, 22–9 December 1737). By the end of the 1730s Hawkins suggests that the *Gentleman's Magazine* had reached a monthly circulation of fifteen thousand (Hawkins, 1787 edn, 27–30).

12. *Yale*, VI, 40–3; Norma Clarke, *Dr Johnson's Women* (Hambledon and London, 2000), 26–7; *Life*, I, 123. Johnson also published epigrams in her praise in the July and August issues of the *Gentleman's Magazine*.

13. *Letters*, I, 14–18; *Life*, I, 124–5, where Boswell accounts for Johnson's dislike of Whitehead by his membership of the 'riotous and profane club', the Monks of Medmenham Abbey.

14. *Yale*, VI, 43–4; (*Humani studium generis cui pectore fervet,/ O! colat humanum te foveatque genus!*), Richard Holmes, *Dr Johnson & Mr Savage* (London, 1993), 177; *Lives*, III, 185.

15. *Lives*, III, 166; *Life*, I, 161 n. 3, 164; Clifford, *Young Samuel Johnson*, 202–3; *The Poetical Works of Richard Savage*, ed. Clarence Tracy (Cambridge University Press, 1962), 234, and Hawkins, 29–30, 49.

16. 'London', ll. 5–6, *Yale*, VI, 48. For a lengthy discussion of the question when Johnson first met Savage, see Holmes, 177–83. He quotes Hester Thrale's annotation of her 1816 edition of Boswell's *Life*: 'I thought we were all convinced that Thales was Savage.' See *The Life of Samuel Johnson*, ed. Edward G. Fletcher (3 vols, London, 1938), I, 77. 'Sir John Hawkins, p. 86, tells us, "The event is *antedated*, in the poem of 'London'; but in every particular, except the difference of a year, what is there said of the departure of Thales, must be understood of Savage, and looked upon as *true history*." This conjecture is, I believe, entirely groundless.' *Life*, I, 125 n. 4; *Letters*, I, 16.

17. *Life*, I, 73; *London*, I, 98; *Yale*, VI, 53, 56.

18. *Yale*, VI, 55, 60; for Savage's trial for murder, see Holmes, 100–32; the popular legend of the peacefulness of Alfred's reign had been revived in Sir John Spelman's *The Life of Aelfred the Great*, ed. Thomas Hearne (Oxford, 1709), 114.

19. *Letters*, I, 17; *Thraliana*, I, 177.

20. *Life*, I, 135–6. The paper, dated 2 August 1738, sets out an 'Account between Mr Edward Cave and Sam. Johnson, in relation to a version of Father Paul' between that date and 21 April the year following.

21. *Letters*, I, 18; *Yale*, VI, 62.

22. *Gentleman's Magazine* (1739), 166.

23. Thomas Birch, Diary, British Museum Add. MS 4478c; *Letters*, I, 20.
24. See Kaminski, 201–3.
25. *Yale*, I, 38; *Daily Gazetteer*, 25–31 August, 2–7 September 1738.
26. *Gentleman's Magazine* 8 (1738), 581–3.
27. It is important to remember that these were two distinct works, something which the first writers on Johnson did not realise. See *Yale*, XVII, xxii–xxviii.
28. *Gentleman's Magazine* 8 (1738), 496. Similar advertisements appeared in the *Daily Advertiser* and *London Evening Post* for 9 September. Nicholas Carter's letter for 26 September is quoted from A. D. Barker's DPhil thesis, 'Edward Cave, Samuel Johnson, and the *Gentleman's Magazine*' (1981), 274.
29. *Letters*, I, 20–1; *Yale*, XVII, xxviii–xxxii; *Life*, V, 67, for 19 August 1773; James Boswell, *Laird of Auchinleck 1778–1782*, ed. Joseph W. Reed and Frederick A. Pottle (1977), 375. For a discussion of what 'six sheets' may have meant, see *Yale*, XVII, xxii–xxiii.
30. Elizabeth Carter possessed one of the few copies of the 1739 *Commentary*. Kept in Yale University's Beinecke Library, it bears the inscription in her hand: 'E Libris Elizae Carter'. For Johnson's annotations, I am grateful to O M Brack for the use of his MS typescript, part 1, p. 51. *Letters*, I, 17; Clarke, ch. 2.
31. *Lives*, IV, 76; *Yale*, XVII, 42.
32. *Yale*, XVII, xxxv, 23, 51, 75, 64, 175. For Johnson's habitual use of the word 'darling' see O M Brack Jr.'s discussion in the Introduction to the volume, p. xlvii.
33. My own view of the 'trifling distich' is published in *John Gay, A Profession of Friendship* (1995), 538.
34. *Yale*, X, 16. For a discussion of Johnson's part in this letter see also p. 14 in which L. F. Powell (*Life*, II, 483) argues that it 'may have been touched by Johnson, but is not, I think, wholly his'. I take the text of these 'Observations', printed in No. 8 of the the *Gentleman's Magazine* (640–1) in December 1738, from the manuscript by O M Brack Jr. (60–3). Johnson claimed, late in life, that Cave achieved monthly sales of ten thousand (*Life*, III, 322) and Hawkins puts the figure higher, estimating a circulation of 'ten to fifteen thousand copies' (abridged edn, 1962, 57). Attributed to Johnson by Boswell (*Life*, I, 139), the Preface was published in *Works* (1823), vol. XI, 24–8. Further pieces continuing these arguments and possibly by Johnson are 'Letters' (see *Life*, I, 139n and Arthur Sherbo, *Journal of English and German Philology* 52 (1953), 543–8); editorial Notes (see Sherbo, ibid.); Proposals (see Fleeman, *A Bibliography of the Works of Samuel Johnson* (Oxford, Clarendon Press, 2000), I, 37); and 'An Appeal' (see *Life*, I, 140).
35. *London Evening Post*, 9–12 April 1737.
36. *Gentleman's Magazine* 9 (1739), 37–8, 72–3, 114–16, 172–6.
37. *Yale*, X, 22, 25, 49, 50.
38. Hawkins, 72; *Life*, I, 141–2 and MS of *Life* (Yale Boswell Papers).

39. *Yale*, X, 52–73, 69. No press comments on the *Vindication* have been found.

40. *Yale*, X, 63, 73. The pamphlet was ascribed to Johnson in the *European Magazine*, January 1785, 9; '. . . the attribution has never been questioned, and is not likely to be' (D. J. Greene, *Yale*, X, 54).

41. See John Nicholls's first printing of these 'Considerations' in *Gentleman's Magazine* 57, July 1787 (555); *The Country-Journal, or the Craftsman* and *Read's Weekly Journal*, 28 April 1739.

42. Holmes makes much of the ambiguous non-specificity of the phrase; 'Tears in *whose* eyes?' he asks, noting that Johnson adds, in a marginal correction to the second edition, 'I had then a slight fever' (14–15); *Lives*, III, 173.

43. *Life*, I, 143, 133–4, 533; *Read's Weekly Journal*, 12 May 1739.

5 Love

1. Sir Roger Bannister, speaking at the 'Celebrating Johnson's Dictionary' conference at Pembroke College, Oxford, on 27 August 2005; *Life*, I, 143. Further discussions of Johnson's symptoms may be found in T. J. Murray's 'Dr Samuel Johnson's Movement Disorder', *British Medical Journal* 1 (1979), 1, 610–14, and in John Wiltshire's *Samuel Johnson in the Medical World* (Cambridge University Press, 1991).

2. See Clifford, *Young Samuel Johnson*, 333 n. 43.

3. *Thraliana*, I, 538–9; *Anecdotes*, 113.

4. *Yale*, VI, 369–70; *Poems*, 71–2 and Notes, 202–6. See also Holmes, 29.

5. *Anecdotes*, 113.

6. *Yale*, VI, 83–4; *Poems*, 73; Holmes, 30.

7. *Gentleman's Magazine* 10 (February 1740), 78; *Daily Post*, 1–15 January 1740; *The Country Journal*, 2 February 1740.

8. Clifford, *Young Samuel Johnson*, 214–15; Robert DeMaria Jr. *The Life of Samuel Johnson* (Oxford, 1993), 73; Bate, 185; Holmes, 28, 32.

9. *Thraliana*, I, 178.

10. *Letters*, I, 23; *Anecdotes*, 110.

11. Notes left by Richard Farmer, Cave's friend, state that £100 per annum was paid to Johnson for at least the latter half of the period 1738–45; *General Biographical Dictionary* (1812–17), XIX, 53.

12. Davies, I, 43; *Richard III* opened at Goodman's Fields on 19 October 1741. The poem, which appeared in the *Gentleman's Magazine* for September 1740, is in *Yale*, VI, 68–9; *Poems*, 76, and is discussed in *Life*, I, 148–9.

13. *Yale*, I, 10. *Memoirs of Richard Cumberland* (1807), I, 357–8; *Life*, I, 313.

14. *London Daily Post*, 26 and 28 November 1740; 'The Life of Admiral Blake', 1740, in *Early Biographical Writings of Dr. Johnson*, with an introduction by J. D. Fleeman (1973), 67–85.

15. 'The Life of Admiral Drake' (1740–1), *Gentleman's Magazine*, 10–11 and *Early Biographical Writings*, 36–66.
16. *London Daily Post*, 22 October 1740; *Letters*, I, 24–7.
17. Boswell's *Life*, 18 April 1778 (p. 964).
18. *Anecdotes*, 119, 100; British Library Stowe MS 748, f. 181.
19. *London Daily Post*, and *General Advertiser*, 13 August 1740, 7 September 1741.
20. *Life*, IV, 187.
21. *Gentleman's Magazine* 10 (December 1740), 593–6.
22. *Yale*, X, 74–110; *Life*, I, 150 n. 2; *Gentleman's Magazine* 11 (1741), 202–8; *Life*, I, 153; *Gentleman's Magazine* 11 (1741), 477–9. Boswell has no doubts that the *Jests* are by Johnson (*Life*, I, 150); Hill disagrees: 'This piece is certainly not by Johnson' (I, 150n.) but Donald Greene has the last word: 'Hill's rejection should be rejected' ('Some Notes', 81). The question of attribution is discussed by O M Brack in *The Shorter Prose Writings of Samuel Johnson* (MS, 36–8).
23. *The Literary Magazine*, in Allen T. Hazen, *Samuel Johnson's Prefaces and Dedications* (New Haven, Yale University Press, 1937), 129; *Johnsonian Miscellanies*, I, 378–9. Arthur Murray seems to have been wrong about where Johnson was living at the time. *Letters*, I, 28–32; Reade, 'A New Admirer for Dr Johnson', *London Mercury* xxi (January 1930) 248.
24. *Gentleman's Magazine* 8 (1738), 627; ibid., 12 (1742), 3–11; *Life*, I, 504.
25. *Gentleman's Magazine* 8 (1738), 181; *Johnsonian Miscellanies*, I, 379; *Life*, II, 355; *Gentleman's Magazine* 12 (1742), 14.
26. *Gentleman's Magazine* 11 (1741), 13, 62, 56.
27. *Life*, I, 152.
28. *Gentleman's Magazine* 12 (1742), 128–31; ibid., 11 (1741), 375–7; ibid., 12 (1742), 206–10. *Early Biographical Writings*, 159–88; *Gentleman's Magazine* 12 (1742), 320–3; 353–7, 484–6; ibid., 354–7; *Life*, I, 467.
29. Birch to Philip Yorke, British Library Add. MS 35,396; letter of 16 September 1742; *Life*, I, 154. The bookseller was William Oldys; *London Daily Post*, 16 December 1740.
30. The proposal appeared (in slightly different versions) in *Gentleman's Magazine* 12 (1742), 636–9, the *London Evening Post* for 7 December 1742, and the *Daily Advertiser*, 5 January 1743.
31. Hawkins, 133; Oldys was later thrown into the Fleet prison, for which he developed such a liking 'that he constantly spent his evenings there'. *Life*, I, 175.
32. The texts of items are taken from O M Brack's MS, which cites Fleeman, 'Proposals', 221 and 1 : 111–18 (44.4HM/1); *Life of Pope* in *Lives*, III, 187.
33. *Daily Post*, 30 December 1743; Boswell says 'the Latin accounts of books were written by him', *Life*, I, 154. See Thomas Kaminski, 'Johnson and Oldys as Bibliographers: An Introduction to the Harleian Catalogue', *Philological*

Quarterly 60 (1981), 439–53.

34. *Life*, I, 154. For variants see ibid., 534; Hawkins, 149–51; *Thraliana*, 195; and Clifford, *Young Samuel Johnson*, 345 n. 10. Also *Letters*, I, 36.

35. *Early Biographical Writings*, 99–158. For a detailed discussion of Johnson's contributions to the *Medicinal Dictionary*, see O M Brack Jr. and Thomas Kaminski, 'Johnson, James, and the *Medicinal Dictionary*', *Modern Philology* 81 (1984), 378–400.

36. *Life*, V, 67; *Letters*, I, 34–6; *Life*, I, 165 n. 1 ('An Account of the Life of Mr Richard Savage'); *Poetical Works of Richard Savage*, 89.

37. *Life*, I, 169, 167.

38. *Letters*, I, 39–40; see also *Gleanings*, VI, 32–5, VII, 87–94; and *Life*, I, 95–6n.

39. *Life*, I, 163. *Yale*, I, 40–1.

40. R. W. Chapman, *London Mercury*, May 1930, 439–41.

41. *Yale*, VII, 1–45; ibid., 'Macbeth', 1.iv.27; 1.v.45; 5.v.42; 5.iii.22–3; 3.iv.122; 4.i.153; 2.iii.116; *Life*, II, 96.

42. *Miscellaneous Observations* were published 6–8 April; Tonson wrote to Cave on the 11th; see Samuel Pegge, *Anonymiana* (1809), 33–4.

43. *Life*, I, 106; Hawkins, 391–2, second edition, which corrects his earlier statement of 'a guinea' to 'two guineas'. Hebrews xiii.16: the text is from the *Book of Common Prayer*, which has this reading, rather than the King James Bible in which the relevant verb is 'communicate' not 'distribute'. Clifford, *Young Samuel Johnson*, 274. For accounts of the ceremony see *St James's Evening Post* and *London Evening Post*, 4 May 1745. The sermon is published in *Yale*, XIV, 287–99.

44. *Westminster Journal*, 24 August, 7, 14 and 28 September, 5 October, 2 and 16 November, 14 and 28 December 1745.

45. Clark, 175.

46. *Letters*, I, 40; *Life*, I, 176–7, 182; *Life*, I, 310.

47. *Johnson's Journey to the Western Islands and Boswell's Journal of a Tour*, ed. R. W. Chapman (Oxford, 1924), 6, 10, 23.

48. ibid., 237–40 and 281; *Life*, I, 430. Boswell gives Johnson's thoughts in 1763, *after* he had gained his pension, but notes that 'Mr. Topham Beauclerk assured me, he had heard him say this before he had his pension.'

6 A Harmless Drudge

1. *Life*, I, 186.

2. *Life*, III, 405; ibid., I, 182.

3. Pope, 'Essay on Criticism', in *Pastoral Poetry and an Essay on Criticism*, vol. I of the Twickenham Edition of the Works of Alexander Pope, general editor, John Butt (11 vols, London, 1943–69), l. 483; *The Prose Works of Jonathan Swift*, ed. Herbert Davis (16 vols, Oxford, 1939–74), I, 132; *A New Dictionary of the*

Terms Ancient and Modern of the Canting Crew by 'B.E.' was published in 1698. Addison's remarks in favour of an English academy are in the *Spectator* 135 and 165; see Mary Segar, 'Dictionary Making in the Early Eighteenth Century', *RES* 7 (1931), 210–13.

4. See note 3 to the Prelude, above; Walpole's opinion is quoted by James K. Sledd and Gwin J. Kolb, *Dr Johnson's Dictionary: Essays in the Biography of a Book* (Chicago, 1955), 136.

5. British Library Add. MS 33,397, f. 67; *Life*, III, 19; *Letters*, I, 40.

6. Hawkins, 175. Johnson is first listed in the rate books in December, 1747. The house, 17 Gough Square, EC4, still exists and is the principal museum of Dr Johnson in London.

7. *Life*, I, 328–9, where can be found this further note from Frances Reynolds: 'a gentleman who frequently visited him whilst writing his *Idlers*, always found him at his Desk, sitting at one with three legs; and on rising from it, he remark'd that Mr. Johnson never forgot its defect, but would either hold it in his hand, or place it with great composure against some support, taking no notice of its imperfection to his visitor . . .' *Johnsonian Miscellanies*, II, 259.

8. *Life*, I, 187; Reddick, *Making of Johnson's Dictionary*, 205 n. 38; Hyde MS, ed. J. D. Fleeman, *Preliminary Handlist of Documents and Manuscripts of Samuel Johnson* (Oxford Bibliographical Society Occasional Pub. no 2, 1967), no. 35. Baretti's remark is scribbled on Johnson's letter, *Letters*, 393.

9. *Letters*, V, 23; James L. Clifford suggests a date 'as early as late 1749' for the letter (*Dictionary Johnson* (New York, 1979), 55); *Yale*, I, 41.

10. The Oxford Authors, *Samuel Johnson* (ed. Donald Greene, 1984), 165–74.

11. *Yale*, VI, 87–90; *Poems*, 81–2; Johnson's recollections are reported by George Steevens in *Johnsonian Miscellanies*, II, 313.

12. British Library Add. MS 35,397.

13. *Life*, I, 192, 238; III, 406 n. 1. This conversation was cancelled from the original edition of the *Life* as late as February 1791. Boswell writes to Malone that 'Windham etc. were struck with its *indelicacy,* and it might hurt the book much. It is, however, mighty good stuff.'

14. 'Tacenda', in *Boswell: The Applause of the Jury, 1782–1785* (Yale, 1981), 110–13; *Yale*, I, 41.

15. *Yale*, VI, 90; *Life*, I, 192–4; II, 15.

16. *Life*, I, 193; II, 15. The number of polysyllabic rhyme words (that is, words which have not been shortened, as 'pray'r' or 'tow'r', to make them monosyllables) is eighty-one, from 368 rhymes. *Yale*, VI, 97–9; *Poems*, 86–7 and 171–2.

17. *Anecdotes*, 50.

18. *London Evening Post*, 1 January 1747; British Library Egerton MS 2185, ff. 5–6; *A Criticism on Mahomet and Irene in a Letter to the Author* (1749), pp. 5–6. James Miller republished his play *Mahomet and Pamira* simultaneously, no

doubt hoping to benefit from the publicity.

19. *Life*, I, 196, 538.
20. Bertrand Bronson first suggested this in *Johnson Agonistes* (Berkeley, University of California Press, 1946), 136–7; *Letters*, I, 23; *Life*, I, 201, 539.
21. *Life*, I, 197; *Yale*, VI, 160–8.
22. *Life*, I, 197–200; 'I have observ'd that in all our Tragedies, the Audience cannot forbear laughing when the Actors are to die; 'tis the most Comick part of the whole Play.' (Dryden, *Of Dramatick Poesie* (1668), 32); *Gentleman's Magazine* 19, 76–81; *The Works of Aaron Hill* (1753), II, 355; British Library Egerton MS 2185, ff. 9–10.
23. *Life*, I, 198–9.
24. British Library Add. MS 35,397, f. 140. *Life*, I, 186; Sotheby's Catalogue, 7 June 1855.
25. Bodleian MS. Percy d.11, ff. 6–18; *Life*, I, 183–9; I, 295–6; I, 304. For a detailed assessment of all these references and a slow retrieval of Johnson's processes of working, see Reddick, *Making of Johnson's Dictionary*.
26. *The Early Biographies of Samuel Johnson*, ed. O M Brack Jr. and Robert E. Kelley (Iowa City, IA, 1974), 82; *Thraliana*, 34.
27. Hawkins, 175; *Life*, III, 284–5; IV, 4.
28. Quoted in De Witt T. Starnes and Gertrude E. Noyes, *The English Dictionary from Cawdrey to Johnson* (Chapel Hill, NC, 1946; repr. 1960), 160; British Library Add. MS 35,397, f. 222.
29. *Letters*, I, 43–4; Hazen, 171–89.
30. In a final paragraph the *Essay* solicited subscriptions 'for the relief of Mrs Elizabeth Foster, grand-daughter to John Milton' which were to be taken in by, among others, Mr Dodsley at Pall Mall and Mr Cave at St John's Gate.
31. *Lives*, I, 108–9; *A Series of Letters between Mrs Elizabeth Carter and Miss Catherine Talbot*, ed. Montagu Pennington (2 vols, 1808), I, 372; Clifford, *Dictionary Johnson*, 64–5.
32. Hazen, 79; *Works* (1788), XIV, 125–55; *Life*, I, 227–8; *Yale*, VI, 239–41; *Poems*, 92–3; *Life*, II, 120, V, 229, III, 271, II, 298.
33. Clarke, 66–74; *Johnsonian Miscellanies*, I, 158, 204; *Life*, I, 27 n. 2; *Diary & Letters of Madame D'Arblay*, ed. Charlotte Barrett with Notes by Austin Dobson (6 vols, 1904–5), I, 58–9; Hawkins, 219–20, 286–7, 250; *Works*, IV, 55–60, 69.
34. *Letters*, I, 50–1, 73; V, 23, which clarifies the dating; *Gentleman's Magazine* 69 (Supplement, 1799), 1,171.
35. *Life*, III, 37; Shiels, who was the true author of Theophilus Cibber's *Lives of the Poets* (1753), died in December 1753.
36. *Yale*, I, 42–3; *Letters*, I, 48–9; *Yale*, III, 7; *Life*, I, 202–3; *Letters*, I, 45–6. In the 1756 edition of the *Rambler* Johnson, in addition to thanking Elphinston for his 'many elegant translations', mentions that he keeps an academy for 'young

gentlemen' in Kensington.

37. *Yale*, III, 10, 32, 35; see *Yale*, III, xxii for details. *Life*, I, 217. Bedford County Record Office, L30/9A/5.

38. *Rambler* 10, 13, 11, 18 and 14; *Yale*, III, 35–103.

39. British Library Add. MS 35,399 f. 190; *Johnsonian Miscellanies*, II, 414; *Yale*, V, 75–80.

40. Johnson wrote the entire *Rambler*, save for No. 30, by Catherine Talbot, No. 97, by Samuel Richardson, and Nos 44 and 100, by Elizabeth Carter. For occasional contributions, in the form of letters, see D. Nichol Smith, *Bodleian Quarterly Record* 7 (1934), 508–9; No. 20, *Yale*, III, 112, and No. 14, ibid., 74–80.

41. *Yale*, III, 125–30; *Gentleman's Magazine* 20, 465; Bedford CRO, L30/9A/5; *Memoirs of the Life of Mrs. Elizabeth Carter*, ed. Montagu Pennington (1808), I, 146, 244, 295; Hagley MSS, II, 143.

42. *Yale*, III, 114; ibid., IV, 153–9; *Life*, I, 210; *Selected Letters of Samuel Richardson*, ed. John Carroll (Oxford, Clarendon Press, 1964), 165; *Correspondence of Samuel Richardson*, ed. Anna Letitia Barbauld (1804), I, 164–5, 168, 169; *Letters*, I, 47–8.

43. *Yale*, III, 319, No. 60; III, 114, No. 20, 216, No. 40; V, 315–20, No. 208.

44. *Life*, I, 256; *Yale*, IV, 197, 356, Nos 105, 136.

45. *Yale*, V, 145; V, 95; IV, 290; V, 13, 84; V, 125–9; IV, 121–9; IV, 186; III, 258.

46. *Yale*, IV, 192; III, 354; V, 203.

47. *Yale*, III, 103; V, 45, No. 152; 135, No. 169.

48. *R. B. Adam Library*, III, 172; *Letters*, I, 60. The point about republication rights is a sensible conjecture, first made by G. B. Hill (ed.), *Letters of Samuel Johnson, LL.D.* (2 vols, Oxford, Clarendon Press, 1892), I, 29, and repeated by Clifford, *Dictionary Johnson*, 98.

49. *Diary and Letters of Madame D'Arblay*, I, 86; Duncan Isles, 'The Lennox Collection', *Harvard Library Bulletin* 18, 317–44, and 19, 416–33; *Letters*, I, 58–9.

50. *General Advertiser*, 13 March 1752. The dedication was openly acknowledged by Johnson (*Life*, I, 367) but nothing further. For a discussion of the authorship issue, see Miriam R. Small, *Charlotte Ramsay Lennox* (Yale, 1935), 77–82 and Hazen, 94–8. *Letters*, I, 59–60, 43–4.

51. See *Gentleman's Magazine* 57, 1,157–9; Clifford, *Dictionary Johnson*, 92–5; Albert J. Kuhn, 'Dr Johnson, Zachariah Williams, and the Eighteenth-Century Search for the Longitude', *Modern Philology* 82 (1984), 40–52; *Yale*, III, 108, 356; *Idler* 58; *Yale*, II, 182.

52. *Gentleman's Magazine* 57, 757–9, 1,041–3.

53. In private hands. Tetty's name is inscribed on volumes II, III and IV, and the date included in volume III. There is no signature on volumes I, V and VI, which did not appear until the summer, and there may possibly be a doubt whether the volumes were actually signed by Tetty or by Johnson. See

Clifford, *Dictionary Johnson*, 97 and 327 n. 22.

54. *Life*, I, 238; *Letters*, I, 61–2.

55. Hawkins, 314. According to Tyers, Johnson 'sent for Hawkesworth, in the most earnest manner, to come and give him consolation and his company'. Brack and Kelly, 75, 274; John L. Abbott, *John Hawkesworth: Eighteenth-Century Man of Letters* (University of Wisconsin Press, 1982), ch. 3, n. 8.

56. See Clifford, *Dictionary Johnson*, 328 n. 30; *Thraliana*, 178; *Letters to and from Samuel Johnson*, ed. H. L. Piozzi (1788), II, 384–5; *Yale*, XIV, Sermon 25, 261–71; *Life*, I, 241. The words written on a piece of paper, and kept beside her ring, were: '*Eheu! Eliz. Johnson, Nupta Jul. 90 1736, Mortua, eheu! Mart. 170 1752*'.

57. Susan M. Radcliffe, *Sir Joshua's Nephew* (London, 1930), 86–8; *Yale*, I, 44–8.

7 Frank Barber

1. Deed 131 of the Jamaica Archives, Spanish Town, Jamaica records the conveyance to Bathurst of 'a negro woman slave named Grace and her two children Luckey and Quashey. Consideration 5£ currency.' Bathurst sold his plantation to William Lamb of Kingston in August 1749. See Lyle Larsen, *Dr Johnson's Household* (Hamden, Connecticut, Archon Books, 1985).

2. *Life*, I, 242. Bathurst's closeness to Johnson at this time is recorded by Mrs Piozzi who recalls Johnson referring to him as 'my *dear, dear* Bathurst, whom I loved better than ever I loved any human creature'; *Anecdotes*, 66.

3. Colonel Bathurst's will, dated 24 April 1754, granted 'to Francis Barber, a negroe whom I brought from Jamaica aforesaid into England, his freedom and twelve pounds in money'. See A. L. Reade, 'Francis Barber: The Doctor's Negro Servant', in *Gleanings*, II, 4; J. Hawkins, 326.

8 The *Dictionary*

1. *Yale*, I, 48–9.

2. ibid., 49–50. The Gregorian calendar replaced the Julian one in England in September 1752, with the 'loss' of eleven days, 2 September being immediately followed by 14 September. The fact that Johnson does not quibble over or even remark the fact, other than to resolve, after writing 'JAN. 1, 1753, N.S.' boldly among his prayers, 'which I shall use for the future', seems to indicate a wish to get on with living. His immediate subsequent failure to observe this resolution would seem to confirm this.

3. *Dr Campbell's Diary of a Visit to England in 1775*, ed. J. L. Clifford (New York: Macmillan, 1947), 68.

4. *Yale*, I, 50–14. Hill Boothby died on 16 January 1756: *Anecdotes*, 114; *Letters*, I, 118–19.

5. *Anecdotes*, 114

6. *Letters*, I, 116–24.

7. *Yale*, I, 59–60.

8. Archibald Campbell, *Lexiphanes* (1767), 108–9. For details of working progress on the undertaking, see Reddick, *Making of Johnson's Dictionary*, 70–2.

9. J. D. Fleeman notes that some cross-references from the letters A and B (such as that for *Aurora Borealis*) are simply not followed up. See 'Dr Johnson's Dictionary, 1755', *Bodleian Library Record* (1964), 39–40; J. A. Cochrane, *Dr Johnson's Printer* (London, 1964), 102. *Letters*, I, 80–2.

10. *Letters*, I, 67–8; Johnson had written just one *Adventurer* paper by that time (8 March 1753) and in the end provided twenty-nine.

11. ibid., 69–70.

12. ibid., 62–6.

13. ibid., 74–80; *Yale*, XVIII, 25–6.

14. Hawkins, 435; *Life*, I, 243–4, 247.

15. *Letters*, I, 67–8; for a discussion of the authorship of the Misargyrus papers (Nos 34, 41, 53 and 62) see *Yale*, II, 323–36; *Letters between Mrs Elizabeth Carter and Miss Catherine Talbot*, II, 1–2. See David Fairer, 'Authorship Problems in *The Adventurer*', *Review of English Studies*, n.s. XXV, 137–51 for a discussion of their contributions to the periodical.

16. Hawkins, 310.

17. *Yale*, II, 400–5, 417, 435, 450, 460, 468, 476–7, 487, 492–7.

18. *Letters*, I, 80–2; *Life*, I, 270; Cave died on 10 January 1754 and Johnson's *Life* is in *Gentleman's Magazine* for February and *Early Biographical Writings*, 407–10.

19. *Life*, I, 271–4.

20. Reddick, *Making of Johnson's Dictionary*, 74, where Johnson's borrowings from John Wallis and George Hickes are examined. *Yale*, XVIII, 127, 282–5; *Letters*, I, 82.

21. *Letters*, I, 116–19.

22. Reddick, *Making of Johnson's Dictionary*, 77.

23. The episode is described in detail in Clifford, *Dictionary Johnson*, 128–33, and in Clifford's essay 'Johnson and Foreign Visitors to London: Baretti and Others' in *Eighteenth Century Studies Presented to Arthur M. Wilson*, ed. Peter Gay (University of New England Press, 1972), 99–115. See also Lacy Collison-Morley, *Giuseppe Baretti* (London, 1909), 82–93. The letter, in Italian, is in Giuseppe Baretti, *Epistolario*, ed. Luigi Piccioni (Bari, 1936), I, 100–7, and the loose leaves from Holloway's diary are in the Trinity Warton Papers.

24. *Letters*, I, 83–6.

25. ibid., I, 88–91; *Yale*, XVIII, 343; *Letters*, I, 92.

26. *Yale*, XVIII, 73–113.

27. *The World* 100 and 101 (28 November and 5 December 1754).

28. *Life*, I, 264–5. See Dille, 198–211.

29. *Life*, I, 287; *Letters*, I, 100–1; see the *Daily Advertiser* for 16, 17 and 18 April and later issues, and the *Monthly Review* which gives the date of publication as 15 April. Hawkins, 345–6; *Life*, I, 304.

30. *Gentleman's Magazine* 25, 147–51; *Monthly Review* 12, 292–324; *Edinburgh Review* 1, 61–3. Smith identifies himself by some handwritten annotations; Warton, *Biographical Memoirs*, 230–1; 'The Letter Book of Thomas Edwards' in the Bodleian Library, ff. 208–11.

31. *Letters*, I, 102–7.

32. *Letters*, I, 109–10; see Reddick, *Making of Johnson's Dictionary*, 84–8, and Dille, 199.

33. *Life*, I, 293–6. One might ask whether the definitions given in the current *New Shorter Oxford Dictionary*, though clearly more accurate, are significantly better: *Network*: 'Work in which threads, wires, etc., are crossed or interlaced in the fashion of a net; *esp.* light fabric made of threads intersecting with interstices.' *Pastern*: 'The part of a horse's foot between the fetlock and the hoof.'

34. *Johnsonian Miscellanies*, II, 404, 390; Henry Hitchings, *Dr Johnson's Dictionary* (London, 2005), 129.

35. ibid., 235–6.

36. *Life*, I, 293; *Yale*, XVIII, 292, 287; *Public Advertiser*, date unknown; see Clifford, *Dictionary Johnson*, 334 n. 14; *Life*, I, 300; *Letters*, IV, 378–9.

9 Nothing Is Concluded

1. *Letters*, I, 105–10, 111.

2. *Yale*, I, 56; *Life*, I, 284.

3. *Letters*, I, 112–13; *Yale*, I, 57–8; *Letters*, I, 114.

4. *Letters*, I, 126; the *Account* was published on 29 January 1755, but sold badly. I have taken my version of it from Brack, *Shorter Prose Writings*, SAM. 249. Williams died on 12 July 1755, and the 'Obituary', printed in 'an unidentified newspaper', is taken from a copy pasted into the *Account* in the Bodleian Library, SAM. 250.

5. *Letters*, I, 124, 126–9. The benefit performance was 22 January 1756; see *The London Stage, 1600-1800*, ed E. L. Avery, A. H. Scouten et al. (11 vols, Carbondale, 1960–5), Part IV, ii. 522. Baretti's work was published on 19 July 1755. See Hazen, 110–16 and 146–51.

6. The work was published on 12 February 1756; see *Early Biographical Writings*, 105; *Life*, I, 359, and Brack, SAM 254.

7. *Letters*, I, 116; *Yale*, I, 60; *Letters*, I, 114–19; *Letters*, I, 116–24; *Anecdotes*, 114; *Yale*, I, 59–60.

8. *Letters*, I, 128–33; ibid., 158; *Life*, I, 304n; *Christian Morals* was published on

18 March 1756 and the copy in the British Library is inscribed: 'Tho. Birch, 20 March 1756. Donum Samuelis Johnsoni.' *Early Biographical Writings*, 421. The book was probably Anthony à Wood's *Athenae Oxonienses*, which he had borrowed the previous November and was returning; *Letters*, I, 115, 133. He may, possibly, have meant William (not Richard) Cave in his letters to Paul; it is not possible to be clear.

9. Hawkins, 360; *Life*, I, 397; see Arthur Sherbo, *Christopher Smart: Scholar of the University* (Michigan, 1967), Edward A. Bloom, *Samuel Johnson in Grub Street* (Providence, R.I., 1957), and *Yale*, X, 116–25. The first issue of the *Universal Visiter* appeared on 2 February 1756.

10. *Yale*, X, 120–5; Fleeman, *Bibliography*, 1: 660–9; *Letters*, I, 133–4.

11. *Life*, II, 345; *Yale*, X, 126–50; 171.

12. *Yale*, X, 177–83; Pitt's speech was on 15 December 1755, resulting in his (temporary) dismissal from power.

13. *Letters*, I, 135–7; Johnson was unable to place a review in the *Gentleman's Magazine*, and it appeared in the October issue of the *Literary Magazine*.

14. *Yale*, VII, 49; *Letters*, I, 71; *Yale*, VII, 56, 58.

15. *Yale*, VII, 51–8; *Letters*, I, 135, 140–3; *Life*, I, 329.

16. *The Correspondence of Samuel Richardson*, ed. Anna Laetitia Barbauld (6 vols, London, 1804), III, 136; Warton Papers, Trinity College, Oxford; *Letters*, I, 155; ibid., 157–60.

17. *Letters*, I, 138–9, 141–2, 146–7; *Life*, I, 86–7. Hector's transcription of Johnson's dictated translation of Lobo's *Voyage to Abyssinia* may owe something to legend. Paul J. Korshin, for one, doubts whether this version of events is quite accurate: 'A 416-page translation is rather a long book to dictate from one's bed; no matter how fast Edmund Hector could write, this task would have taken him a minimum of forty hours . . . It is clear, I think, that this story is part of the myth of the procrastinating author which surfaces repeatedly in accounts of his early writings.' 'The mythology of Johnson's *Dictionary*', in Lynch and McDermott (eds), 13.

18. *Letters*, I, 145–6; ibid., 150–1.

19. ibid., 147–9; Clifford, *Dictionary Johnson*, 181. See also *Life*, I, 239.

20. *Yale*, X, 197–212, 213–40, 241–60. Voltaire's view is taken from *Candide*, ch. 23.

21. *Early Biographical Writings*, 475–93.

22. *Life*, 311–12; for a detailed account and presentation of the thirty-eight short pieces that he wrote in 1756, see Brack's forthcoming *Shorter Prose Writings*.

23. Greene (ed.), *Samuel Johnson*, 522–43.

24. *Life*, I, 313–14; see the detailed account by Ruth K. McClure in *Review of English Studies*, n.s. 27 (1976), 17–26.

25. *Literary Magazine* 13 (May 1757); *Yale*, X, 261–5.

26. *Letters*, I, 157; ibid., 149–50. This was a settled conviction. Years later, writing *The Lives of the Poets*, he reiterated it many times; 'About things on which the public thinks long it commonly attains to think right' (II, 132).

27. *Letters*, I, 152–3, 153–4, and *R. B. Adam Library*, III, 198; *Gleanings*, IV, 8–9.

28. *Letters*, I, 155–6, 158.

29. ibid., I, 159; *Yale*, VII, xx–xxvi.

30. J. D. Fleeman, 'The Revenue of a Writer: Samuel Johnson's Literary Earnings', in *Studies in the Book Trade in Honour of Graham Pollard* (Oxford Bibliographical Society, 1975), 214; *Life*, I, 320, III, 19; the Hawkins anecdote is contained in *The Letters of Horace Walpole*, ed. Mrs Paget Toynbee (16 vols, Oxford, Clarendon Press, 1903–5), XII, 158.

31. *Life*, I, 330; *Yale*, II, xix, xxii.

32. The average length of *Idler* papers is one thousand words, whereas the *Ramblers* reach fifteen hundred and the *Adventurers* almost eighteen hundred. Nos 40 and 56 are devoted to advertisements, No. 11 to the weather. *Idler* Nos 5, 6 and 13 are specifically addressed to female readers and Nos 7, 8 and 20 are devoted to the war.

33. *Yale*, II, 95 (No. 30), 84 (No. 27), 71 (No. 22), 117–121 (No. 38).

34. *Letters*, I, 174–5.

35. ibid., I, 160–4; 166; 169–70 and *Life*, I, 242.

36. 27 June 1758: Nichols, *Illustrations*, VII, 259.

37. The rent was apparently reduced from £26 to £24. Guildhall Records indicate that Johnson paid 'impropriation tythes', 'augmentation tythes' and land tax for the summer of 1758, but is not listed for the Poor Rate, although two years earlier, in September 1756, he had paid 17s 4d 'for and towards the cleaning repairing and beautifying' of St Bride's Church. Thomas Bodward, who took over from Johnson as tenant, is not listed for payments, and the next person listed at the Gough Square residence is William Addenbrooke who had certainly taken over by Lady Day (25 March) 1759. See Clifford, *Dictionary Johnson*, 200–1, and *Life*, I, 350 n. 3.

38. *Life*, I, 328–9 n. 1; *Johnsonian Miscellanies*, II, 259.

39. *Life*, I, 350 n. 3, 421; 350 n. 1. Barber was taken on board the *Golden Fleece*, was transferred to the *Princess Royal* and thence to the *Stag*, from which he was discharged on 8 August 1760; Grainger's letter of 20 July 1758 is in the Hyde Collection.

40. *Letters*, I, 171–4; Garrick declined the play, which he called 'cruel, bloody, and unnatural' (Davies, I, 251), whereupon Johnson supported it, exclaiming, 'I will write a copy of verses upon [Anne Bellamy] myself' from the pit; G. A. Bellamy, *An Apology for the Life of George Anne Bellamy* (1785), III, 77–80. See also *Life*, IV, 20.

41. *Letters*, I, 174–9.

42. *Yale*, I, 65–8.
43. *Yale*, II, 128–31 (No. 41), 134–9 (Nos 43, 44); the text is from John 2.4.
44. *Letters*, I, 181–2, 183–4.
45. *Life*, I, 341.
46. *Yale*, XVI, xxvi, xlix, and *Life*, I, 340 n. 3, 341 n. 2. 'Thus, by the end of its first year of publication, the tale reached, from the proprietors' editions alone, the substantial figure of 3,500' (*Yale*, XVI, xlix).
47. *Life*, I, 331.
48. The quotations are from Irvin Ehrenpreis, Arieh Sachs, Earl R. Wasserman, W. J. Bate and Carey McIntosh, all taken from '*Rasselas* and the Traditions of "Menippean Satire" ' by James F. Woodruff in *Samuel Johnson, New Critical Essays*, ed. Isobel Grundy (1984), 158–85.
49. See *Rambler* 38, 65, 120, 190, 204 and 205 (1750–2), and *Idler* 75, 99 (1758–60); *Yale*, XVI, 28, 43–6, 119–41, 100.
50. *Yale*, XVI, 77, 83, 74, 33, 50; the endured/enjoyed antithesis with regard to human life was a favourite trope, repeated in *Life*, II, 124, *Rambler* 165 and elsewhere; see *Yale*, XVI, 50 n. 2.
51. *Yale*, XVI, 58; see n. 7 for details of Johnson's obsessive need of such detailed computation to prevent 'his mind from preying upon itself' (*Life*, I, 72); *History of Rasselas, Prince of Abyssinia*, ed. G. B. Hill (1887), 174; *Anecdotes*, 77.
52. *Yale*, XVI, 118 and *Idler* 30; *Yale*, II, 92; see also *Rambler* 104 and *Adventurer* 119.
53. *Yale*, XVI, 99 and *Life*, II, 128, 109.
54. *Yale*, XVI, 111–12; *Rambler* 41, 203; *Yale*, XVI, 142, 144–9, 150.
55. *Life*, I, 66; *Anecdotes*, 199.
56. *Yale*, XVI, 157, 164, 175–6.
57. *Yale*, I, 66–9; II, 101.

10   The Pensioner

1. *Yale*, II, 156; *Life*, III, 29; *Yale*, II, 261.
2. *Letters*, I, 184–5; *Lloyd's Evening Post and British Chronicle* 4 (2–4 May 1759); *The Critical Review, or Annals of Literature*, April 1759, 372–5; *Monthly Review* 20 (May 1759), 428–37. The reviewer in the last is identified by B. Nangle, *The Monthly Review, First Series, 1749–1789* (Oxford, 1934), 180.
3. *Yale*, II, 184–5, 180–2.
4. *Yale*, I, 69–70. It is not certain that the 'Scruples' mentioned here were written at this time. Transcribing the undated note in June 1768 Johnson confesses 'nor can I conjecture when it was composed'. 1759 seems a realistic choice, partly from the repetition of the 'chain' metaphor. *Yale*, II, 139.
5. *The Posthumous Works of Mrs. Chapone* (1807), 108–11; Percy Diary, British Library Add. MS 32,336, ff. 19–21.

6. *Letters*, I, 186–7 and Boswell's *Life of Johnson*, ed. J. W. Croker (1832), I, 151 n. 1.

7. *Life*, I, 250–1; the lines are a misremembering of Lord Lansdowne's 'Drinking Song to Sleep'.

8. *Yale*, II, 201–3, 217, 232; *evacuate* is given the meaning 'to void by any of the excretory passages' as a third signification.

9. ibid., 235 n. 1.

10. ibid., 260, 261–4.

11. ibid., 266, 270; Francis Barber, who had joined the navy in the summer of 1758, was not discharged until August 1760, despite Johnson's best efforts, who got Tobias Smollett to write on behalf 'of that great CHAM of literature, Samuel Johnson' on 16 March 1759. *Life*, I, 348–50.

12. *Considerations of the Plans offered for the construction of Black-Friars Bridge*, 3 Letters, 1–15 December 1759, *Works* (1825), V, 303–10; *Life*, I, 348.

13. *Yale*, II, 312.

14. 'The World Displayed', in Hazen, 216–37.

15. *Letters*, I, 187–8; *Life*, I, 350; *European Magazine* 30, 161.

16. *Yale*, X, 278–84.

17. *Life*, I, 353 n. 2; *Revue Internationale de la Croix Rouge* 32 (1951), 969–71; *Yale*, X, 285–9.

18. *Life*, IV, 97; Murphy is quoted in *Life*, I, 350 where Johnson's promissory notes to Newbery are given as £42 19s 10d on 19 May 1759 and £30 on 20 March 1760. This would not quite be earned by contributions to the *Idler*, which ceased to appear after 5 April 1760.

19. *Life*, I, 246; Stebbing Shaw, I, 324; *Life*, I, 356 n. 2.

20. *The Diary of Joseph Farington*, ed. Kathryn Cave (Yale University Press, 1979), II, 307; John L. Abbott, 'Dr Johnson and the Society', *Journal of the Royal Society for the Encouragement of Arts, Manufactures & Commerce* 115, 395–400, 486–91.

21. *Life*, I, 351–2; *Letters*, I, 196–201; *Life*, II, 364–5.

22. *Life*, I, 546; Nichols, VI, 147–8; *Johnsonian Miscellanies*, II, 400.

23. *Yale*, I, 71; British Library Add. MS 35,399, f. 190v; Nichols, VI, 147–8; *Gentleman's Magazine* (January 1763 and December 1768); see James Walvin, *The Black Presence* (London, 1971) and William M. Wiecek, '*Somerset*: Lord Mansfield and the Legitimacy of Slavery in the Anglo-American World', *University of Chicago Law Review* 42 (1974), 86–146.

24. *Letters*, I, 196–7.

25. *Works of Arthur Murphy* (1786), VII, 3–12; 'Anningait and Ajutt', a versification of *Rambler*s 186 and 187, was written by Anne Penny and reviewed, favourably, in the *Gentleman's Magazine* (March 1761) and the *Critical Review* (April 1761).

26. *Letters*, I, 196–201.

27. ibid., 192–4; *London Journal*, 136–7; *Thraliana*, 1, 177; *Letters*, I, 199.

28. *Letters*, I, 205–6; *Life*, I, 417.

29. *Letters*, I, 190–2, 194–5; Percy Diary, British Library Add. MS 32,336; *The Percy Letters*, ed. Cleanth Brooks and A. F. Falconer (New Haven, 1977), 96.

30. *Miscellaneous Works of Oliver Goldsmith* (1801), I, 62–3; *Transactions of the Lichfield Johnson Society* (1976), 22; British Library Add. MS 42,560, f. 89v; *Letters*, I, 205.

31. *Yale*, I, 73; Hayward (ed.), *Autobiography*, 23; the first two volumes of *Tristram Shandy* were published in December 1759; *Letters*, I, 200, 205; Johnson received £84 2s 4d as his two-thirds share of a new edition of the *Idler* which appeared in 1761 (Fleeman, 'Johnson's Literary Earnings', 214); *St James's Chronicle, or the British Evening-Post*, 15 and 22 September 1761.

32. *Lloyd's Evening Post and British Chronicle*, 16–23 September 1761; *St James's Chronicle*, 15–24 September 1761; *Letters*, I, 201; *Yale*, X, 290–300; *London Chronicle*, X, 720, 124; *Public Advertiser*, 8,402 (8 October 1761); *Annual Register* (1759), 479.

33. *Letters*, I, 205–7, 285.

34. *Yale*, I, 74–5.

35. *Life*, III, 230; see Douglas Grant, *The Cock Lane Ghost* (London, 1965) and *The Poetical Works of Charles Churchill*, ed. Douglas Grant (Oxford, Clarendon Press, 1956), 98, 483–5; Johnson's report appeared in the *St James's Chronicle, London Chronicle, Daily Advertiser, Public Advertiser* and several other papers.

36. *Universal Museum* (1762), 158–61; Augustan Reprint Society (1974) No. 163, edited by O M Brack; *Edinburgh Magazine* (1762), 222–5.

37. For extended discussions of this, see Clifford, *Dictionary Johnson*, 263–5 and *Studies in the Eighteenth Century, III*, ed. R. F. Brissenden and J. C. Eade (1976), 1–19. Clifford suggests that Richard Farmer, scholar of Emmanuel College, Cambridge, may have been the author.

38. *Life*, I, 374–5n.; *St James's Chronicle*, 20–22 July 1762; *Letters*, I, 208–9.

39. James M. Osborn Collection at Yale, 4 August; Blakeway to Thomas Percy, Northamptonshire Record Office (X 1079/ E(S) 1206, f. 42), 31 July.

40. See George Nobbe, *North Briton* II (1939), 74–5, 83–4.

41. *St James's Chronicle*, 31 August–2 September; Reynolds's engagement book for 1762 is kept at the Royal Academy, London, from which this itinerary is traced; *Gentleman's Magazine* 32, 379.

42. *Poetical Works*, 126–7.

43. *Life*, I, 429 n. 2; PRO, 30/8/229, pt 1. I am indebted to James L. Clifford for this information: see Clifford, *Dictionary Johnson*, 275 and 350.

44. *Johnsonian Miscellanies*, II, 274–5. The manuscript of Frances Reynolds's 'Recollections of Dr. Johnson' is in the Hyde Collection; *The General Correspondence of James Boswell, Research Edition*, ed. David Hankins and James J. Caudle (Yale University Press, 2006), IX, 129, 308–9.

45. *London Chronicle*, 2 May 1769, 410; *Life*, I, 378–9.
46. *Letters*, I, 212; 212–15; 215–17. Alan T. McKenzie, 'Two Letters from Giuseppe Baretti to Samuel Johnson', *Publications of the Modern Language Association* 86 (1971), 220.
47. Alicia LeFanu, *Memoirs . . . of Mrs Frances Sheridan* (1824), 324–7. Johnson made frequent, ineffectual attempts to recover his relationship with Sheridan. *St James's Chronicle*, 15 January and 27 January.

11 Enter Boswell

1. *Correspondence of James Boswell*, 303, 156.
2. ibid., 308–9, 225.
3. ibid., 391, 225, 241, 321–2.
4. *Life*, I, 378, 377n.; *London Journal*, 43–4.
5. *London Journal*, 59, 97; *Letters*, I, 221; *London Journal*, 94–101, 137–40.
6. *Letters*, I, 219; *London Journal*, 155–6.
7. *London Journal*, 259 n. 1; 260.

12 Shakespeare

1. *London Journal*, 260; *Letters*, I, 220, 222–3, 223–4; *Life*, II, 462.
2. Hazen, 74–7; *Letters*, I, 224–5.
3. *Letters*, I, 225–30, 232–4, 235–7.
4. *Life*, I, 419, 425, 463. One can find an earlier expression of all three sentiments in *London Journal*, 287, 294 and 331.
5. *London Journal*, 272–3; *Life*, I, 457; *London Journal*, 327, 332–3.
6. *Letters*, I, 237–40; *Life*, I, 475.
7. *Letters*, I, 241; *Life*, I, 477n, V, 511; *Letters*, I, 186; *Johnsoniana* (2 vols, London, 1836), 435.
8. *Life*, I, 477–80; *Letters*, I, 231–2, 243; British Library Add. MS 32,336. Johnson and Miss Williams arrived on 25 June; Miss Williams left on 7 August and Johnson remained until 18 August; Frances Reynolds, 'Recollections of Dr Johnson', in *Johnsonian Miscellanies*, 273.
9. Hazen, 170; the allegations of a mirthful reading of the poem are discussed in ibid., 168–71, and *Life*, II, 453, 532–4.
10. *Yale*, I, 76–80; *Life*, I, 435–6.
11. *Yale*, I, 81–3.
12. *Letters*, I, 244–7.
13. *Thraliana*, I, 158–9 and n. 5; for further discussion about difficulties with the date of Johnson's first meeting Mrs Thrale, see James L. Clifford, *Hester Lynch Piozzi* (Oxford, Clarendon Press, 1941, 55 n.1, and *Life*, I, 520–1.

14. John Rylands Library, Ry. 533, 1; Mainwaring, *Piozziana*, I, 50; Hayward (ed.), *Autobiography*, II, 19–20; *Johnsonian Miscellanies*, II, 169, 374; *Thraliana*, I, 159.

15. *Thraliana*, I, 159; *The Gazetteer, and New Daily Advertiser*, 21 November 1764; *The Public Advertiser*, 4 March 1765.

16. Hazen, 158–68, 167; *Letters of David Garrick*, ed. D. M. Little and G. M. Kahrl (Oxford, 1963), II, 460; *Hebrides*, in *Yale*, IX, 207; *Life*, II, 14–15.

17. *Letters*, I, 248–50; *Poems*, 123, 218; *Yale*, VI, 257–63; *Johnsonian Miscellanies*, I, 233.

18. *Yale*, VII, xxiii–xxiv; *Letters*, I, 253–5.

19. Kate Chisholm, in unpublished research; *St James's Chronicle*, articles from 22 October, but specifically 19 November. See also *The Court Miscellany; or Ladies New Magazine* 1 (1765); *Boswell For the Defence 1769–1774*, ed. W. K. Wimsatt Jr. and Frederick A. Pottle (1959), 123–4.

20. *Public Advertiser*, 18 October 1765; *The Public Ledger; and the Daily Register of Commerce and Intelligence*, 12 November 1765.

21. *Letters*, I, 257–8.

22. *Yale*, VII, 61–2; VI, 91; XVI, 43.

23. *Yale*, VII, 98, 186; VIII, 528; VII, 193, 302–3, 368.

24. *Letters*, I, 254; *Yale*, VIII, 764, 996, 704; *Thraliana*, I, 161.

25. *Letters*, I, 259–61; *Yale*, VII, 522; see *Letters*, I, 291.

26. *Letters*, I, 261–2; Boswell's mother died on 11 January, which occasioned his leaving Paris.

27. *Letters*, I, 263.

28. *Yale*, I, 83–98, especially 86, 89 and 87.

29. ibid., 92–5.

30. ibid., 98; Thomas Birch wrote to Lord Hardwicke about William Hamilton's maiden speech in November 1755, 'which I hear to have been the performance of Sam. Johnson, with whom, I know, he is very intimate' (British Library Add. MS 35,400).

31. *Letters*, I, 259; see E. L. McAdam, *Dr. Johnson and the English Law* (Syracuse, 1951), 55, and *Yale*, I, 97.

32. Clifford, *Hester Lynch Piozzi* (1952 edn), 60 and n. 3.

33. *Letters*, I, 264–6; *Yale*, I, 99–103; Hazen, 213–16; Clifford, *Hester Lynch Piozzi* (1952 edn), 61–2.

34. Hazen, 33–8, 1–4, 38–40; *Yale*, I, 103–6. The editors of *Yale* vol. I follow Hill in guessing this entry 'is not continuous with the foregoing but was clearly written in late September or October' (103n.). This point seems not so obvious to me, and would seem to imply that Johnson chose to deceive himself (or his reader?) since six pages further on he clearly writes '[SEPT] 18. 1766. AT STREATHAM'. Moreover, a line from his letter to Langton of 8 March ('I have risen every morning since Newyear's day at about eight') (265), seems to

echo a line from his Easter Saturday prayer ('Since last Newyear's day I have risen every morning by eight') (106), which seems to imply a close connection between them, not one delayed by six months.

35. Frances Reynolds, 'Recollections of Dr Johnson', in *Johnsonian Miscellanies*, II, 274–5; *Life*, I, 485–6.
36. *Yale*, II, 98; *Life*, II, 5n.
37. *Yale*, X, 301–12, 305. For the discovery of this piece, and arguments about its dating, see ibid., 301–4.
38. *Letters*, I, 264–6.
39. *St James's Chronicle*, 25–28 January and 6–9 September 1766; *Gazetteer*, 18 January 1766.
40. *Yale*, I, 107–8.
41. *Johnsonian Miscellanies*, I, 234; for a full discussion of the date of these events, see *Life*, I, Appendix F, 520–2.
42. *King Lear* V.iii.

13 Club and Country

1. *Letters*, I, 284; *Yale*, I, 110, 127.
2. *Johnsonian Miscellanies*, I, 339; Hayward (ed.), *Autobiography*, I, 16.
3. *Letters*, I, 266; *Yale*, III, 320–1.
4. 'The Children's Book, or rather Family Book', a MS of 186 pages, from 17 September 1766 to the end of 1778, in the possession of Sir Randle Mainwaring; Mainwaring, *Piozziana*, I, 56; Sir Joshua Reynolds's notebooks, Royal Academy, London.
5. *Letters*, I, 269, 273.
6. *Yale*, I, 111; *Early Biographical Writings*, 498; for the date of composition, see *Life*, I, Appendix G, 550–2.
7. *Letters*, I, 274–5.
8. ibid., 276–8; see I, 319–20 for Hester Thrale's knowledge of the collaboration.
9. *Life*, II, 33–41, 15; *Letters*, I, 278–9.
10. *Letters*, I, 280–2, 282–5.
11. *Letters*, I, 286–8; see T. M. Curley, *A Course of Lectures on the English Law* (Oxford, Clarendon Press, 1986), 23.
12. *Yale*, I, 113–16; *Letters*, I, 288–9.
13. *Letters*, I, 291–3.
14. *The Sale of Authors, A Dialogue; In Imitation of Lucian's Sale of Philosophers*; though anonymous, the work is known to be by Archibald Campbell; *St James's Chronicle*, 8–10 December 1767.
15. *Letters*, I, 293–8, 300; Anna Maria, the Thrales' fourth child, lived for two years, dying in 1770.
16. McAdam, 69; *Yale*, I, 113.

17. *Letters*, I, 320; McAdam, 83, 100, 101.

18. *Yale*, VII, 82; McAdam, 93.

19. *Yale*, I, 118; *Letters*, I, 300–5.

20. *Letters*, I, 307, 298; *Life*, II, 49, 60.

21. *Gazetteer*, 28 May 1768.

22. *Letters*, I, 307–14, 315–18; *Public Advertiser*, 8 August and 18 August 1768; *Yale*, I, 119–20.

23. *Letters*, I, 318–20; *Yale*, I, 120.

24. *Yale*, I, 121; *Thraliana*, I, 384–5.

25. *Letters*, I, 322–6.

26. ibid., 326–9; *Life*, II, 68.

27. *Gazetteer*, 23 September 1769; *Public Advertiser*, 16 September 1769; *Life*, II, 92; *Yale*, VII, 79.

28. *Life*, I, 470; II, 75, 66, 100, 330, 341–5.

29. *Independent Chronicle*, 18–20 October 1769; see H. W. Liebert, *A Constellation of Genius* (1958), for a full record of the trial. *Life*, II, 97.

30. *Life*, II, 94; I, 471.

31. Hazen, 151–2, 60–8; *Early Biographical Writings*, 519; *Lloyd's Evening Post*, 8–10 March 1769.

32. *Johnsonian Miscellanies*, I, 173; *Boswell in Search of a Wife 1766–1769*, ed. Frank Brady and Frederick A. Pottle (London, 1957), 156. For further details of the whole affair see *Yale*, X, 313–17; George Rudé, *Wilkes and Liberty* (Oxford, Clarendon Press, 1962); A. H. Cash, *John Wilkes: The Scandalous Father of Civil Liberty* (New Haven, 2006). From the evidence quoted, Johnson must have written the pamphlet on 10 and 11 January.

33. *Life*, II, 111–12; see *Letters*, I, 343, 346; *Yale*, X, 319, 338.

34. *Public Advertiser*, 17 February 1770; *The Middlesex Journal: or, Chronicle of Liberty*, 22 February 1770; *Independent Chronicle*, 23–26 February 1770.

35. *Letters*, I, 332–4, 315; *Thraliana*, I, 101–2; see John Sainsbury, *John Wilkes, The Lives of a Libertine* (Ashgate, 2006), 204; on Frank Barber, consider Hawkins's reactions, *Life*, IV, 370, 444.

36. *Letters*, II, 168–71.

37. *Yale*, X, 401–11; *Letters*, II, 184–6; *Life*, II, 317; R. W. Chapman, 'Boswell's Revises of the Life of Johnson', in *Johnson and Boswell Revised* (1928), 37.

38. *Yale*, X, 411–55; see Coleridge's *Table Talk*, 16 August 1833, and the views of R. L. Schuyler, L. H. Gipson and D. J. Greene which come to the conclusion that 'Americans have, in practice, come around to Johnson's view' (*Yale*, X, 405–6).

39. *Letters*, III, 71; *Life*, III, 167, 178, 200.

40. *Life*, III, 64–7, 69–76; *Letters*, II, 331–4.

14 Strawberries and Fetters

1. *Yale*, I, 125–6.
2. ibid., 122–4; *Gazetteer*, 22 December 1769.
3. *Letters*, I, 336–9; *London Evening-Post*, 27–29 March 1770; *Life*, II, 119, 168.
4. *Letters*, I, 343–9; *Yale*, I, 127; *Gazetteer*, 9 July 1770.
5. *Yale*, I, 127–32.
6. ibid., 133–4; ibid., 6; *Letters*, I, 350–1, 355.
7. *Letters*, I, 350, 353; *Life*, II, 119; 'The Doctors: A Literary Anecdote', *General Evening Post*, 7 May 1771; it is taken from *Town and Country Magazine* (April) and repeated, with variants, in *The London Packet, or New Evening Post*, 3 July. For Goldsmith's arrest, see *Life*, I, 415–16.
8. *Letters*, I, 356; the softened version has 'and if he sometimes erred, he was likewise sometimes right'; see *Life*, II, 135 and *Yale*, X, 346–9, 383.
9. *Yale*, X, 350, 357, 353; Debrett, *History, Debates, and Proceedings of Parliament* (1743–74), 1792, v. 345.
10. *Yale*, X, 370–1; 'Literary Intelligence' in *Gazetteer*, 29 August 1771; *Cadenus* is Swift's rather obvious disguise for *Decanus* (Dean), by which he indicated himself.
11. Parodies of Bishop Percy's 'Hermit of Warkworth', in *Poems*, 128. There were several versions of his parodies; see *Yale*, VI, 268–70 and *Life*, II, 136; also *Lyrical Ballads* (1800), Preface.
12. *Letters*, I, 358–9, 373–4, 362–3.
13. ibid., 364; 345; 366-8.
14. ibid., 343, 367–74; *The Correspondence of Jonathan Swift*, ed. Harold Williams (5 vols, Oxford, 1963–5), II, 427.
15. *Letters*, I, 369–76; the quotation, by Foresight, is from Congreve's *Love for Love* (II.i.35); the quotation concerning the literate swan refers to Dryden's 'Dido to Aeneas', ll. 1–2, from his translation of *Ovid's Epistles*. Johnson had quoted it under *elegy* in the *Dictionary*; John Rylands Library, Ry. 539–40.
16. *Letters*, I, 378–9, 372–3, 380–1.
17. *Yale*, I, 138–40. Dating of these prayers is arbitrary, but I see no good reason to challenge that assigned to them by the Yale editors on these pages.
18. *Yale*, I, 142; *Thraliana*, I, 384–5; John Rylands Library, Ry. 629, 7.
19. *Letters*, I, 381–2; *Anecdotes*, 78; *Life*, II, 498.
20. See *Samuel Johnson's Unpublished Revisions to the Dictionary of the English Language*, ed. Allen Reddick (Cambridge, 2005), which prints facsimiles of all 122 pages; ibid., xvi.
21. See a fuller discussion in Reddick, *Making of Johnson's Dictionary*, 105–6.
22. *Yale*, I, 142–4; *Letters*, I, 383–5; Little and Kahrl (eds), II, 778.
23. *Life*, II, 144–5; *Letters*, I, 388–9; *Boswell's Letters*, ed. C. B. Tinker (Oxford, 1924), I, 173.

24. *Yale*, I, 146–50; *Letters*, I, 395; *Life*, II, 191–2.

25. *Letters*, I, 392; *Gentleman's Magazine* 42 (1772), 293.

26. *Thraliana*, April 1778, and Hayward (ed.), *Autobiography*, II, 27; Clifford, *Hester Lynch Piozzi*, 93–4.

27. *R. B. Adam Library*, III, 261; *Letters*, I, 400–1.

28. *Letters*, I, 395–6, II, 8–9; *Gazetteer*, 18 July 1772; *Yale*, I, 154.

29. MS: John Rylands Library, Ry. 539.II. *Letters*, I, 398–9, 403; John Rylands Library, Ry. 539, misdated 'Sat. 7 Oct'; *Letters*, I, 403–4.

30. *Letters*, I, 406–9, 410–11, 413–15.

31. *Yale*, I, 152; *Private Papers of James Boswell*, VI, 92.

32. Letter to Johnson, 19 March 1773, John Rylands Library, Ry. 539, 19; *Letters*, II, 31; *Westminster Magazine or the Pantheon of Taste*, 1 (2 April 1773), 178, 374.

33. John Rylands Library, Ry. 616; Hayward (ed.), *Autobiography*, II, 25–6.

34. *Idler* 72, *Yale*, II, 227; *Letters*, II, 3–4, 11–16; *Thraliana*, I, 184–5, 532; John Rylands Library, Ry. 539, letter 19.

35. *Letters*, II, 5–6, 18–20, 23; John Rylands Library, Ry. 539, 17–19 (19 March 1773).

36. *Life*, II, 217, 227; *Letters*, II, 8–10, 25; the masquerade was actually the second to be held in Scotland (*London Magazine* 43 (1774), 82–3). The first was given by Sir Alexander and Lady Macdonald, who were Johnson's and Boswell's hosts on Skye. Boswell attended as 'a Dumb Conjuror' (*Gentleman's Magazine* (1773), 43).

37. *Life*, II, 240, V, 76; *Yale*, I, 156; *Letters*, II, 24, 29.

38. *Life*, II, 258; John Rylands Library, Ry. 538, 4; *Letters*, II, 32; the couple were married in Holland and returned to England by the summer.

39. *Letters*, II, 34–7; *R. B. Adam Library*, III, 15.

40. The dating of this letter is conjectural, but I agree with Bruce Redford, J. D. Wright and J. L. Clifford in placing it at 'a date between SJ's arrival at Streatham on 1 June and the 18th'. See *Letters*, II, 37–9 and n. 1. '*Est ce trop de demander d'une ame telle qu'est la vôtre, que, maîtresse des autres, elle devienne maîtresse de soy-même, et qu'elle triomphe de cette inconstance, qui a fait si souvent, qu'elle a negligée l'execution de ses propres loix, qu'elle a oubliée tant de promesses, et qu'elle m'a condamnè a tant de solicitations reiterèes que la resouvenance me fait horreur. Il faut ou accorder, ou refuser; il faut se souvenir de ce qu'on accorde. Je souhaite, ma patronne, que vôtre autoritè me soit toûjours sensible, et que vous me tiennez dans l'esclavage que vous sçavez si bien rendre heureuse.*'

41. See *Thraliana*, I, 384–6 n. 1, 415 n. 4; ibid., II, 625 and Katherine Balderston, 'Johnson's Vile Melancholy', in *The Age of Johnson*, ed. F. W. Hilles and W. S. Lewis (1949), 3–14; John Rylands Library, Ry. 539, 30. The letter is not dated, and in a more formal hand than usual, allowing the suspicion that it was written at a later date.

42. *Letters*, II, 39–42; John Rylands Library, Ry. 616.

43. Hazen, 152, 132–6; *Yale*, I, 158–9.

44. John Rylands Library, Ry. 542, 1; *Letters*, II, 44–5.

15 'A Wide Sail'

1. *Life*, V, 20; Boswell to Temple, 10 May 1775, in *Johnson's Journey to the Western Islands of Scotland*, ed. R. W. Chapman (London, Oxford University Press, 1924), xvi.

2. *Letters*, II, 49–50; *Yale*, IX, 40.

3. *Letters*, II, 54; *Yale*, IX, 30, 33, 60, 145–6. Like Johnson, Wordsworth used measurements to guarantee the authenticity of his feelings: in 'The Thorn' he writes of a pond, 'I've measured it from side to side:/ 'Tis three feet long, and two feet wide.' Subsequently these lines were altered.

4. *Yale*, I, 27; *Life*, V, 138; *Yale*, IX, 56, *empyreumatical*: 'having the smell or taste of burnt substances'; ibid., IX, 50, *proceleusmatic* (not included in either the first or fourth editions of the *Dictionary*) means 'serving for incitement'; ibid., IX, 130, *succedaneous*: 'supplying the place of something else' (*Dictionary*).

5. *Life*, V, 124; *Yale*, IX, 39, 45, 66.

6. *Life*, V, 21–3, 60; *Yale*, IX, 9–10; *Letters*, II, 63; see *Life*, V, 69–70.

7. *Life*, V, 54, 60; *Yale*, IX, 9.

8. *Yale*, IX, 22; *Life*, V, 109–10.

9. *Yale*, IX, 32–3; *Life*, V, 132–3.

10. *Life*, V, 112, 141, 159, 178, 183; *Yale*, IX, 100, 154, 128; *Life*, V, 211.

11. *Life*, V, 186; I, 430; *Letters*, II, 72; *Yale*, IX, 63, 90, 131–2.

12. *Letters*, II, 62–4, 70–1, 75; *Yale*, I, 160; *Samuel Johnson, The Latin Poems*, trans. and ed. Niall Rudd (Associated University Presses, 2005), 56–7.

13. *Letters*, II, 74–7; *Life*, V, 307; *Letters*, II, 78–81.

14. *Letters*, II, 81, 92, 99, 101; *Life*, V, 261–2, 272, 290; *Latin Poems*, 56–7.

15. *Letters*, II, 96–8.

16. *Life*, V, 344–6; *Glasgow Journal*, 14–21 October 1773; *Letters*, II, 102.

17. *Letters*, II, 108, 113–15; *Life*, V, 358, 318, 368.

18. *Life*, IV, 183; II, 126; V, 150, 388, 241; *Yale*, IX, 117–19.

19. *Life*, II, 511–12, 307–8 n. 4; *Letters*, II, 168–9; *Life*, V, 117.

20. *Life*, V, 376, 382, 385; *Letters*, II, 113; *Yale*, IX, 162–4.

21. *Life*, V, 405; *Letters*, II, 117–19.

22. *Letters*, II, 119–21, 122; *Yale*, I, 162; 'The Children's Book' 1766–1778, MS 94ff.

23. *Life*, II, 270–1; *Anecdotes*, 78; *Letters*, II, 125, 128, 129–31, 132–4; *Life*, II, 275.

24. *Letters*, II, 138, 140–1, 142–4; *Johnsonian Miscellanies*, I, 274; MS of Mrs Thrale's (Piozzi's) 'New Commonplace Book', in the possession of Mrs Donald F. Hyde (see Clifford, *Hester Lynch Piozzi*, 112–13, 464).

25. *Letters*, II, 144–5, 147; *Life*, V, 292.

26. *Life*, V, 427 n. 1; Mrs Thrale's diary, edited by A. M. Broadley in *Dr Johnson and Mrs Thrale* (London, 1910), 158, 160; *Yale*, I, 163–4; *Life*, V, 427–9.

27. Croker, *Boswell's Life of Johnson* (1831), III, 126; *Yale*, I, 164–9; *Life*, V, 429–31, 579–82; Broadley, 166.

28. *Yale*, I, 170–8; *Life*, V, 431–5, 582–5; Broadley, 177; *Johnsonian Miscellanies*, I, 215; Croker, *Boswell's Life of Johnson* (1831), III, 131–3.

29. *Thraliana*, I, 222, 424; *Yale*, I, 179–80; *Life*, V, 436–7, 585–7; Broadley, 182–4.

30. *Yale*, I, 183–4; *Life*, V, 438–40 n. 2.

31. *Yale*, I, 185–7; *Life*, V, 440 n. 3–442.

32. *Anecdotes*, 139; *Life*, V, 136, 143.

33. *Life*, V, 442–9; *Yale*, I, 188, 200, 204–5; Broadley, 190, 196–200; *Letters*, II, 148–9.

34. *Life*, V, 450–8; *Yale*, I, 206–22; Broadley, 201, 203, 210, 215; *Letters*, III, 68.

35. Broadley, 217–18.

36. *Letters*, II, 149–52; *Life*, II, 348; *Yale*, X, 387–400; see also Clifford, *Hester Lynch Piozzi*, 116–17n.

37. *Letters*, II, 153–6, 159: Johnson was probably thinking of the report in the *Caledonian Mercury*, 30 October 1773.

38. *Letters*, II, 152–66; Clifford, *Hester Lynch Piozzi*, 118: Johnson was concerned lest his censure of the Dean and chapter at Lichfield should be taken to reflect on John Addenbrooke, who had recommended him as a tutor many years before.

39. *Letters*, II, 168–70, 174.

40. ibid., 174–82, 203–7; *Life*, II, 299–300 n. 1.

41. *Letters*, II, 197–8; *Life*, II, 335, 337, 378.

42. *Letters*, II, 198, 187, 195, 188–9, 205; *Yale*, I, 224–6.

43. *Letters*, II, 208–16, 219–20.

44. ibid., 221–6, 228–40.

45. ibid., 243, 265; John Rylands Library, Ry. 539, 46.

46. *Letters*, II, 245, 248–9; John Rylands Library, Ry. 600, 23; *Thraliana*, I, 43.

47. *Letters*, II, 246–60; Mary Hyde, *The Thrales of Streatham Park* (Cambridge, Mass., 1977), 127–8.

48. *Letters*, II, 266, 253; *Poems*, 132–3; *Yale*, VI, 292–3.

49. Hazen, 8–11; *Poems*, 131; *Yale*, VI, 291–2; *The French Journals of Mrs. Thrale and Doctor Johnson*, ed. Moses Tyson and Henry Guppy (Manchester, 1932), 70; *Poems*, 129; *Yale*, VI, 285–6; *Life*, II, 404.

50. Tyson and Guppy (eds), 84–5, 106–7, 101–3, 113, 130, 125; *Yale*, I, 229–39; *Letters*, II, 272.

51. *Yale*, I, 241–5; Tyson and Guppy (eds), 131; *Thraliana*, I, 333.

52. *Yale*, I, 235–8, 255–6; Tyson and Guppy (eds), 143.

53. *Life*, II, 403; *Letters*, II, 273–7.

16 Biographer of the Poets

1. *Letters*, II, 274, 284, 289, 282, 294–7.
2. *Yale*, I, 257; *Letters*, II, 296, 299; Hazen, 29; *Life*, II, 409, I, 423.
3. *Letters*, II, 301–3, 309; 'Here, too, there are tears for misfortune' (Virgil, *Aeneid* I. 462, trans. H. R. Fairclough, Loeb edn).
4. *Life*, II, 427, 434, 444, 451–2n., 457–60, 462–4.
5. ibid., 446, 468.
6. *Private Papers of James Boswell*, XI, 212; diary entry for 18 September 1777, in James L. Clifford, *Hester Lynch Piozzi* (2nd edn, reissued with additions, Oxford, Clarendon Press, 1968), 124.
7. *Life*, II, 469, III, 23; *Letters*, II, 311–15; *Yale*, I, 258.
8. *Letters*, II, 318; Piozzi (ed.), *Letters to and from Samuel Johnson*, I, 318; Hayward (ed.), *Autobiography*, I, 103–8; *Life*, III, 29; Clifford, *Hester Lynch Piozzi* (1968 edn), 138.
9. MSS of 'Children's Book', April 1776; *Life*, III, 26, 51; *Letters*, II, 323–4.
10. *Life*, III, 52, 479; *Letters*, II, 328.
11. *Life*, III, 41–2; *Letters*, II, 331–4.
12. *Letters*, II, 340, 346, 338–9, i; Clifford, *Hester Lynch Piozzi* (1968 edn), 141.
13. *Letters*, II, 340, 365.
14. *Private Papers of James Boswell*, XI, 202; *Letters*, II, 348–9, 360; *Life*, II, 362; *Monthly Review*, May 1776.
15. *Letters*, II, 358; *Life*, II, 299; 'Children's Book', 21 December 1776, 7 January 1777.
16. *Yale*, I, 262; *Letters*, III, 4, 5–9; John Rylands Library, Ry. 540, 86.
17. *Letters*, II, 361, III, 142; *Yale*, I, 266; *Life*, III, 103, 486.
18. *Letters*, III, 13–15; John Rylands Library, Ry. 539, 12; *The Early Diary of Frances Burney, 1768–1778*, ed. Annie Raine Ellis (2 vols, 1913; original edn 1889), II, 152–3.
19. *Life*, III, 116n., 299; Clifford, *Hester Lynch Piozzi* (1968 edn), 153; *Yale*, VI, 290–1; *Poems*, 133–4, 224–5.
20. Hazen, 154–7; *Letters*, III, 19–20; *Yale*, I, 264.
21. *Life*, IV, 34n.; *Yale*, I, 264, 143, 267; *Letters*, I, 256.
22. *Letters*, III, 15; *Yale*, I, 268–9.
23. MS in Boswell Papers (*Catalogue*, C 1075); *Life*, III, 111n.; John Nichols, *Literary Anecdotes of the Eighteenth Century* (9 vols, 1812–16), VIII, 416–17n.; *Johnsonian Miscellanies*, I, 271–2.
24. *Letters*, III, 24–5, 30, 33–4; 'Histories of the Tête-à-tête Annex'd', in *Town and Country Magazine*, supplement for 1773; *Life*, III, 140 n. 2, 143, IV, 208; O M Brack, *The Macaroni Parson and the Concentrated Mind* (privately printed, 2004), 30.
25. John Rylands Library, Ry. 539, Ry. 540; *Letters*, III, 24–7, 35–6, 43; *Johnsonian Miscellanies*, I, 298; *Life*, IV, 34–5.

26. *Letters*, III, 38–51, V, 240; Advertisement to 'Prefaces, Biographical and Critical' (1779) in *Lives of the Poets*, I, 15. The memory is of Pope's 'Eloisa to Abelard'.

27. Clifford, *Hester Lynch Piozzi* (1968 edn), 154; Chapman (ed.), *Letters*, II, 209; *Letters*, III, 52–62.

28. *Letters*, III, 63–8; *Yale*, I, 274; *Life*, III, 154, 137, 155, 191–2; Gilbert Burnet, *Some Passages of the Life and Death of the Right Honourable John Earl of Rochester* (1680).

29. *Letters*, III, 71; *Life*, III, 167, 178.

30. *Yale*, I, 278–9; Clifford, *Hester Lynch Piozzi* (1968 edn), 155–6; *Letters*, III, 81–9.

31. *Yale*, I, 280–2; *Letters*, III, 90–5.

32. *Yale*, I, 285; *Letters*, III, 98–9, 69, 103.

33. *Letters*, III, 122; *Lives*, I, 195, 198, 200–1, 220; *Life*, IV, 38; T. S. Eliot, *Selected Essays* (London, 1951), 287.

34. *Lives*, I, 224, 237, 241; *Letters*, III, 106–10: *Morning Post*, 27 February 1778; receipts for the performance on 27 May came to almost £200 (*London Stage*, Part V, I, 177).

35. *Life*, III, 231, 272, 260, 341, 305, 345; *Lives*, I, 6–7; *Letters*, III, 118–19.

36. Hazen, 195–7; *Yale*, I, 288–9, 291–2; *Lives*, I, 53.

37. *Yale*, I, 292; John T. Smith, *Nollekens and His Times* (1828), I, 114; *Early Diary of Frances Burney*, II, 284–7; *Letters*, III, 122, 124; John Rylands Library, Ry. 540, 80; Clifford, *Hester Lynch Piozzi* (1968 edn), 166.

38. Barrett (ed.), I, 48–9, 65–80, 112–14.

39. *Letters*, III, 140, 125–7, 134; 'Children's Book', unpublished MS; *Letters*, Hester Thrale to SJ, 28 October 1778.

40. *Lives*, I, 30–1; *Letters*, III, 140–1, 131, 134; *Life*, IV, 197.

41. *Yale*, I, 293; *Correspondence and Other Papers of James Boswell*, ed. Waingrow (2001 edn), 13; *Letters*, III, 146, 151, 153.

42. *Lives*, I, 266, 275, 282, 276, 290, 295.

43. ibid., 155, 118, 120

44. Little and Kahrl (eds), 995; *Letters*, III, 150, 156; *Life*, I, 393 n. 1, III, 371, 373; *Lives*, II, 179; Boswell's 'Register of Letters' MS: Beinecke Library; *Yale*, I, 294.

45. *Yale*, I, 295–6; *Life*, III, 376; *Letters*, III, 157–9.

46. John Rylands Library, Ry. 540, 87; *Thraliana*, I, 375; *Life*, III, 375; *London Evening-Post*, 30 March–1 April 1779; Mary Delany, *Autobiography and Correspondence*, ed. Lady Llanover (1862), V, 493; Horace Walpole, *Correspondence*, ed. W. S. Lewis et al. (48 vols, New Haven, 1937–83), XXIX, 100.

47. *Life*, III, 391; *Letters*, III, 164–78; *Thraliana*, I, 390.

48. *Thraliana*, I, 399, 393, 400; Barrett (ed.), I, 248–50; *Yale*, I, 298–9.

49. *Life*, III, 395, 399–400; *Letters*, III, 181–208; Burney, III, 360.

50. *Letters*, III, 209; *Thraliana*, I, 409–10, 414.

51. *Yale*, I, 300; *Life*, III, 418; *Lives*, III, 18; *Thraliana*, I, 423; *Letters*, III, 223–31.

52. Barrett (ed.), I, 364; *Letters*, III, 237; Clarke, 145; *Lives*, III, 1, 18 (translating Horace, *Odes*, II.i.7–8, and Cicero, *De Oratore*, II.xv.62), 15, 38; *Life*, III, 155.

53. *Letters*, III, 254, 244, 252; *Thraliana*, I, 436–7.

54. *Letters*, III, 236–7, 244, 239, 250; *Lives*, III, 70, 72, IV, 184.

55. *Letters*, III, 250–3, 258.

56. *Letters*, III, 256, 262, 266, 280 ('time glides on with speedy foot', Ovid, *Ars Amatoria*, III.65), 269, 272–3, 275, 282 and n. 6; Hazen, 136–42; *Yale*, I, 300; Barrett (ed.), I, 435.

57. *Thraliana*, I, 441, 445–6, 451–2; *Letters*, III, 289, 285; Barrett (ed.), I, 443.

58. *Letters*, III, 296–303.

59. *Thraliana*, I, 453–4.

60. *Yale*, I, 301–2; *Thraliana*, I, 461–2; *Letters*, III, 318.

61. *Lives*, III, 206, 191, 208.

62. *Letters*, III, 320; *Thraliana*, I, 465.

63. *Morning Herald*, 19 January 1781; Barrett (ed.), I, 460–1; W. H. Hutton, *Burford Papers* (1905), 49; *Yale*, I, 302–3.

64. *Lives*, IV, 54–6, 3.

65. ibid., 16, 28, 36, 68, 72, 76, 66.

66. *Letters*, III, 325; *Yale*, I, 303–4.

67. *Johnsonian Miscellanies*, I, 298.

17   'The Town Is My Element'

1. *Letters*, III, 327–8; *Thraliana*, I, 487.

2. *Letters*, III, 330, 328; *Thraliana*, I, 492; *Life*, IV, 96.

3. *Letters*, III, 331, 349, 351, 356; *Thraliana*, I, 492; *Life*, IV, 87, 101; Clifford, *Hester Lynch Piozzi* (1968 edn), 202; Barrett (ed.), II, 23.

4. *Private Papers of James Boswell*, XIV, 196, 198; John Rylands Library, Ry. 545, 23; *Walpole Letters*, XI, 455; Barrett (ed.), II, 28; *Yale*, I, 307.

5. *Thraliana*, I, 489 n. 4; Hayward (ed.), *Autobiography*, II, 46–8; Barrett (ed.), II, 2.

6. *Letters*, III, 361–70; *Yale*, I, 310; *Latin Poems*, 121–2.

7. *Letters*, III, 375, 378; *Yale*, I, 308; John Rylands Library, MSS; *Thraliana*, I, 519.

8. *Thraliana*, I, 523–6, 531–2; *Letters*, IV, 3–4; *Yale*, I, 312, VI, 313–15; *Poems*, 139–40.

9. *Letters*, IV, 7–10; *Thraliana*, I, 528; *Yale*, I, 312–13, 316, 319.

10. *Morning Herald*, 19 March 1782; Barrett (ed.), II, 66; *Thraliana*, I, 531; *Letters*, IV, 28; *Boswell's Letters*, II, 312–13.

11. *Thraliana*, I, 535; Hannah More, *Memoirs* (1835), I, 249; *Letters*, IV, 48, 50, 64; *Yale*, I, 312.

12. *Thraliana*, I, 540–1, 544–6; *Yale*, I, 337–8.

13. *Morning Post*, 15 and 18 October 1782; *Yale*, I, 343–9, 351; Barrett (ed.), II, 122; *Thraliana*, I, 549–50.

14. *Letters*, IV, 90–2, 94, 88, 96; *Thraliana*, I, 553–4, 555; *Yale*, I, 355–7.

15. *Letters*, IV, 103–4, 107; *Thraliana*, I, 557–8, 560–1; *Private Papers of James Boswell*, XV, 174; *Life*, IV, 164; *Yale*, I, 358–9.

16. *Letters*, IV, 124–9, 133, 134–5; John Rylands Library, Ry. 540, 108; *Thraliana*, I, 563; *Life*, IV, 204.

17. *Letters*, IV, 138–9, 142–3, 145–6, 148–9, 150–3; *Life*, 521–2; *Thraliana*, I, 568.

18. *Public Advertiser*, 21 June 1783; *Letters*, IV, 154–68; see *Life*, IV, 227–33; *Yale*, I, 313–14.

19. *Letters*, IV, 172, 168, 174–84, 186–8; the quotation is from David Mallet's 'William and Margaret' in *The Works of David Mallet* (1759), I [B2r], ll. 3–4.

20. *Thraliana*, I, 569, 574; *Yale*, I, 362–3, 366; *Letters*, IV, 191, 176, 203–7.

21. *Letters*, IV, 210–11, 216, 219, 229, 232–5.

22. ibid., 238–9, 254, 259; *Thraliana*, I, 580–2.

23. *Letters*, IV, 256–7, 261, 265.

24. ibid., 272, 274, 285, 293; *Thraliana*, I, 583–4, 588.

25. *Thraliana*, I, 591; *Letters*, IV, 305, 303, 301, 312, 317–21.

26. *Life*, IV, 275–7; Barrett (ed.), II, 258; *Letters*, IV, 328–9.

27. *Thraliana*, I, 593–4; for Mrs Thrale's suspicions of Fanny Burney see Clifford, *Hester Lynch Piozzi* (1968 edn), 225; *Life*, IV, 283, 336–7; *Letters*, IV, 334, 331.

28. *Letters*, IV, 336–7, 337–8; *The Queeney Letters*, ed. Marquis of Lansdowne (1934), 148–9; *Thraliana*, I, 599–600.

29. *Yale*, I, 371; *Letters*, IV, 343–4; John Rylands Library, Ry. 540, 110; *Queeney Letters*, 170–1; R. Blunt, *Mrs. Montagu* (2 vols, 1923), II, 274; *Morning Herald*, 18 August 1784; Barrett (ed.), II, 271; for further commentary on Mrs Thrale's remarriage, see *Life*, IV, 339–47 and Clifford, *Hester Lynch Piozzi* (1968 edn), 229–31.

30. *Letters*, IV, 344–51, 351–3, 436.

31. ibid., 351, 355–7, 381, 358, 367; *Yale*, I, 382–3.

32. *Letters*, IV, 369, 374–5, 383, 389, 399–400.

33. *Letters*, IV, 391–2, 401–2, 407; *Yale*, I, 391–3, 396; *Georgina: Extracts from the Correspondence of Georgina, Duchess of Devonshire*, ed. Earl of Bessborough, (1955), 92.

34. *Letters*, IV, 408–11; *Letters of Sir Joshua Reynolds*, ed. F. W. Hilles (1929), 112.

35. *Letters*, IV, 418, 421–9, 432, 434; *Yale*, I, 407–15.

36. *Letters*, IV, 434–6, 438.

37. ibid., 440–6; *Thraliana*, II, 617; *Life*, IV, 417.

38. *Yale*, I, 417–18; *Life*, IV, 401–5 and n. 2, 408–9, 417–18.

18 Epilogue

1. *Life*, IV, 419–20n., 430.

2. ibid., 402–6n.

3. *Correspondence and Other Papers of James Boswell*, ed. Waingrow (2001 edn), II, 221–3, 226–7.

4. *Life*, III, 421, 536–7, I, 237.

5. There had been various short 'Lives' of Johnson since his death; see Robert E. Kelley and O M Brack, *Samuel Johnson's Early Biographers* (University of Iowa Press, Iowa City, 1971). *Thraliana*, II, 624; *Life*, IV, 405n.

6. Frank Brady, *James Boswell: The Later Years, 1769–1795* (1984), 351–4; *Life*, I, 27n.

7. *Boswell: The Applause of the Jury 1782–5*, ed. Irma S. Lustig and Frederick A. Pottle, 75; Donald J. Greene, 'Johnson without Boswell', *Times Literary Supplement*, 22 November 1974, 1, 315–16, and ''Tis a Pretty Book, Mr Boswell, But –', in John A. Vance (ed.), *Boswell's Life of Johnson: New Questions, New Answers* (Athens, Ga., 1985); *Life*, IV, 430.

8. *Letters*, IV, 254; *Yale*, III, 318–23.

List of Illustrations

Index

SJ is Samuel Johnson, HT is Hester Thrale